Graphic Arts Photography

Frederick D. Kagy
Illinois State University

J. Michael Adams
State University of New York, Oswego

Delmar Publishers Inc.®

For information, address Delmar Publishers Inc.,
2 Computer Drive West, Box 15-015
Albany, New York 12212-5015

Library of Congress Cataloging in Publication Data

Kagy, Frederick D.
Graphic arts photography.

Includes index.
1. Photomechanical processes. 2. Graphic arts.
I. Adams, J. Michael. II. Title.
TR925.K26 1983 686.2′32 82–22691
ISBN 0-8273-2702-1 (Previously 0-534-01295-7)

Printed in the United States of America
Published simultaneously in Canada
by Nelson Canada,
A Division of International Thomson Limited

10 9 8 7 6 5 4

GRAPHIC ARTS PHOTOGRAPHY was prepared for publication by the following people: Pamela Byers, copy editor; Eleanor Connolly, cover designer; Barbara Gracia supervised production. The book was set in Times Roman by Modern Graphics, Inc.; cover and insert printing was by New England Book Components; text printing and binding was by Halliday Lithograph. The sponsoring editor was Jay Bartlett.

Contents

Preface

This book is intended to serve as an introduction to the broad field of graphic arts photography. It is designed to be used in the classroom or by individuals working on their own to update or upgrade their skills. It can also serve as a useful reference guide for individuals employed in the industry. Several important features make it valuable in such different settings.

Each chapter begins with a detailed list of objectives and skills to be gained by working through the information covered. Topic coverage within each chapter begins with basic concepts and builds toward more sophisticated understandings. New terms are set in boldface type, and new sections are set off by a large, descriptive headings. At the end of every chapter are lists of key points, review questions, and activities. The key points summarize the language and ideas contained within the chapter and are an excellent review of the information. The review questions can be used to check the information learned and to identify weak areas needing further study. The activities suggest practical ways to apply the information in the darkroom. A special feature at the back of the book is a glossary containing concisely defined terms for quick reference.

Our intent in this book was to organize the field of graphic arts photography so that the user could effectively and efficiently perform in the printing industry. We believe we have accomplished this goal and that readers will find the book to be both useful and enjoyable. It contains theory and practice. The language is understandable. Step-by-step directions are given for every operation. The illustrations reinforce the ideas and procedures discussed. The full range of all contemporary darkroom tasks are covered. When used as part of a class, the reader should be able to develop entry-level skills to find employment in the exciting field of graphic arts photography.

During the writing of this book, many individuals and companies willingly provided information, illustrations, and support, for which we are grateful. The illustration sources are acknowledged throughout the book in the figure captions, but special recognition must be extended to the E.I. duPont deNemours and Eastman Kodak companies. Thanks are also due to Kimberly Conover-Loar for her work on the line art and to Vivian Golding for her typing. Several reviewers, including Joseph W. Truex of the California Polytechnic State University at San Luis Obispo, William A. Romano, Jr., of Vincennes University, and James F. Herr of the University of Wisconsin—Stout, helped us to refine the contents and presentation of our manuscript. Barbara Gracia of Woodstock Publishers' Services and Sylvia Dovner and Jay Bartlett of Breton Publishers, and their respective staffs, are responsible for crafting that manuscript into a book. Finally, we want to express our heartfelt appreciation to our wives, Bernice Kagy and Mignon Adams, for their understanding and support throughout the several years of this project.

Fred Kagy
Mike Adams

Chapter 1

Photography in the Graphic Arts

• Objectives

In this chapter you will cover:

- The printing cycle,
- How photography is used in the printing cycle,
- The photographic steps,
- Some common printing terms.

After reading the chapter you should be able to:

- List and describe the six basic steps in the printing cycle,
- Explain why photography is an important printing tool,
- Briefly describe the basic photoconversion steps,
- Recognize and use in conversation the most common printing terms.

Ours is a visual world. While we hear, smell, taste, and touch, seeing is the most important way we get information from the world around us. Printing is a visual industry; it produces products that people use to obtain information through the sense of sight. When we talk about photography and printing, most of us think of printed photographs in magazines, newspapers, or books. The role of photography in the graphic arts, however, goes far beyond illustration or pictures. Most of today's modern print technology uses photography in nearly every step of the printing cycle.

• Printing Cycle

There are six basic steps, called the **printing cycle**, through which every printing job must go:

1. Image design,
2. Image assembly,
3. Image conversion,
4. Image carrier preparation,
5. Image transfer,
6. Finishing.

Image Design. Every printed piece begins as an idea (figure 1.1). The design step brings the idea from the artist's mind to a piece of paper. Type sizes and styles, placement of the

Figure 1.1. Planning a design. Designers create images that are reproduced by printers.

Figure 1.2. Preparing a mechanical.

words on the page, use of illustrations, and the kind of paper and color or ink are determined by the designer. Sometimes artists use photography to test ideas. They might decide to enlarge or reduce a drawing photographically to compare sizes, or they might make what is called a **stat**, or a **velox**, which is a rapid photoreproduction of the originial. Artists might also use photography to get an idea of what the finished product will look like by pasting pictures onto a comprehensive. A **comprehensive** is a same-size artist's layout that is used to display to the customer a sense of the final product.

Image Assembly. Once the artist has created the design, drawings or photographs to be used in the design are made. Someone must then bring together the type and pictures that will make up the message of the final reproduction. Thus paste-up artists assemble the different images into a final form, called a mechanical (figure 1.2).

Image Conversion. After the design has been made and the type and illustrations are put together as a mechanical, the paper image of the mechanical is converted to a film image (figure 1.3). The point of this book is to examine the photographic processes that make this conversion.

Image Carrier Preparation. The converted film image will be used to make a printing plate. Many jobs, however, require several different pieces of film. Some jobs combine type (words) and photographs that will print in one color, while others use several film images, each to print in a different color. The process of bringing together all of the different film images into their required positions is called stripping (figure 1.4). The person who does the work of putting the film images together is called a stripper.

After the several pieces of film are combined into a larger piece of film (called a film flat), they are placed over a light-sensitive print-

Figure 1.3. Image conversion. A vertical process camera is used here to transfer the paste-up image to film.

Figure 1.4. Image assembly. A stripper combines different film images in the image assembly step of the printing cycle.

ing plate, and light is passed through the film image openings to expose the plate.

Image Transfer. At this stage of the cycle, the printing plate (image carrier) is placed on some kind of press, and ink is used to create the printed piece (figure 1.5). Photography is not used in this step.

Finishing. All products must be prepared for delivery to the customer. Some are trimmed, stapled, bound, punched, stitched, folded, inserted, or even padded, and others are merely inspected and packaged (figure 1.6). Following this step, the printer moves back to the beginning of the cycle with another customer's order, and the process is repeated. Only the last two steps do not use the photographic process in one form or another.

Figure 1.5. Image transfer. We begin to see the results of the production effort when a job reaches the press.

Figure 1.6. Trimming the printed job.

• Role of Photography in the Production Processes

Gutenberg invented movable type sometime around 1452. For almost three hundred years after that invention, the word **printer** meant only one thing: someone who worked with individual pieces of type by hand and who transferred images onto paper from a raised surface. Since the invention of lithography by Alois Sensfelder in 1789, and the introduction of screen process and gravure as industrial processes, the meaning of the title printer has not been so clear. An important concept that we must understand is that the skills used for all the printing processes are similar in many ways. The following sections discuss how photography can be used in the preparation of relief, litho, screen, or gravure printing plates.

Relief Printing

Some relief image carriers such as hand-set foundry type, linotype composition, or duplicate plates (stereotypes are still used in the newspaper industry) are still prepared manually; however, the trend has been to use photomechanical plates. There are many different types of photomechanical relief plates, but the preparation procedures are all basically the same.

A piece of smooth material or plate is coated with a light-sensitive emulsion. A sheet of film (usually a negative) is placed in contact with the dry emulsion coating, and the coating is exposed using a powerful light source (figure 1.7). The light passes through the image openings on the film and hardens the emulsion, but it does not reach the coating in the nonimage of black portions of the film negative. This unexposed nonimage emulsion area is then washed away in a developing step, leaving only the image areas covered with a hardened emulsion. The nonimage areas are next removed by chemical etching until the image area is higher than the nonprinting area. The hardened emulsion is finally dissolved, using a special solvent, and the relief plate is ready for the press.

Photo-engraving has been used for many years by relief printers to etch away, with acid, the nonimage portions of a metal plate. More recently, printers are using *photopolymer* plates that are formed by the bonding of a hard, light-sensitive polymer to a film or metal base. Many of these new photomechanical relief plates can be used for extremely long press runs; literally millions of impressions can be transferred from the same printing plate.

Lithographic Printing

Ever since lithographers stopped drawing directly on their heavy pieces of limestone and began using metal as the image carrier, photography has been employed as an important tool. There are many different kinds of litho plates, but the basic processing procedures are essentially the same. A light-sensitive emulsion is coated onto a flexible sheet of thin metal. After the image to be printed has been recorded on a piece of transparent film, it is placed in contact with the dry plate. Light is directed through the openings in the film, which hardens the emulsion; light does not reach the areas of the plate that are blocked by the sheet of film in the nonimage areas. The soft emulsion is then washed away, leaving the hardened coating in the shape of the image to be printed (figure 1.8). Sometimes a special material is made to adhere to the image area to increase the length of press run, but the exposed emulsion is still the factor that allows the process to work.

Some litho plates use film negatives and others use film positives; some types require three or four processing steps, while others need only one; some carriers have a paper base, some are made from a sheet of plastic, and still others use metal (usually aluminum). However, the important idea to understand is that, all industrial lithographic image carriers use photography as a means of creating the final printing image.

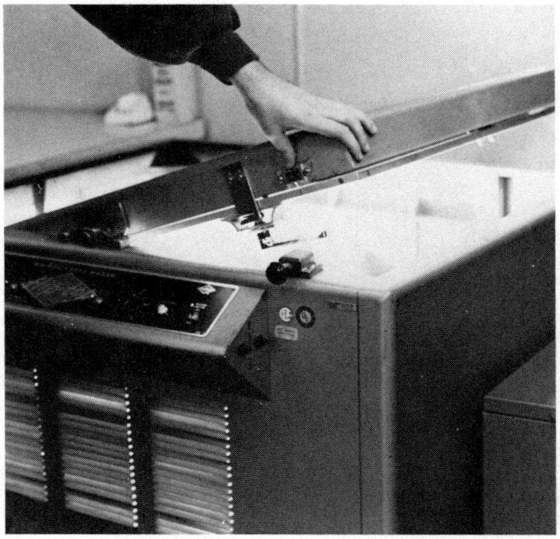

Figure 1.7. Exposing photographic emulsions in a platemaker.

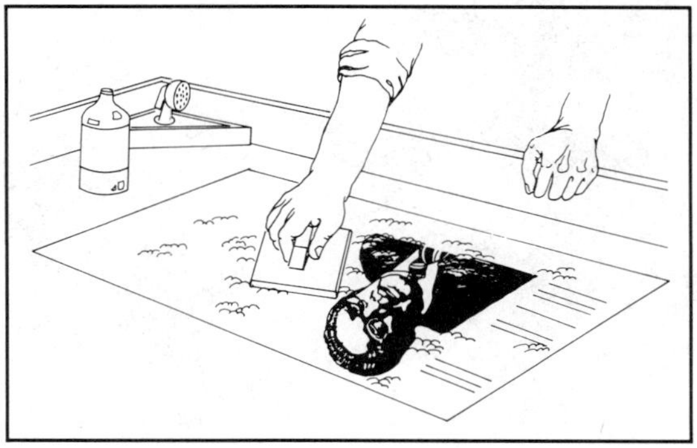

Figure 1.8. Washing away unexposed emulsion. (Kimberly Conover-Loar)

Screen Process Printing

Screen process printing stencils traditionally have been cut by hand, using a sharp knife to remove the printing areas from some kind of masking materials. Hand-cut stencils are still common, but the use of photographic stencils is now an important industrial process.

The basic procedure for preparing a stencil is first to coat a relatively thick layer of light-sensitive emulsion upon a piece of plastic or, alternatively, directly upon the screen fabric. A transparent film positive, carrying the desired image, is placed against the dry emulsion (figure 1.9). Light is allowed to pass through the film, hardening the nonimage areas, but does not reach the coating where the image blocks its passage. The soft, image emulsion is then washed away, leaving a clean opening in the shape of the printing design (figure 1.10). If the emulsion is coated onto a piece of thin plastic film, the emulsion

Figure 1.9. Exposing a transparent film positive to the emulsion in screen process printing.

Figure 1.10. Washing away unexposed screen emulsion with warm water.

side of the film is pressed against the screen fabric while still moist and then allowed to dry. When the coating is dry, the plastic film is carefully pulled away, leaving a perfect stencil on the screen. If the emulsion is coated directly onto the screen, then it is simply allowed to dry, and the stencil is ready to print.

Again, photography is used to control the passage of light to create the image carrier.

Gravure Printing

Intaglio printing is an old process, used today by artists to create images by cutting into a printing plate. Ink is forced into the sunken image and then transferred to paper. The industrial application of intaglio is called **gravure** (figure 1.11).

One way to make a gravure printing surface is to expose a film positive to a special light-sensitive masking material (figure 1.12). Light passes through the clear areas of the film and hardens the mask. The mask remains soft under the postitive image. Next the mask is mounted onto a special copper-plated cylinder and developed so that the unexposed areas dissolve away. Finally, the mask-covered cylinder is rotated through an etching bath. The acid eats away the copper where the mask is open (where the positive image did not harden the mask). When the mask is removed, the printing image remains, sunken into the surface of the cylinder.

It is important to remember that photography is a tool used by almost all printers. It makes no difference that they are using relief, lithographic, screen process, or gravure plates; photography can be used to prepare image carriers that are placed on a printing press.

• The Photoconversion Process

While this book is concerned with the use of photography for printing reproduction, a brief overview of the basic photographic steps is valu-

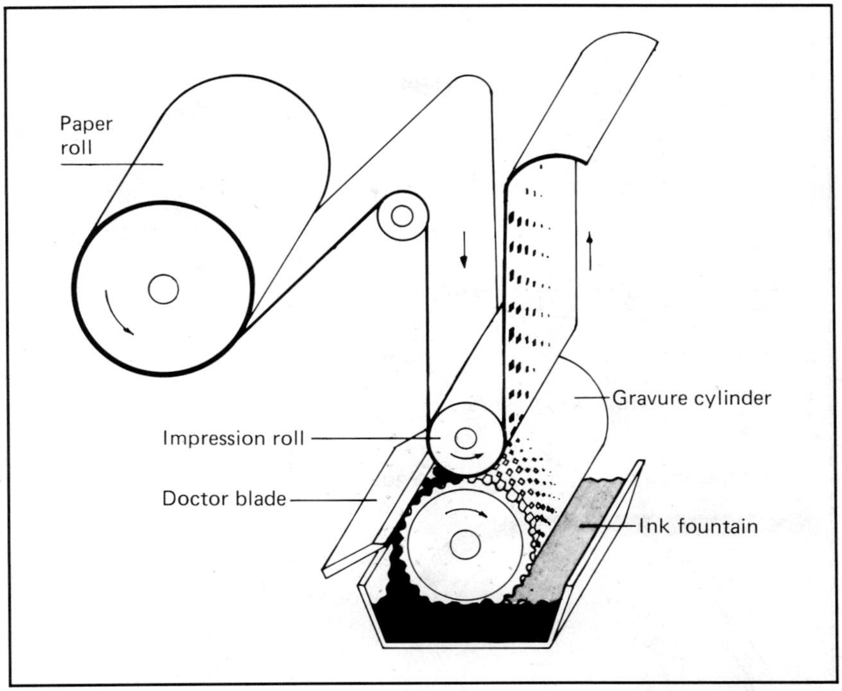

Figure 1.11. Gravure printing. Most industrial gravure prints from sunken images.

able. After the designer has created the desired image and the type and illustrations have been brought together in the image assembly step, the process photographer is ready to convert, or transfer, the form, or image, to a sheet of transparent film.

The photoconversion process begins by mounting the design on the **copyboard** of a large camera. The photographer then places a sheet of film on the vacuum back (sometimes called **filmboard**). Film is nothing more than a flexible sheet (usually plastic) that has been coated with a special chemical formulation, emulsion, that reacts or changes when light strikes it.

Most cameras used by printing photographers can be set up so the image that is recorded on the film is either larger, smaller, or exactly the same size as the original layout. Once the camera enlargement or reduction has been established and the proper camera adjustments made, the camera operator turns on the camera lights. When the light strikes the copyboard, it is reflected by the white areas of the artist's layout, back through the camera lens, until it reaches the film. The light that strikes the black lines (illustrations and type) is absorbed—that is, it is not reflected back. Almost any dark color absorbs more light than it reflects. Where light is absorbed, no light reaches the film (figure 1.13). This works out very well: When light reaches the film, it changes the chemical emulsion in the nonimage areas of the original design; when light does not reach the film, the image areas remain unchanged.

After the camera lights go out, it is not possible to see the change in the chemical emulsion. At this point the change is invisible, or latent. To make the change real (so that we can see it) the photographer must begin the developing process.

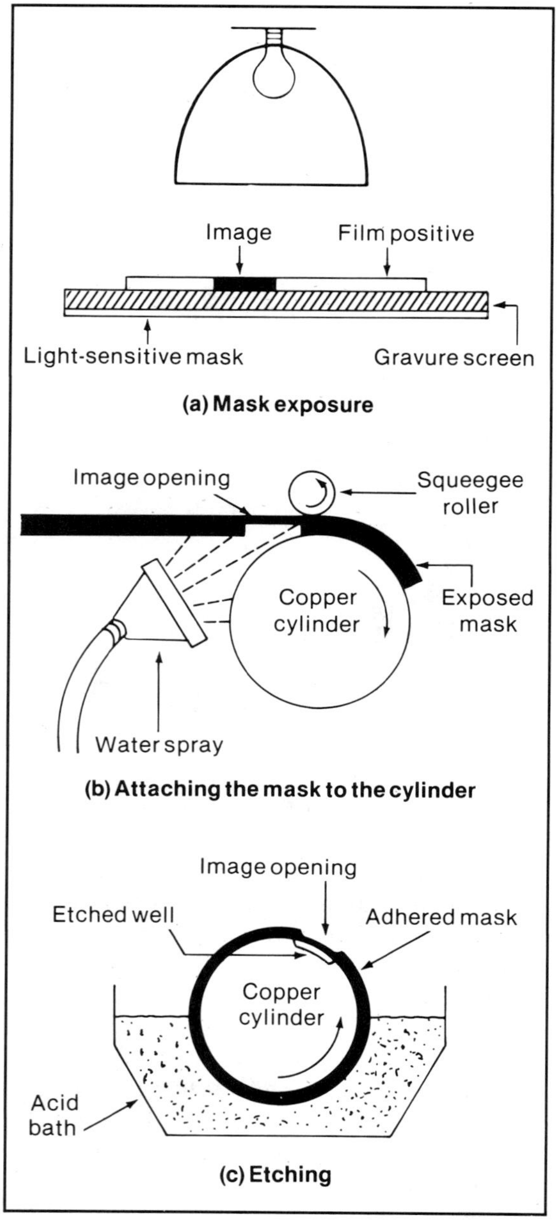

Figure 1.12. Preparation of a gravure cylinder. (a) Expose a light-sensitive mask to a film positive, (b) attach the mask to the cylinder, and (c) etch the cylinder.

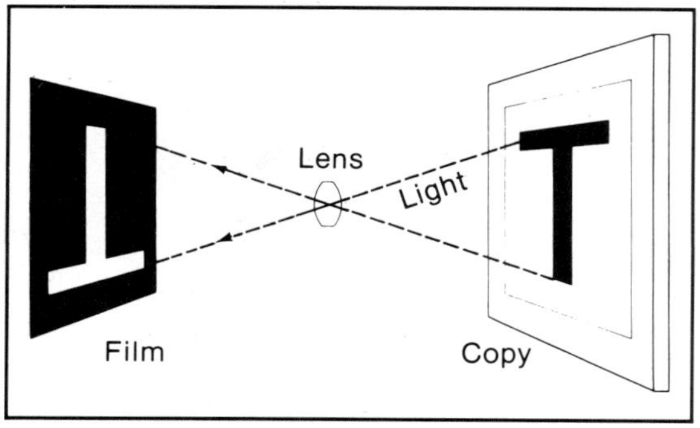

Figure 1.13. Light reaches the film through the camera lens. (Kimberly Conover-Loar)

The first step in the developing process is to place the film in the **developer**. The developer is a liquid chemical that makes the exposed areas of the film turn solid black. The unexposed, or image areas, remain unchanged. The next step is to halt the developing action and to neutralize the developer chemicals; this step is called the **stop bath**. Next, the unexposed emulsion must be removed in a liquid chemical called the **fixer** (fixer is also called **hypo**). The fixer leaves the sheet solid black in the nonimage areas but clear, or transparent, in the image areas. The final step is to wash the film until all traces of the suspended hypo or fixing bath are removed and the sheet is dry.

The remainder of this book deals with helping you to understand how to control these procedures. The goal is to enable you to produce high-quality pieces of film that can be used to make printing plates.

• Establishing a Common Language

One of the most difficult parts of learning a new subject is trying to understand the special language unique to it. Language that is commonplace to individuals who have worked in a field for many years might be totally new to someone just beginning to study the field. Sometimes there are even problems between two people who have a great deal of experience but who have worked in different parts of the country where different words or terms are used to describe the same idea. In this book most new words are defined when they are used. However, a glossary is provided at the back of the book to help you remember the meaning of difficult terms.

Since this book is intended for use by students who have some background in printing, an additional problem with language arises. A great many basic terms used throughout these pages probably have been covered in earlier coursework, but the authors have no idea of the level of understanding of every reader. Thus, we must come to a common definition of some basic words.

Paste-up refers to the materials prepared by the artist and compositor and is the final image that will be converted to the transparent film by the photographer. Other terms that mean the same thing are **mechanical** and **final layout**. Sometimes the printer might say, ''Please give me the copy.'' The **copy** might be the information from which the paste-up is prepared, but the same term might also be used to describe the paste-up itself. Confusing? You will get used to it.

A **film negative** is a sheet of transparent-based material, and when the image is **right reading** (so you can read the printing from left to right, just as we read these lines) the emulsion side is away from the viewer (figure 1.14).

A **film positive** is defined as a sheet of transparent-based material, and when the piece is held so the image is **right reading**, the emulsion side is on top, or facing, the viewer (figure 1.15).

A **window** in a clear opening in a film negative (figure 1.16). It typically is prepared on the paste-up as a large block of red or black. That area of the film is not exposed and remains clear during development. The purpose of a window is to hold another piece of film (usually a halftone during carrier or plate preparation) and

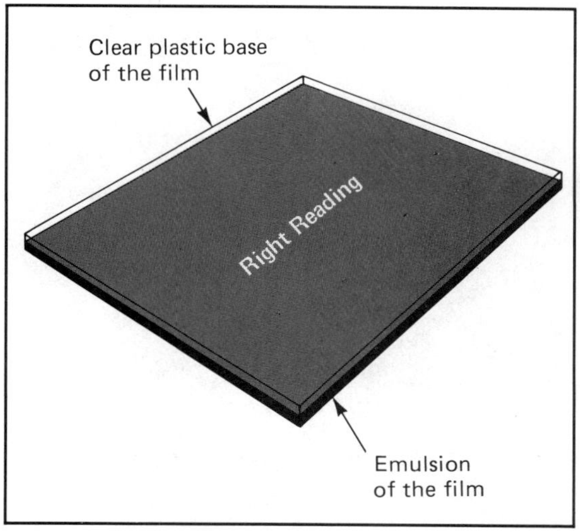

Figure 1.14. Film negative—right reading through the film base.

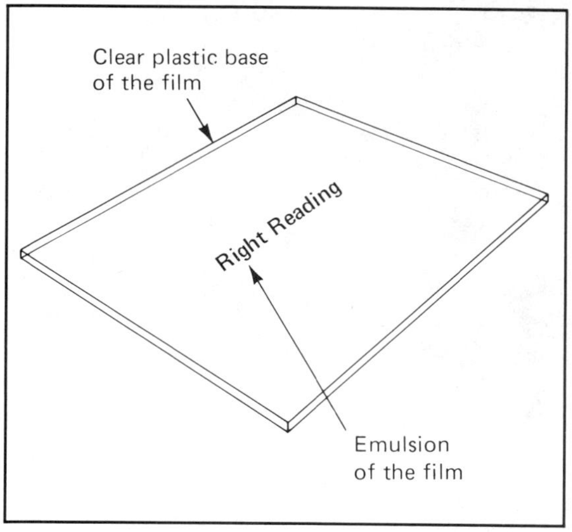

Figure 1.15. Film positive—right reading through the film emulsion.

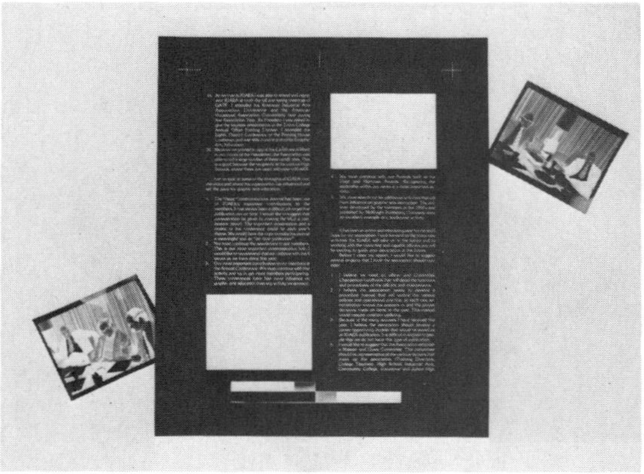

Figure 1.16. Example of windows on a negative.

Figure 1.17. Example of a surprint

to provide border lines when the images are plated.

A **surprint**, or **overprint**, is an image that has been positioned over another design (figure 1.17). It is usually printed as a solid, but it could be reproduced as a tint. A surprint is created by simply exposing the same plate to two different film images, one after the other.

Figure 1.18. Example of a reverse.

A **reverse** is an image that has been positioned over another design but that is created by the absence of ink (figure 1.18). It is created by positioning a transparent film positive that carries the image to be reversed over the film negative. When the plate is made, the positive blocks the passage of light wherever the image appears, preventing any image from being formed on the plate.

A **tint** is an image created by a special piece of film. A screen tint is usually made up of a series of many small dots, all of the same shape and size. By putting the screen between a film negative and the printing plate, the solid open area is changed to dots (figure 1.19). These small dots appear to the human eye as a lighter color than solid ink. Tints can be purchased in many dot sizes and areas.

A **halftone** is a line conversion of a continuous-tone photograph. A special screen (different from a screen tint) breaks the tones into dots of varying shapes and sizes, with varying amounts of space between the dots (see figure 4.9). The combination of shape, size, and position of these dots tricks the human eye into thinking it is seeing an image with many different tones.

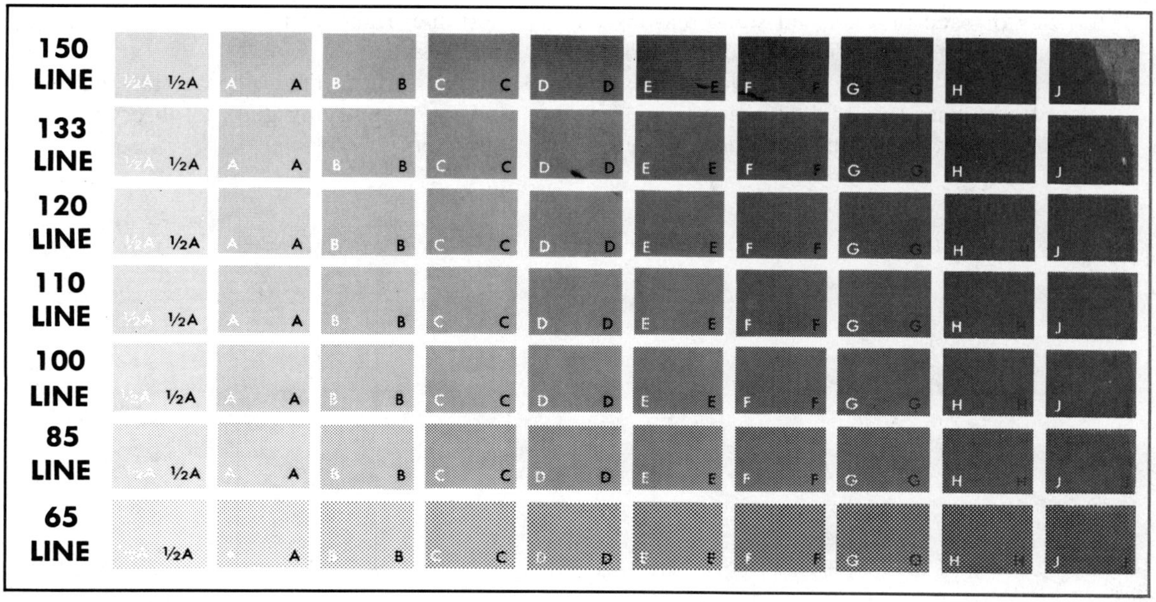

Figure 1.19. Screen tints. These tints are formed from small dots of uniform size, shape, and position. (Courtesy of ByChrome Co., Inc.)

• Key Points

- There are six steps in the printing cycle. They are image design, image assembly, image conversion, image carrier preparation, image transfer, and finishing.
- Photography is an important printing tool. It can be used in relief, screen process, lithography, or gravure to prepare printing plates.
- Film images are created by light being reflected from an image, or passing through a sheet of film, onto a sheet of light-sensitive film. The image is made permanent by the following developing steps: developer, stop, fixer, wash, and drying.
- It is important that common printing terms be thoroughly understood. Several important ones are paste-up, mechanical, copy, negative, positive, right reading, window, surprint, overprint, tint, reverse, drop, and halftone.

• Review Questions

1. What are the six steps in the printing cycle?
2. What are the main steps in the photoconversion process?
3. Without looking back at the chapter, explain each of these terms:

paste-up	reverse
right reading	surprint
window	

• Activities

1. Identify several examples of printed products that represent uses of each of the four major printing processes. Discuss charac-

teristics of each product and some reasons for choosing that specific method of reproduction.
2. Identify the base side and emulsion side of a film negative. Examine both sides to determine right-reading and wrong-reading images.
3. Examine a printed photograph (halftone) with a magnifying glass to observe the dot structure.

Chapter 2

Photoconversion Equipment

• Objectives

In this chapter you will cover:

- Camera structures and types,
- Types of light sources,
- Exposure control devices,
- Common darkroom equipment,
- Filters,
- Registration control,
- Darkroom design.

After reading the chapter you should be able to:

- Identify the major camera parts;
- Explain the difference between horizontal and vertical process cameras;
- Recognize and explain light measurements such as millimicrons or nanometers and angstrom units;
- Explain the differences between common graphic arts light sources;
- Recognize and explain the function of repeating timers, sweep timers, and integrated unit systems;
- Recognize and explain the purposes of safelights, darkroom sinks, temperature control units, tray and automatic processors, stabilization processors, photomechanical processors, vacuum frames, point light sources, and registration punches and tabs;
- Explain the difference between filters that transmit and absorb light;
- Identify the wet and dry sides of a process darkroom and explain the idea of work flow in the darkroom area.

This chapter provides you with some basic understandings about the equipment that is used in the darkroom area for graphic arts photography. If you do not read this chapter first—and understand it—you will have trouble understanding the rest of the book. When discussing more advanced ideas in later chapters, the authors might say, "Refer to chapter 2 for a review of the basic equipment to perform this operation." If, at that point, you are not sure what the basic

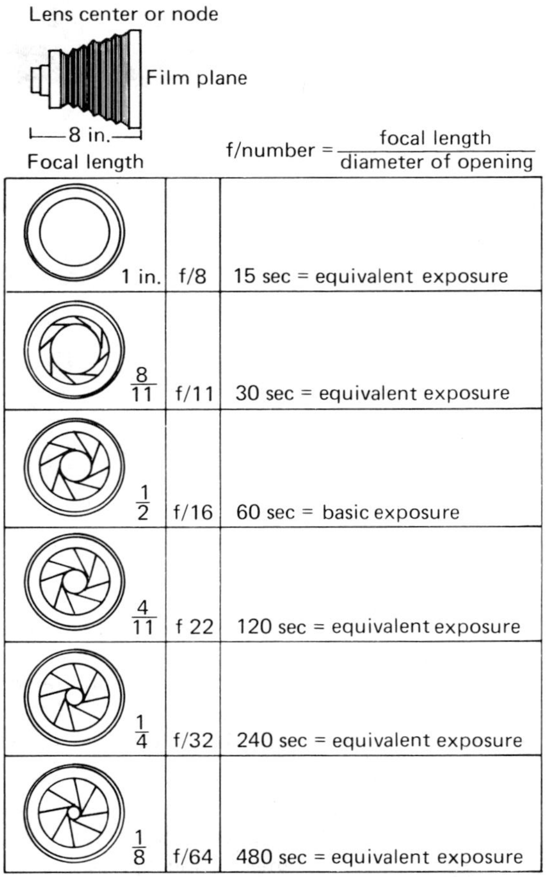

Lens center or node
Film plane
8 in.
Focal length
f/number = focal length / diameter of opening
1 in. f/8 15 sec = equivalent exposure
8/11 f/11 30 sec = equivalent exposure
1/2 f/16 60 sec = basic exposure
4/11 f 22 120 sec = equivalent exposure
1/4 f/32 240 sec = equivalent exposure
1/8 f/64 480 sec = equivalent exposure

Figure 2.1. Camera f/stops. Camera f/stop is the relationship between focal length and lens opening size. In this figure the focal length is 8 inches and the lens opening sizes vary from 1 inch to 1/8 inch. The basic exposure time is 60 seconds at f/16. Equivalent exposure times are given for the remaining steps.

equipment is, then stop and come back to these pages. This information is important.

• Cameras

Camera Structure

Cameras are machines that control the passage of light—that is, they either let light in or keep it out. All camera structures begin with a light-tight box (light-tight means that light cannot seep in through the corners or edges). Next, a hole is added to allow light to enter. This opening is called an **aperture**. Usually, a special device called a lens is placed in the hole, but a lens is not absolutely necessary. In the early days of photography, so-called pinhole cameras were used that had nothing more than a pinhole punched through the box. A lens is valuable, however, because it helps to focus the image (or to make it sharp and clear).

It is possible to adjust the size of most apertures to help control the amount of light that enters the camera. If the size of the aperture is adjustable, the camera is said to have a **diaphragm control**. The amount of light controlled by the diaphragm is measured by the f/stop system. The **f/stop system** is based upon the ratio of the size of the aperture opening (diameter) to the focal length of the camera lens. Focal length is the distance from the center of the lens to the film plane (filmboard) when the lens is focused at infinity (maximum reduction for graphic arts process cameras) (figure 2.1). If the lens has an 8-inch focal length, a 1-inch opening is said to have the f/stop value of f/8; a half-inch opening is f/16. The numbers and openings are selected so that adjacent numbers differ by a factor of two in the quantity of light they pass into the camera. Notice that the larger the f number, the smaller the opening. Changing from f/32 to f/22 will double the amount of light that reaches the film (times 2). Moving from f/16 to f/22 will halve it (divided by 2). It is important to understand that an f/stop number will always pass the same amount of light whatever the size of the camera or lens.

After a lens has been added, light can easily enter the camera, but there must be some way to turn off the light entering the camera. The purpose of the **shutter** is to control the length of time that light is allowed to enter the camera through the lens.

Next, some sort of device (called the filmboard, or vacuum back) must be placed in the back of the light-tight box to hold the film during the exposure (when the light is passing through the lens). Additionally, the film-holding system must support the film so that it is at a right angle to the line that passes through the center of the lens (figure 2.2). Most cameras are designed so that the filmboard folds down, away from the camera, to mount the film and then swings back into place for the exposure (figure 2.3). Many camera manufacturers use a vacuum system to hold the film on the filmboard in which suction draws the film against the back of the camera.

With graphic arts, or process cameras, it is necessary to add a special unit that will hold the mechanical; this is called the **copyboard** (figure 2.4). The copy must be held exactly parallel to the filmboard so that the film image will be exactly in focus. Additionally, the copyboard must hold the mechanical so that it does not move during the exposure. Again, many companies build cameras that use a vacuum system to hold the final layout in place.

In graphic arts photography, the photographer often needs to enlarge or reduce the size of the film image from the original layout size. The photograph supplied to the printer is rarely the size needed for the printed piece. Thus, the graphic arts photographer must adjust the size so that it fits into the required area. On graphic arts cameras, the size of the film image is adjusted by changing the ratio (the fractional relationship) between the distance from the filmboard to the lens and the distance from the lens to the copyboard.

Figure 2.2. Film-holding system. The filmboard and copyboard are parallel to each other and at a right angle to an imaginary line that runs through the lens.

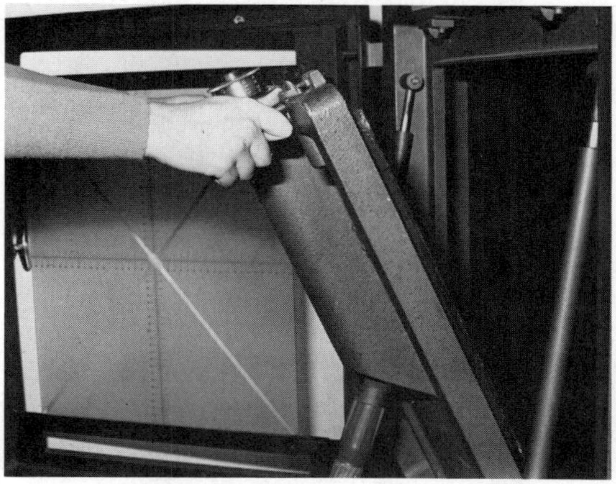

Figure 2.3. Filmboard. Most filmboards fold down and away from the camera.

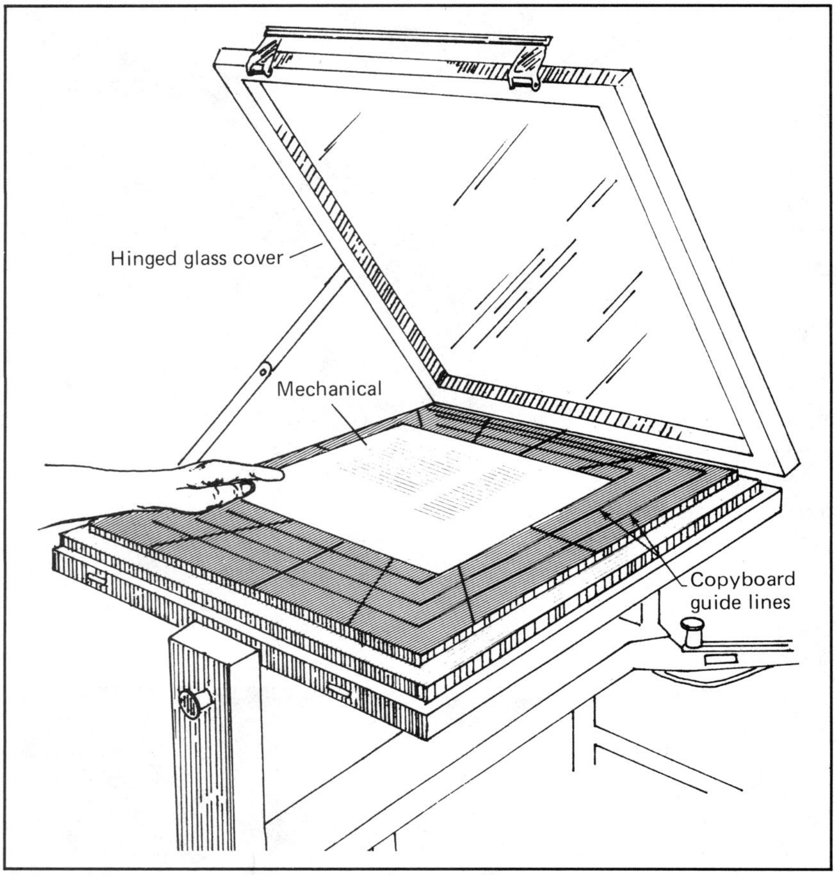

Figure 2.4. Copyboard. The purpose of the copyboard is to hold the paste-up in position during exposure. (Kimberly Conover-Loar)

To review, the basic parts of any graphic arts camera are a light-tight box, lens, aperture, shutter, filmboard, copyboard, and enlargement/reduction controls. A variety of additional devices are available, but these six parts are found on every process camera. Some of these components are discussed in much greater detail later in the book.

Types of Process Cameras

There are two basic types of graphic arts cameras. The first is called a **horizontal process camera** (figure 2.5). It is called horizontal because the imaginary line that passes through the center of the lens is always parallel to the ground or floor. Additionally, it is designed so that the filmboard end of the camera is housed in the darkroom and the copyboard end is outside, in a normally lighted room (see figure 2.30).

The second type of graphic arts camera is called a **vertical process camera** (figure 2.6). With this camera design, the line that passes through the center of the lens is at a right angle to the floor. Vertical cameras are intended to be housed entirely in the darkroom so that both

Figure 2.5. Horizontal process camera. (Courtesy of Brown Service and Parts, Inc.)

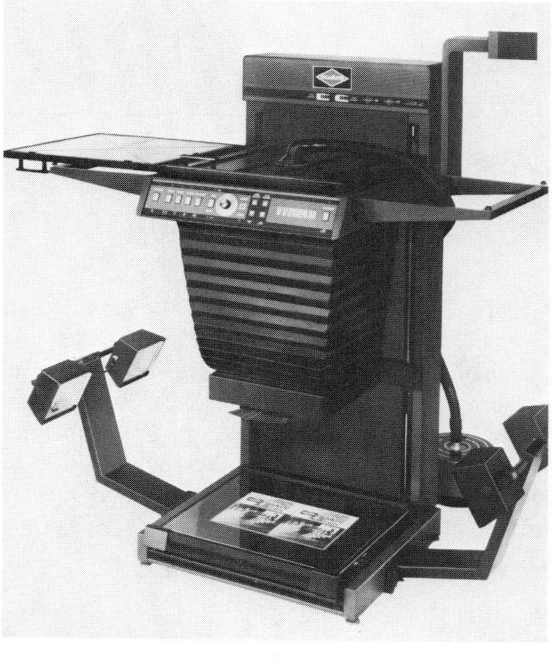

Figure 2.6. Vertical process camera. (Courtesy of nuArc Company, Inc.)

camera exposure and film processing take place in the same area (see figure 2.30).

In addition to the two basic types, some process cameras are used for special purposes. Two examples are the **stat** camera and the **camera/plate system**. Stat cameras are special devices that are used to prepare opaque (opaque means that you cannot see through the base—like the paper in this book) positives from opaque positive originals.

They are valuable in the composition stage of the printing cycle when an original must be enlarged or reduced and then added to a paste-

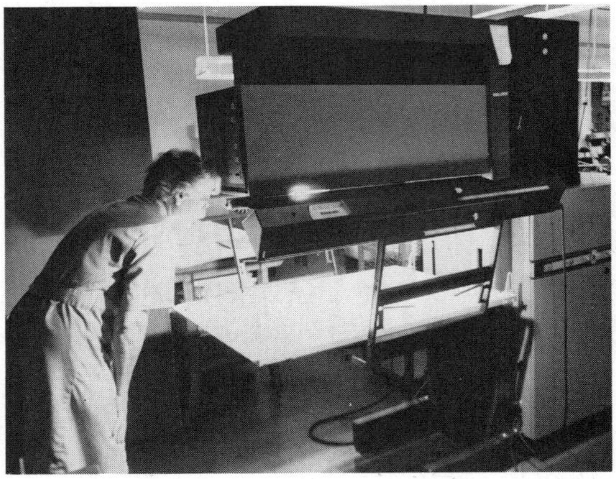

Figure 2.7. Camera/plate systems for direct-image plates.

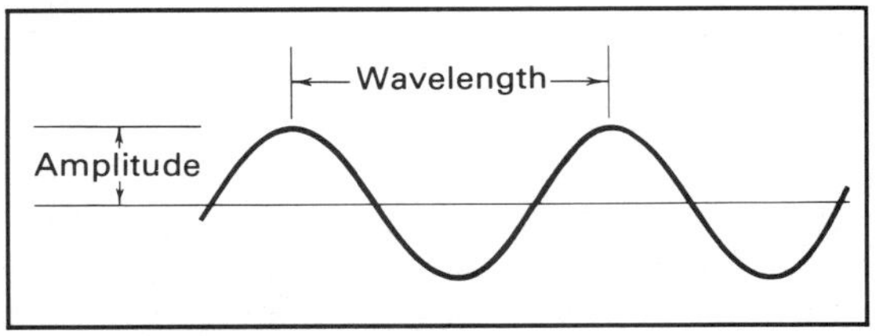

Figure 2.8. Diagram of a lightwave. Energy is measured by wavelength.

up. The camera/plate system is a technique that prepares a lithographic plate directly from the mechanical, without making a film conversion (figure 2.7). While these devices most appropriately belong with a discussion on platemaking or copy preparation, they are mentioned here because the process photographer is frequently responsible for their operation.

• Light Sources

You can see the words and pictures in this book because light is reflected from these pages back to your eyes. It is important to have a basic understanding of light and how printers control it to produce film images.

Understanding Light

Light is a form of energy that we can see. Heat is energy waves we can feel, and radio waves are energy we can hear if we use a special receiver. All energy is measured by **wavelength**. Wavelength is the distance from one wave crest to the next (figure 2.8). When an object (such as the sun or an electric heater) gives off energy, it is said to radiate; energy is also called **electromagnetic radiation**. Figure 2.9 shows the known spectrum of electromagnetic radiation. Notice that most of the spectrum uses centimeters as the unit of measure. Figure 2.10 shows the size of a centimeter compared to an inch. Next, observe that most of the numbers have exponents (for example, in 10^3, 3 is the exponent). This system is merely a special way to write big numbers. 10^2 means $10 \times 10 = 100$; 10^3 means $10 \times 10 \times 10 = 1{,}000$. Table 2.1 shows the values of some exponential numbers. Exponential notation is a relatively simple system.

Many of the terms in figure 2.9 are probably familiar to you. TV transmissions that you receive on your television set are nothing more than electromagnetic radiation that is made up of wavelengths of about 100 centimeters in size. The X-ray used to determine if a bone was broken is radiation with a very short wavelength.

One very narrow section of the electromagnetic spectrum has been expanded to show you a clearer picture as the **visible spectrum**. The visible spectrum is defined as any electromagnetic radiation that the human eye can see. Because light waves are very small, and because we want to divide a narrow area into very specific parts, a new measure is used. Light is measured in **millimicrons**, or **nanometers**. One millimicron equals one-billionth of a meter, or twenty-five millionths of an inch. Sometimes another measure is used, called **angstrom units**.

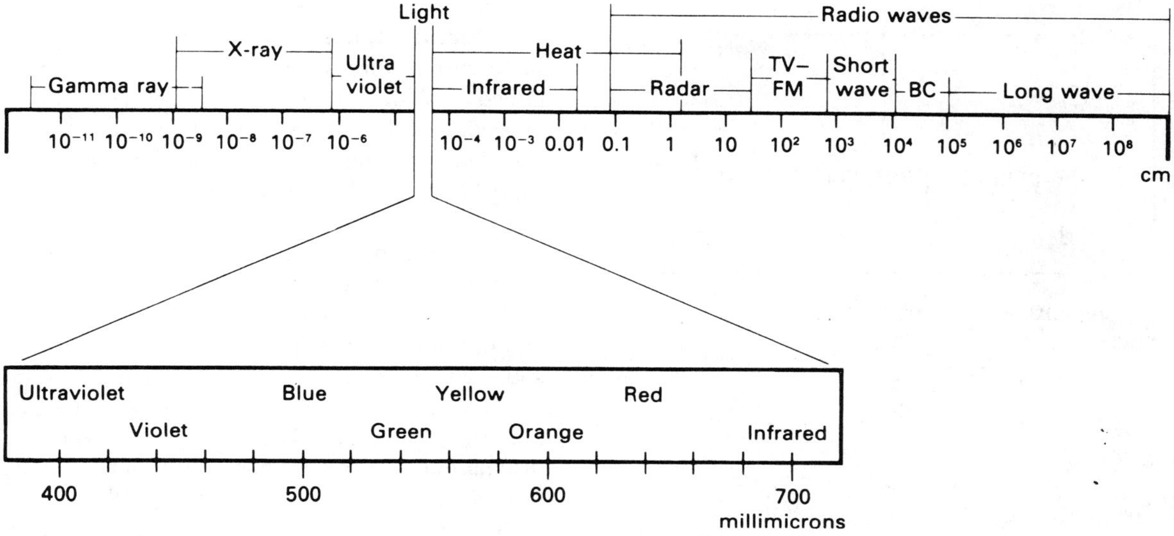

Figure 2.9. Diagram of electromagnetic radiation spectrum.

One millimicron equals ten angstrom units. Regardless of which measure is used, it still measures the wavelength of energy from one wave crest to the next.

Look again at figure 2.9. Notice that each specific color has a special wavelength; blue is about 500 millimicrons, red is approximately 640 millimicrons, and green is around 540 millimicrons. The point is that we see different colors because of the differences in wavelength in the visible spectrum. It is possible to measure the exact wavelength of any color we can see. White light is the balanced mixture of all wavelengths of energy in the visible spectrum. This topic is discussed in greater detail in later chapters when you need to know more.

Table 2.1. Exponential numbers

$10^1 = 10$
$10^2 = 100$
$10^3 = 1000$
$10^4 = 10,000$
$10^5 = 100,000$
•
•
•
$10^{27} = 1,000,000,000,000,000,000,000,000,000$
$10^{-1} = .1$
$10^{-2} = .01$
$10^{-3} = .001$
$10^{-4} = .0001$
$10^{-5} = .00001$
•
•
•
$10^{-27} = .000000000000000000000000001$

Common Graphic Arts Light Sources

Anything that gives off light is called a **light source**. Graphic arts photographers once used

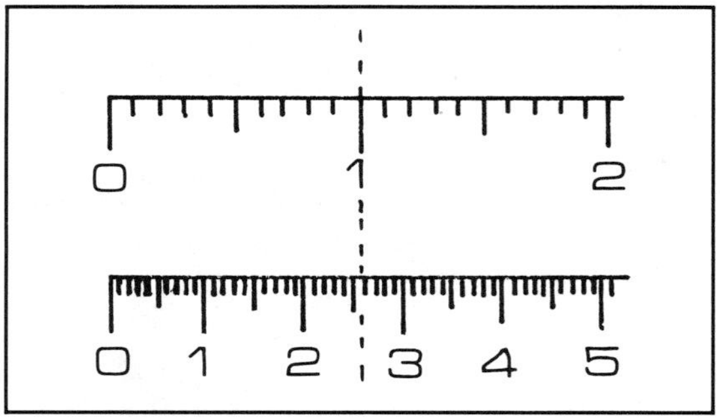

Figure 2.10. Inch/centimeter conversion scale. One inch equals 2.54 centimeters.

the sun as their only source of light. Our sun is the most ideal light source since it is balanced white light. The problem, however, is that the sun is not predictable. The intensity changes from morning to night; if a cloud passes over the sun, then the photographer has to wait; during rainfall, it cannot be used at all. Process photographers now use artificial (manmade) light sources.

Carbon arc is perhaps the oldest artificial light source used in the graphic arts industry. Light is created by passing an electrical current through two carbon rods (figure 2.11). The same procedure is used in arc welding, only the goal there is to create heat. Although carbon arc is a very good light source, it has several limitations. For example, voltage changes in the electrical current can affect the quality of the light output. In the process of creating light, the carbon rods are consumed, which gives off noxious fumes and a great amount of dirt. The dirt is a special problem in the darkroom because that area must be kept as clean as possible.

Tungsten lights are similar to the light bulb you place in your reading lamp to study this book after the sun goes down. A vacuum is created in a hollow glass bulb. A thin wire, called the filament, is contained in the vacuum. When electricity is passed through the filament, light is created.

Mercury vapor lamps create light by passing a current through a mercury gas that is contained in a quartz bulb. The vaporization and ionization of the gas generates the powerful light. The lamps require a short warm-up time and must be cooled down before they can be started again.

Pulsed xenon lights were first developed as electronic flashes for continuous-tone photography (*continuous-tone* is a term that describes another branch of photography, including snapshots and family portraits). The lamp is constructed by filling a quartz tube with a low-pressure xenon gas. The xenon is charged and discharged (a current is passed through it) at the rate of the power line frequency (in the United States, that is 120 times each second). Even though the light is pulsed (turned on and off) during the camera exposure time, the light appears to be constant. The lamp does not require a warm-up time and is similar to the natural white light given off by the sun.

Metal halide is a recent invention. It is basically a mercury vapor design with a special chemical additive called metal halide. The advantage of metal halide lamps is that they have an extremely high intensity (therefore exposure times can be shortened) and can be used in platemaking, proofing, photofabrication, and many other areas in addition to the camera room.

Many other special types of light sources are used by the graphic arts photographer. These five, however, form a good classification system for the beginning printer.

• Exposure Control Devices

Earlier we said that the purpose of the shutter is to control the length of time that light is allowed to enter the camera. A shutter is like a door that can be opened and closed either to pass or block the passage of light. Early photographers merely took the cap off the front of the camera lens and either guessed, watched a clock, or counted to a certain number, then put the cap back on. Graphic arts photographers want to be able to control exactly the length of time that the door is open. Two basic types of exposure control devices are in common use.

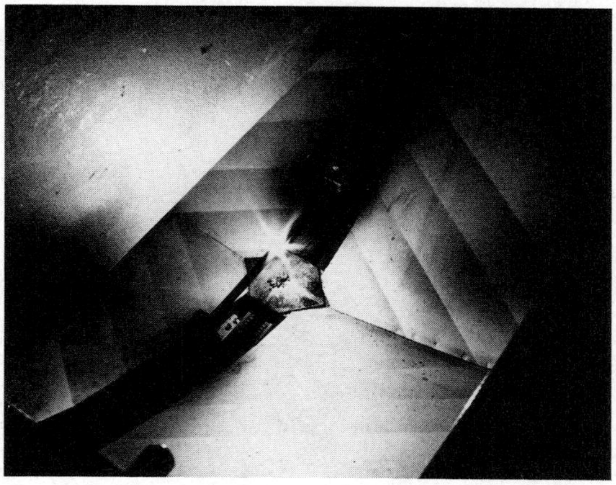

Figure 2.11. Carbon arc. Light can be generated by passing an electrical current through two carbon rods.

Repeating Timer

A **repeating timer** is shown in figure 2.12. It can normally be set to the nearest second, although some types can be adjusted to less than one-second time intervals. A pointer is turned to the required time. A button is usually pushed to start the timer and, at the same time, to open the shutter automatically. When the desired exposure time has passed, the device closes the shutter. The timer then automatically resets itself so that another exposure can be made immediately, without resetting the pointer—that is why it is called repeating.

Figure 2.12. Repeating timer.

Sweep Timer

A **sweep timer** (figure 2.13) is much like a clock. The desired time is set on a large dial. Most sweep timers can be adjusted to a one-second accuracy but have the potential to time for as many as sixty minutes. When the timer is started, the second hand sweeps around the dial, followed by the minute hand, working backward from the preset time. It is always possible, then, to be able to see how much time remains. When the desired exposure or time interval is over, the device automatically shuts off. When a new time measure is required, then the time must be reset on the dial.

Integrated Unit Systems

One problem with any interval timer that opens and closes the shutter after a passage of time is that it does not take into account any variation in light intensity. Changes in voltage coming

Figure 2.13. Sweep timer.

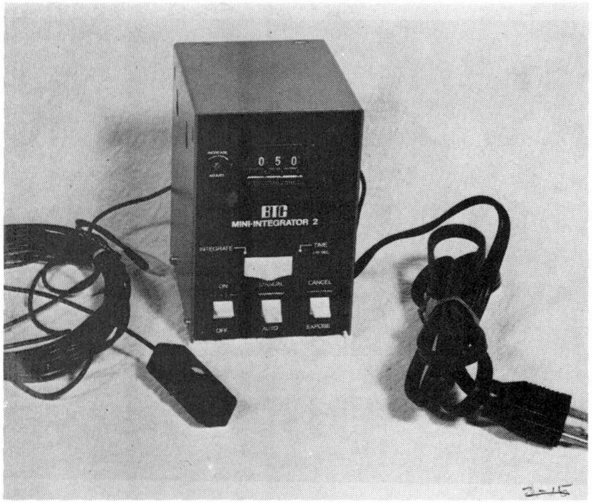

Figure 2.14. Light integrator with photoelectric cell.

from the power source will cause changes in the intensity of the light reaching the film. A more accurate method of controlling film exposure is with a **light integrator** (figure 2.14). A photoelectric cell (a device that converts light energy to electrical energy) is placed in line with the light that passes through the lens. The cell is connected to a device that measures the quantity of light that reaches the film. Instead of time, the camera operator sets the integrator for the quantity of light necessary to expose the film being used properly. The lens is automatically closed when that quantity of light has reached the photoelectric cell. Thus, any changes in copy or light characteristics will be compensated for.

• Darkroom Equipment

Graphic arts photographers work in a darkroom but are rarely in the dark. Beyond the process camera that has already been discussed, a variety of pieces of equipment are commonly found in every printer's darkroom area.

The area is called a **darkroom** because the photographer can control the kind of light that is used and can completely close the room off from any outside light. Most graphic arts photographic operations are performed under **safelights**. Most film used in photo conversion is only sensitive to a small part of the visible spectrum—mostly around the blue end. The photographer, then, can use safelights that emit radiation of a wavelength that does not expose the film. Most darkrooms are equipped with a **white light** system that consists of normal incandescent light bulbs and a separate safelight system. Figure 2.15 shows one example of a darkroom safelight.

All graphic arts films must be processed (developed) chemically at a certain temperature. Most film manufacturers produce their materials to give the best results when developed at 68°F (20°C). The purpose of the darkroom sink is to hold a water bath at a specified temperature. There are several possible ways to control tem-

Figure 2.15. Darkroom safelight.

Figure 2.16. Dial thermometer. A mixing valve can be used to control bath temperature.

perature. The simplest way uses a mixing valve that passes both cold and hot water over a dial thermometer (figure 2.16). The photographer adjusts the amount of water from each faucet until the desired temperature is reached. With this design, water is constantly flowing through the sink area. More advanced systems fill the sink with water and then use a heating element to recirculate it at a constant temperature. This last design is more accurate and less expensive to operate since it does not pump such large quantities of fresh water down the drain.

The temperature of the processing chemicals is usually controlled by floating trays or tanks in the sink water. Stainless steel trays are the most efficient since they rapidly adjust to any temperature fluctuation. However, they are somewhat expensive. Recently, plastic trays have become popular with graphic arts photographers. They are inexpensive, strong, and do not stain or otherwise react to chemicals.

Usually attached to the darkroom sink is some sort of film-washing system (figure 2.17). All traces of the fixer must be removed from the film before it can be used in the next step of the printing production. Usually, good results can be obtained if the water in the washing system is changed every two to three minutes, but always follow the manufacturer's recommendations. Use of a chemical called **hypo eliminator** can greatly reduce washing time.

Most graphic arts darkrooms have a special wet-viewing system that allows the user to examine pieces of film as soon as they come out

Figure 2.17. Film-washing system.

Figure 2.18. Automatic film processor.

of the fixer. Most are a sheet of frosted glass sealed over a box that holds both a white light and a safelight.

Other specialized pieces of darkroom equipment are discussed in each chapter as part of the detailed discussion.

• Processors

Tray Processing

Tray processing is a common technique in the graphic arts industry. The photographer sets a timer and then inserts the sheet of exposed film into the first bath. After the appropriate time, the film is moved to the second bath and finally to the third. Variables that can affect this procedure include exactness of time, rate of agitation (rocking the tray), how the film is inserted in the bath, and activity level of the chemicals. Tray processing is discussed in greater detail in chapter 5.

Conventional Automatic Processors

Many different automatic film processors are available to the graphic arts photographer (figure 2.18). All conventional processors, however, have the same basic structure. Figure 5.11 shows a cross-sectional view of a typical machine. Notice that the film is carried by a moving belt through three separate deep chemical tanks. These tanks correspond to the same steps followed for tray processing. The difference is that, with the automatic devices, the chemical activity level (freshness), exact temperature, rate of agitation, and length of time in each bath is exactly controlled. Additionally, most manufacturers advertise dry-to-dry processing, in which a dry sheet of exposed film is placed in the device and a short time later a dry, developed piece of film drops out.

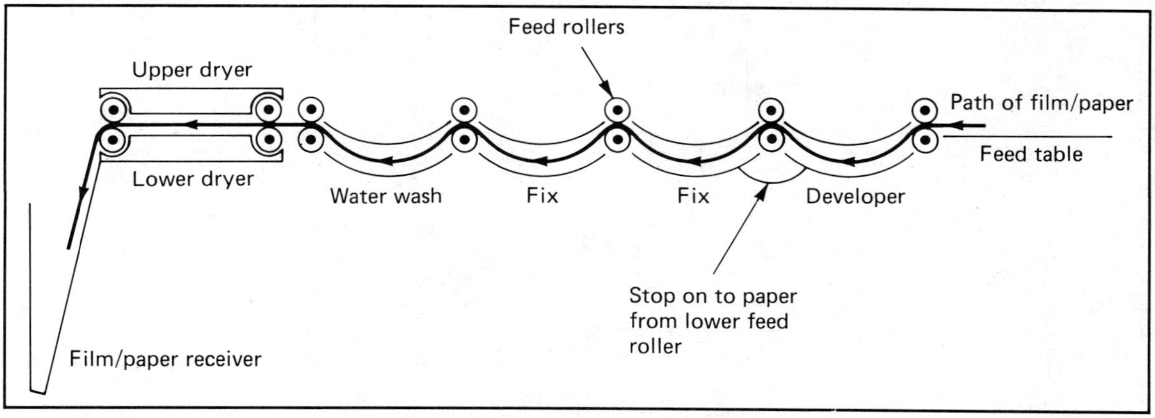

Figure 2.19. Diagram of a rapid access processor. These processors are of a different design than the traditional deep-tank automatic systems.

One major concern with automatic processing is the control of the chemical activity. With most machines, the operator dials in the number of square inches of film being entered, and the device automatically adds a replenisher to the developer and fixer tanks. It is necessary to send control strips through the machine frequently to insure that the device is operating correctly and processing high-quality pieces of film.

Until recently, separate machines had to be maintained for graphic arts film and continuous-tone materials. With the development of machine processing films (called MP), special chemicals can be used to process any type of film used in the graphic arts darkroom.

Rapid Access Processors

Rapid access equipment and materials are part of a relatively new development that allows the photographer great latitude in both exposure and processing. Film materials, called **daylight working**, can be handled under normally lit working conditions for a limited length of time. Rapid access processors are of a different design than the standard deep-tank automatic processors (figure 2.19). Notice in figure 2.19 that the film passes through the processor in a relatively straight line rather than being moved by a belt system. Rapid access is a system rather than a specific machine; the processor must be used with the special film materials designed for the process. The film, however, may be tray processed using rapid access chemicals.

Stabilization Processors

Stabilization processing is a special technique used to prepare opaque film materials. The technique is used widely in copy preparation to prepare camera-ready enlargements or reductions, to develop paper used in photographic composition, to proof negatives, and sometimes to prepare prescreened halftones (see chapter 9). The exposed sheet is passed through two chemical baths in the processor (figure 2.20). The first bath is an activator that starts the developing action and that makes the sheet no longer light sensitive. The second bath is a stabilizer that halts development and makes the image per-

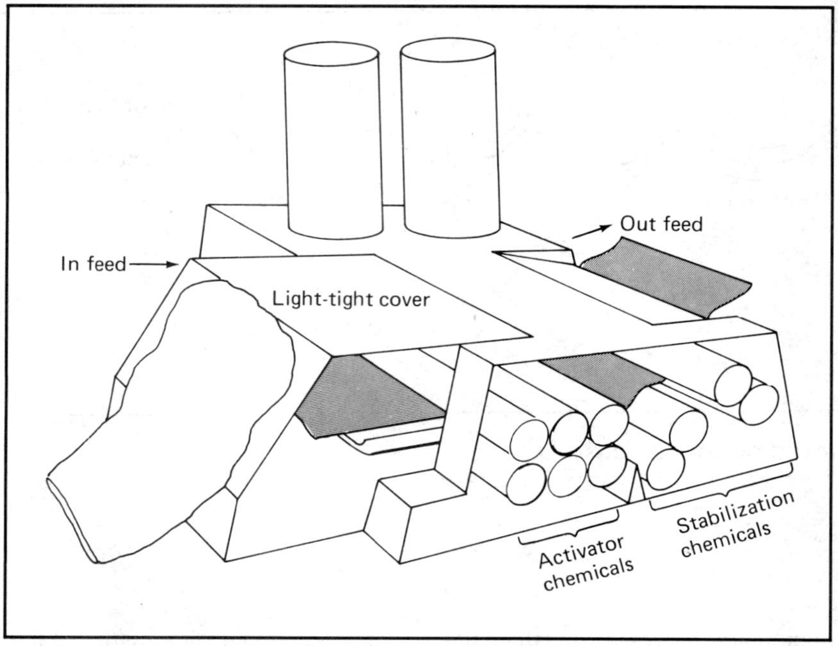

Figure 2.20. Stabilization processor. This processor passes an exposed sheet through two separate baths. (Kimberly Conover-Loar)

manent. If the film is to be used over a long period of time, it should be placed in a separate fixer tray and then washed before being allowed to dry.

Diffusion Transfer Processors

Diffusion transfer (sometimes called **photomechanical transfer**) is a process that has application in both photography and platemaking. Basically, the process involves a light-sensitive negative image sheet and a chemically sensitive receiver sheet. The negative sheet is exposed to the camera copy (see chapter 7). The emulsion of the negative is then placed against the receiver and is passed through an activator solution in a special processor (figure 2.21). The material on the negative sheet, in the image area, is transferred to the receiver sheet. Once dry, the receiver is ready to be placed directly on the paste-up, or mechanical. This process is discussed in greater detail in chapter 10.

• Filters

A **filter** is a material used to control the passage of light. Some filters are used to block or pass certain wavelengths (colors) of the visible spectrum selectively. These are commonly called **color-correcting** (CC) filters. Other types of filters are used merely to diminish the intensity of light; these are called **neutral density** (ND) filters. CC filters are used by the graphic arts photographer in the color separation process.

It is sufficient for you to understand only two ideas at this point. First, printers normally use only red, green, and blue filters in the color separation process. Each filter transmits (allows to pass) its own color and absorbs (blocks) all other colors. For example, we see the world as red through a red filter because all wavelengths of light except red are being absorbed—only radiation of a certain wavelength is transmitted. Safelights are merely cage filters placed in front of a light bulb. The second idea that you should remember about filters concerns handling. Fil-

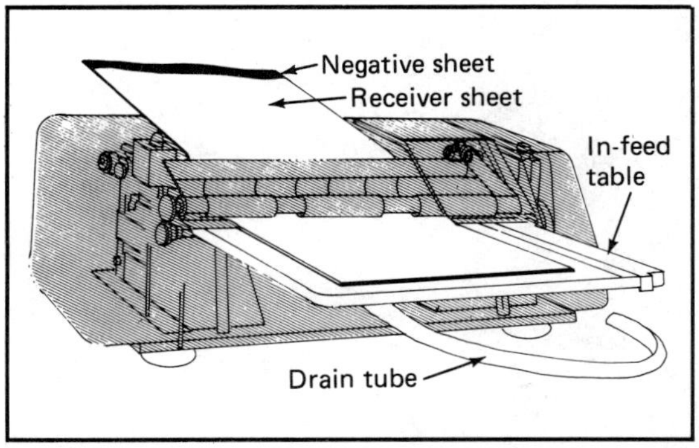

Figure 2.21. Diffusion transfer. The emulsion of the negative sheet is placed against the emulsion of the receiver sheet and sent through a diffusion transfer processor. (Kimberly Conover-Loar)

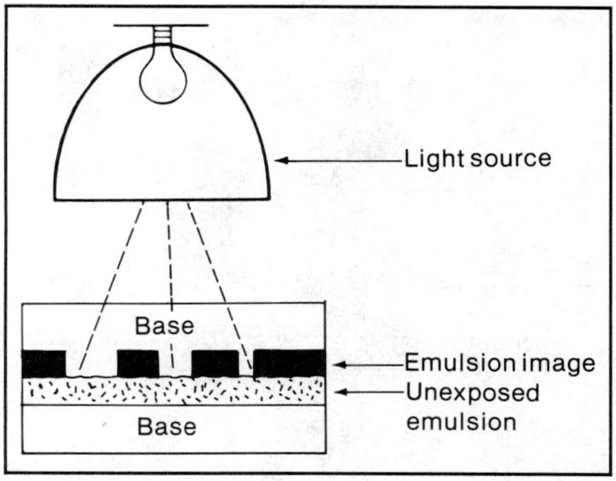

Figure 2.22. Contacting. Light is passed through the film image onto the new film.

ters are expensive and, thus, should be handled with great care. Water can change a filter's light-transmitting characteristics. Skin oil on a filter can also change its characteristics. No matter how well we wash our hands, there is always a certain amount of oil on the surface of our skin; thus, handle filters only by the edges.

ND filters are sometimes placed in front of a camera lens to reduce the intensity of light reaching the film. In the graphic arts, ND filters are usually classified by density. For example, a filter might be marked ND-0.3. The 0.3 means that the filter has a density of 0.3 and will, therefore, reduce the amount of light passing through it by 0.3 units. ND-1 means it has a density of 1. It is possible to place ND filters together and then to add their densities in order to create a desired result. If ND-1 and ND-0.3 filters are both placed over a camera lens, the light will be reduced by 1.3 units of density.

• Contacting

Contacting is a process of placing one transparent film image directly against an unexposed sheet of film (called a **sandwich**) and then passing light through the film image (figure 2.22). Contacting can be used to make film positives from film negatives, to make **duplicate** film images (that means if you start with a film negative, the result is another film negative exactly the same as the original), or to produce something called a **lateral reverse** (see chapter 8).

Vacuum Frames

The most basic piece of contacting equipment is a vacuum frame. A **vacuum frame** is a device similar to a camera copyboard (figure 2.23). A glass frame is hinged on a frame that holds a flexible rubber blanket. When the sandwich is placed on the blanket, and the glass is locked in place, a vacuum pump is used to remove air from the frame. The result is that the blanket is pressed against the glass, drawing the two pieces of film into intimate contact. The point of this procedure is that if the sheets were not held firmly together, then the new film image would be distorted (figure 2.24).

Some contact frames use only spring pressure to hold the sheets together, but the vacuum system is far more dependable.

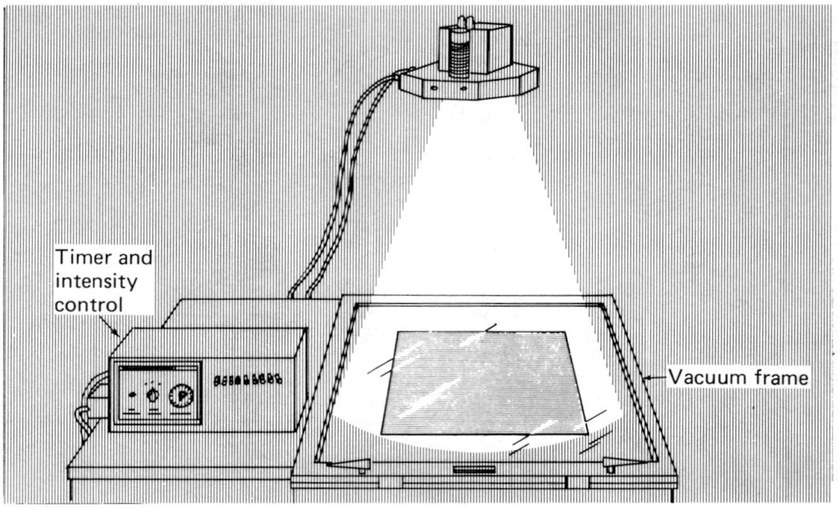

Figure 2.23. Vacuum frame. This device is used to hold film sandwiches in place during exposure. (Kimberly Conover-Loar)

Point Light Sources

A **point light source** is a device that projects a small, controlled beam of light (figure 2.25). It is important that the circle of light provide uniform intensity over the entire vacuum frame surface. The value of a point light system is that contacting can take place in the darkroom, but since the light is so well controlled, other film activities can take place without exposing film being handled in other parts of the room.

Filter Control/Exposure Control Systems

Many operations in the contacting area require a change of filter or an adjustment in the intensity of the light. Several different systems have been designed that allow the operator to control easily both filtration and exposure. Figure 2.26 shows a convenient rotating filter system. The small filters are mounted in the open frames, and the entire device is turned until the required filter is placed between the light source and the vacuum frame. Some systems are electronically remote controlled, so the contact printer merely presses a button (or turns a point) and the required filter is rotated into position.

Each different film material used in contact printing typically requires a special exposure time. There are two ways to adjust for those differences: (1) change the length of time the point light source is turned on or (2) change the amount of intensity of the point light source. A repeating timer commonly is linked to the contact room light as a convenient way to change exposure time. Intensity of the light can be controlled in several ways. Some photographers merely insert ND filters into the rotating filter system; when a change is required in the amount of light, the wheel is rotated until the desired intensity is reached. Another method is to connect a rheostat to the light. This device controls the amount of electrical current that is sent to the light bulb; as the amount of current decreases, so does the light intensity.

• Registration Control

In many instances, more than one piece of film is used to produce a single printing plate (figure 2.27). **Registration** is the process of assembling and securing all film pieces so that each image is in the required position on the printing plate. While this is basically the job of the **stripper** (during the image assembly phase of the printing cycle), several steps can be taken in the darkroom to improve registration control.

Register Marks

Register Marks are devices that the photographer can use to help control registration (figure 2.28). If several film images are to be produced from the same original (such as in the color separation process), the camera operator places several preprinted register marks on the original in the copyboard. The minimum number is usually three, and they are placed at various points on the copy, but sometimes a row of fifteen or twenty marks is placed on both the top and bottom of the copy to increase accuracy.

Once the different pieces of film are exposed and developed, the register marks became aids for the stripper. If the marks were not moved between camera exposures, then they would appear as images on the film, in the same position (in relation to the printed image), on each piece of film. The stripper lines up the register marks, and the film images should be in the required printing positions. Before platemaking, the register marks are usually covered with red tape so they do not appear on the plate.

Punched Film System

A more exact method of registration control than the register marks is a **punched film system**. The system is relatively simple. Under the safelights, the photographer uses a special punch to place two or more holes in a sheet of unexposed film (figure 2.29). Once the camera is set up, the punched film is placed on the filmboard so that the holes are placed on two tabs that have been taped to the camera back. As long as the original on the copyboard is not moved, and each new piece of film is positioned over the tabs, then the images will always be in the same position

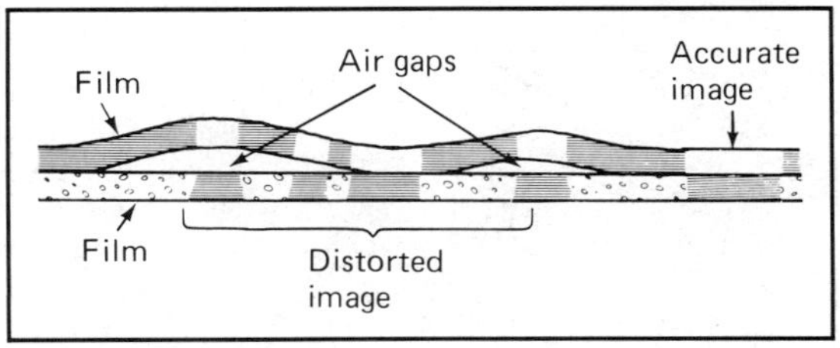

Figure 2.24. Film sheets held firmly together prevent distortion.

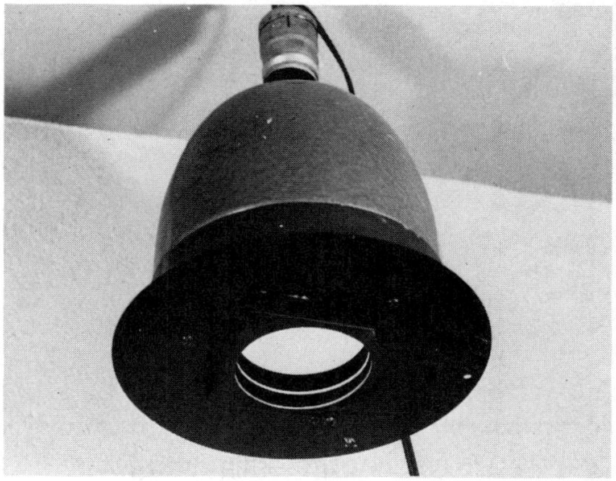

Figure 2.25. Point light source.

Figure 2.26. Rotating filter system. This system can be used to change filters rapidly between exposures.

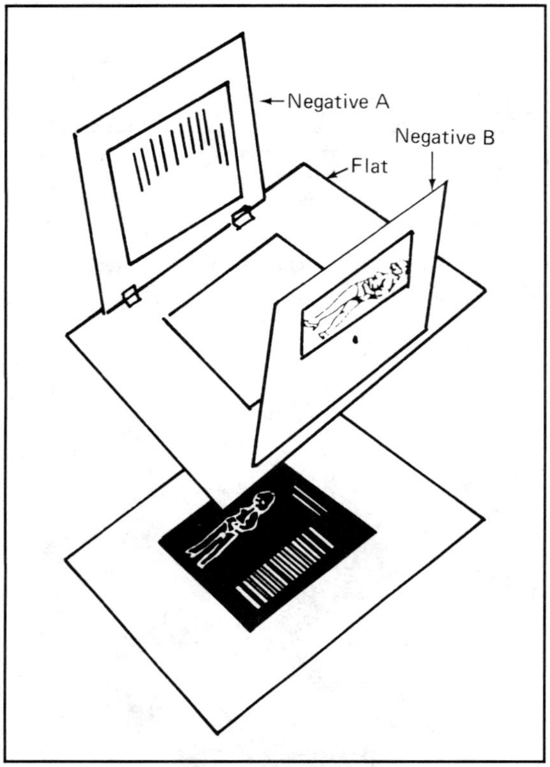

Figure 2.27. Two separate film images exposed to the same plate. (Kimberly Conover-Loar)

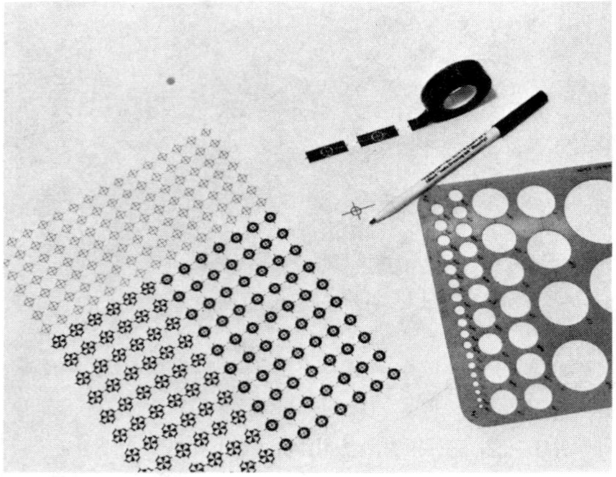

Figure 2.28. Example of register marks.

Figure 2.29. Film punch.

in relation to the punched holes. The stripper then has two tabs taped to the light table and can easily register any number of film images together. With this system, the punched tabs are also carried to the platemaking area and used to prepare the printing plate.

• Darkroom Layout and Design

Designing a Darkroom

The layout of a darkroom is very important. If the film is stored across the room from the camera, or if the film cutter is not next to the film container, then additional steps will have to be taken for every exposure. If the sinks are next to the film storage, then there is a chance of water damage to unexposed film materials. Poor placement of both equipment and supplies can cause the photographer to spend more time than necessary for every operation.

When beginning to design any darkroom, the designer must keep in mind the two distinct areas: the wet area and the dry area. The **wet area** includes the sink, the wet-viewing board, and the film-drying system. The **dry area** includes the film storage container, the film cutter, the screen and filter storage system, the contact area, and the camera. Water is allowed only in the wet area and is never carried into the dry area. Thus, all darkroom designs should separate the two areas.

The next step in designing a darkroom is to consider limitations. Usually the company already owns the equipment that will be placed in the new darkroom, or at least certain specific pieces have been ordered; companies all have size limitations that must be considered. Also, the photographer rarely has unlimited space; usually a certain room has been identified in the physical plant, and the size of that area becomes a very important limitation.

A good way to remember these limitations is to use a process called **scaling**. Measure the size of the area that has been identified as the darkroom and do a scaled drawing. Every one-quarter inch equals one foot. Figure 2.30 shows a scaled drawing of a room as it would appear if you were looking straight down through the ceiling.

Next, drawings of any equipment are made to the same scale as the room layout; again, each drawing is made as the object would look from the top of the room. If the drawings of equipment are carefully cut out, then it is possible to place the drawings on the room layout. By moving these cutouts, it is easy to consider different positions for each piece without moving the equipment. This process of moving the cutouts to different locations within the room layout is important. By considering different equipment

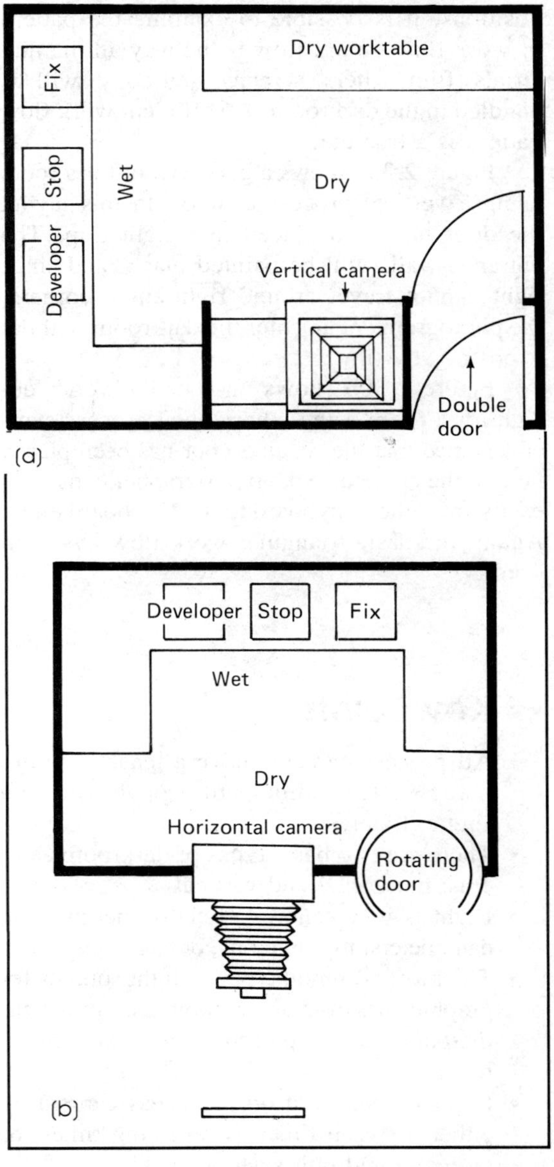

Figure 2.30. Scaled drawings of a darkroom. (a) Layout with a vertical camera and (b) layout with a horizontal camera. (Kimberly Conover-Loar)

positions, it is possible to examine the pattern of work flow. Work flow is the way all the materials (film, filters, screens, and copy) will be handled in the darkroom. An efficient work flow pattern is a triangle.

Figure 2.30a shows a good layout for a room using a vertical process camera. In this layout the door has been placed in a light trap. The entrance walls will be painted black, and since light cannot travel around right-angle corners, the photographer can enter the darkroom without exposing any film.

Figure 2.30b shows another darkroom design for a room using a horizontal process camera. Notice that the rotating door has been placed next to the camera so the photographer can move easily from the copyboard to the filmboard ends. Again, the basic triangular work flow has been used.

• Key Points

- All process cameras have a lens, aperture, f/stop system, filmboard, copyboard, and shutter/timer.
- There are two basic types of darkroom cameras: horizontal and vertical.
- Light is wave energy, usually measured in nanometers, millimicrons, or angstrom units.
- The most common types of light sources for graphic arts use are carbon arc, tungsten, mercury vapor, pulsed xenon, and metal halide.
- Light is measured on a process camera by either a sweep timer, a repeating timer, or an integrated unit system.
- Most films are designed to be processed in a sink with temperature controlled to 68°F (20°C).
- The two most common methods of film processing are shallow tray or automatic processing.
- Stabilization is a process used to prepare opaque film materials.
- Diffusion transfer is a special process used in both photography and platemaking.
- There are two types of graphic arts filters: color correcting (CC) and neutral density (ND).
- Contacting is the process of exposing one sheet of film through another one in something called a sandwich, which usually is held together in a vacuum frame.
- A point light source projects a small, controlled beam of light.
- Registration is the process of assembling and securing film in the required printing positions; process photographers sometimes use register marks or a registration punch.
- Every process darkroom has a wet side and a dry side.
- Work flow is the way materials are handled in the darkroom.

• Review Questions

1. What are the major camera parts?
2. What is the difference between a horizontal and vertical process camera?
3. How is light measured?
4. What is the difference between repeating and sweep timers?
5. What is the function of a light integration unit?
   Why is it different than an ordinary timer?
6. Briefly explain the functions of the following:
   a. Safelight,
   b. Vacuum frame,
   c. Register punch,
   d. Point light source.
7. Why is it important to have wet and dry sides in the darkroom?

• Activities

1. Examine the process cameras available in your shop. Identify:
   a. Filmboard and copyboard,

  b. Percentage control,
  c. Lens and aperture controls,
  d. Timer units.
2. Review the darkroom setup in your shop. Identify the wet and dry sides, safelight controls, darkroom sink organization, processor units, and the film storage system.
3. Locate the vacuum frame and point light source in the shop. Familiarize yourself with the tap and timer system.
4. Locate the registration punch and tab equipment. Punch several scrap sheets of film and use the tabs to practice use of the registration control system.

Chapter 3

Sensitized Materials

• Objectives

In this chapter you will cover:

- The structure of film,
- Spectral sensitivity,
- Emulsion characteristics,
- Film-handling techniques.

After reading the chapter you should be able to:

- List and explain the purpose of the major parts of any film material;
- Explain the difference between opaque and transparent materials;
- Explain the purpose of and interpret wedge spectrograms;
- Explain the characteristics of pan, ortho, and blue-sensitive emulsions;
- Define color sensitive, speed, and contrast;
- Identify the purposes of the most common sensitized materials used by graphic arts photographers;
- Handle film safely in a darkroom.

Photographers work with a light-sensitive emulsion that has been coated over the surface of a stable carrier such as glass, metal, paper cellulose, or plastic. The term **light sensitive** means that the chemical compound reacts, or changes, when light reaches it.

The purpose of this chapter is to examine some of the characteristics of today's common light-sensitive materials and to review some of the elementary procedures used when handling film.

• The Structure of Film

Light-sensitive materials are available in two basic forms, classified according to the base material used to hold the chemical emulsion. If it is not possible to see through a sheet of paper or other material, then we say that it is **opaque**. The first class of light-sensitive material, then, is when the emulsion is placed over an opaque base. The snapshots you took with your Instamatic or Nikon camera (and sent to the local photography shop for processing) are photographic prints made on a special paper base. Printing plates used in lithography are also examples of a light-sensitive emuslion coated upon an opaque base; so are PMT materials (see chapter 10), stabilization prints, and many types of proofing sheets.

If it is possible to see through a piece of base material, then we say that it is **transparent**. The second classification of light-sensitive material is when the emulsion is placed over a transparent base. We usually use the common term **film** to label this class, although the term is sometimes used to describe all types of light-sensitive materials. Film, as it is used in this book, always refers to transparent-based materials. Graphic arts photographers use a variety of different kinds of film. Line film is probably the most common (see chapter 7), but there are also reversal films, halftone films, separation films, pan-masking films, and a long list of others.

Early film materials usually were prepared by the photographer. A liquid coating was adhered to a clean sheet of glass, and the film was rushed to the camera for exposure. Light would pass through the camera lens to the film emulsion and expose it. The problem with this film was that light could be reflected from the camera back, which would expose the emulsion a second time (figure 3.1). The solution we use today is literally to paint a light-absorbing layer on the back of the sheet of film so any light that passes through the emulsion and base is absorbed. This layer is called the **antihalation backing** (figure 3.2). This also makes it easy to tell which side of the sheet is the emulsion. When working with transparent-based film, the light side is the emulsion and the dark side is the antihalation backing.

Figure 3.2 also shows two other major changes that modern filmmakers have made since the days of wet-glass plates. First of all, very little commercial or graphic arts photography requires glass as a base sheet, although several areas of scientific photography still use the material. The main advantage of glass is that it is a stable material; it does not change size with changes in temperature and during the developing process. One of the first substances to take the place of glass was a cellulose-nitrate-based material. The main problem was that the stuff would change shape or size whenever the temperature changed, and if the temperature got really hot, it would easily burst into flame. The most common approach today is to use a plastic-based or cellulose-acetate-based material that is relatively stable and gives little danger of fire.

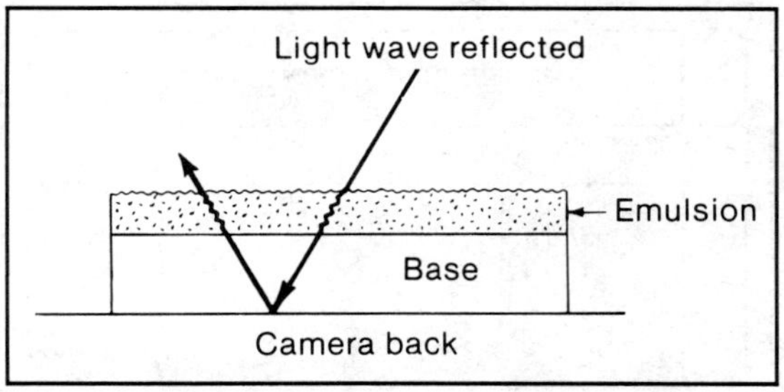

Figure 3.1. Early film materials

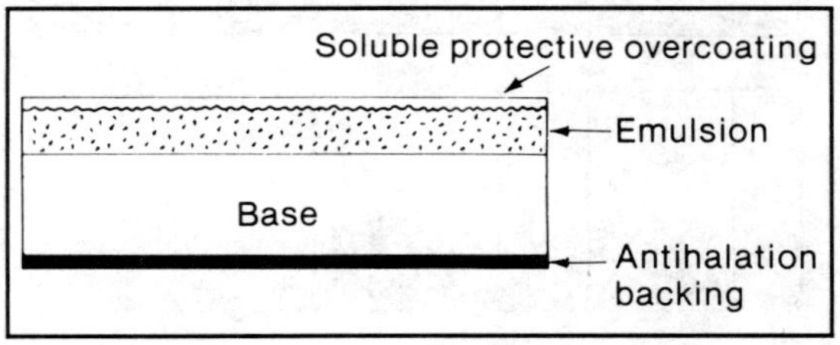

Figure 3.2. Typical contemporary film structure

The second major change is the addition of a top coating over the emulsion, called an **overcoat**. The purpose of the overcoat is to protect the fragile emulsion from human hands. No matter how well we wash our hands, they are always covered with an oily substance that can be transferred to film emulsions and that will ruin any

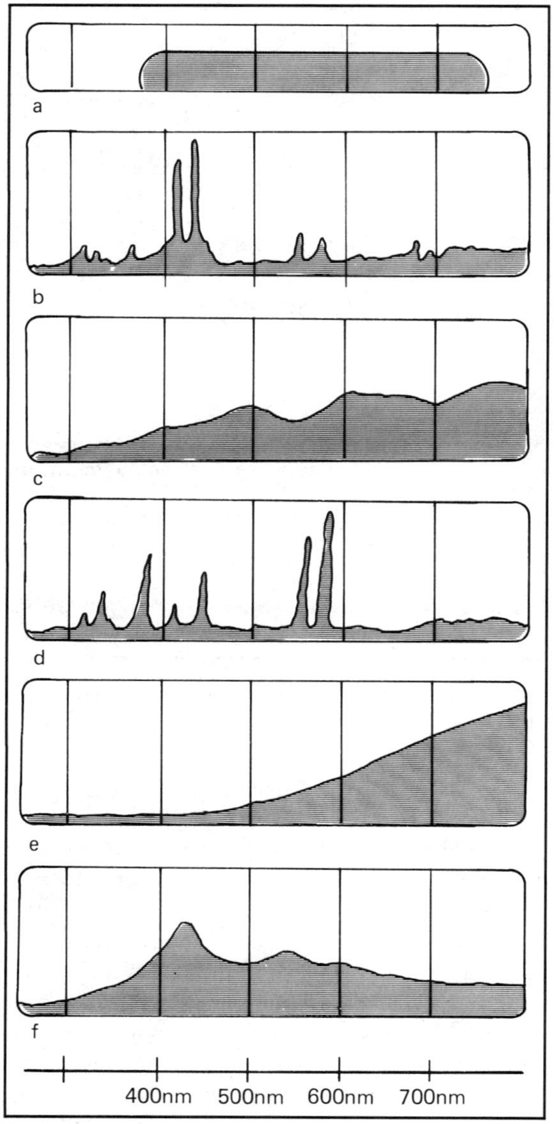

Figure 3.3. Graphs of the output of different light sources. Vertical height indicates intensity, horizontal shading indicates output across the visible spectrum. (a) The sun, (b) metal halide, (c) pulsed xenon, (d) mercury vapor, (e) tungsten, (f) carbon arc. (Kimberly Conover-Loar)

film image. Additionally, the overcoat tends to protect the emulsion from minor scratches and abrasions.

• Spectral Sensitivity

Light Source Emissions

Chapter 2 introduced the idea of light sources. Recall that light is wave energy that we can see (see figure 2.9). The important thing to understand is that humans see different colors because of differences in wavelength.

It is possible to make a graph of the wavelengths of light that any light source gives off. The sun is sometimes called the perfect light source because it gives nearly equal amounts of all wavelengths in the visible spectrum (figure 3.3a). Notice that the horizontal shading represents the wavelength and that the vertical portion, or height, of the plot represents intensity or quantity (see chapter 4 for more detail).

Now look at figure 3.3e, which shows the spectral emission of a tungsten light bulb. Observe that there are not equal amounts of visible spectrum being produced; more red than blue is being emitted. Figure 3.3 also shows the emission of several common light sources. The main point is that different light sources give off different amounts of light in different areas of the visible spectrum. Both the human eye and photographic film can see these differences.

Wedge Spectrogram

Wedge spectrogram is a complicated-sounding word, but it is really a simple idea. "Gram" means drawing or graph, "spectro" means spectrum; thus, a **wedge spectrogram** is a graph that shows how much light the eye or a type of film sees across the visible spectrum. Figure 3.4a shows a wedge spectrogram for the human eye. Most individuals see the most at the middle of the spectrum, about 550 millimicrons, and less at either end (infrared and ultraviolet).

Types of Light-Sensitive Material

It is possible to plot a wedge spectrogram for any type of light-sensitive material. Most manufacturers classify such materials into three categories: (1) panchromatic, (2) orthochromatic, and (3) blue sensitive.

Figure 3.4b shows a wedge spectrogram for a **panchromatic** emulsion. Observe that the emulsion sees relatively equal amounts of light across the visible spectrum and, in fact, is similar to what the human eye can see (compare figure 3.4a with figure 3.4b). Another name for panchromatic is simply **pan**. Pan films are used for continuous-tone photography in your home camera and in graphic arts color separation.

Orthochromatic emulsions are sometimes referred to as **ortho**. Figure 3.4c shows a wedge spectrogram for a typical ortho emulsion. Notice that the graph does not extend into the red end of the spectrum. In other words, this emulsion is blind, or cannot see light weavlengths that are longer than around 600 millimicrons. This works out very well in the darkroom. Humans can see in red light, but the film cannot. If all the light bulbs are painted red (or put behind red filters), then the photographer can see to work with the film and camera, but the red light will not expose the ortho film. Although it is possible to use orthochromatic emulsions to produce continuous-tone images, the most common use is in the area of high-contrast photography for printing production. Basically, high contrast means the recording of lines (see chapter 7).

Figure 3.4d shows a wedge spectrogram for a **blue-sensitive** emulsion. It can only see light with wavelengths between approximately 390 and 490 millimicrons. Many opaque-based materials for making continuous-tone photographs are blue sensitive—we call them **photographic papers**. Becauses the film emulsion is blind over most of the visible spectrum, the photographer can work under relatively bright safelight conditions.

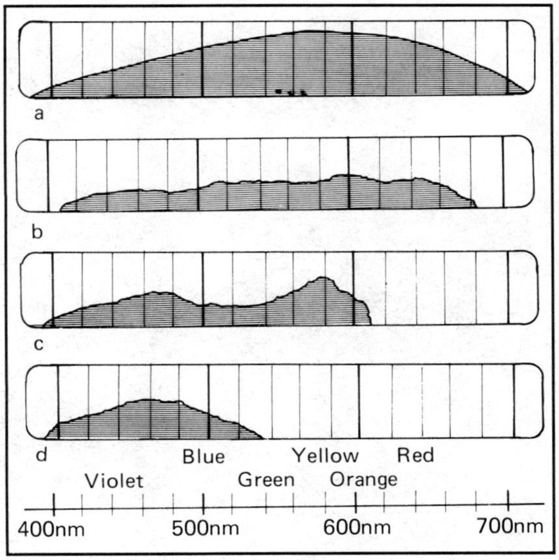

Figure 3.4. Wedge spectrogram. (a) Human eye, (b) panchromatic, (c) orthochromatic, (d) blue sensitive. (Kimberly Conover-Loar)

Selection of Films and Papers

Sometimes the new photographer can become confused when trying to decide what kind of film to use for any given job. Film manufacturers publish lists of literally hundreds of different products, each chemical emulsion being designed for a specific purpose. Several ideas will help the apprentice process photographer begin to learn about these differences and purposes.

Color Sensitivity

Color sensitivity describes the portion of the visible spectrum that will expose a particular emulsion. Another term, **spectral sensitivity**, was discussed in the previous section. The color sensitivity of almost all films can be classified as either panchromatic, orthochromatic, or blue sensitive.

Figure 3.5. Normal-contrast photograph.

Speed

Film **speed** refers to the amount of light that is necessary to cause an image to be recorded on a particular emulsion. Materials that require very little light are called fast, and those that need a great deal of light to record an exposure are called slow. The problem with these expressions, however, is how fast or how slow? Is very fast film faster than very, very fast material?

The solution to this problem was the development of a concept called **exposure index**. Film manufacturers now assign a number to each of their films that indicates the speed. The most popular system is called ASA. The ASA standards were developed by the American Standards Association (now called the American National Standards Institute). With this system, the higher the numer, the faster the film. For example, an emulsion that is assigned an ASA of 125 requires twice as much light to record an exposure as a material with an ASA of 250. Common ASA ratings for continuous-tone pan films that are used in the amateur photographer's camera are 32, 64, 125, 250, and 400. Ortho films, used by printers for line photography, are normally much slower, in the range from 6 ASA to 12 ASA.

Contrast

Contrast describes the range of tones in a photographic image. Figure 3.5 shows a photograph with normal contrast. Normal contrast means that there is a range of tones from clear whites to dense blacks, in a relationship that we tend to see with the human eye. Figure 3.6 is a photograph with low contrast. Notice that there are no dense blacks and that everything looks gray and washed out. *Washed out* is a photographer's expression to describe a low-contrast scene. Printers also sometimes say that a low-contrast print is flat.

A high-contrast photograph is illustrated in figure 3.7. Notice that, in this example, there appear to be only a few tones—that is, clean white paper and solid black ink; there are little or no grays. The range of tones has been compressed. Printers find that high-contrast emulsions are convenient for the printing processes. Printers do not print shades of gray (unless something is wrong with their equipment); their main goal is to print dense, solid layers of ink on clean sheets of paper. The letters that form the words you are now reading were photographed by using high-contrast film. If the typesetter spilled coffee on the copy, or if the sheet was smudged, the photographer could still drop the defects because the film will only hold a record of the dense type characters and the open background area.

One reaction to this discussion of contrast might be that the reader has seen many photo-

Figure 3.6. Low-contrast photograph.

Figure 3.7. High-contrast photograph.

graphs, like figure 3.5, that are printed with shades of gray. While it may appear to be made up of different tones, examination of any printed photograph with a magnifying glass will show that the grays are merely many small dots, spaced closely together.

Common Sensitized Materials

It is important to understand that, individually, color sensitivity, speed, or contrast do not define a particular type of film. It is possible to have any combination of the three, depending upon the desired sensitivity of the materials. Just because a film is orthochromatic does not mean that it must be also high contrast with a low ASA. Although that is a common combination, it is still possible to make an ortho film that gives results of normal contrast with a high ASA.

However, several common combinations of characteristics are commonly used by printers. The most common is called **line film**. Line film can be used to produce a high-contrast negative, on a camera, from a positive original or to make contact positives from film negatives in a contact frame. Although there are many more uses, the point is that line materials make high-contrast film images that are the negative of the original. If the original is a positive, then a negative is produced; start with a negative, and a positive will be the result.

Reversal film is the exact opposite of line film. This material is sometimes called dupe film because it duplicates the original. If the camera copy is a positive, then the reversal film result will be a high-contrast film positive of the original. If the original is a negative, then the reversal film will give a duplicate negative.

Some printers use **stabilization paper** to proof negatives, make prescreened halftones, or produce camera stats (enlargements or reductions of the copy that can be pasted onto the mechanical.) Most stabilization material is orthochromatic or blue sensitive but has the potential to produce normal-contrast images. All stabilization papers are machine processed (see chapter 5 for additional detail).

Diffusion transfer is a process that can be used to prepare either opaque paper positives, transparent film positives, or even lithographic plates. It is a two-step process that uses an orthochromatic, high-contrast negative sheet and a special receiver sheet. The negative is exposed and then processed in contact with a non-light-sensitive receiver sheet (paper, film, or aluminum plate). Chapter 10 deals exclusively with diffusion transfer.

Pan separation and **pan-masking** films are both used in the area of color separation for multicolor printing reproduction. Since the materials are panchromatic, they must be used in total darkness. These color separation materials are used in conjunction with filters and can be used either on the camera or in the contact frame. Chapters 12 and 13 cover the use of these separation materials.

• Handling Techniques for the Darkroom

It is very frustrating, when first beginning to work in the darkroom, to make mistakes because of poor handling of film or paper materials. Experienced photographers, as a result of their early mistakes, have developed key points or techniques that reduce handling errors. Here are some such techniques that might save you some time and frustration.

Water

Water belongs in the darkroom sink—nowhere else. Recall from chapter 2 that every darkroom has a wet side and a dry side. Any moisture that contacts an emulsion before the developer step will ruin an emulsion. Always check the dry areas before the white light goes out. If there is the least bit of moisture, wipe it up.

Also, try to get in the habit of never setting a piece of film down unless it is absolutely necessary. Wait until everything is set for the exposure before removing a sheet from storage, cut it if necessary, and then move it immediately to the camera or contact frame.

Controlling the Light

Film manufacturers always pack a spec sheet (specification sheet) with their product (figure 3.8). Always check to be sure that the proper safelight is being used. Too bright a safelight, or the incorrect safelight filter, can result in fogging. Fogging is a light background exposure over the entire emulsion surface that ruins the piece of film.

Of course, turn off the white light before removing the film or paper from storage, but be aware of another possible error. Always close the film box, or storage container, immediately after removing the piece. Too often the novice photographer takes a sheet out, places it on the camera, makes the exposure, and then glances over to see the box open, with all the sheets being exposed by the camera lights—an expensive mistake.

Holding the Sheet

No matter how well or often you wash your hands, there is always a slight oily coating over your fingers. This oily material can ruin light-sensitive emulsions. Always hold the sheet of film or paper by the edges (figure 3.9).

Storage of Film and Paper

A light-tight storage container is important in the darkroom. For short-term use in the darkroom situation, the container should be able to be opened and closed easily. Sometimes, however, it is necessary to store a large quantity of film over a long period of time.

All film and papers have an expiration date printed on the package when purchased from the manufacturer. Emulsions change sensitivity over time. The purpose of the expiration date is to identify the period of time during which the emulsion will react predictably to light as photographers have come to expect it to. With some types of commercial-grade films, the manufacturer ages the film before selling it to the photographer so it is in its period of peak sensitivity.

It is possible to control this aging process. Placing film in an extremely hot, damp area increases changes in sensitivity. Reducing the temperature of the film storage area slows down the change. If the plant got a bargain on 20,000 sheets of film but rarely uses more than 600 pieces a month, it is possible almost to halt the aging process. First, tightly wrap the film container in plastic, and seal it so that air cannot enter or excape. Then put the package in the freezer. At temperatures near 0°F, film can be so stored almost indefinitely—for years—without changes in emulsion sensitivity. Be careful, however, when the package is removed from the freezer. Allow it to warm up slowly to the room temperature before opening the plastic. Otherwise, condensation will form inside the package, and the moisture will ruin the film.

Figure 3.8. Film spec sheet. Always check to ensure the correct safelight is used before opening a box of film.

Figure 3.9. Holding a sheet of film or paper by the edges. Notice that the dark, or base, side of the sheet is away from the viewer. (Kimberly Conover-Loar)

• Key Points

- It is not possible to see through opaque materials.
- It is possible to see through transparent materials.

- The structure of most film is overcoat, emulsion, base material, and antihalation backing.
- A wedge spectrogram is a graph that shows how much and what wavelength of light a film sees.
- There are three basic kinds of photographic emulsions: orthochromatic, panchromatic, and blue sensitive.
- Three characteristics of film are color sensitivity, speed, and contrast. Each can be varied for different film results by a manufacturer.

Review Questions

1. What is the definition of opaque? Transparent?
2. What are the main parts of any film material?
3. What is a wedge spectrogram?
4. What are the characteristics of the following materials?
   a. Orthochromatic,
   b. Panchromatic,
   c. Blue-sensitive.
5. What is film speed?
6. What is contrast?
7. Name two common sensitized materials. Where are they used in the graphic arts?
8. Name three film-handling techniques.

Activities

1. Examine the label on a film box in your shop. Identify:
   a. Safelight condition,
   b. Type of film,
   c. Expiration date,
   d. Base thickness.
2. Find a reject piece of processed film. Locate the emulsion side (try scraping the emulsion off with a razor blade). Where is the emulsion when the image is right reading?
3. Find the manufacturer's data sheet from a film box in your shop. Examine the wedge spectrogram. Where is peak sensitivity for the film?

Chapter 4

Sensitometry and Quality Control

• Objectives

In this chapter you will cover:

- The language of sensitometry,
- How to measure the density of different materials,
- Classification and use of gray scales,
- Characteristic curves.

After reading the chapter you should be able to:

- Explain the difference between reflected and transmitted light;
- Define transmittance and density;
- Measure the density of opaque and transparent copy using reflection and transmission densitometers;
- List the different types of gray scales;
- Explain the use of a gray scale as a predictive tool;
- Identify the toe, shoulder, and straight-line portions of a characteristic curve and explain the visual effect of contrast.

Sensitometry is the area of photography that is concerned with the measurement of film reaction to light. A sheet of film is said to be light-sensitive because when light strikes the emulsion a chemical change takes place. Several kinds of sensitivity were discussed in chapter 3. Color sensitivity is a film's reaction to different parts of the visible spectrum; speed is a reaction to the quantity of light. These measures are used by photographers to predict a film's reaction to light.

Sensitometry is a science the process photographer can use to measure the result of the reaction to light on a finished piece of film. The measurement can also be used to determine necessary changes in exposure that will give corresponding changes on the film.

Sensitometry is an important topic. It is possible to push buttons and process film without understanding sensitometry. When problems occur, however, the tools of sensitometry are necessary resources.

• The Language of Sensitometry

Printers often use the word **density**. They are usually using the term to refer to how black, or dense, the emulsion or ink is on the film or paper. Unfortunately, the word density is often casually used without an understanding of its meaning or purpose.

When light is directed at an object, it is called **transmitted light**. When light is reflected back from an object, it is called **reflected light**. We know that different colors and materials absorb and reflect different amounts of light. A white roof on a house in Florida is much cooler than a black roof; white reflects light and black absorbs it.

It is possible to measure quantities of light using a **light meter**. With such a device we can measure the amount of tramsmitted light and reflected light and therefore know how much light is absorbed. For example, if we directed 100 units of light at an object, and if only 80 units were reflected back, then 20 units were absorbed. If another object absorbed 30 units, then it is denser than the first.

This method of measuring density can be very confusing. If one researcher uses 200 units, and if another uses 110 units, then a comparison of the amounts transmitted is not possible. The solution is to express the amount a material reflects as a ratio:

$$T = \frac{I_r}{I_t},$$

where

I = transmittance,
I_t = intensity of transmitted light,
I_R = intensity of reflected light.

With this approach, if the 100 units of light directed at a material reflect back only 80 units, transmittance is 0.80, or 80 percent:

$$T = \frac{80}{100} = 0.80 = 80 \text{ percent.}$$

This is a simple concept but very difficult in practice. Examples in a textbook always seem to work out perfectly, but in the shop the math never comes out evenly: $T_r = 63$, $T_t = 87$, $T = 71.145$ percent. Numbers like 71.145 percent are hard to interpret, difficult to manipulate, and almost impossible to plot on a graph.

It is possible to change large numbers to small ones without losing information with logarithms (sometimes called logs). You need not be a mathematician to understand logarithms. There are tables that convert raw numbers into logs, and most printers have machines that automatically read out density in logs. It is important, however, to know where the numbers come from. Printers define density as the log of the inverse of transmittance:

$$\text{Density} = \log\left(\frac{1}{T}\right)$$

The resulting changes look like this:

Transmittance (percent)	Density
100	0
10	1
1	2
0.1	3
0.01	4
0.001	5
0.0001	6
0.00001	7
0.000001	8
•	
•	
•	

Printers do not work with the formula when measuring density. The point that should be understood is that as transmittance decreases, density increases. A material that reflects back all of the light that strikes it (100 percent reflectance) has no density. Although theoretically there is no maximum density, materials used by printers fall within a practical maximum of 0 to 3 density range.

• Measuring Density

In practice, the measurement of density is a simple operation in the shop. It is measured by a device called a **densitometer**. Densitometers are classed according to the type of copy being measured. Remember that printers deal with images in two different forms: opaque and transparent. We see opaque copy such as a continuous-tone print or a printed page by reflected light. When reading this book, light from the desk lamp strikes the pages and is reflected back to our eyes. Printers call this **reflection copy**. When looking at a transparent-based negative on a light table, we see the image because of transmitted light. Light passes from the light table through the openings in the film to our eyes. This is called **transmission copy**.

Reflection Copy

There are several forms of reflection densitometers. A **visual densitometer** is a simple gray scale that is placed on the copy to be measured (figure 4.1). The printer visually compares the steps on the scale with the image. When a step appears to match the image, then the density (printed on the tablet next to each block) is recorded as the image density. The accuracy of using a visual density guide is limited by the skill of the printer. Results can also vary from individual to individual and can be affected by fatigue of the reader's eye.

A more accurate and common method of dealing with the density of opaque copy is with an **electronic reflection densitometer** (figure 4.2). The hand-held device can be moved to any position on the sheet, with provisions for measuring extremely small areas. A small beam of light is directed at a 45° angle onto the sheet. The device records the amount of light that is reflected back and then displays the logarithmic density on the read-out scale.

When using a reflection densitometer, it is important to zero the scale before beginning to take measurements. Since there is really no such

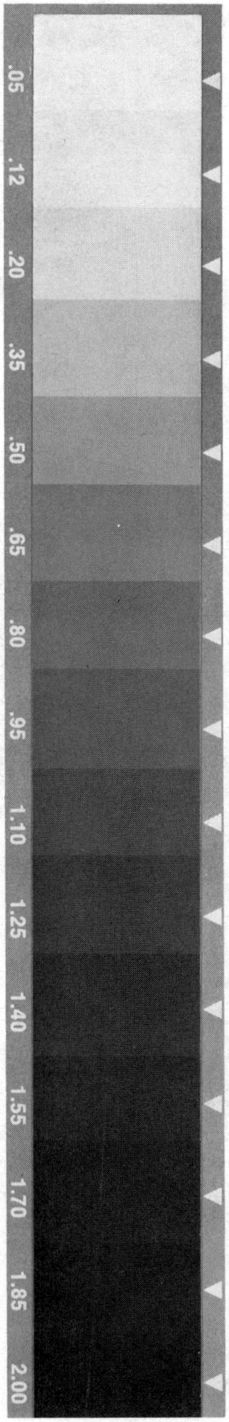

Figure 4.1. Calibrated gray scale used as a visual densitometer.

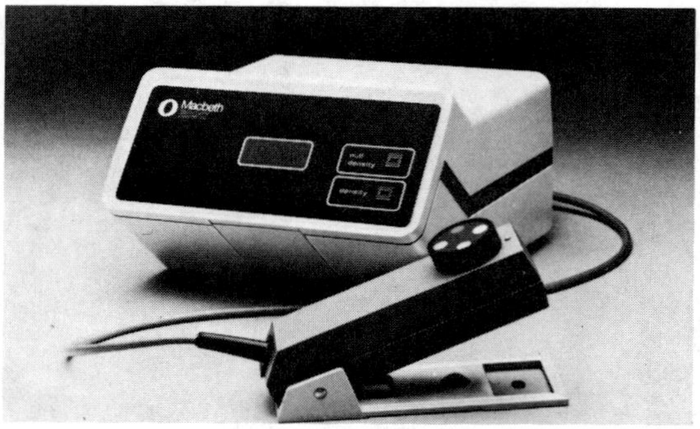

Figure 4.2. Electronic reflection densitometer. (Courtesy of Kollmorgen Corp., McBeth Division.)

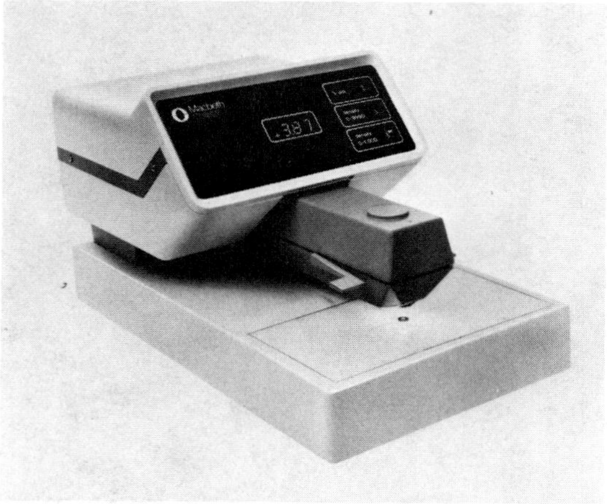

Figure 4.3. Electronic transmission densitometer. (Courtesy of Kollmorgen Corp., McBeth Division.)

thing as a perfect zero density (all papers, no matter the color or whiteness, have density), the idea of a density range is relative to the object we are measuring. Most printers use a special wedge or block of white as a standard starting point. Before each group of readings, the photographer places the standard sheet under the light and then adjusts the read-out scale to 0. With this approach, all readings in the shop will be measured against the same starting point.

Transmission Copy

The basic device used to measure the density of transparent copy is an **electronic transmission densitometer** (figure 4.3). With this system, a sheet of film is placed on the machine, and an arm is pushed into position against the sheet. A small beam of light is directed through the film, and a reading is made of the amount that reaches the other side. The measure is then converted to transmittance and displayed on the read-out scale as a log density.

The transparent material that makes up the base of the film has density. Even though we can see through it, the plastic does record a certain amount of light. When setting up to make density readings, it is necessary to zero the densitometer in order to subtract out this base amount. Position the film so that a clear section is under the beam of light, then adjust the read-out scale to 0. This will insure that only the density of the emulsion is being recorded.

• The Gray Scales

Types of Gray Scales

A **gray scale** is a basic tool used by the photographer to control, check, and predict the quality of the image recorded on a sheet of film (figure 4.1). Different names are used, such as gray scale, step wedge, step tablet, and density scale. The device comes in several forms, but all types have the same basic structure and purpose: A series of blocks are positioned next to each other in order of increasing density. The typical range is from nearly 0 to nearly 3.

The first way to classify types of gray scales is by the number of blocks. The most common are 10, 12, 14, or 21 steps. The range is still the same, but the differences between each step can be smaller for the greater the number. In other words, dividing 3 by 10 steps gives an average difference of 0.30 between each step; dividing 3 by 21 steps gives 0.14 average difference between each step.

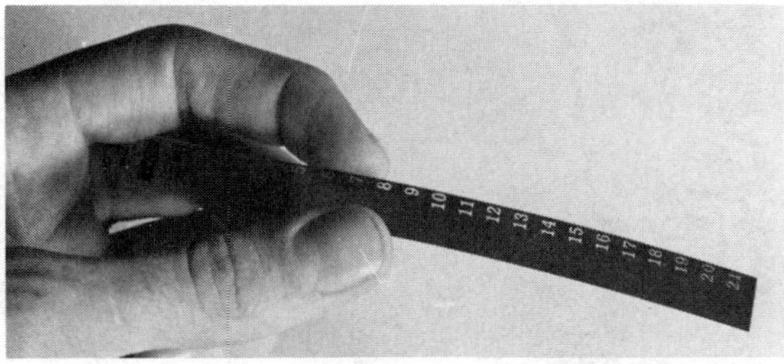

Figure 4.4. Transparent gray scale.

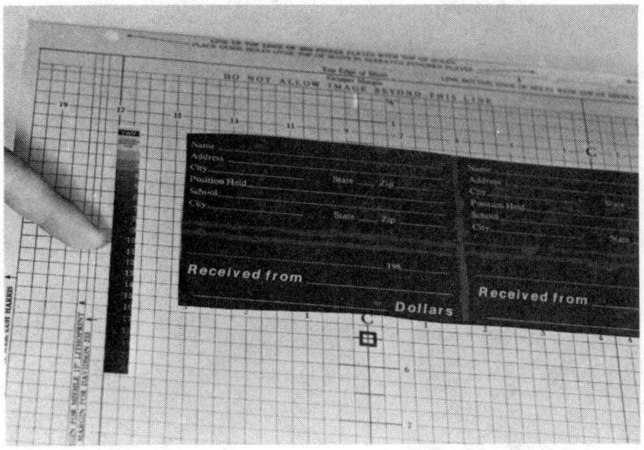

Figure 4.5. Transparent gray scale stripped into a flat.

A second way to classify types of gray scales is by intended use. Some scales are designed to be placed on camera copyboards as a quality control instrument. When an exposure is made, light is reflected from both the copy and the scale, and these are recorded on the film. This type of scale is called an **opaque gray scale** (figure 4.1). Other scales are designed to be stripped into a film negative (figure 4.4). **Transparent gray scales** can be stripped into a flat to expose a scale on a plate (figure 4.5), placed next to negatives when contacting to record a scale onto a film positive or color proof, or stripped into a carrier for use in color separation.

Gray scales can also be purchased as either calibrated or uncalibrated. Calibrated scales are tablets with density readings written next to each step. It is not possible to manufacture scales such that readings will be the same for every scale. The density of step three for one scale will be different than the reading for step three on another scale. The value of calibrated scales is that the manufacturer warranties the density of each step. Uncalibrated scales are merely the blocks positioned next to each other without the densities noted. Because calibrated scales must be measured individually and recorded by hand, they tend to be much more expensive than uncalibrated devices.

The Gray Scale as a Predictive Tool

As an exercise, place an opaque gray scale next to a continuous-tone photograph. Move the scale around and locate a tone in the print that matches each step of the scale. This is important to understand. A gray scale is merely a mechanical way of expressing the range of tones found in most photographs or artist's drawings. If a scale is placed next to the same picture and a line reproduction is made, it is interesting to observe what has taken place. Notice in figure 4.6 that a step four has been recorded on the ten-step scale. This means that the first four steps have been totally exposed, with only a partial record in the other steps. If you look at figure 4.7, you will see that all of the tones that you compared to steps one, two, three, and four have been reproduced in figure 4.6. Another way of saying this is that if, for example, step four on this scale had a density of 0.42, then everything on the copy that was 0.42 density or less was recorded on the film.

This understanding can be used to predict exposure changes when problems occur or when a special effect is desired (see chapter 11). Photographers know, from research in sensitometry, that doubling or halving the amount of light that reaches the film will result in a change of 0.30

Figure 4.6. Solid step four recorded on gray scale.

Figure 4.7. Any density less than step four has been dropped from figure 4.6.

density on the film. For example, assume a solid step four was recorded, with a density of 0.47, after a 22-second exposure at f/16. If the exposure was doubled to 44 seconds at f/16 (or 22 seconds at f/11), the new scale would show a density reading of 0.77 (0.47 plus 0.30). If the exposure was halved to 11 seconds at f/16 (or 22 seconds at f/22), the new density would be 0.17 (0.47 minus 0.30). This process assumes that all processing variables such as time, temperature, agitation, type of developer film, and developer activity level are the same.

The idea of a 0.30 density shift can be used for all types of photography. It works for line, halftone, special effects, and color separation darkroom work.

• Density Measurement of Halftones

The measurement of the density of halftone negatives or positives is a unique sort of problem. You will learn, in chapter 9, that a halftone is a special manipulation of continuous-tone images into a series of dots. These dots are of different sizes and are placed next to each other with varying amounts of space (figure 4.8). The problem is that, when making density readings with a transmission densitometer, the device reads only the amount of light absorbed by the emulsion. Because of the varying amount of space between the dots, inaccurate readings take place. However, it is very important that the photographer be able to read the size of dots recorded on the film.

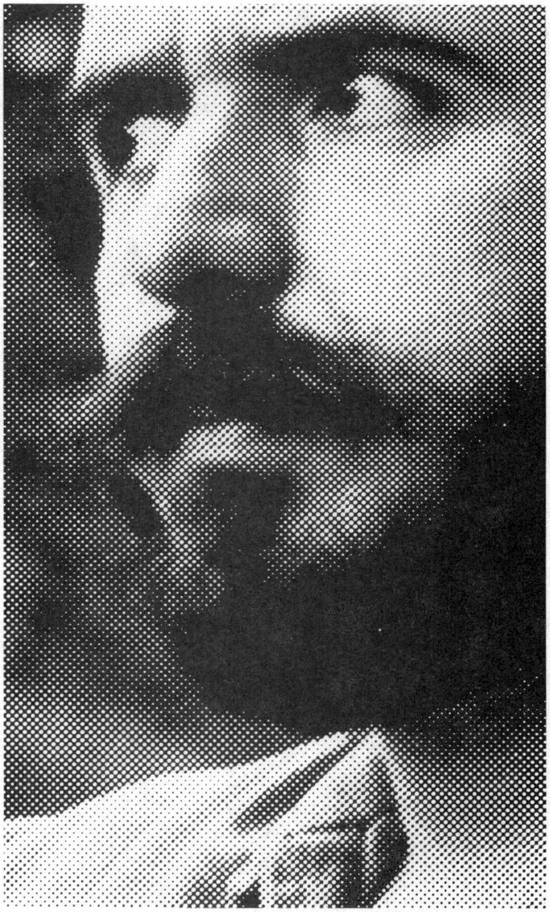

Figure 4.8. Halftone dot structure.

Two methods can be used to measure the size of haltone dots. The first is with an **integration conversion scale** (see table 4.1). When the photographer wants to read a dot size, he or she places the area under the light on the densitometer and records a density reading. That reading is then located on the integration conversion scale, and the dot size is determined. For example, if a highlight area was measured as a density of 0.05, then from table 4.1 this would be an 11 percent dot.

The integration conversion scale presents some difficulties. The first is the inaccuracy of the density reading because of the varying space between dots; at one point within the light beam the density of the dot is being read and, at another, light is passing directly through the clear film. The amount of light being absorbed by the dots is not being measured critically. The second problem is with the scale. The table is con-

Table 4.1. Integrated halftone density to percentage

Integrated halftone density	Percent dot area	Integrated halftone density	Percent dot area
0.00	0	0.36	56
0.01	2	0.38	58
0.02	5	0.40	60
0.03	7	0.42	62
0.04	9	0.44	64
0.05	11	0.46	65
0.06	13	0.48	67
0.07	15	0.50	68
0.08	17	0.54	71
0.09	19	0.58	74
0.10	21	0.62	76
0.11	22	0.66	78
0.12	24	0.70	80
0.13	26	0.74	82
0.14	28	0.78	83
0.15	29	0.82	85
0.16	31	0.86	86
0.17	32	0.90	87
0.18	34	0.95	89
0.19	35	1.00	90
0.20	37	1.10	92
0.22	40	1.20	94
0.24	42	1.30	95
0.26	45	1.40	96
0.28	48	1.50	97
0.30	50	1.70	98
0.32	52	2.00	99
0.34	54		

structed with inexact precision since density readings are not really convertible to dot size; some averaging is involved, resulting in a relatively large margin of error.

A much more accurate and dependable method of working with halftones is to use a **dot area meter** (figure 4.9). This is a special device designed with the express purpose of measuring the size of halftone dots. It can be purchased as a separate machine, or it is available as a unit that can be added to a transmission densitometer. With this technique, the film is inserted under the light beam, and the dot size is shown on the read-out scale. Dot area meters cannot be used to measure density of film; they are intended only for work with halftones.

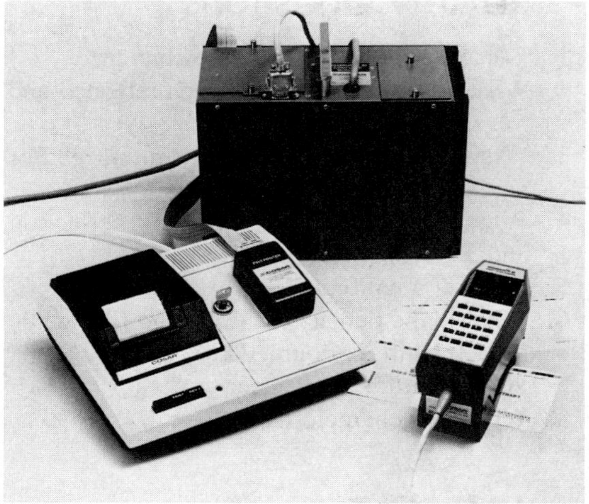

Figure 4.9. Dot area meter.

• Characteristic Curves

Film manufacturers often want to communicate the sensitometric characteristics of their emulsions in a way that shows changes over the full range of tones. One method they use to create a picture is by use of a **characteristic curve**. These are also referred to as *H & D* curves. *D*-$\text{Log}_{10}E$ curves, Log *E* curves, and sensitometric curves. Figure 4.10 shows the characteristic curve for Kodak's Ortho, Type III, litho film.

Any characteristic curve is made up of three parts: toe, straight-line portion, and shoulder (figure 4.12). The main piece of information obtained from a curve is shown by the straight-line portion. Contrast is defined by the angle of this line, called gamma, average gradient, or contrast index. The steeper the line, the greater the angle, and the greater the contrast.

Contrast describes the expansion or compression of tones. One way to understand this is by plotting the tonal change on a characteristic curve. Pick any two points on the horizontal axis, project up to the curve. Where the lines intersect the curve, draw over to the ver-

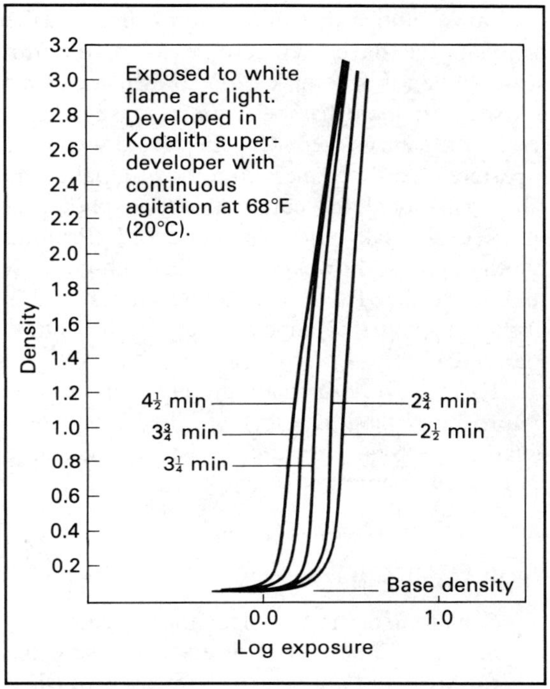

Figure 4.10. Characteristic curve for Kodak's Ortho, Type III litho film.

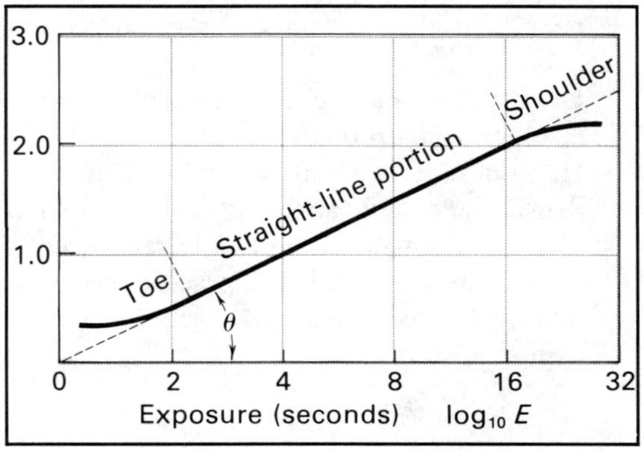

Figure 4.11. The three parts of a characteristic curve. Toe, straight-line portion, and shoulder.

tical axis. Notice that the range of tones on the original scale have been compressed on the film scale. When this compression takes place printers say that there has been an increase in contrast. If the curve were 45°, then there would be a perfect record of tones from the original to the film. The ideal for continuous-tone photographers is to make this perfect record. Printing photographers, however, want a high-contrast record. Notice from figure 4.11 that Kodak's Ortho, Type III is an extremely high-contrast material.

Further work in photography is necessary before understandings can be formed about characteristic curves. They are, however, a valuable tool for the photographer.

• Key Points

- Sensitometry is a tool of the process photographer that can be used to measure the result of the reaction to light on a finished piece of film.
- Density of opaque material is measured by a reflection densitometer.
- Density of transparent material is measured by a transmission densitometer.
- A gray scale is a series of blocks positioned next to each other in order of increasing density.
- Gray scales can be used to predict exposure changes when problems occur.
- Halftone dot size can be measured using a densitometer and an integrated conversion scale or a device called a dot area meter.
- A characteristic curve is a graphic representation of sensitometric characteristics of a film emulsion.

• Review Questions

1. What is a definition of sensitometry?
2. What is the difference between reflected and transmitted light?
3. What is the equation for transmittance? For density?
4. What is the difference between a reflection and a transmission densitometer?
5. What is a calibrated gray scale?
6. What is the density result on the film when the exposure is doubled?
7. What is a dot area meter?
8. What is a characteristic curve?

• Activities

1. Obtain an opaque gray scale from the instructor. Zero a reflection densitometer using step one as the standard. Then record, on a separate sheet of paper, the densities of each step.
2. Obtain a continuous-tone photograph. Pick two steps on the gray scale used in the first experiment. Try visually to match up areas in the print with the two steps. Measure the densities of the two print areas, and compare the results with the actual step densities. Is visual densitometry as exact as electronic?
3. Obtain a transparent gray scale from the instructor. Zero a transmission densitometer, using step one as the standard. Record, on a separate sheet of paper, the densities of each step.

Chapter

5

Photographic Processing

• Objectives

In this chapter you will cover:

- Manual and automatic processing,
- Processing variables,
- Stabilization processing,
- Diffusion transfer processing,
- Photographic reduction.

After reading the chapter you should be able to:

- Explain the difference between automatic and manual photographic processing,
- List the common steps for all photographic processing,
- Set up the darkroom for shallow tray processing and develop a line negative,
- Control the variables for both manual and automatic photographic processing,
- Process stabilization materials,
- Process photomechanical materials,
- Reduce overdeveloped film negatives.

When the photographer exposes a sheet of film on a process camera, it is not possible to see any difference on the emulsion even though a chemical change has taken place. This change is called a latent image. The task of changing the latent image, which we cannot see, to a real image, which we can see, is called **photographic processing**.

The purpose of this chapter is to classify and to review the various methods used by graphic arts photographers to process film that can be used by the printing industry.

• Methods of Photographic Processing

There are many different kinds of photographic materials, each available with a variety of characteristics such as color sensitivity, speed, color temperature rating, base thickness, contrast, and type of base (opaque or transparent). The processing of these different films can be classified as either manual or automatic.

Manual processing refers to the methods by which the photographer uses his or her hands to control image quality directly. Visual judgment of image development is also usually associated with this method, although for panchromatic films this is not possible (pan films must be developed in total darkness). The main advantages of manual processing are direct control of each step and low equipment cost.

Automatic processing is development by machine. With most systems, the photographer inserts an exposed piece of film in one end of the processor, and in a few minutes, a dry, ready-to-use sheet drops into a receiving basket at the other end. The processing variables are controlled by continual monitoring of the machine functions. The primary advantage of automatic processing is consistency; as long as the machine is operating within a narrow set of tolerances, the film image will always be acceptable for printing production. The main disadvantage is cost—machines are expensive and must be in nearly continual use to be cost-effective.

• Common Elements of Photographic Processing

No matter if it is manual or automatic, all photographic processing passes through five distinct steps: (1) developing, (2) stopping, (3) fixing, (4) washing, and (5) drying (figure 5.1). Some processes, like stabilization, combine the function of several steps in a single bath.

The purpose of the **developing** step is to change the latent image on a piece of exposed film to a real image. The developer solution is a complex chemical that can be purchased in a variety of formulations to produce many different results with a film emulsion. All developers, however, are made up of varying proportions of water, developing agent, activator, restrainer, and preservative. Most common graphic arts developers are sold to the printer stored in two separate containers (usually labeled "Part A" and "Part B") (figure 5.2). When kept apart, the two solutions may be stored indefinitely without deterioration; a printer would say they have a long shelf life. Once mixed together, however, the activity level necessary to process a sheet of film is very short. When an active solution loses its ability to process film, it is said to be exhausted. Development is a process of the chemicals in the solution working upon the silver crystals contained in the emulsion of the film.

All solutions eventually reach a point at which the developing agent is so used up that it cannot continue to cause the chemical change. One reason, then, for developer exhaustion is that too much film has been pushed through the solution.

Developers also become exhausted because of time and air. If a small amount of Parts A and B were mixed together in a shallow tray, the solution would easily become exhausted by the end of the workday, even if no film had been developed. By being mixed together, the chemicals interact with each other. With a shallow tray, a large surface of the liquid is exposed to air, resulting in chemical exhaustion by a process called "aerial oxidation."

The **stop bath** is a weak acid solution, usually formulated from a combination of water and a very small quantity of acetic acid. Chemically, the developer is a base. If the film is moved from a basic solution to an acidic bath, then all developing action will halt immediately. The main purpose of the stop bath (sometimes called the short stop), then, is to be able to control development time accurately.

A second purpose, though, is to help extend the working life of the third step, called the **fix**. When a sheet of film is lifted from the developer, a certain amount of solution is always carried with the sheet. If each sheet of film were moved directly from the developer to the fix, then eventually the amount of developer in the third tray would be so great that the fixer could no longer function. Thus, the stop bath, also dilutes the developer that is carried on the film.

Once in the stop bath, all developing action is halted, but the film emulsion is still light sensitive. The unexposed emulsion must be removed to make the final image permanent. The purpose of the fixer is to perform this important

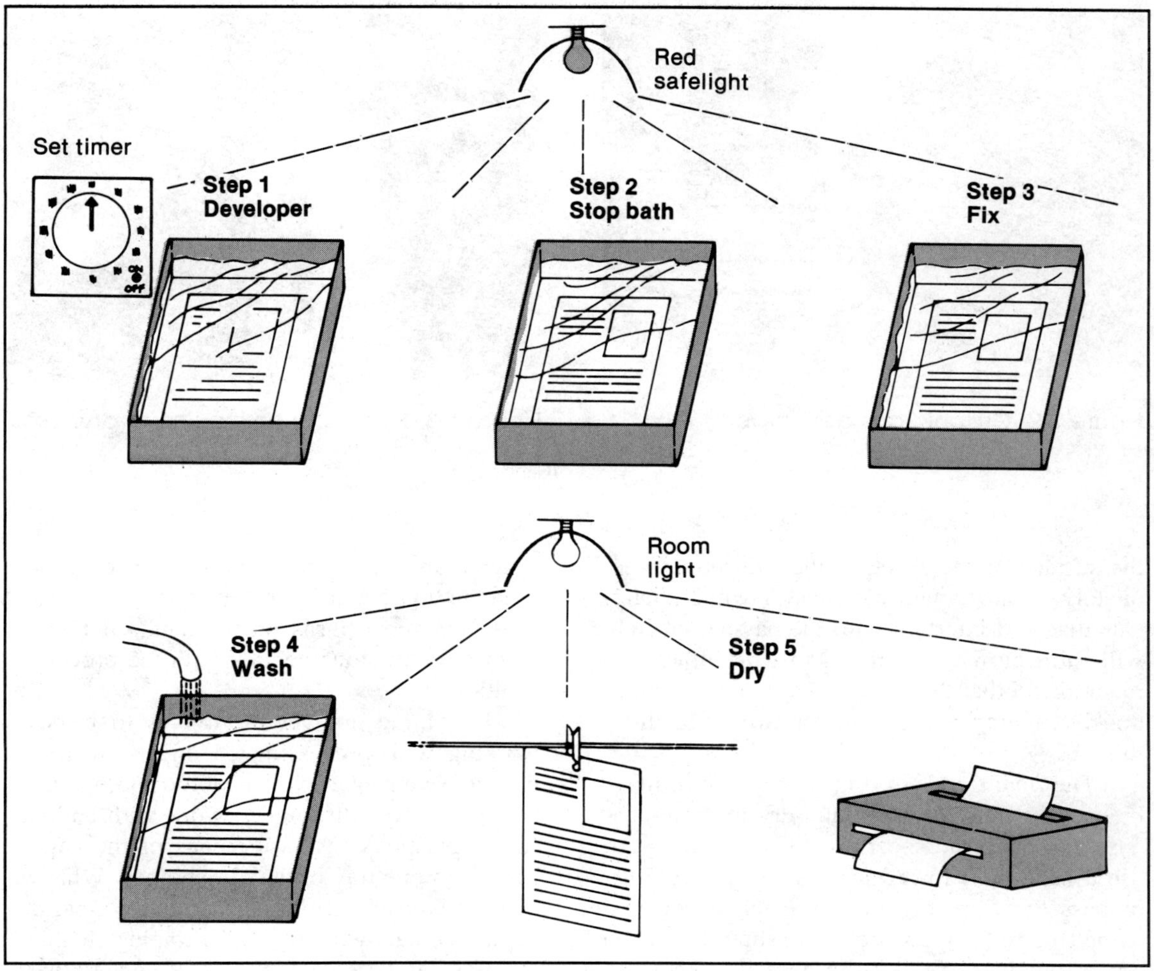

Figure 5.1. Five steps of photographic processing

function. The terms **hypo** and **fixer** are used here interchangeably.

The unexposed emulsion, on transparent-based films, appears milky white. When the milky white emulsion is dissolved by the hypo, to show the clear base, the film is said to have cleared. While it is possible to leave film in the fixer for several hours, it should remain in the bath at least twice as long as the film takes to clear.

Be extremely careful when working with fixer. The dried chemical can leave white stains on clothes, the floor, or the edge of the processing sink. Always rinse your hands after coming in contact with fixer, and never carry a piece of film away from the tray without rinsing the sheet in water.

The fourth step for photographic processing is **washing**. Once the film has been fixed, it is necessary to remove all traces of the hypo from

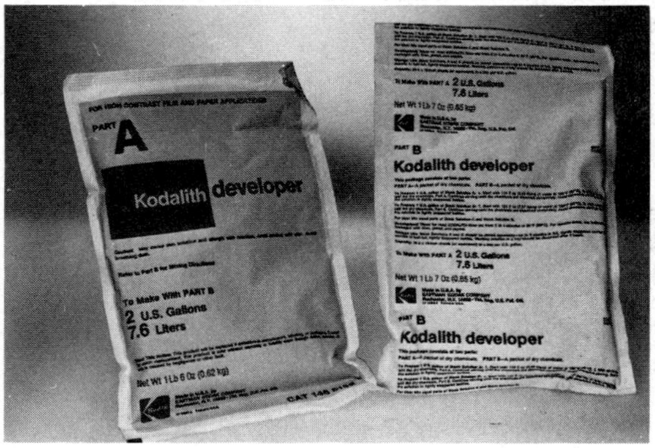

Figure 5.2. Graphic arts developers.

Figure 5.3. Film hung on the line to dry.

the surface of the sheet. If the film is not adequately washed, then blotches of white chemicals that will interfere with the passage of light will form on the dry film. Most manufacturers recommend that the film be washed in a continuously running water bath for twenty to thirty minutes.

The final step is **drying**. Before the film can be used, it must be clean and dry to the touch. You can hang the sheet on a line (figure 5.3), use a hand-held forced air system (figure 5.4), or pass the film through a special drying machine (figure 5.5). Extreme care should be taken not to overheat the film because if it becomes too hot, it could buckle out of shape, melt, or even burst into flame.

These steps, then, take place in any chemical processing. Some functions might be combined into a single bath, but they all occur.

• Processing Safety

Darkroom safety is an important area that deserves special attention. Some individuals have special problems because of their skin's sensitivity to the processing chemicals. It is possible to have an allergic reaction to repeated contact with the liquid materials. Overexposure can also cause chemical burns on the hands if they remain in continuous contact with the processing solutions.

If a large amount of time is to be spent working with processing chemicals, then it is wise to wear rubber gloves. Some photographers find the gloves difficult to work with and substitute plastic tongs as a means of moving the film from one tray or tank to another. Whatever method is used, it is wise to avoid a great deal of skin contact with any photographic chemical.

Eye safety is another area of concern in the darkroom. Splashed chemicals can do great damage to the human eye. It is best to use safety glasses when working with processing chemicals. Be extremely careful when mixing or moving liquid chemicals. Before beginning to work, examine the manufacturer's instructions that are printed on the chemical containers. You should always know what actions to take in case of an emergency.

Always mix any chemicals in a well-ventilated room. Always add acid to water to form a solution, never the reverse. Some darkroom chemicals are very poisonous. A solution might look like water, but even a small taste could make you very sick. Never drink any processing chemicals.

Another thing to check in the darkroom before beginning chemical processing is ventilation. If air does not circulate, then it is possible to become overwhelmed with chemical fumes and pass out. If there is no special system in your darkroom to provide the necessary ventilation, then stop processing frequently and open the door to allow a fresh exchange of air.

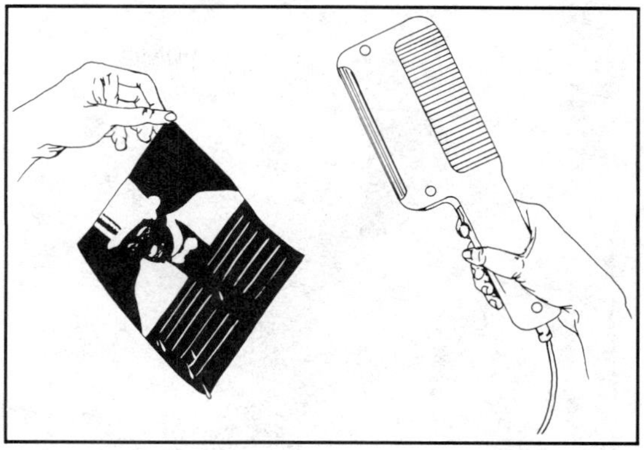

Figure 5.4. Film dried by a hand-held drier.
(Kimberly Conover-Loar)

• Manual Chemical Processing

Methods

The two basic manual processing techniques are shallow tray and deep tank. Shallow tray development involves the use of three trays that are slightly larger than the film being processed and only a few inches deep. Usually, only enough chemicals are added just to cover the sheet as it lies in the bottom of the tray. During development, the tray is rocked back and forth to move the solution constantly over the surface of the sheet. Shallow tray developing is the most common of all the manual processing methods.

Deep-tank photographic processing usually employs large rectangular stainless steel tanks to hold the chemical solutions. The film is usually inserted into a metal holding frame and then dipped into the tank (figure 5.6). The tanks typically hold a great deal of liquid and are employed when the solutions will be used for more than several days with the help of replenisher. Replenisher is a chemical that is added to a solution to return it to a usable activity. Deep-tank processing, because of the reduced liquid surface area, reduces the effects of aerial oxidation.

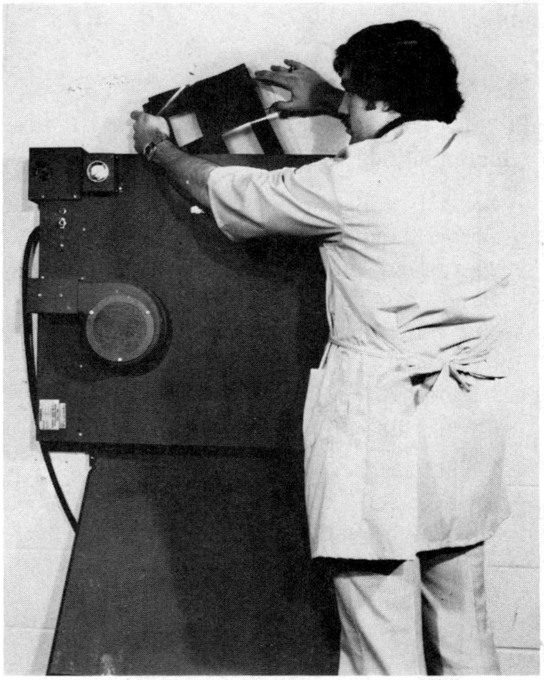

Figure 5.5. Special film-drying machine.

A variable in chemical processing is anything that can be changed by the photographer that will affect the quality of the final photograph. In discussing processing variables, sev-

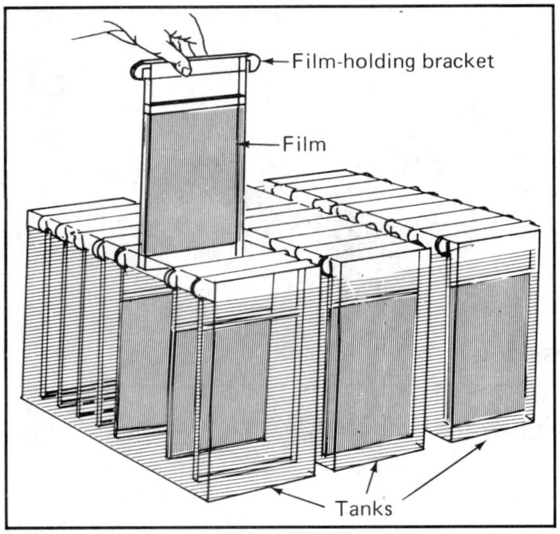

Figure 5.6. Deep-tank processing. Film is dipped into the solution. (Kimberly Conover-Loar)

eral things should always be assumed before development begins:

- Fresh film is being used that will function as the manufacturer predicts.
- The brand and type should always be the same for each class of job.
- The camera exposure has been made accurately and correctly.
- Fresh chemicals are being used in the processing sink.

With these factors always assumed, the photographer directly controls only three variables to obtain high-quality film negatives and positives—namely, time, temperature, and agitation.

Time refers to the exact number of minutes and seconds the developer solution acts upon the film emulsion. Most printers use a sweep timer to measure the length of time the film is immersed in the bath (see figure 2.13). Time is a critical variable. With some films, even a slight change in time will give drastically different results.

Temperature refers to the temperature level of the chemical processing solutions. Most manual processing is done with the trays or tanks placed in a large sink where water is allowed to flow around the containers (figure 5.7). The temperature of the water is regulated to the specifications supplied by the film manufacturer (usually 68°F, or 20°C).

Some systems adjust the amount of hot and cold water passing through pipes into the sink. With this approach the water is exchanged every few minutes. Other devices have heating and cooling elements that are immersed into a stationary pool of water. These devices automatically recirculate and heat the water to the desired level and then shut off. One reason that most trays and tanks are stainless steel is that metal easily transfers the temperature of the sink water to the processing solutions. Also, stainless steel resists being damaged by the chemicals or rusted by the bath water.

Agitation describes the movement of the chemicals over the surface of the film. This is very important. When the chemical action takes place between the developer and the emulsion, the developing agent rapidly becomes exhausted. By moving the tray, fresh developer will replace the developer that is exhausted by contact with the exposed film. The key to predictable image results is consistent agitation. The photographer must perfect an agitation rate that is the same throughout each development time period and for every sheet of film that is processed. It is relatively easy to control temperature and time using a clock and a temperature gauge, but it is not as easy for agitation. Everyone agitates at a different pace, so this becomes an individual variable that must be rigorously controlled by each photographer.

Basic Exposure

The idea of a **basic camera exposure** is a fundamental understanding for all process camera line work. In general, basic exposure is the camera aperture and shutter speed combination that

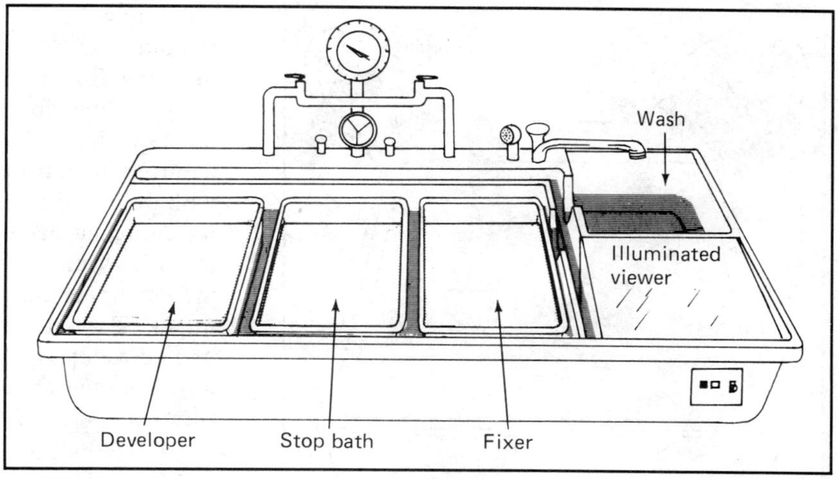

Figure 5.7. Using a water bath to control temperature. (Kimberly Conover-Loar)

will produce a quality film image of normal line copy with standardized chemical processing. This combination will vary from camera to camera, depending on many variables. The idea is discussed in detail in later chapters, but you need to know that this is the basic exposure from which all line exposures are determined.

The calculation of basic exposure is based upon the consistency of time, temperature, and agitation. It is possible to predict image changes as a result of exposure only because all processing variables are always the same. The goal for the photographer is to have every variable in such control that the exposure (f/stop and shutter speed) becomes the only adjustment made for any desired image change. The process is covered in detail in chapter 6.

Typical Manual Processing Procedures

Since shallow tray processing is the most common manual method, we shall review each step in detail. Assume that the photographer is beginning the day's work, and it is necessary to set up the darkroom to develop the first sheet of film.

The first step is to fill the sink with water. Using whatever controls are available, bring the bath to the desired temperature level. Next, rinse out three trays with water, and float them in the sink. Most photographers label each tray so the same one is used each day for the same chemicals. If one day a tray is used to hold the fixer, and then the next to hold the developer, it is possible eventually to contaminate one of the solutions. The trays ae always rinsed to remove any particles of dust or dirt and to dissolve any dried chemicals that might have been missed from the last shift.

For the same reason, rinse out the measuring flask. Then mix the processing chemicals from the working solutions. **Stock solutions** are the concentrated materials supplied by the manufacturer in either powder or liquid form. **Working solutions** are made by mixing stock solutions and water. If ordinary line film is to be used, then mix equal parts of developer A and B (figure 5.8). The quantity will depend upon the size of tray to be used. For a small 8″ × 10″ tray, a total of sixteen ounces would probably be sufficient—eight ounces of Part A and eight ounces of Part B. Measure Part A first and pour it into the first tray, then measure the same amount for

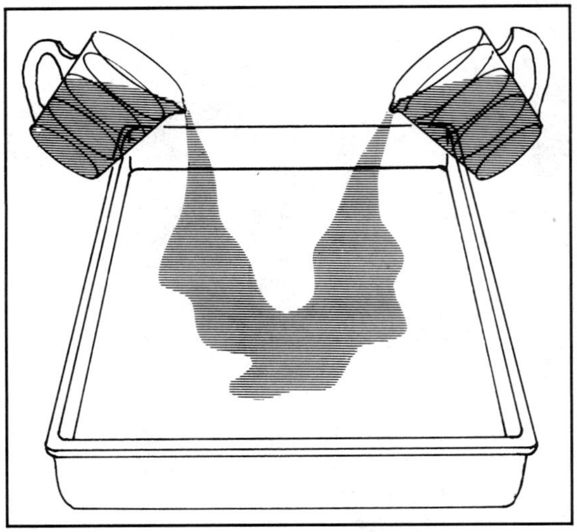

Figure 5.8. Setting up a working solution. Mix equal parts of A and B working stock. (Kimberly Conover-Loar)

Part B and pour it into the tray. Again rinse out the flask. Next, measure out enough stop bath to fill the second tray to a level of approximately one-half inch. Finally, measure out enough fixer to fill the third tray to a level of about one-half inch. Since the order of processing is developer, stop, then fix, photographers always place the trays in the same order, moving from left to right (see figure 5.7).

With the sink and the three chemical solutions at the desired temperature, turn off the white lights and make the first camera exposure under safelight conditions. Remove the film from the camera, and set the timer to the required time. The film manufacturer will always specify a recommended development time—for line film, usually two and three-quarters minute.

There are several methods of inserting the film into the developer. One technique is to hold the film in the right hand, with the emulsion up, and with a sweeping motion, to turn the film over so that the entire surface of the sheet emulsion is pushed against the developing solution. The film is then turned over so the emulsion is up, facing the photographer. Another method is to hold the film by alternate corners and then to drag the film under the surface of the liquid, with the emulsion up (figure 5.9). There are still other methods, but the goal is the same: The entire emulsion of the film should be covered with the solution as rapidly as possible. Ideally, the entire surface would become wet at the same instant. With most line films, if one part is in the developer longer than another, that section might be overdeveloped, with the later section underdeveloped. Whatever approach is used, however, the timer is turned on the instant the film is covered with developer.

Immediately begin agitating the tray. Rock in several directions, never just back and forth. If the solution is moved in only one direction, developer streaks that interfere with the final image might form. One technique is to hold the tray by alternate corners (figure 5.10). Rock the tray so the solution flows from front to back, then from left to right, from back to front, and finally from right to left, beginning the pattern over again. Whatever pattern and rate is used, be consistent.

Always view the image through the emulsion. If the film is seen through the base in the developer, the photographer easily can be tricked into thinking that the film is developing too rapidly. It is always helpful to have placed a graphic arts gray scale on the copy so it is possible to watch the density build during development. Although it varies, depending upon the type of original copy, many photographers use a solid step four (on a ten-step scale) as target. The true test of development, of course, is the quality of the image, but if all variables are in control, then the scale can be a good predictor of the final product.

It is best not to wait until the timer is off to remove the film from the developer. It takes time to move the sheet from one tray to another, which means that the film will be developing during the change. One approach is to lift the film out of the developer when ten seconds remain on the timer. The sheet is allowed to drain

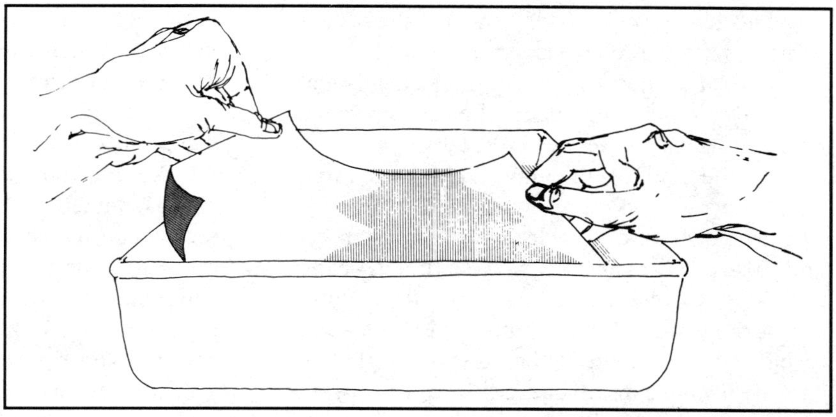

Figure 5.9. Inserting film into the developer. One way to insert dry film into the developer is to drag the film under the surface of the liquid with the emulsion up. (Kimberly Conover-Loar)

over the tray and then is moved over the stop bath so that it is plunged into the short stop just as the timer goes off.

The film should be agitated also in the stop bath. Always follow the film manufacturer's recommendations, but normally, five to ten seconds should be sufficient time to be in the short stop. At this point it is possible to examine briefly the image and gray scale more critically than when the film was in the developer. Many darkroom sinks have a wet-viewing system. Most viewing tables come equipped with both a white light and a red safelight. With the red light on, look at the fine line detail and the gray scale. Are the lines closed or open? Is the desired step solid? If the image is acceptable then the sheet may be moved immediately to the fixer. If it has not developed quite enough, it is possible to return the film to the developer, but always first rinse the sheet with water. The acid in the stop bath could pollute the developing agent if it were not washed off.

When the necessary time has passed, immerse the film in the third tray and begin agitating. Watch the film, and time the period it takes the image to clear. When it is clear, continue agitating the same length of time it took to clear. The reason this time is variable is that as the solution continues to work it loses its ability to accept the unexposed silver emulsion into solution. When the hypo has taken all the silver that it will hold, it is said to be saturated and must be replaced.

Figure 5.10. Agitating the solution. Hold the tray by alternative corners and rock the tray. (Kimberly Conover-Loar)

Next, place the film in the wash, and allow water to flow over the sheet. Following manufacturer's recommendations, twenty minutes should be sufficient.

The last step is to dry the finished sheet, using whatever method is available in the shop. One way of diminishing water marks is to squeegee both sides of the sheet when it is removed from the wash to the wet light table.

At the end of the day, the photographer clears up the darkroom and empties the trays. The developer is always discarded. The stop bath and fixer, however, are saved. If a so-called indicator stop bath is being used, the solution will turn purple when the bath has lost its ability to halt development. If the stop is purple, discard it; if not, carefully return it to the working solution container. Some companies empty the fixer into a special silver recovery device that removes the silver from the hypo; this reclaimed silver can then be sold to help lower production costs. If such a device is not being used, pour the fixer back into the washing solution bottle. Finally, turn off the temperature control unit, and empty the sink. Rinse out the trays and turn them over to dry.

• Automatic Film Processing

One of the most recent developments in the darkroom has been automatic processing of film by machine. The variables that were mentioned under manual processing remain the same with automatic units. It should be emphasized that just because the label ''automatic'' is used it does not mean that these variables are forgotten. With automatic systems the photographer can control them more critically, consistently, and accurately than with manual processing.

Almost all machines carry the film through deep tanks of chemicals using a moving belt (figure 5.11). With deep tanks, exhaustion due to aerial oxidation is diminished. Further, the activity level of the developer is controlled by the addition of replenisher. The amount of development time is controlled by the rate of speed of the belt. The slower the movement, the longer the develoment time; the faster, the shorter the development time. This rate is usually adjusted by the machine's manufacturer, although with some units it can be adjusted in the darkroom.

Agitation is effected through the use of pumps, attached to each tank, that continually recirculate the solution. Some machines are set up so that the pumps are activated as a sheet of film enters the device and are shut off when the processing is completed. The result of this is a savings in energy, which reduces operating costs.

All devices are equipped with an automatic temperature control device that heats or cools the solutions to the desired temperature. These are usually attached to the recirculating system.

As the sheet moves from the wash into the drying unit, most machines automatically turn on a fan and heating element that force warm air onto both sides of the film.

Most machines are designed for dry-to-dry delivery. This means that the elapsed time from when a dry, exposed sheet of film is inserted to when a dry, developed sheet is dropped into the output bin is very short. For some machines this is as short as six minutes and, for others, as long as twelve minutes. While this might initially seem to be a long time, it should be realized that once the film enters the machine, the photographer is free to make another exposure. It is possible to feed one sheet after another through the device as rapidly as the moving belt accepts the film.

Keeping the Machine in Control

While the photographer must check to insure that the agitating pumps are working, that the temperature control unit is holding the solution at the correct level, and that the belts are moving, these variables are not of continual concern during the workday. The activity level of the

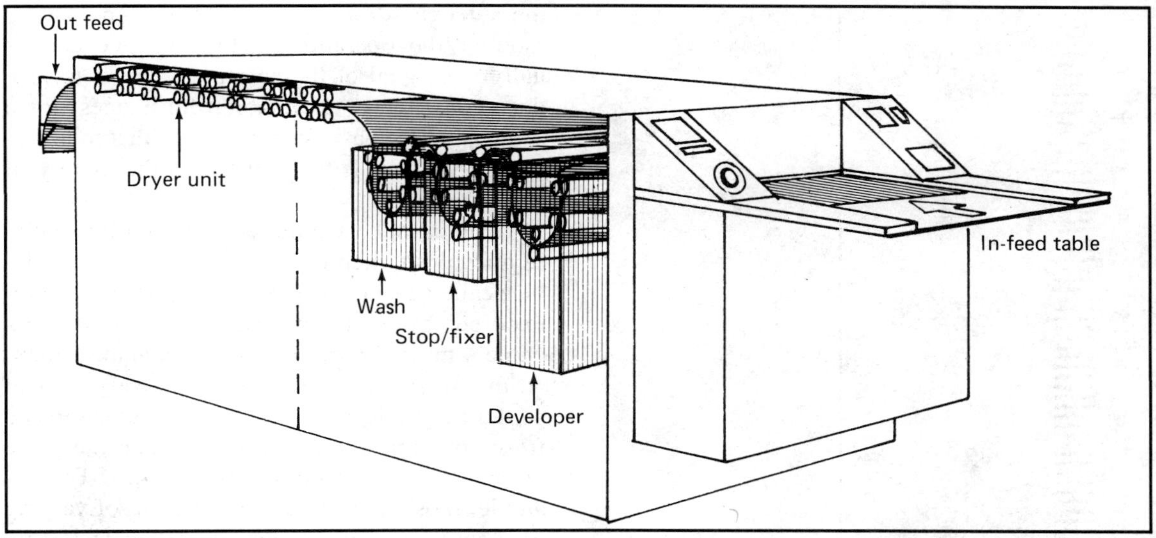

Figure 5.11. Automatic film processor. The film is moved through deep tanks of solution using a complex belt system. (Kimberly Conover-Loar)

developer solution, however, demands frequent and careful checking. When the question is asked, Is the machine in control?, reference is being made to activity level. With automatic processing, this variable is the main concern of the photographer.

Recall that developer activity level is controlled through the addition of replenisher. The amount added is proportional to the surface area of the film being processed. Processor manufacturers calculate how much developing agent is consumed to develop a square unit of area (say, for example, one square inch). The same amount of replenisher must then be added to the developer solution after that area is processed in order to return the solution to the original activity level.

Several methods are used to calculate the amount of replenisher to add. One common way is to have the photographer dial in the size of sheet being processed, and then the device calculates and adds the appropriate amount. Remember, the developer agent only works upon the exposed areas of the film—if a large sheet is sent through with only a minute portion exposed, then it is possible for too much replenisher to be added. The point is, with machines in which the size is dialed in and the device adds replenisher for an average exposure, it is possible to bring the machine out of control if the exposed areas are not within the machine's average range.

A second method used to add replenisher to the developer is with the use of a densitometer. Some devices have a transmission densitometer (see chapter 13) attached to the output end of the machine. As the dry film drops into a bin, density readings are made, and replenisher is added proportional to the amount of exposure.

Even with the most careful attention, machines get out of control. The main solutions eventually become exhausted and must be flushed out and replaced. When the machine is shut down overnight, activity level goes down. If an operator forgets to dial in several sheets,

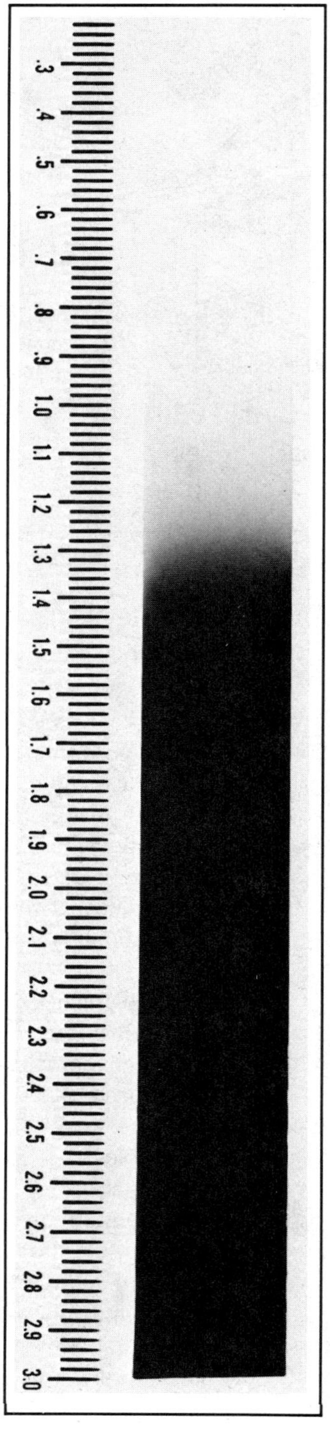

Figure 5.12. Control strip.

the level can drop. There must be some way to monitor the operation of the machine continually. The goal of the automatic unit is to produce consistently acceptable film images. Even if the machine has a special device that monitors the activity level, the real test is the quality of the film image.

Photographers commonly check film quality as a result of chemistry activity level with a device called a **control strip**. Control strips are pre-exposed sheets of film that are sold by the machine's manufacturer or by film manufacturers. At the beginning of each day and every hour or so during production time, the operator sends a fresh strip through the device. When the piece drops out, several things are checked. For example, most control strips show lines of varying thickness and carry a large gray scale (figure 5.12). Density readings are made of specific steps to make sure, as specified by the manufacturer, that the density is within certain tolerance levels.

If the density readings are acceptable, then machine adjustments are not necessary. However, if the readings are not within the tolerances, adjustments must be made. For example, if the activity level is too low, then replenisher must be added. How much? The amount depends upon the degree of variation from the desired density reading. Manufacturers usually supply charts that recommend quantities to effect different increases in density level. If the activity level is too high, then scrap sheets of exposed film must be sent through the machine without adding replenisher. Again, the amount of film depends upon the degree to which the machine is out of control.

Once adjustments are made, the operator must send through another control strip and again take density readings. The process of making adjustments and taking readings continues until the machine is again in control.

Automatic processing is not magic, but it is also not something the photographer can assume will function without human control. As with other sophisticated machines, it frees the technician from routine tasks but still requires attention and care.

• Special Types of Photographic Processing

Several processes and techniques are used by the graphic arts photographer to prepare special types of materials for printing reproduction. Even though they are labeled as special, they are so common that it is important to explain them.

Stabilization Processing

The camera operator is called upon frequently to produce images using opaque-based materials like paper. These can be camera enlargements or reductions or simple proofs of existing negatives by contacting (see chapter 9). One method of rapidly processing paper-based materials is called **stabilization**. Stabilization processing recently has become widely used in the composition area to develop rolls of paper that were exposed on photographic composing machines.

All stabilization development is done automatically by passing the exposed material through two chemical baths in the processing unit. The first solution is an activator that starts the development process. The emulsion of the special stabilization sheet has a built-in chemical that interacts with the activator solution. If properly exposed, the image density will develop to a maximum density level and then stop. The second solution is a stabilizer that dissolves any unexposed emulsion and fixes the print.

The actual operation of a processor is relatively simple. First, turn on the machine and allow it to run for a few seconds. Sometimes crystals build up on the rubber rollers in the device. Running the machine allows the chemical solutions to dissolve any buildup and insures that nothing is jamming the system. Next, place the exposed paper on the in-feed table, emulsion up. Slowly push the sheet forward into the machine. When the rollers begin to pull the paper, release the sheet and allow the device to feed at its own rate. It is wisest to center the sheet in on the machine rather than to place it near the edge of the roller. It is possible to jam the paper in the gears that drive the system, or to wrinkle the sheet if it gets too close to the edge. Gently hold the paper as it leaves the machine, but do not attempt to pull it out faster than the rotation of the rollers.

Most stabilization processors are housed directly in the darkroom (on the wet side of course). If the processor is placed in a totally white light situation, then a special cover must be added (see figure 2.21). The paper is then carried to the machine in a special light-tight container, placed inside the cover, and then fed into the machine.

Most stabilization prints are intended to be used immediately and then discarded. If, for some reason, it is required to be saved, place the sheet in a tray of fixer as soon as it leaves the processor. Fix the sheet as if it were a piece of film, then wash and dry. Fixing and washing will insure the permanence of the sheet and will prevent yellowing or spotting over time.

Diffusion Transfer

Diffusion transfer is gaining widespread use in the printing industry. Its primary purpose is to produce opaque positives from positive originals. However, the process can be used in the areas of copy preparation, proofing, making film positives, and even offset lithographic platemaking. The process is called by a variety of trade names such as PMT (photomechanical transfer), TR (transfer), and copy rapid.

In the darkroom, diffusion transfer has several important uses that can save the camera operator both time and trouble. Consider three examples:

Example One. The paste-up department is behind on a job. They have an illustration to fit into a small area on a layout, but the artist's copy is too large. This is a normal sort of task with which photographers have had to deal for years. Before diffusion transfer, they would take the illustration to the camera, reduce it onto a sheet of transparent-based film, process the film, allow it to dry, then take it to the contact table, expose it to a sheet of opaque-based print paper, process the print, and finally, allow it to dry. It might take an hour to perform these steps. With diffusion transfer, however, the camera exposure is made onto a special negative sheet. The negative sheet image is then transferred to a special receiver sheet in an automatic processor. The process, from camera to dry, paste-up copy, can be completed in as little as three minutes.

Example Two. The sales staff just received the artist's copy for a special rush job from the company's most important customer. During a coffee break the production director set a wet coffee cup on the pile of illustration boards. When the mistake was discovered, the top sheet was dropped on the floor and someone stepped on it. Now the customer's expensive original copy has both a coffee ring and footprint, and nobody wants to tell the boss. The solution is to use diffusion transfer. By slightly overexposing, it is possible to drop background scum or dirt from the original when a diffusion transfer print is made.

Example Three. Some copy has been received that is made up of several different-colored lines. Each piece would reproduce differently if they were all shot together on ortho film. By adjusting exposure, it is possible to record each different copy image on diffusion transfer so that the line densities are consistent. The diffusion transfer copies can then be pasted back together to obtain a final film image that is of uniform quality.

Diffusion transfer materials are purchased in two parts: a light-sensitive negative sheet and a chemically sensitive receiver sheet. The negative sheet can only be worked with in a safelight situation, but the receiver can be handled in normal white light. The negative sheet is exposed to the original copy on the camera.

To process diffusion transfer, the negative sheet is placed against the receiver, emulsion to emulsion, and is then passed through an activator bath in a diffusion transfer processor. Always place the negative on the bottom, slightly leading the receiver. The sheets must pass around a separator bar and are then pulled by rollers into the activator. Let the rollers move the sheets at their own rate; do not try to push them into the machine faster than the device is set.

As the sheets move into the processor, they pass through the activator and are pressed together by the out-feed roller. The latent image on the negative sheet acts as a chemical mask that allows the activator to cause a change in the nonimage areas. A special chemical built into the negative emulsion changes the nonimage area, which then allows the image area to transfer to the receiver sheet.

As the sandwich passes out of the back of the processor, hold it by the edges, and try not to bend or crinkle the two sheets. Allow them to remain together for at least thirty seconds, then pull them apart (figure 5.13). If the exposure was correct, then a perfect image should have been formed on the reciever sheet. Discard the negative and allow the receiver to dry. It should be dry to the touch within a minute.

If the image is not acceptable, it will be necessary to adjust the camera exposure. Because it is a transfer process, the exposure changes are the exact opposite of those when working with line film. To increase the density of the image on the receiver sheet, decrease the exposure time. To decrease density, increase the exposure.

Diffusion transfer receiver sheets are also available in forms other than the white opaque paper. Transparent receiver sheets commonly are used to obtain a film positive, like when making a reverse. Special plate material also can be purchased that will receive an image from a negative diffusion transfer sheet. The plate then can be used on an offset lithographic duplicator.

The basic steps in photographic processing are present in diffusion transfer but are not as easily identifiable as trays setting in a sink. The developer is built into the emulsion; the stop and fix are combined in the process when maximum transfer takes place. Rinsing is still necessary for long-term use, but the action of the squeegee rollers serves to remove a sufficient quantity of activator for normal use. Drying is the final step. Even though all photographic materials use the same processing steps, they might not all be recognizable. Diffusion transfer is covered in greater detail in chapter 10.

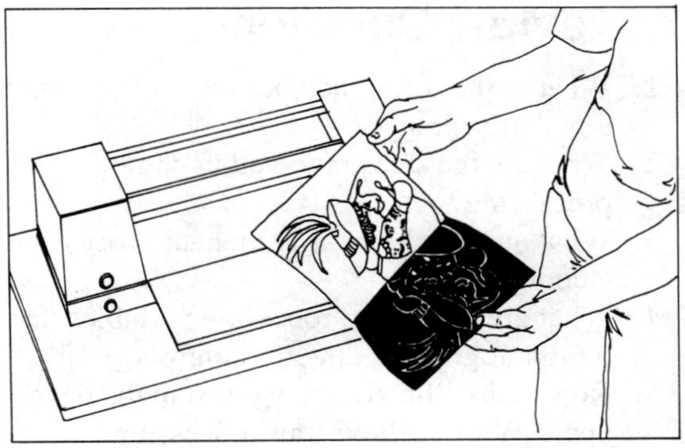

Figure 5.13. Finished diffusion transfer. After allowing the two sheets to remain together for thirty seconds, carefully peel them apart. (Kimberly Conover-Loar)

Reduction

It is possible sometimes to save an overdeveloped negative through a process called **reduction**. A reducing agent removes density from the film emulsion. The process is basically one of oxidation, which changes a portion of the emulsion to a solution that can be washed away in a rinse (usually water).

The most common type of reducer is called a cutting (or subtractive) reducer. Cutting reducers remove density equally from all parts of a negative. The result is that thin areas are most rapidly affected. A popular reducing agent, called Farmer's Reducer, is a mixture of potassium ferricyanide, sodium thiosulfate, and water.

To reduce a negative, first mix the reducer chemicals using the directions supplied by the manufacturer. Place the reducer in a tray, and then insert the film, emulsion up. Agitate the solution over the negative for thirty to sixty seconds. Then remove the film and rinse until the yellow reducer stain is gone. Examine the image. If more reduction is necessary, return the sheet to the tray, and again agitate for the same time period. If the image is acceptable, then refix, wash, and dry the film.

Selective reduction of negatives is a common procedure for the retouching of separation negatives or positives in process color work. Sometimes a special resist (protective coating) is painted over all parts of the negative, except the areas that need to be reduced. The film is then processed to the desired density, and when dry, the resist is removed.

• Key Points

- The two basic ways to process photographic materials are by either manual or automatic processing.
- All processing must pass through five separate steps: developing, stopping, fixing, washing, and drying.
- Automatic film processors are kept in control by the careful addition and monitoring of replenisher.
- Stabilization processing is a method of producing paper-based film images by automatic means.
- Diffusion transfer is a two-part process of producing opaque positives from positive originals.
- Reduction is a method of removing density from a film emulsion after normal processing.

• Review Questions

1. What is the difference between a latent and a real film image?
2. What are the steps involved in photographic processing?
3. What are the three basic manual processing techniques?
4. What are the three processing variables that the photographer directly controls?
5. How is the film always viewed in the developer? With shallow tray processing?
6. What is the purpose of a control strip with automatic processing?
7. What is the purpose of replenisher?
8. What type of product is produced with stabilization processing?
9. What materials are used with the diffusion transfer process?
10. List three purposes of diffusion transfer.
11. What is the result of reduction?

• Activities

1. Mix working solutions from stock solution of developer, stop, and fixer for line film processing.
2. Set up a darkroom sink for shallow tray development.
3. Run an activity test on an automatic film processor, and take any necessary steps to insure that it is in control.
4. Process a film negative to a solid step four on a ten-step gray scale.
5. Process a stabilization print.
6. Make a diffusion transfer copy of a smudged original, removing all background marks.
7. Take a piece of slightly overdeveloped negative, and using Farmer's Reducer, open the closed image areas.

Chapter 6

Basic Camera Operations

• Objectives

In this chapter you will cover basic camera operation.

After reading the chapter you should be able to:

- Calculate size changes using a proportion wheel;
- Adjust process camera size controls;
- Mount camera copy so that the required image and gray scale will be reflected through the lens to the filmboard;
- Check and adjust camera focus, illumination, and image size;
- Explain the idea of basic exposure;
- Adjust the f/stop and shutter time to maintain required exposures;
- Mount film on the camera back;
- Mount contact screens over film on the camera back;
- Make process camera exposures.

The most important equipment for the graphic arts photographer is the process camera. While other pieces of equipment are frequently used in the darkroom, most merely support the operation of the camera. Unlike the common Instamatic camera used around the home, the industrial device has several controls that are used to control the quality of the final image critically. When size changes are specified, then settings must be checked carefully; even the smallest setting error on the camera could result in an image not fitting on the final press sheet. Errors in size of the lens opening or exposure time can result in an unacceptable piece of exposed film. If there are quality control problems with the photographer's work, they are usually caused by poor camera operation.

The purpose of this chapter is to review the procedures that are fundamental to the operation of any process camera. The skills outlined here should be mastered before any attempt is made to move to more advanced work such as halftone or color separation photography.

• Determining Enlargement/Reduction

One of the main advantages of the process camera is that it can be adjusted to produce sizes other than that of the original copy. Frequently, designers or artists produce illustrations larger than the required size. The advantage of this

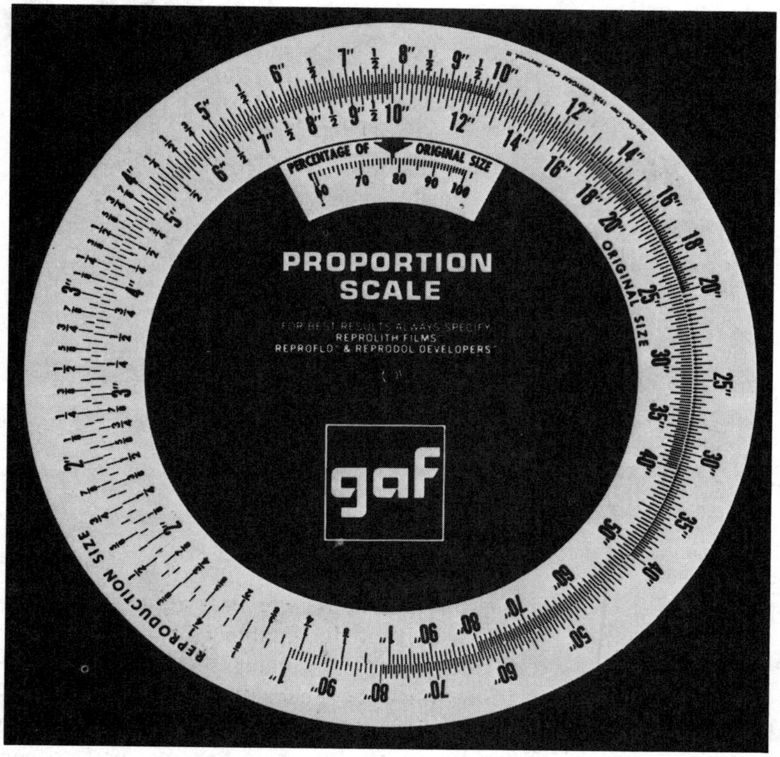

Figure 6.1. Proportional wheel.

procedure is that it enhances the quality of the final product; reducing the size of an image sharpens the line quality. Other times images must be manipulated to fit an existing space on the paste-up. If the line of display type is six inches long but the space on the layout is five inches, then the original must be reduced to 84 percent so that it fits into the required area.

Sometimes the designer writes instructions on a work order that specifies the required percentage change. Other times the photographer must calculate the setting. One of the easiest methods of determining size changes is with the use of a proportion wheel (figure 6.1). Assume that we have a line drawing that measures 10 1/4 inches × 6 3/8 inches that must fit into a width of 8 inches. What percentage reduction must be made? To use the wheel, first locate the original size (10 1/4) on the inner wheel. Next, identify the desired size on the outer wheel (8). Then line up the two new numbers, and read the percentage change at the arrow in the window—in this example, 78 percent. The reproduction height measures 5 inches.

The wheel can also be used to determine size changes that will result from specific percentage settings on the camera. Say we wanted to know the length of the line drawing in the last example. Set the wheel at 78 percent, locate the original length on the inner wheel, and then read the results (8 inches) on the outer wheel (see figure 6.1).

Sometimes a proportion wheel is not available when a quick percentage calculation must be made. What percentage setting must be made on the camera if we have a headline that measures 8 1/2 inches but that must fit into a 4-inch space? The answer can be found by making a fraction, with the desired size on top, and the original size on the bottom:

$$\frac{4}{8.5}$$

Then divide:

$$8.5\overline{)4} = 85\overline{)40.000} = 0.470 = 47 \text{ percent.}$$

```
        0.470
85 ) 40.000
     340
      600
      595
       50
```

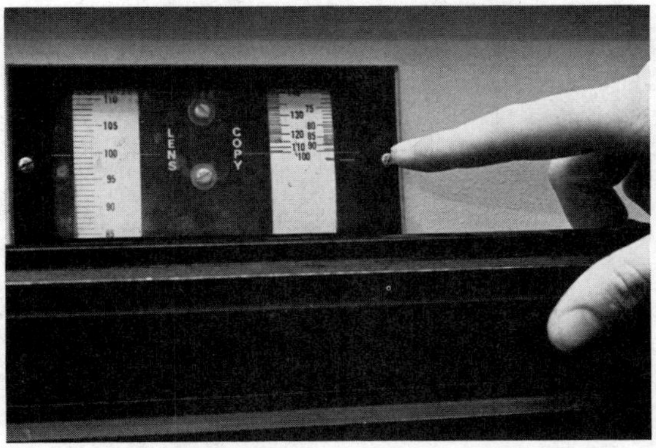

Figure 6.2. Process camera percentage tapes. Line up both percentage tapes at the desired percentage of enlargement or reduction.

• Setting the Camera Controls

Two common systems are used to control size changes on process cameras: percentage tapes and the ratio system. Both involve moving the camera copyboard and lensboard to different positions in relationship to each other and to the filmboard.

Percentage tapes are merely numbered scales that move as the lens or copyboard is moved. Most tapes have a range from 25 percent to 300 percent and can be adjusted accurately to the nearest 1 percent—that is, it is not possible to set the tapes at 58 1/2 percent; it will have to be either 58 percent or 59 percent, the nearest 1 percent.

Tape systems are calibrated so that, when both scales read 100 percent, the image that is formed on the filmboard is the exact size as that of the original copy on the copyboard. A 50 percent setting is one-half the original size; 200 percent is double (in each direction). All percentage tape systems have two tapes, one connected to the lensboard and the other connected to the copyboard. If both tapes are lined up at the same percentage reading, then an image that is the desired size should be formed (figure 6.2).

A somewhat similar method of adjusting percentage changes is the ratio system. This is normally found on the largest, most precise cameras. When the camera is installed by the manufacturer, careful tests are performed to determine exactly what ratios of copy to lens and lens to film distances give what percentage changes. These ratios are then recorded and supplied to the company for use with their particular camera. When a certain image size is required, then the camera operator looks up the ratio settings from the list and moves the lens and copyboard to the required positions. These positions can be either measured on a track or located by numeric scales that change as the boards move.

• Mounting the Copy

Most process camera copyboards are equipped with either a vacuum, spring-loaded, or gravity holding system. Copy is mounted on the board while it is in a horizontal position and is then swung into a vertical orientation so that it is parallel to the filmboard (see figure 2.2).

Almost all vertical cameras use the gravity-holding method. A glass plate is usually hinged

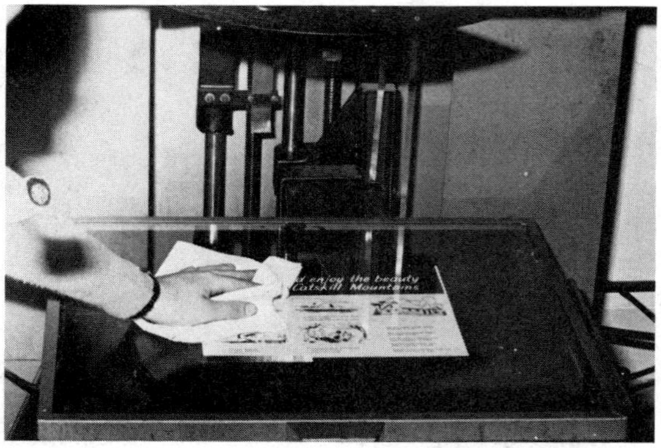

Figure 6.3. Gravity holding system. A clear piece of glass usually covers the copyboard to hold the paste-up in place.

in place from the back of the board so that the copy can be held perfectly flat (figure 6.3).

No matter the system, however, the procedures for mounting camera copy are basically the same.

Cleaning the Glass

The first step is to clean the glass cover, both inside and out. Dust can collect on the outside surface even between exposures and can end up as bothersome pinholes on the film. The inside of the glass cover sometimes picks up pieces of wax or rubber cement from contacting the paste-up board. Wax will absorb light and will therefore be recorded as a large open area on the film.

It is best to use a single-edged razor blade to scrape the large pieces of wax from the inside of the frame. Be sure to brush away carefully any pieces that fall to the copyboard. Then use a commercial liquid glass cleaner on the glass. Use a lintless cloth to polish both surfaces—inexpensive paper towels often cost more in time to remove the stray lint than they save when purchased. The importance of clean glass cannot be overemphasized. Light must travel through the glass, strike the copy, and then be reflected back through the lens. Anything that interferes with that passage of light will end up as a defect on the piece of film. It is far wiser to spend two minutes doing a thorough cleaning job than to spend fifteen minutes reshooting a negative.

Centering the Copy

Most copyboard surfaces are covered with black or gray felt cloth. Remember, dark black absorbs light and reflects very little back to the film. Additionally, all surfaces are marked with some sort of centering system.

All centering systems are calibrated by the camera manufacturer so that the guidelines on the copyboard line correspond to the lines that are etched into the surface of the filmboard. If a photograph is centered according to the copyboard guidelines, then it should be centered perfectly on the filmboard (see figure 2.4).

Too many new photographers are not careful when centering the copy. It is very discouraging to be tray processing an important piece of film and, when the image begins to come up, only to notice that part of the image missed the film. Remember that the camera lens reverses the image, so place the copy upside down on the copyboard.

Positioning the Gray Scale

The **gray scale** is an important device that aids the photographer in judging the quality of the final negative or positive. Get in the habit of always including a gray scale on the copy, no matter how simple the shot.

Place the gray scale next to the copy but not covering any image. It is wisest to stay at least one-quarter inch away from any image area. Be careful, however, that it is not so far away from the board that it is not recorded on the film (figure 6.4).

If there is a large open area on the copy, some camera operators place the gray scale directly on the board. This is acceptable as long as the scale is well away from an image.

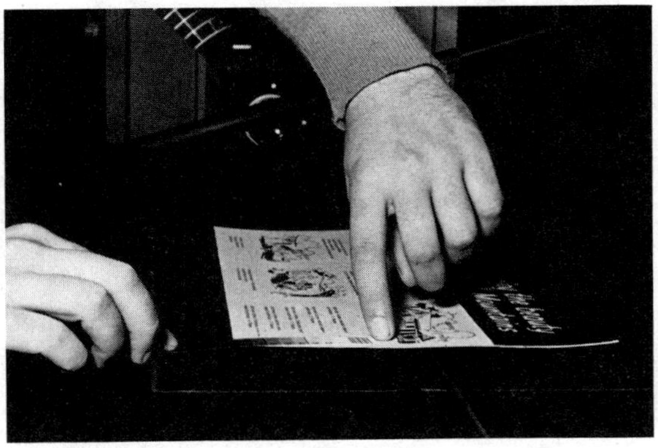

Figure 6.4. Positioning the gray scale. Always place a gray scale next to the image on the paste-up.

Closing the Frame

The final step is to close the glass cover over the camera copy. With most vertical cameras, gravity holds the glass against the paste-up and prevents it from moving. With this type of system, always check to be sure that the copy was not accidentally moved when the glass was lowered into place.

With the vacuum systems, there are several additional steps. First, lower the glass into position, and check to be sure that any latches have been engaged or closed. Next, turn on the vacuum pump and watch the copy as it is forced against the glass. Check to be sure that the copy has not shifted and that the gray scale is still in place, away from any image.

Sometimes, if there is still moisture left on the glass from cleaning, an optical effect called Newton's rings can be formed. These will appear as a faint bull's eye target, radiating out from the center of the copy. Unfortunately, the rings will interfere with the passage of light and will result in a defective film image. One solution to this problem is first to reduce the vacuum pressure so as to diminish the effect. The second solution is to open the glass frame and thoroughly dry the inside surface with air. Use a small fan or an electric hair-dryer-type blower.

Once the frame is closed, the copy positioned properly, and the glass clean and dry, the frame should be swung into a vertical position and locked into place.

• Checking Focus and Illumination

Camera Viewing Systems

All process cameras are equipped with some system that allows the photographer to check the size, focus, and illumination of the image prior to making a film exposure. All cameras employ a ground glass screen that is placed in the filmboard position. Some cameras are equipped with a hinged frame that holds the glass, others roll the glass along a track, and still others require that the photographer place the sheet of glass onto the camera back.

Checking Illumination

It is important that the camera lights evenly cover the entire copyboard. If one portion of the surface receives more light than another, exposure will be inconsistent—that is, more light will be reflected from one part of the copy, giving an overexposure; less light will be reflected from another part, giving an underexposure.

To check illumination, place the ground glass in the filmboard position, lay a large piece of white paper on the copyboard, and turn on the camera lights. Look closely at the ground glass. Check to see if the glass appears to be uniformly bright in the areas on which your copy will be placed. Are there spots of glare? Is it possible to see a reflection of the camera lights on the copyboard? As a final check, take several light meter readings, using a hand-held meter, at different points on the ground glass. The readings should be nearly the same over the image area. If the illumination is not consistent, or if

Figure 6.5. Checking the illumination. Use a guage stick to check the image illumination.

there are spots of glare, then the lights will have to be adjusted.

Most camera lights are adjustable by both distance and angle from the copyboard (figure 6.5). Many camera manufacturers give specifications as to distance and provide gauges to make necessary corrections. There is some discussion on the ideal camera angle for light angle. A typical recommendation is that all lights should be set at a 45- or 60-degree angle to the surface of the copyboard. As with many things, however, whatever works in a particular shop is considered acceptable.

Checking Size, Position, and Focus

While the ground glass is in position, and the camera lights are on, it is always wise to check that the image is perfectly centered, is the required size, and is in sharp focus. Most ground glass systems have centering lines on the glass that correspond to the marks on the filmboard. If the image is correctly centered on the glass, then it should be centered on the film.

One common error for new photographers is to center the paste-up and not the image. The edges of the illustration board are not being printed and, in fact, will probably not even show up on the film. Always be sure that it is the image that lines up with the center marks.

Some cameras have controls that raise or lower and move the image from side-to-side without shifting the copy. This is usually accomplished by a gear system that moves the lens. If the camera has such controls, then it makes centering especially easy. Simply watch through the ground glass while turning the controls to position the image.

If the camera does not have such controls, then it is necessary to open the copyboard glass and to move the copy to make any changes in image position. Remember that the lens is reversing the image. If it appears on the screen that it must be moved to the left, then on the copyboard it must be adjusted to the right.

Checking Image Focus

Focus can be checked easily through the ground glass. Since the inside of the glass is on the exact same plane of the filmboard, then if the image appears to be in focus, it will also be in focus on the film.

With large line detail on the copy, it is easy to tell at a glance if the image is sharp or fuzzy. While looking through ground glass, slightly turn the copyboard percentage control. Notice how, as the copyboard is moved back and forth, the image comes in and out of focus.

With fine-line detail it is not always so easy to judge focus by the naked eye. Some photographers use a small magnifying glass (sometimes called a linen tester) to check a critical focus (figure 6.6). With this method the sharpest possible line detail can be obtained.

It should be emphasized that focus is not a major problem if the percentage tapes are in adjustment. The camera manufacturer sets the system, and unless someone forces the copyboard or lensboard off the camera track, it should remain accurate.

Figure 6.6. Checking image focus. Use a magnifying glass on the ground glass screen to check the focus.

Checking Image Size

Image size is always an important variable. Graphic designers specify sizes, and the photographer is expected to supply the images to fit exactly into the required space. Again, if the percentage tapes are in adjustment, then there should be no problem with size.

There are, however, some jobs for which the size tolerance is so critical that the photographer must supply evidence of accuracy (such as in map making). A simple method to provide such evidence also can be used occasionally to check the camera settings for routine darkroom work.

If a critical job is assigned, then rule an inked H line on the edge of the illustration board, away from the image. If the goal is just to check the camera calibration, then rule a similar line on a scrap piece of illustration board. Choose a convenient length like 10 inches. Make all necessary camera adjustments for size, f/stop, and exposure, and make a film negative or positive. When the film is dry, compare the film image with the illustration board image. If the size setting is 100 percent, then the two lines should line up perfectly; if they do not then the camera is out of adjustment. If the size is other than 100 percent, then the film image can be measured with the required tolerance (such as to the nearest one-sixty-fourth of an inch) and then compared to the expected size.

• Setting the Aperture and Shutter

Basic Exposure

The idea of basic exposure is very important to understand. **Basic exposure** is the combination of aperture opening and shutter speed that will produce an acceptable film image, of normal line copy, when standardized chemical processing is used. Once determined, basic exposure is the starting point for all camera operations. The basic exposure for the process camera is not necessarily the same for any other, even if it is housed in the same shop.

The basic exposure for every camera is determined by experimentation. It begins with several fixed factors that are assumed not to change: for example, type and brand of film, type of camera lights, type and brand of processing chemicals, and absolutely standardized development procedures. Whenever one of the factors changes, then the photographer must redetermine basic exposure. A detailed description of the method to determine basic exposure is given in chapter 7.

Working with the F/Stop-Shutter Relationship

As discussed in chapter 2, the purpose of both the aperture and the shutter is to control the amount of light that enters the camera. The aperture controls the quantity by adjusting the size of the opening; the larger the opening, the more light enters; the smaller, the less. The shutter controls the amount of light by opening and closing the lens; the longer the lens is open, the more light enters; the less it is open, then the less light enters the camera. It is important to understand that the aperture and shutter always work together to pass just the correct amount of light to expose the film properly.

The shutter usually measures light passage by seconds. The aperture measures light by the f/stop system. Again, recall from chapter 2 that each f number differs from an adjacent number by a factor of two. Common f/stop openings for process cameras are: f/64, f/45, f/32, f/22, f/16, f/11, and f/8. F/64 is the smallest opening, f/8 is the largest. In this example, f/16 passes two times the light that f/22 does in the same time period, but it passes only one-half the light of f/11.

The fact that f openings pass twice or half the light of adjacent openings makes it easy to predict the amount of exposure with different settings. For example, if it was found that an acceptable exposure was recorded at f/16 for eighteen seconds, it is easy to find an equivalent combination that will pass the same amount of light. If we change the f opening from f/16 to f/11, then we are doubling the opening and therefore must halve the exposure time. If one setting is doubled, then the other must be halved. F/11 for nine seconds is considered, then, to be an equivalent exposure to f/16 for eighteen seconds. They will both pass the same amount of light.

When is this information useful? Two examples:

Example One: Say that, after experimentation, a process photographer determined that the basic exposure for a new camera was f/8 for four seconds. There are some problems with such a short exposure time. The main one is that the camera times are usually accurate to only within one second. It is difficult to set a timer's pointer to exactly the same position every time. If the operator sets the timer even only one-half a second off, that is a 12.5 percent error rate if the basic exposure is four seconds. If the same error one-half second mistake were made for an eight-second basic exposure, then it would be only 3.1 percent off—a much more acceptable error rate.

To solve the problem, the photographer could calculate an equivalent exposure with the goal of using a longer shutter speed: f/8 at 4 seconds equals f/11 at eight seconds equals f/16 at sixteen seconds. F/16 for sixteen seconds could then be used as the camera's basic exposure.

Example Two: Say that the photographer is making a halftone negative and that the halftone computer suggests an exposure of f/32 for seventy-two seconds (see chapter 9 for a discussion of halftone procedures). The problem is that most repeating timers can only be set to a maximum time of sixty seconds. How can the required exposure be made? Determine an equivalent exposure with a shutter time of less than sixty seconds: f/32 at seventy-two seconds equals f/22 at thirty-six seconds. The problem is solved.

Understanding how to work with aperture-shutter relationships is an important skill for the process photographer.

Diaphragm Controls

Whenever a size change is made on a process camera, the distance between the copyboard and lensboard and between the lensboard and filmboard are also changed. This means that the distance the light must travel when it is reflected from the copy is different for every percentage setting. This also means that for every percentage setting the amount of light necessary for an acceptable exposure is different.

The distance that light travels is an important consideration. Intensity diminishes with changes in the distance light has to travel. The **inverse square law** says that the change in intensity of light is related inversely to the square of the change in distance:

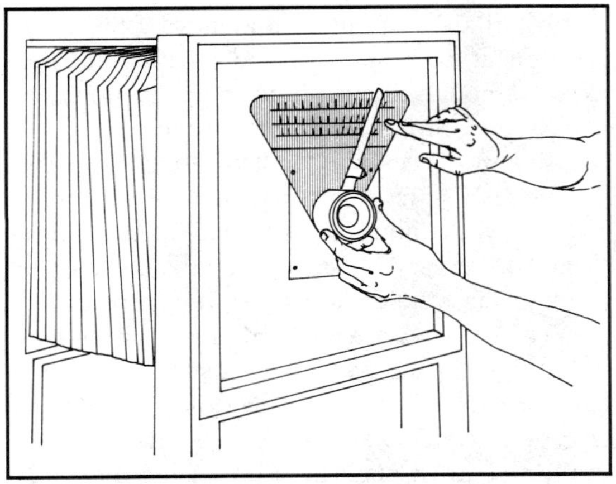

Figure 6.7. A diaphragm control. The lens opening can be adjusted automatically for changes in enlargement or reduction. (Kimberly Conover-Loar)

Figure 6.8. Mounting film. The filmboard swings out and away from the camera back.

$$\text{Change in intensity} = \frac{1}{(\text{Change in distance})^2}$$

This means that if we measure the intensity of a light bulb at 6 feet and found it to be 16 lumins (a measure of light), then at 12 feet it would be only 4 lumins:

$$\text{Change} = \frac{1}{2^2} = \frac{1}{4}$$

(since 6 to 12 is a change by a factor of two). Thus, 1/4 of 16 = 4 lumins. This means that for every percentage setting on the camera, a different quantity of light must pass through the lens for the film to receive an acceptable exposure.

This problem once required the photographer to make a special calculation whenever the image size was changed. Some camera manufacturers supplied a special set of tables showing what time and aperture changes to make, depending upon the percentage setting. It was also possible to use a special dial that would predict exposure changes with size adjustments. Most cameras today come equipped with a diaphragm control that automatically adjusts the lens opening (figure 6.7).

The process of setting a diaphragm control is straightforward. A large scale, showing f/stop numbers and percentages, is set up. If, for example, the basic exposure is twelve seconds at f/16 for 100 percent, and you need to make a 50 percent reduction, then simply move the diaphragm pointer to 50 percent on the f/16 scale, and expose for twelve seconds.

• Mounting the Film

Vacuum Systems

The back of almost all process cameras hinges back so that the photographer can mount film on the filmboard (figure 6.8). The filmboard then swings back into position, sealing the camera and placing the film plane perfectly parallel to the copy plane (see figure 2.3).

Some camera manufacturers sell camera options that allow for mounting a roll of film over the filmboard. With this system, the camera op-

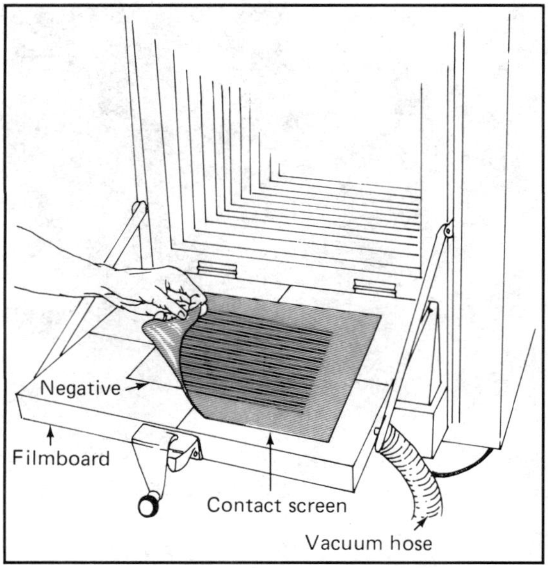

Figure 6.9. Contact screen. The screen must be larger than the film being exposed.

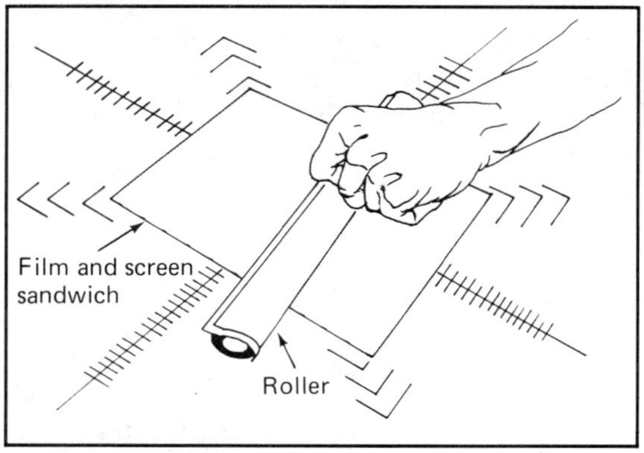

Figure 6.10. Using a rubber roller. Always carefully roll the screen to remove trapped air that will create a distorted image.

erator pulls the required amount of film down, positions it over the back, and slices off the necessary amount. Most photographers, however, still mount film one piece at a time.

The most common filmboard-mounting system today is the vacuum back. The board is covered with thousands of small holes, all attached to a vacuum pump. The suction of air through these holes holds the film in place.

To use a vacuum board, first turn off the white light in the darkroom, and then open the camera back. Remove a sheet of film from the storage container, and place it, emulsion up, on the filmboard. Center the piece using the guidelines that are etched into the board. Next, set the control system to the size of film being used. If an 8″ × 10″ sheet is to be held in place, then only those holes within an 8″ × 10″ area of the center should be activated.

Now turn the vacuum pump on. Carefully roll a rubber-covered roller over the film to make sure that it is perfectly flat and that the vacuum has taken hold. There is usually an obvious sound change when the vacuum is operating correctly. When the film is not held securely, there will be a loud hissing noise; when it is functioning correctly, there will be a quiet hum.

Some vacuum backs are equipped for automatic adjustment of the vacuum holes. With this system the film is simply placed on the board, and the vacuum is turned on. Only those holes under the film continue to provide suction, while all others close down.

Screens

The photographer frequently must work with contact screens that are placed over the film on the camera back. The halftone screen breaks the continuous-tone image into small, printable dots (see chapter 9), and special effects screens and screen tints are an important part of special effects photography (see chapter 11). Contact screens cannot be used without a vacuum system.

With a vacuum filmboard, the contact screen always must be significantly larger than the film (figure 6.9). If it were the same size or smaller, the vacuum would not hold it in place. Air cannot be sucked through the piece of film. Always allow several inches of screen completely around the film. The vacuum must both hold the film in place and draw out air from between the film and screen so that everything is held flat against the camera back.

When working with a contact screen, first mount the film into position on the center of the board. Adjust the vacuum control to the size of the screen. Then carefully place the screen over the film, emulsion down, and turn on the vacuum pump.

Air can be trapped easily between the screen and the film so it is important to use a rubber roller, carefully and thoroughly, on the screen (figure 6.10).

One last caution: Because the screen and film are held so closely together, sometimes a static electricity discharge occurs when the pieces are separated. To diminish the chance of spark exposure, first slowly peel away the screen and place it back into its container. Then turn off the vacuum pump, and slowly peel the film from the board.

• Making the Exposure

The final step is to make the exposure with a push of the timer button. Even if all controls have been carefully set, it is wise to make several small checks before the camera lights go on:

- Touch the film storage container; make sure that it is completely closed and that no film mistakenly has been left out.
- Look at the copyboard; if it is a vacuum system, make sure that it has been swung into position and that the copy is still in place.
- Look at the lens; make sure that the lens cap has been removed.
- Look at the timer; make sure that the switch is on exposure and not focus (if it is on focus the lights either will not come on or, if they come on, will not shut off until the operator realizes something is wrong).

• Key Points

- The main advantage of the process camera is that it can be adjusted to produce sizes other than that of the original copy.
- A proportion wheel can be used to determine enlargement or reduction sizes.
- The sequence of normal camera operation is the following:
  - Mount copy with gray scale,
  - Set percentage size,
  - Set timer,
  - Set f/stop,
  - Check focus and illumination,
  - Mount film,
  - Make exposure.

• Review Questions

1. Why are process cameras equipped to make enlargements and reductions?
2. If the original measures 8″ × 12″ and a 50 percent reduction is required, what will be the reproduction size? For a 25 percent reduction?
3. Why should pieces of wax or rubber cement be removed from the copyboard glass?
4. Where should the gray scale be positioned?
5. How are most camera lights adjusted?
6. Describe a method of checking image size accuracy.
7. What is basic exposure?
8. If you are given f/16 at twelve seconds as a camera exposure, what are two different equivalent exposures?
9. Why must a contact screen be larger than the film?

• Activities

1. Using a proportion wheel or simple arithmetic, calculate the following percentage changes:

Original size	Reproduction size	Percent
10 × 15	8 × 12	———
8-3/8 × 14	4-3/4 × 8	———
6-1/8	5	———
9	14	———
9-1/2	7	———
4-1/2	5	———

2. Locate a process camera and make the following adjustments:
   - Set the camera reproduction size to 85 percent;
   - Expose at f/8 for twelve seconds (or the basic exposure for your shop);
   - Mount a piece of typical shop copy on the copyboard:
     a. Clean glass,
     b. Center,
     c. Include a gray scale;
   - Check image illumination and position;
   - Mount a sheet of scrap film on the camera filmboard;
   - Have your instructor check your setup.

Chapter 7

Line Photography

• Objectives

In this chapter you will cover:

- The different types of copy,
- Basic line exposure procedures,
- Working with unusual copy.

After reading the chapter you should be able to:

- Describe the characteristics of line copy,
- Set up a process darkroom for production,
- Determine the basic line exposure for any process camera,
- Make line negatives,
- Make camera or processing changes to allow for unusual line copy.

• Line Copy Defined

Recall that copy was defined in chapter 1 as something prepared by the designer that was intended to be reproduced by one of the printing processes. To the printing process photographer, there are only two kinds of copy: **line copy** and **continuous-tone copy**.

Line copy is easy to identify (figure 7.1). It is usually delivered to the darkroom in the form of sharp, black, dense lines on clean white paper or illustration board. The lines could take many forms. They might be letters typed on a sheet, generated in a photocomposition device; copy burnished on using dry transfer letters; inked proofs from relief type; or even penned hand-drawn characters. Other lines might appear as artist's illustrations or drawings using a brush or a pen or could be something called clip art which is commercially printed artwork sold to printers. Whatever method is used, however, all line copy has the same characteristics: The image is formed by dark, solid areas, with the nonimage areas (or background) clear.

We are all familiar with one type of continuous-tone copy—namely, photographs. A continuous-tone photograph is made up of many tones or shades of gray from solid black to the base white of the paper (figure 7.2). It is not possible to identify any one area as black and another as clear because the density fades from nearly solid black to only wisps of gray. Other examples of continuous-tone copy are wash

Figure 7.1. Examples of line copy.

Figure 7.2. Example of a continuous-tone photograph.

drawings, watercolor drawings, and charcoal sketches.

• The Need for Line Negatives

An important point must be made: Printers only print line copy on their presses. It is not possible (except with special conditions or techniques) to print images other than solid lines on clear backgrounds. Printers do reproduce what appears to be continuous-tone copy, but actually, the original photograph was first made into a series of lines or dots. This process is called halftone photography and is discussed in detail in chapter 9.

The graphic arts industry uses about two or three times more line copy than continuous-tone or halftone copy. This means that the basic skill of the process photographer centers around line photography. The techniques of exposing and developing line originals is a fundamental skill.

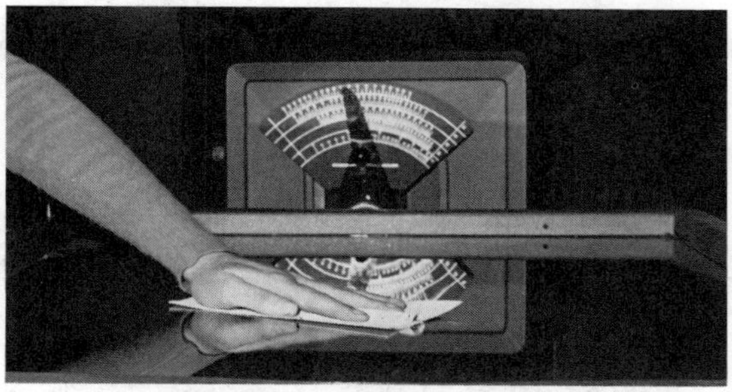

Figure 7.3. Cleaning copyboard glass to remove dust and finger prints.

• Review of Procedures for Making a Line Negative

In order to understand the fundamentals of line photography, it is important to follow through the various darkroom operations. Although some of this information has been introduced in previous chapters, this section brings together important understandings.

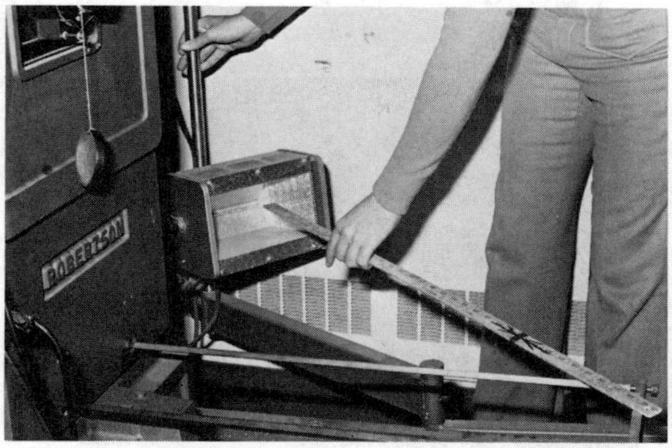

Figure 7.4. Adjusting camera lights for proper illumination.

Setting up the Darkroom

Caution: Use only a good camel hair brush to clean dust off the lens. The lens should never be touched with your hands. If you determine the lens is dirty, report this condition to your instructor or supervisor.

- Make sure the copyboard glass and lens are clean (figure 7.3).
- Make sure the camera lighting is adjusted for even illumination (figure 7.4).
- Review the location of the various controls: timer, aperture (f/stop) control, vacuum back and control switch, copyboard and lensboard adjusting devices, and the copy percentages setting (figure 7.5).

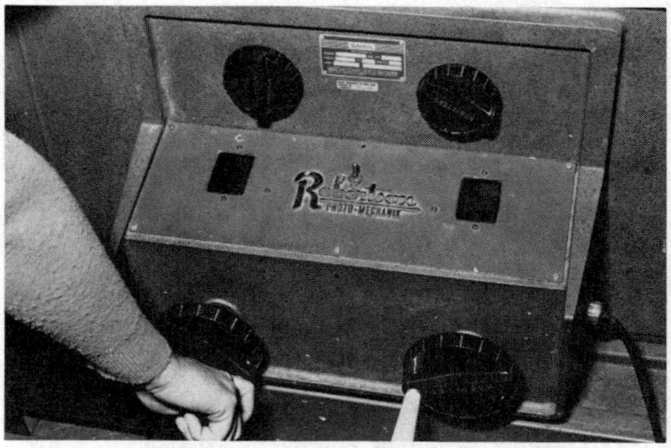

Figure 7.5. Adjusting percentages on copyboard and lensboard tapes to control image size.

When you are familiar with the camera, go into the wet or developing area of the darkroom and set up the darkroom sink for processing the film. Here again, review the location and the function of the following items:

- Safelight and room light switches,
- Water-circulating switches if the sink has temperature control,

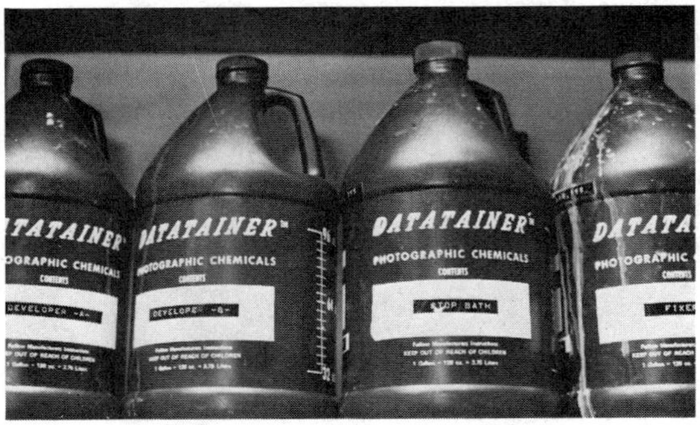

Figure 7.6. Storing mixed chemistry for easy access.

Figure 7.7. Processed film hung for drying.

Figure 7.8. Darkroom sink setup. In this area, developing, stopping, fixing, and washing film take place.

- Viewing lamp and its control switch,
- Film-processing trays,
- Chemistry that will be used in the developing process (figure 7.6),
- Film dryer or a line where the wet film will be hung after processing (figure 7.7).

Setting up the Chemicals

To set up the sink with the proper chemicals will require three trays and a film-washing area (figure 7.8). Select trays slightly larger than the film you will be using. In the first tray will be the developer. This should be mixed according to the instructions provided by the manufacturer. Pour in enough developer so you can completely cover the film. The developer for making line negatives should be a high-contrast litho film developer. Mix only the amount of developer needed for a particular negative or for the day if continuous development will be carried on.

The second tray holds the stop bath. This, if you remember from previous chapters, is a dilute acetic acid bath. The purpose of the stop bath is to halt the action of the developer.

The third tray should contain the fixing bath. This bath will clear the film and wash away the unused emulsion silver crystals.

The washing area or washing tray needs running water to wash away the chemicals left on the film. This washing water, as well as all the chemical baths, should be held at a constant temperature of 68°F (20°C).

The darkroom processing area is now ready; turn out the white lights and turn on the safelights.

Selecting the Film

The next task we have is to select the correct film to make a line negative. The film should be orthochromatic film with a high-contrast litho emulsion. This means that the film is sensitive to the green and blue wavelengths of light and blind to the red wavelengths (see chapter 3). This is why we use the red (1A) safelights.

Caution: While ortho film is safe in red light for short periods, long exposure under the safelight will fog the film.

Film can be purchased in boxes and then cut to the size needed for the particular job (figure 7.9). Common box sizes are 4″ × 5″, 5″ × 7″, 8″ × 10″, 10″ × 12″, and larger.

In most shops a film cabinet to store the film is located in the darkroom near the camera. Usually on top of the film cabinet is a cutting device to cut the film to the most economical size (figure 7.10). Film is an expensive item and should not be wasted. A good film cabinet has light baffles in the drawers to prevent light from reaching the film when a white light is turned on in the room. The good camera operator always removes the piece of film for the job, places the cover back on the box, and returns the box of film to the drawer. This will insure no accidental exposure of the film.

Figure 7.9. Litho-type film. Manufacturers supply film in a variety of sizes.

Figure 7.10. Typical film cabinet. A cabinet with a film cutter on top of it should be located next to the camera in the darkroom. Notice that the drawer has a light trap.

Making a Basic Exposure Test

Since it is assumed that the equipment has not been used, the process photographer must perform a **basic exposure test** by doing a step-off. This process determines the ideal camera exposure that will be used for nearly all line copy.

Begin by selecting a piece of line copy that is made up of dense black images on a clean white background. The image areas should cover most of the sheet and should represent the best possible copy available in the plant. Then use the following procedures:

1. Center the copy in the copyboard, close the copyboard, and turn it so the copy faces the lens (note: upside down) (figure 7.11).

2. Adjust copyboard and lensboard for a same-size (100 percent) exposure. On some cameras this is done on tapes in the darkroom side of the camera; on other cameras it is done on the gallery or lighted, side of the camera (figure 7.12).

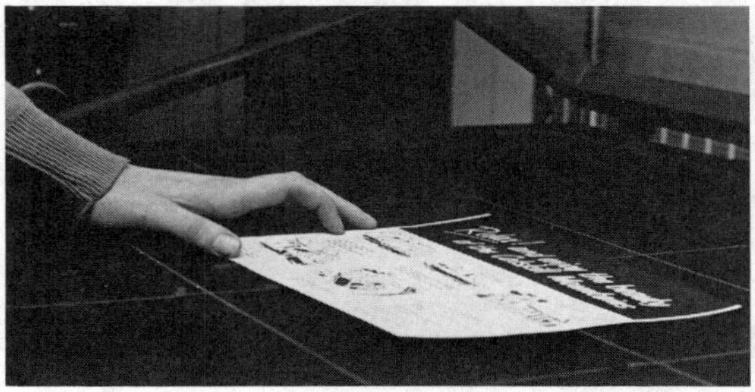

Figure 7.11. Centering the copy in the copyboard.

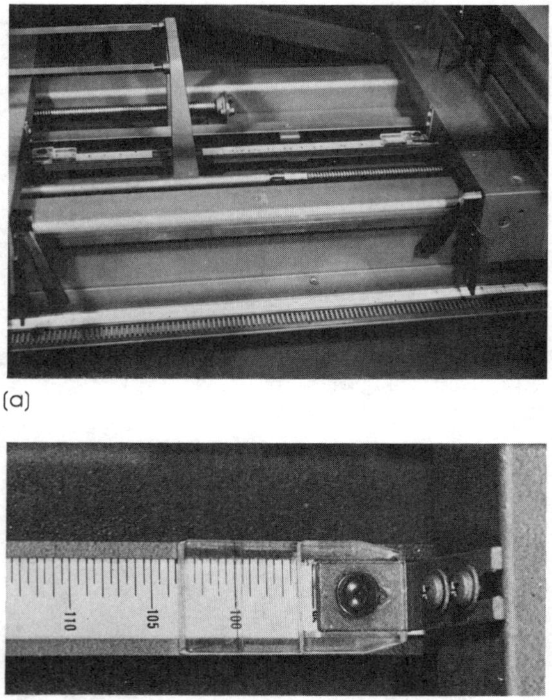

(a)

(b)

Figure 7.12. (a) Adjusting percentage tapes. (b) The hairline alignment unit.

Figure 7.13. Camera aperture (f/stop) adjusting scale. Each stop scale is marked in percentage size of reproduction.

3. Set the f/stop (aperture) on the f/22 scale for 100 percent. The f/22 aperture was selected as a starting place because it is usually two to three stops from wide open on the process lens. Tests by lens makers have determined this to be the best starting aperture (figure 7.13).

4. Set the timer for a five-second exposure (figure 7.14) and turn out all but the red safelights.

5. Remove a sheet of film from the box and determine the emulsion side; the lighter of the two sides is the emulsion.

6. Center the film on the vacuum back so the emulsion side is facing the lens (figure 7.15). Turn on the vacuum pump to hold the film in place. Close the back so the film is parallel to the copyboard.

7. Begin by making a five-second exposure. Then open the camera back (keeping the vacuum on), and place a piece of opaque (this means no light will pass through it) paper over all but approximately 1 1/2 inches of the film (figure 7.16). Close the back and make another five-second exposure. Repeat this procedure, moving the opaque paper 1 1/2 inches each time until you have five exposures on the single piece of film (figure 7.17). The purpose of this step-off procedure is to make exposures ranging from five seconds to twenty-five seconds on one piece of film so you can determine which exposure time will produce the most satisfactory image.

8. Turn off the vacuum after you have completed the fifth trial exposure. Now take the film to the processing area of the darkroom.

Processing

Exposed film is processed in the darkroom using the following steps:

1. Set the timer for 2 3/4 minutes (or the time specified by the film manufacturer), and immerse the film in the developer (figure 7.18). Note the developing solution is tipped in the tray so the film can be covered completely with de-

Figure 7.14. One type of camera exposure timing device.

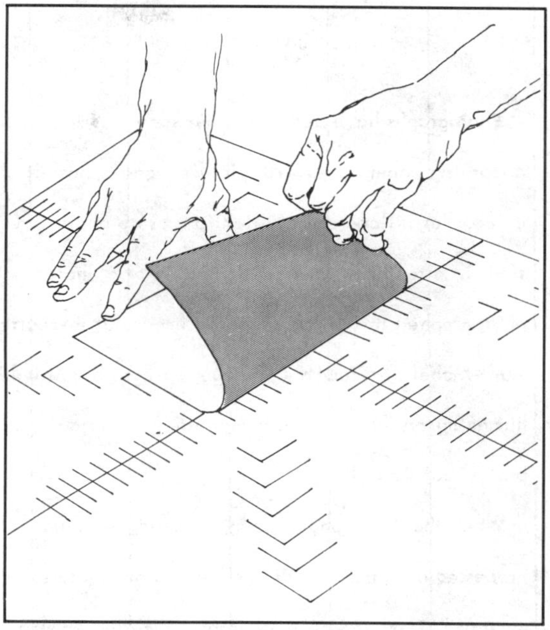

Figure 7.15. Centering film on camera vacuum back. The emulsion of the film must face the lens when the vacuum back is closed.

veloper. Agitate the tray throughout the 2 3/4-minute time that the film is in the developer. Take turns tipping the tray in a rotation from each side. This agitation of the tray, moves the fresh developer over the exposed emulsion. If the developer chemistry were allowed to remain over the film, then the developer would become exhausted and unable to build up sufficient density in the exposed areas.

2. When the developing time is up, lift the film out of the tray and allow the developer to drain off the film for several seconds, then place it in the stop bath tray. Agitate the film in the stop bath for five to ten seconds.

3. Remove the film from the stop bath and allow the solution to drain off the film. Place the film in the fixing bath. The film should stay in the fixing bath for twice as long as it takes to clear. (Actual clock time will vary according to the type of fix being used.)

Before fixing, the film will have a clouded look in the transparent areas of the negative. What you are seeing is the unexposed emulsion (the image areas of the original copy). As the

Figure 7.16. Moving the cover sheet between exposures for a step-off test.

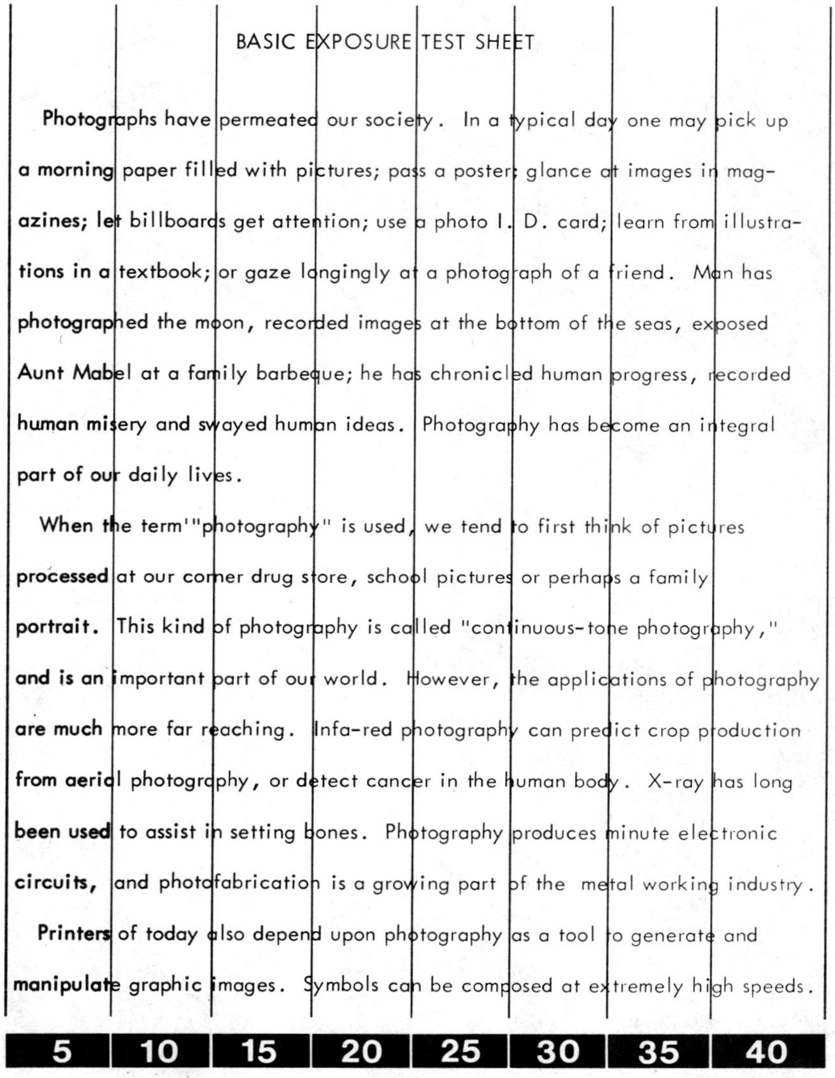

BASIC EXPOSURE TEST SHEET

Photographs have permeated our society. In a typical day one may pick up **a morning** paper filled with pictures; pass a poster; glance at images in mag- **azines; let** billboards get attention; use a photo I. D. card; learn from illustra- **tions in a** textbook; or gaze longingly at a photograph of a friend. Man has **photographed** the moon, recorded images at the bottom of the seas, exposed **Aunt Mabel** at a family barbeque; he has chronicled human progress, recorded **human misery** and swayed human ideas. Photography has become an integral **part of our** daily lives.

When the term'"photography" is used, we tend to first think of pictures **processed** at our corner drug store, school pictures or perhaps a family **portrait.** This kind of photography is called "continuous-tone photography," **and is an** important part of our world. However, the applications of photography **are much** more far reaching. Infa-red photography can predict crop production **from aerial** photography, or detect cancer in the human body. X-ray has long **been used** to assist in setting bones. Photography produces minute electronic **circuits,** and photofabrication is a growing part of the metal working industry.

Printers of today also depend upon photography as a tool to generate and **manipulate** graphic images. Symbols can be composed at extremely high speeds.

Figure 7.17. Step-off pattern obtained in making a line test exposure. 5 seconds, underexposed; 10 seconds, underexposed; 15 seconds, background spots, letters a bit bold; 20 seconds, good exposure; 25 seconds, overexposed, letters closing up.

film remains in the fix, these cloudy areas will begin to clear because the emulsion is being dissolved in the fixer. The reason we keep the film in the bath twice as long as it takes to clear is to insure that all the unexposed and undeveloped silver emulsion is dissolved and will be washed away in the water rinse that follows the fixing step.

4. Rinse the film with water. Allow the film to remain in the water rinse for approximately ten to fifteen minutes (this step may be longer for other film products—be sure to follow the manufacturer's recommendations).

5. Dry the film. After the wash cycle is complete, the film can be hung to dry (see figure

7.7) or placed in a film dryer that speeds the drying process (figure 7.19).

Determining the Best Exposure

The purpose of this work is to determine which time produced a negative with lines the same size as those in the original. Overexposed letters or lines tend to close up and produce lines that are thinner than the original. Underexposure causes lines and letters to appear thicker or heavier than the original (figure 7.20). Determine the time that produced a negative letter or line that matches the original image. This time will be called the **basic line exposure time**.

In order to verify this time, it is necessary to make one or more test negatives—that is, a single exposure at the selected time. For the sake of explanation, assume that the fifteen-second time produced the most ideal letters or lines. For this exposure, add a gray scale sensitivity guide along the side of the copy. Make a fifteen-second exposure (the selected time in our example—your time will probably be different). The gray scale exposed with the copy will become a quality control device. Follow the developing steps just as you did in making the first test negative.

After completing the cycle, make a careful examination of the second negative—a magnifying glass is helpful. Does it match the negative area of the first negative that you selected as the best time? Are the letter weights and line weights a perfect match to the original copy and the first test negative (figure 7.21)?

Let us assume that we now have a satisfactory negative. Look at the gray scale that we included with the copy. Look to see which step in this gray scale is the last fully dark one. In this example, it is step four (figure 7.22). Some operators use an opposed gray scale (figure 7.23). This device is easy to watch in the developing process as the scales come together.

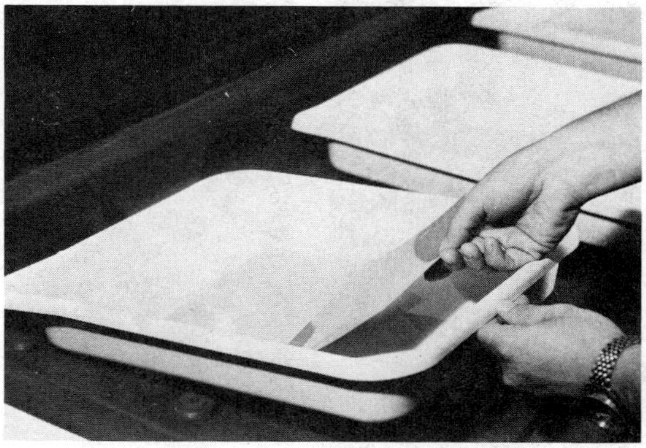

Figure 7.18. Processing. Film is placed in developer tray so that it is completely covered with developing chemicals.

Figure 7.19. Film-drying cabinet.

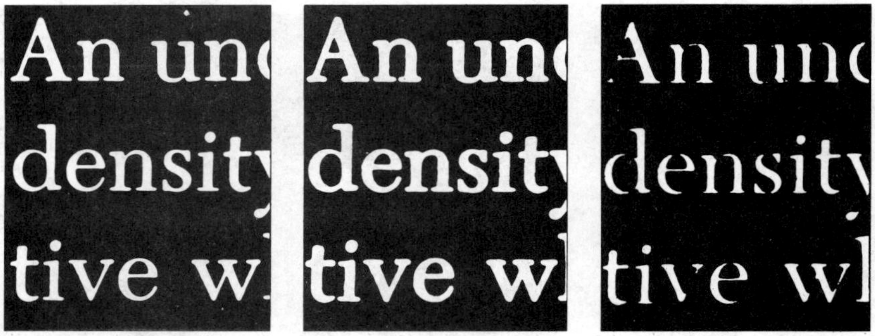

CORRECT EXPOSURE
This segment was exposed correctly. The negative areas are either clearly transparent or densely opaque. Edges are sharp, and detail proportions are true to the original.

UNDEREXPOSURE
This segment was underexposed. Although transparent areas are clear, the dark areas have low density. A positive made from a negative of this type shows thickening of all detail.

OVEREXPOSURE
This segment was overexposed. Although dense areas are opaque, density appears in some areas which should be clear. A positive made from a negative of this type shows loss of fine detail.

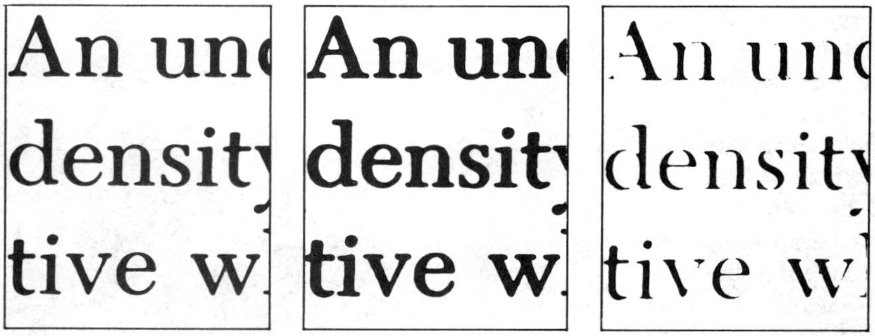

Figure 7.20. Comparison of underexposure, normal exposure, and overexposure on line copy. (Courtesy of Eastman Kodak Company.)

For all future line negatives made, include a gray scale in the border area on the copy so that it does not cover the image area. When developing future negatives, it is possible to determine when the developing is complete by developing to the same solid step as on the test negative. This quality control device will assure you that each negative has been processed the same.

If the developer you are using is a bit old, too hot, or too cold, developing to the proper step will compensate and give an acceptable negative. Always keep the timer set for the 2 3/4 minutes (or whatever time the manufacturer specifies) so that great differences in time to get the required solid step will let you know that your exposures are wrong or that the developer is too old and should be changed.

Summary of Line Negative Preparation Steps

Now that we are satisfied that our tests have provided a satisfactory line negative, we will select a new piece of copy and make a new one. This also will give you a standard procedure to follow for all line negatives. The copy we will

Figure 7.21. Comparing copy with negative.

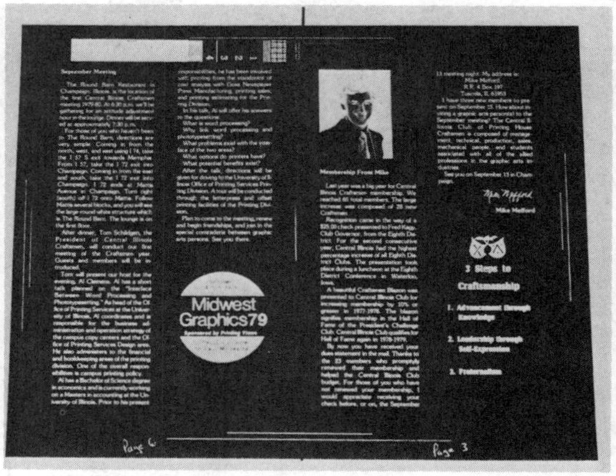

Figure 7.22. Gray scale on copy near image area. Negative with Stouffer gray scale developed to a step 4.

use has a good dense black image on a white background.

- Make sure copy and copyboard glass are clean.
- Center copy on copyboard with a gray scale in margin of the copy. Close copyboard and face it toward lens.
- For this example, set lens aperture for 100 percent on the f/22 scale.
- Set copyboard and lensboard for 100 percent (same size).
- Set time for fifteen-second exposure.
- Make sure lights are properly illuminating the copyboard.
- Set up darkroom for processing film and turn out white lights.
- Remove a piece of litho film (ortho) from the film box. If film is not the proper size, trim it. Return box to drawer in film cabinet.
- Place film (emulsion up) in center of vacuum back. Turn on vacuum.
- Make exposure.
- Develop film, set timer for 2 3/4 minutes, watch for step four to turn black.
- Complete the processing of the film and dry it.

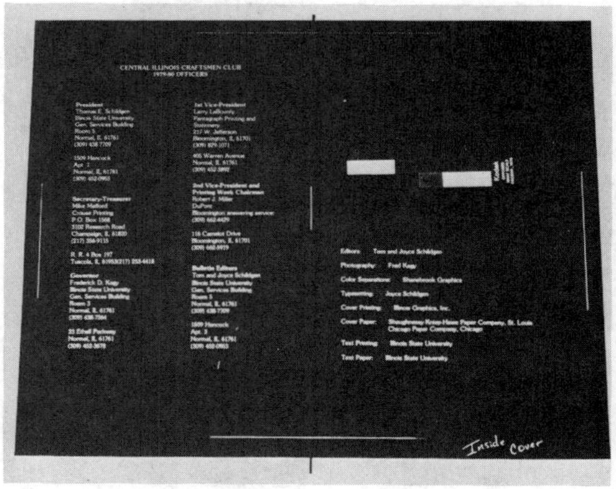

Figure 7.23. Negative with opposed gray scale. The negative is properly developed when the two black portions of gray scale in negative meet.

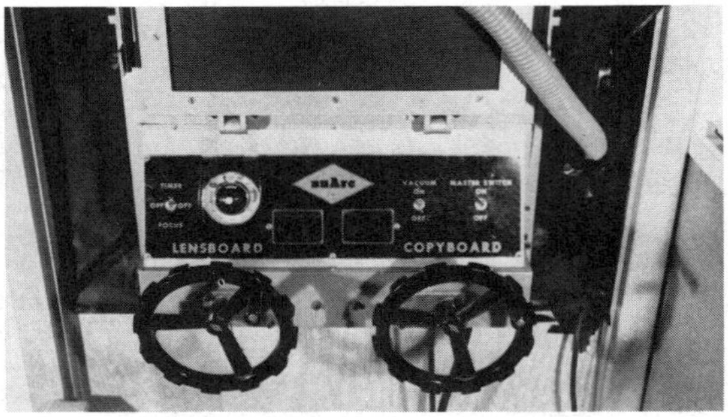

(a)

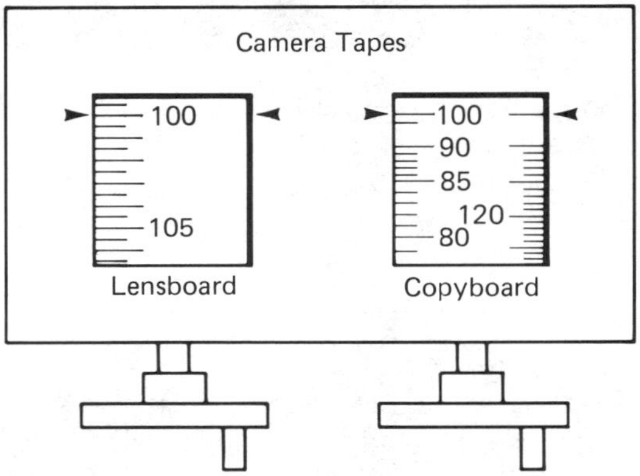

(b)

Figure 7.24. Lensboard and copyboard cranks. (a) These are used to change percentage size. (b) Tapes are shown in window.

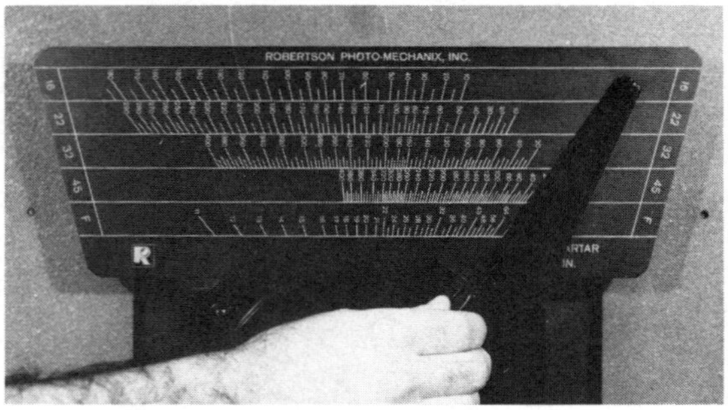

Figure 7.25. Aperture (f/stop) dial to give desired percentage changes.

In the example for determining the basic line exposure, 100 percent was used as the enlargement/reduction size. It is important, however, to understand that many line negatives require some other final size than the original copy dimensions. Chapter 6 covered the procedures for calculating percentage changes using a proportion scale (see figure 6.1). Changes in sizes are not difficult on the camera, but the operator must be sure to check three settings for any size changes: (1) the copyboard, (2) the lensboard, and (3) the f/stop aperture control.

Most cameras now use a tape control system so the operator merely cranks the desired percentage size, moving both the lens and copyboard positions (figure 7.24). Also, most process cameras now come equipped with a diaphragm control. By adjusting the aperture control dial to the desired f/stop and percentage combination, the size of the lens opening is changed to admit more or less light, while keeping the basic exposure time the same (figure 7.25).

• Handling Unusual Copy

So far in this chapter we have only discussed ideal copy—dense black lines on crisp white paper. Unfortunately, as most trade photographers will report, not all copy they are given is ideal. It is important for the camera operator to be able not only to recognize when the original material might present difficulties but also to know the techniques that will solve the problem. The most common unusual copy problems are fine-line copy, colored copy, gray rather than black images, and prescreened originals.

Fine-Line Copy

Fine-line copy is a common problem. The difficulty is that the image is made up of such thin lines that they could easily fill in during the developing process. A sample of this type of copy is shown in figure 7.26. To make a line negative from fine-line copy, it is best to select a halftone-grade film, developed in a special fine-line developer. Halftone films have an especially small grain emulsion structure, and the developer is formulated to keep thin lines open during processing. Several manufacturers make this type of film.

It is possible to use regular high-contrast developer if you are careful in your developing procedures and use the **still development** technique: Make a regular line exposure and place the film in the developer. Agitate vigorously until the image appears on the film. Stop agitating and allow the film to develop without any further movement until the developing time is completed. The very fine lines of the copy should show distinctly in the negative using this procedure.

Colored Copy

Some copy that will arrive at the shop may have images on paper that are colored instead of white. Other pieces may have a good white background but an image of some other color than black. Each of these situations needs to be handled differently, but in every case, the goal is to hold the image. This means somehow to make the colored lines appear as black on white paper to the film. The easiest way to solve this problem is to place a colored filter in front of the camera lens.

Figure 7.27 is a chart that shows how to select the correct filter to hold copy and to make it appear as black or to select a filter that will cause the colored paper to appear as white and thus drop out on the negative.

When using these filters you must adjust your exposures to compensate for holding back a certain amount of light. Each of these filters has a specific factor or number that indicates the additional time or lens aperture adjustment that must be made to allow for the correct exposure.

Figure 7.26. An example of fine-line copy.
(Original art courtesy of Margaret DeCardy)

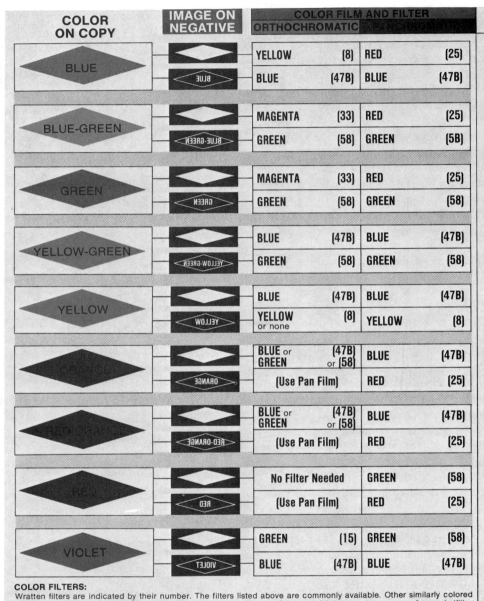

COLOR ON COPY	IMAGE ON NEGATIVE	COLOR FILM AND FILTER: ORTHOCHROMATIC	COLOR FILM AND FILTER: PANCHROMATIC
BLUE		YELLOW (8)	RED (25)
	BLUE	BLUE (47B)	BLUE (47B)
BLUE-GREEN		MAGENTA (33)	RED (25)
	BLUE-GREEN	GREEN (58)	GREEN (5B)
GREEN		MAGENTA (33)	RED (25)
	GREEN	GREEN (58)	GREEN (58)
YELLOW-GREEN		BLUE (47B)	BLUE (47B)
	YELLOW-GREEN	GREEN (58)	GREEN (58)
YELLOW		BLUE (47B)	BLUE (47B)
	YELLOW	YELLOW (8) or none	YELLOW (8)
ORANGE		BLUE or GREEN (47B) or (58)	BLUE (47B)
	ORANGE	(Use Pan Film)	RED (25)
RED-ORANGE		BLUE or GREEN (47B) or (58)	BLUE (47B)
	RED-ORANGE	(Use Pan Film)	RED (25)
RED		No Filter Needed	GREEN (58)
	RED	(Use Pan Film)	RED (25)
VIOLET		GREEN (15)	GREEN (58)
	VIOLET	BLUE (47B)	BLUE (47B)

COLOR FILTERS:
Wratten filters are indicated by their number. The filters listed above are commonly available. Other similarly colored filters can frequently be used for line color separation. It is essential to establish correct exposures for each (filter factor) under shop conditions. Where color contrast of the original is poor, the contrast can be improved by contacting to Du Pont CRW-4, or CRR duplicating films.

DU PONT FILMS FOR LINE COLOR SEPARATION

ORTHOCHROMATIC FILMS

"L" Family of Litho Films are high speed, hard dot films especially suited for high productivity with automatic processors.

CHL-4 and 7
are camera speed films for producing very hard dots and fine line detail.

CLL-4
permits lateral image reversals. It can be exposed to the emulsion or through its back. A fine matte insures contact when used for film or smooth plate exposures.

CDL-4
provides extra halftone dot density for extensive dot-etching.

CLN-4 and CLN-II
are camera speed high contrast films for economically producing laterally reversed images for newspaper production.

AHL-3 and 5
combine the "L" emulsion with tri-acetate base to simplify stripping operations.

"S" Family of Litho Films have wide development latitude in trays and automatic processors.

COS-4 and 7
are general purpose films for camera, line, and halftone exposures and for contact applications.

COD-4
can be exposed to the emulsion or through its back for lateral reversals. It has a fine matte surface that speeds vacuum drawdown to insure excellent contact with films or smooth surfaced printing plates, like DYCRIL®.

COH-4
offers very high dot density when extensive dot-etching is required.

AOS-3 and 5
are triacetate base films that will facilitate stripping operations.

PANCHROMATIC FILM

CPL-4
is a camera speed panchromatic litho film that is required when a red (25) filter exposure is used for color separation.

BLUE SENSITIVE FILMS

CBS-4 and 7
are blue sensitive contact films that can be used on the camera without a filter where a blue (47B) filter is specified for use with other films.

CBL-4 and 7
are improved blue sensitive contact films with excellent abrasion resistance, dot-for-dot replication, fast vacuum drawdown and good dot etching latitude.

(NOTE: All film codes prefixed with "C", such as COS and CHL, are on dimensionally stable CRONAR® polyester base.)

Figure 7.27. A filter selector chart. This chart helps to determine proper filter to hold or drop out colors. (Courtesy of E.I. DuPont)

Copy with Poor Image Quality

Copy often arrives at the shop that appears to be black on white but that is really gray. This type of copy usually requires some underexposure (less than the basic exposure time) and/or some underdevelopment (less than the recommended time in the developer). A good initial procedure is to reduce exposure by approximately 10 to 15 percent and to watch the gray scale carefully in the developing process. Whereas a solid step four is usually obtained for normal copy, develop the weak copy to a solid step three. This will usually improve the quality of the image in the printing. Exact steps and exposure reduction is a relative thing so some experimentation will probably be necessary.

Prescreened Copy

Pictures that were clipped from a printed magazine or book often come to the camera operator. Recall that, in order to print such pictures or photographs, it was necessary to break the tones of gray into dot patterns. (You will learn how to make halftone negatives in chapter 9). The problem is that these printed small dots are not easily recorded from a piece of paper. The best or at least a most usable negative can be produced by making a normal line exposure of the halftone and then following the still development technique as outlined in the section on handling fine-line copy.

• Key Points

- Line copy is made from dense lines or letters on clear, open background; continuous-tone or halftone copy is made up of many tones or shades of gray; the major printing processes only print lines or dots to give the illusion of grays.
- The purpose of the basic exposure test is to determine the ideal camera exposure that will be used for most line copy.
- A gray scale or sensitivity guide is a quality control device used to determine when the development is complete. It should be placed on the border of all line copy for every camera exposure.
- Still development is used to record fine-line detail; filters can be used to hold colored copy; underexposure and underdevelopment can usually improve gray copy.

• Review Questions

1. Describe what is considered to be line copy for making line negatives.
2. Why is it important to set up basic exposure for line photography?
3. Describe the use and purpose of including a gray scale with the copy when making a line negative.
4. How can the camera operator tell which side of the film is the emulsion side?
5. Describe what is meant by still development and when this technique is used.

• Activities

1. Select a suitable piece of line copy and establish basic exposure and processing information for your equipment. Do a step-off exposure as part one. Do an overall evaluation negative as part two. Record your exposure time and gray scale data. Consult with your instructor on your findings.
2. Select a piece of poor copy (your instructor will provide this). Shoot at 100 percent. Expose and develop this to make a usable line negative (see section on difficult copy). Record your data and gray scale step that provided a satisfactory negative. Consult with your instructor on your findings.
3. Select a piece of fine-line copy or a printed

halftone. Shoot at 100 percent. Make proper line exposure and use still development procedure. Repeat until a satisfactory negative is produced. Record your data. Consult with your instructor on your results.

4. Select a piece of suitable copy for a line negative. Shoot two negatives, one at 60 percent and one at 120 percent. Expose and process. Record your data. Consult with your instructor on your results.
5. Develop your own camera-ready art that includes:
   - Reproduction proof of hand-set type,
   - Typewritten line of type from carbon ribbon,
   - Typewritten line of type from cloth ribbon,
   - Hand-drawn-art pencil drawing,
     Hand-drawn-art pen and ink drawing,
   - Clip art,
   - A color wheel made from paint sample book.

Expose at 100 percent and process. Explain your results in writing. Consult with your instructor.

Chapter 8

Halftone Photography

• Objectives

In this chapter you will cover:

- Uses of halftones,
- Scaling procedures,
- Contact screens,
- Halftone exposures,
- Dot measurement,
- Exposure determination methods,
- Working with difficult copy,
- Processing variables.

After reading the chapter you should be able to:

- Explain uses of halftones;
- Recognize characteristics of originals that will produce good halftones;
- Scale copy;
- Explain the purpose of a halftone screen;
- Read original densities;
- Explain the purposes and procedures for making main, flash, and bump exposures;
- Determine halftone dot size;
- Measure highlight and shadow densities of original copy;
- Determine halftone screen density range;
- Determine a basic flash exposure;
- Calculate halftone exposures using several different methods;
- Make a halftone screen density range;
- Describe the procedures for working with difficult copy;
- Explain the major process variables when developing halftones.

• Why Halftones Are Necessary

Halftoning is a specialized photographic procedure used to change a continuous-tone image (such as a photograph or an artist's painting) to a form that can be printed to look like the original. This photographic procedure is necessary because letterpress, lithography (offset), or screen printing processes cannot lay down varying amounts of ink on the material being printed. For example, the light areas of a picture (photo or drawing) that has many tones from black to white cannot be reproduced by putting down a thin layer of ink. The halftone screen was de-

(a) (b)

Figure 8.1. (a) Conventional halftone. (b) Photograph printed without halftone screen.

veloped to solve this problem. If only a solid layer of ink can be laid down on the paper, it is possible to change the appearance of density by using a screen that varies the space between dots and the size of the dots. Figure 8.1 shows one photo printed without the use of a halftone screen and one with a screen. The thickness of ink laid on the paper for each image dot is the same—the space between the dots and dot size have been changed. Figure 8.2 shows an enlarged section of a halftone print. The illusion of light and dark areas is created by the size of the dot and the amount of white space.

While almost all printing processes use this principle, it should be noted that some gravure techniques can vary the amount of ink that is placed on the sheet. In this respect, the gravure printing process differs from the others. The best gravure printing uses the combination of varying the amount of ink with the size of the dots.

• Qualities of Halftone Copy

The best printed halftone images start with excellent photographs and artist drawings. The halftone process rarely improves the quality of any original; in fact, it compresses the range of tones in a photograph.

Copy for the halftone process is a photograph or artist's drawing that is not just solid black images on a piece of paper (remember that this sort of image is called line copy). Good halftone copy has tones from black through white, with intermediate shades of gray (figure 8.3).

The photograph should have good contrast, meaning range of tones. High contrast means just blacks and whites with few grays. Low contrast means just grays (see figure 3.6 and 3.7). High- and low-contrast photographs do not typically give good halftone results. The important idea is the distribution of the tones. The photograph should also have good detail and image sharpness. Out-of-focus photographs cannot be

Figure 8.2. Enlarged dot structure in a halftone.

sharpened or focused by the halftone process.

The subject should not blend into the background. Dark subjects reproduce better if they have a light background. Light subjects are best against a dark background.

Photographs that are not on white-background paper are difficult to work with. If photographs are on textured papers such as silk or rough, the texture will show up on the reproduction and image detail will be lost.

Original images should be covered with a cover sheet of clear plastic or tissue to protect the picture's surface (figure 8.4). Instructions for cropping and sizing should not be placed on the picture. The picture should be mounted on illustration or poster board and the instructions written on the tissue or board.

Paper clips should never be used to hold photos to the information or instruction sheets; they make a crease that will be reproduced. Writing on the back of a photograph with a ball-

Figure 8.3. Samples of halftone copy.

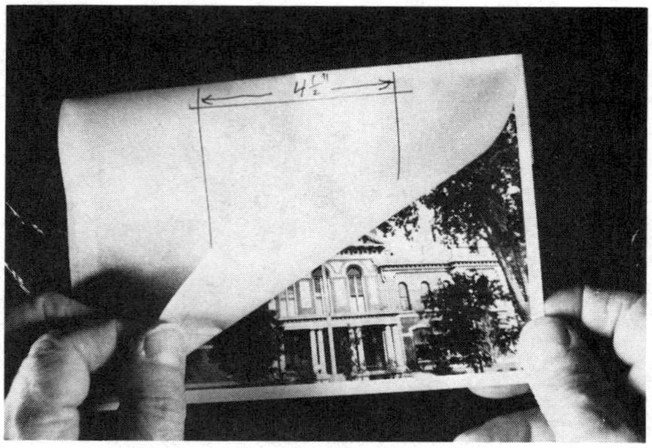

Figure 8.4. Photograph covered with protective cover.

(a)

(b)

Figure 8.5. Airbrushing. (a) This photograph has unwanted background, (b) the same photograph after airbrushing to remove the background.

point pen will damage the photo, and the marking will appear on the reproduction.

To improve photographic copy, advertising agencies and publishers sometimes have an airbrush artist improve the quality of the photo by removing unwanted areas or adding tones (figure 8.5). Copy that has been mistreated, bent, cracked in the emulsion, spotted, or poorly developed or exposed when it gets to the printer cannot be corrected by the graphic arts camera operator.

The point of this discussion is that good halftone copy is a photograph or piece of art that was produced skillfully and handled carefully to preserve its high quality. It should have a defined range of tones from black to white, and the image should be sharp and the detail clear. Unfortunately, printers do not always receive this type of copy. In those cases the camera technician must use the best skills and techniques to make the most acceptable halftone possible from the copy.

• Scaling the Copy

All camera copy that was not prepared for same-size reproduction needs to be scaled. **Scaling** is a frequent operation in the preparation of halftones since most photos must be reduced to fit into defined space on a printed job. Photographers usually prepare photos to one of the standard sizes of photographic paper—8″ × 10″, 5″ × 7″, and 11″ × 14″. Many times the line work paste-up is prepared for same-size reproduction, and the photos are sent along to fit into the places provided on the line art. The places for the halftones often are reserved by black or red blocks (figure 8.6); these will reproduce on the line negatives as clear windows. The halftone negative will have to fit into the window area, and the job of the camera operator is to reduce or enlarge the photograph during the halftone exposure to fit that area.

The quickest and most efficient method for scaling or resizing the photographs for reproduction at the new size is with a proportion scale (see figure 6.1). This scaling device has two dials and a window. The outer scale is for the reproductions or desired new size. The inner scale is the size of the original. The window in the scale shows the percentage of the original size. This reading will tell the camera operator how to set up the camera for size and exposure.

If the photo will not reduce or enlarge in the proper proportions to fit the window, a part of the picture will have to be cropped. Crossed L pieces give the operator the appearance of the new size of the photo (figure 8.7). Most buyers of printing will supply photos that have been marked for cropping by some method like a tissue overleaf. This relieves the camera operator of making this decision.

Let us review the use of a scaling device with a simple problem. The photo supplied is 8″ × 10″ with no margin or border. The line art has a black window area for the photo that is 4″ × 5″. Because a lens will reduce or enlarge proportionately (a fixed amount for both dimensions), choose one measurement to scale. Consider the 8″ side; it should be scaled down to 4″. Place the original size of 8″ on the inner scale to match up with the 4″ mark on the reproduction size scale (figure 8.8). Check on the 10″ size, and it will fall on the 5″ mark on the outer scale. (This is a proportional reduction). Now look in the window of the unit; it will give you the percentage reading of the change. In this case it is 50 percent. For practical purposes, so that you are sure that the picture will overlap the window, increase the percentage to 55 percent (5 percent extra) to insure that the picture is slightly larger than the window.

Most changes will not come out as neatly as the proportional 8″ × 10″ to 4″ × 5″ reduction. When this happens, check the scaling devices and crop the picture so it will reduce to a size to fit the window but still will show the essential parts of the photo.

Most commercial shops charge extra money each time the camera operator must make size changes. To reduce this cost, publishers request

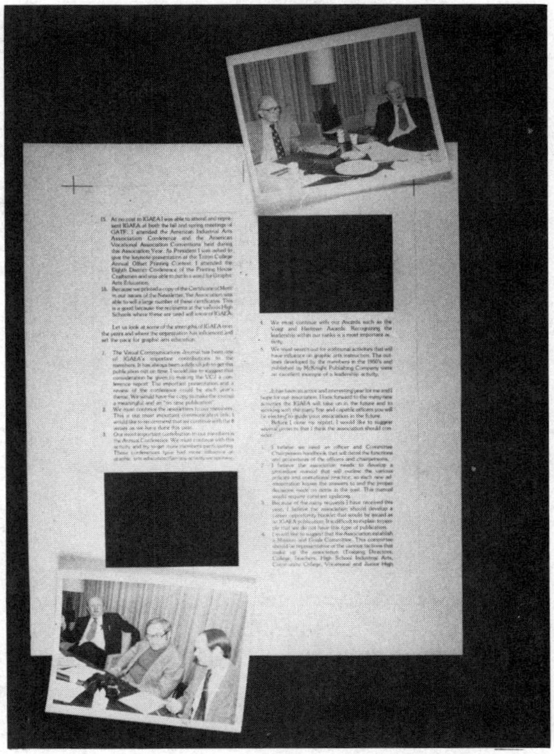

Figure 8.6. Example of windows on copy. Halftones will appear in the space of the windows when job is printed.

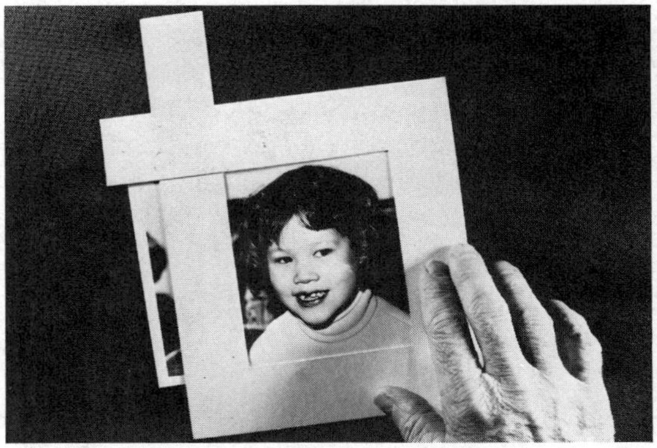

Figure 8.7. Using crossed L pieces to determine cropping of the photograph.

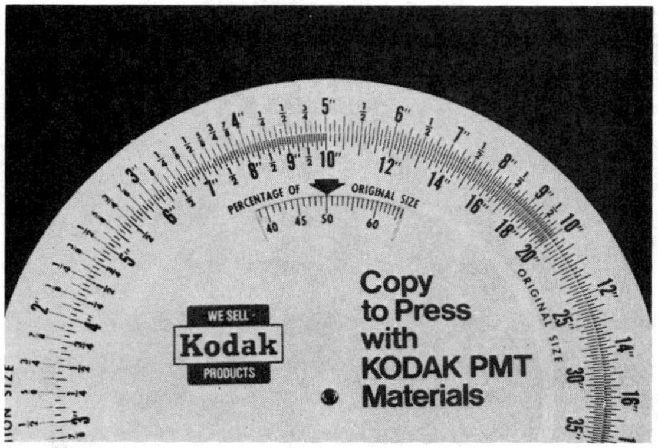

Figure 8.8. Proportion scale set for 50 percent size. The inside scale shows copy size; the outside scale shows the new, or reproduction, size.

the photographers to make the photo to the size specified. This speeds up the operation in the camera department of the printing establishment since many photographs can be ganged upon one board and shot at the same time.

• Types and Function of Halftone Screens

Before discussing the technique of making a halftone, it is important to review the types and function of halftone screens. How does a screen break up a continuous-tone picture into dots of various sizes? Today most halftones are made with **contact screens**. Several different types of contact screens are produced for specific purposes. For example, gray contact screens (negatives) are used to make halftone negatives from black-and-white originals. The gray halftone negative screen is also used for direct screen color separation. The gray screen (negative) has a built-in bump (no screen exposure) effect. This gives better highlight results.

Another type of screen is the **gray halftone screen** (positive). This screen was designed for making halftone positives from continuous-tone negatives. It can be used for making halftone negatives, but in most cases a bump exposure would be required.

A **diffusion transfer screen** (gray) is available for making diffusion transfer halftones. This screen opens the shadow dots. It is best to use it only in this process (see chapter 10).

It is also possible to obtain a **halftone magenta screen**. This screen has a long scale. It can be used for black-and-white halftone negatives, but it should not be used in color work. The magenta screen, used with a rose-colored filter, will shorten the screen range. When the screen is used with a yellow filter, the range of the screen will lengthen.

Screens come with a square dot pattern or an elliptical dot pattern. These patterns are most noticeable in the middle tones of a halftone (figure 8.9). The best screen to use as far as dot structure is concerned is usually just a personal preference, although an elliptical structure does provide a more uniform middle-tone appearance.

Screens must also be selected according to a screen ruling. The ruling indicates the number of dots along a one-inch line (called 11 lines per inch) (figure 8.10). The more dots, a higher screen ruling, the more the halftone looks like a continuous-tone photograph. The screen rulings differ according to the printing process and the type of paper on which the job will be printed, as shown in the following table:

Lines	Use with paper/press
65–85	Newsprint for letterpress,
100–120–133	Newsprint for offset,
120–133–150	Offset stock for offset, Coated stock for letterpress.

Higher line rulings are used for special jobs and in gravure printing.

The halftone screens are expensive and can be damaged easily if they are cared for improperly. It is imperative that the screen be protected from dust, dirt, fingerprints, scratches, chemicals, or any other misuse.

The screen should be stored in the heavy folder that was protecting it when it was purchased. If this is no longer available, a new protective device should be made. Some shops will place the screen in a card stock or film frame so that the screen can be handled by this border material (figure 8.11).

If the screen is dusty, use a dry photo chamois to wipe it. If the screen is dirty, a special screen-cleaning solvent is available to clean the screen. Have your instructor or supervisor give you instruction before you attempt to clean the screen.

The film used for the halftone process is a high-contrast litho material. When the emulsion is developed in a high-contrast developer, the result is either a black image on the film or practically no image at all.

When setting up for a halftone exposure, the film is first placed on the vacuum back of the camera (emulsion up). The contact screen is placed over the film (emulsion of the screen down). The screen, which is a series of vignetted dots, will allow a decreasing amount of light to pass through dot openings from the center out (figure 8.12).

A vignetted halftone dot on a printed sheet is one that shades off from a solid core or center to the white of the paper it is printed on. The vignetted dot in the halftone screen is just the opposite. It has an open center and gains density as it moves away from the open center.

When the exposure is made, those areas of the copy that are white will reflect the most light, pass through the screen, and expose the emulsion of the film. Each shade of gray on the original will reflect less light than white areas and therefore will penetrate less of the screen and expose less of the film. The result is that dot sizes will be formed that are proportional to the density on the copy. When a positive is made of the negative, the light areas will have small dots and the dark areas will have large dots.

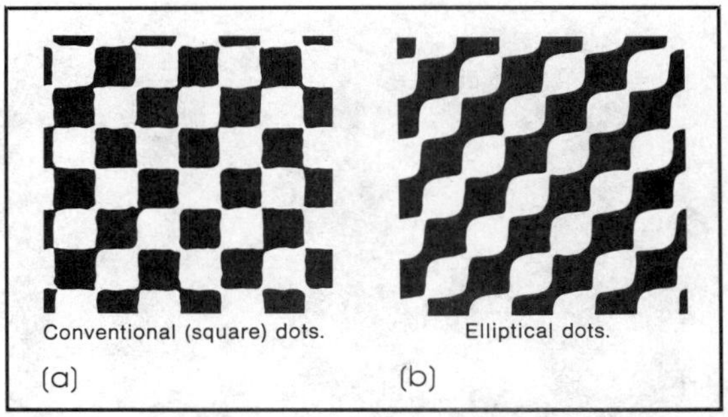

Figure 8.9. Halftone screen dot patterns. (a) The middle-tone dots on a conventional halftone screen, and (b) the middle-tone dots on an elliptical dot screen.
(Courtesy of Eastman Kodak Co.)

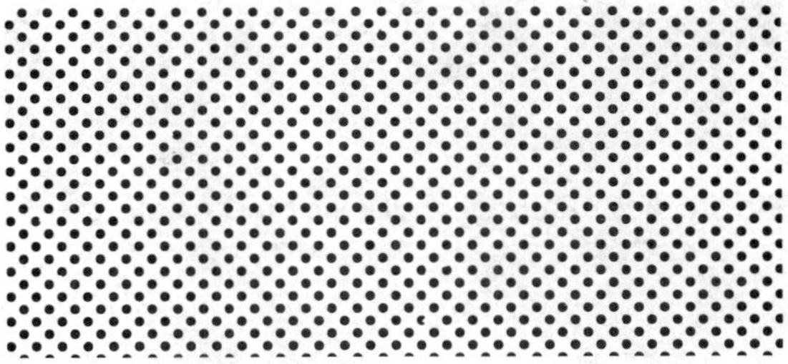

Figure 8.10. 16-line screen. Notice the angle of the dots is 45°.

Figure 8.11. Halftone screen. The screen is in a frame to protect it from fingerprints and damage.

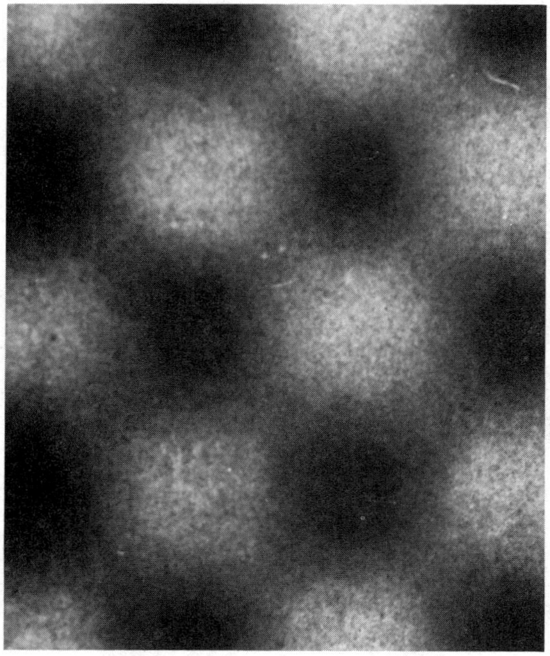

Figure 8.12. Enlarged view of the contact screen dots. These are vignette dots.

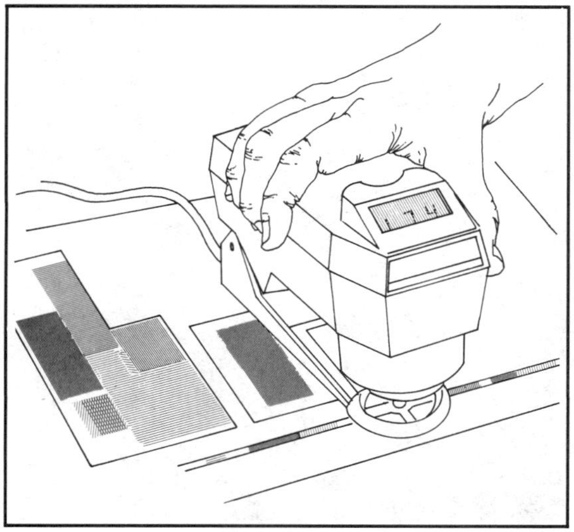

Figure 8.13. Diagram of the use of a reflection densitometer.
(Kimberly Conover-Loar)

• Reading Photo Densities

You learned about density and density readings in chapter 4. The camera operator uses a variety of methods to determine photo densities. A regular densitometer can be used, or an inexpensive method of determining densities is to match the shades of gray with a reflection gray scale that has the density values marked (see figure 4.10). Each of these methods gives the camera operator a knowledge of the tonal range of the picture, called the **copy density range**.

It is important to know the copy density range of the original in order to calculate camera exposures. To determine the print density range, first take a density reading of the lightest highlight area with detail, then read the density of the darkest shadow area with detail (figure 8.13). The numeric difference between the two is the copy density range.

For example, if the highlight is 0.04 and the shadow is 1.65, the copy density range = 1.65 − 0.04 = 1.61.

• Understanding Halftone Exposures

Three types of exposures are used to make halftones: (1) main, (2) flash, and (3) bump. It is important to understand the purpose of each before detailed procedures are discussed.

Main Exposure

The **main exposure** is as the name implies—the most important of the three exposures. It sets the position and size of the highlight dots and defines the range of the middle-tone and shadow areas. The main exposure is made with the screen over the film and the exposure through the camera lens. If the density range of the screen and of the photograph are equal, it is the only exposure that is necessary. Most halftones, however, require some supplementary exposures to produce a good negative. The aperture for the main exposure is usually two f/stops closed from wide open. This usually will be at f/16 or f/22.

Flash Exposure

The **flash exposure** is a supplementary exposure that is given to a negative to put small black dots into the clear area of the negative. Without a flash exposure, the dark areas of the print would be solid black with no detail. The flash exposure is given to the film with a special flashing lamp (figure 8.14). The camera back is opened, the vacuum is left on, and the screen remains over the film. The flashing lamp is turned on for a specific length of time. Most lamps use a 7 1/2-watt frosted bulb in a bullet-shaped safelight with an 00 yellow filter. The lamp should be approximately six feet from the film. If, after testing the exposure of the flash, time is too short—under ten seconds—move the lamp farther away. If the exposures are too long—over twenty-five seconds—place a 15-watt bulb in place of the 7 1/2-watt bulb. Determining basic flash exposures is discussed later in the chapter.

It is extremely important not to move the screen between the main and flash exposures. It is impossible to move a halftone screen and then to replace it in the exact same position.

The flash gives an exposure over the whole piece of film. It will strengthen the shadow dots that received some exposure from the main but not enough exposure to give the dot a solid black base. Overflashing makes the shadows gray instead of black in the printed job. It flattens the halftone. Underflashing produces no detail in the shadow areas. The flash exposure tends to lengthen the range of the halftone (figure 8.15).

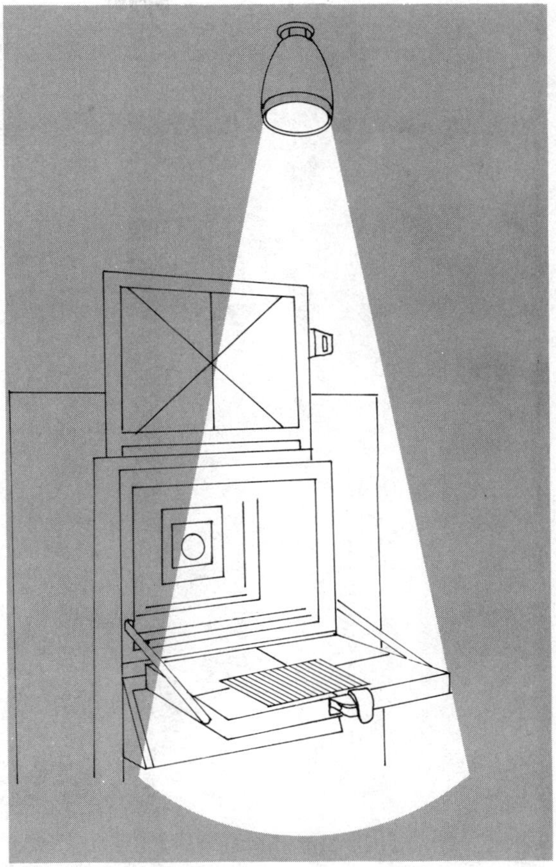

Figure 8.14. Diagram of the flash exposure using the flashing lamp over the camera vacuum back.
(Kimberly Conover-Loar)

Bump Exposure

The **bump exposure** is a supplemental exposure given to the highlight areas. It is a no-screen exposure. After the main and flash exposures have been made through the halftone screen, the screen is removed and a very short no-screen exposure is given. This darkens the highlight areas of the negative, making the highlights on the positive print appear whiter (figure 8.16). This exposure is made through the lens with the copy in the copyboard. After the other exposures are made, the vacuum is left on, the screen is carefully removed, not disturbing the film, the back is closed, and the bump exposure is made. The no-screen exposure is calculated from the main exposure and expressed as a 2 percent, 5

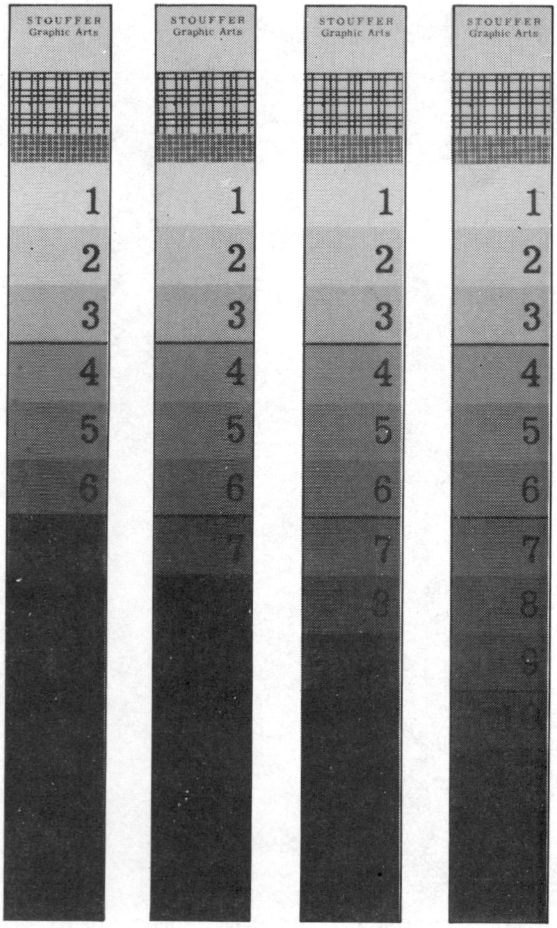

39-sec. main no flash | 39-sec main 5-sec flash | 39-sec main 10-sec flash | 39-sec main 14-sec flash

Figure 8.15. Gray scales showing progressively more flash exposure from left to right.

percent, or 10 percent bump. The bump exposure can also be the first exposure in the sequence. It is important that the camera operator develop a sequence of the exposures. In this way none of the steps will be forgotten. Bump, main, and flash is one sequence. The other would be main, flash, and bump.

The most practical way to make the bump exposure is using ND filters. The filters are placed in front of the lens, the f/stop remains the same, and the exposure time remains the same as the main exposure. The following table shows the filters to use to keep the exposure for specific percentage bumps:

Bump	Filter
2½ percent	1.60
5 percent	1.30
8 percent	1.10
10 percent	1.00

The bump exposure compresses (shortens) the print density range and tends to whiten the highlights. Most camera operators will reduce the main exposure if a bump is to be used. This exposure requires practice and experimentation to insure high-quality results.

While complex formulas are available to help the camera operator determine the exact amount of reduction of the main exposure when using the bump, the beginner will have satisfactory results if a 25–30 percent reduction of the main exposure is used. It is best not to bump over 10 percent. The reduction of the main exposure moves the middle-tone dot toward the highlight end of the scale. The bump exposure affects the highlights to the greatest degree but does, to some degree, affect the entire range of tones. A slight 2–3 percent reduction of the flash is also important when the bump exposure is used. Exact calculations of these exposures are worked out for the camera worker who uses the Kodak Halftone Negative Computer or the new Q–700 data center. Both of these are discussed later in this chapter.

• Recognizing Halftone Dots

An important skill to develop is recognition of dot size when viewing halftone negatives. Most graphic arts photographers use the highlight and shadow dots as the target areas to judge acceptability of the halftone negative. The goal, with most halftone images, is to record the smallest printable highlight dot and to leave a small open area in the shadows, so that the shadows do not print as a solid. It is sometimes confusing for a printer-in-training to work with negatives since the dot size is the exact opposite of the size when printed as a positive.

It is best always to talk of halftone dots as they would appear on the final printed sheet. With this procedure a 5 percent dot is always a highlight, whether it is a small spot of light on a negative or a spot of ink on the press sheet. A 95 percent dot will appear as a large open area, with a small black dot (that does not print) on the negative that will print as almost solid black on the final job.

Figure 8.17 shows examples of halftone dots. Notice that the highlight areas on the negative are small open areas, and that those on the positive are solid dots. The shadow areas on the negative appear as large, open areas, with small black dots. The small dots in the shadow areas will block light and create a large black dot on the positive. Remember, in all cases, the open area on the negative is the halftone dot. Light must pass through the openings on the negative to form positive dots on the printing plate.

The goal with most halftone images is to record the smallest printable highlight dot and to leave a small open area in the shadows so they do not print as a solid.

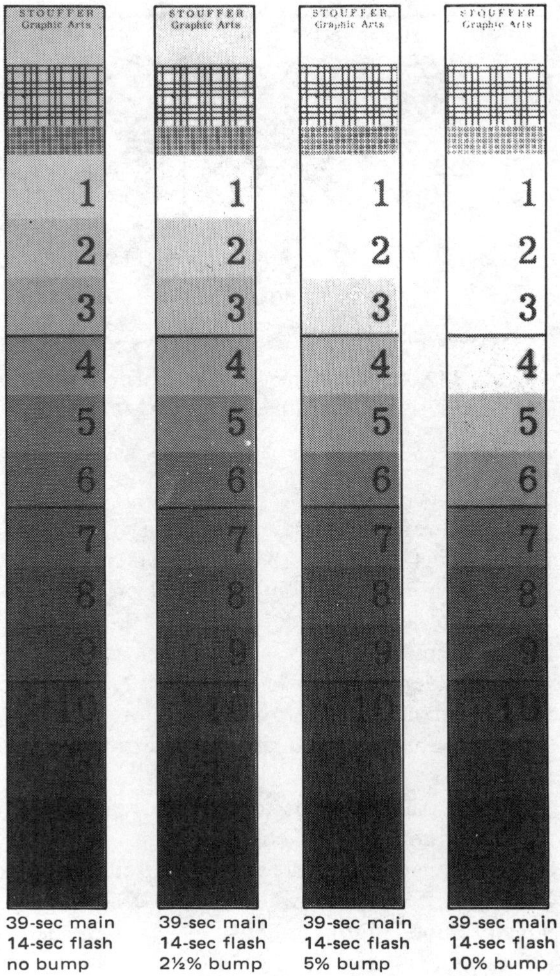

Figure 8.16. Gray scales showing progressively more bump exposure from left to right.

• Reading Reflection Copy Densities

The camera operator can determine the density readings of continuous-tone copy in several ways. One is to punch holes in the patches of a

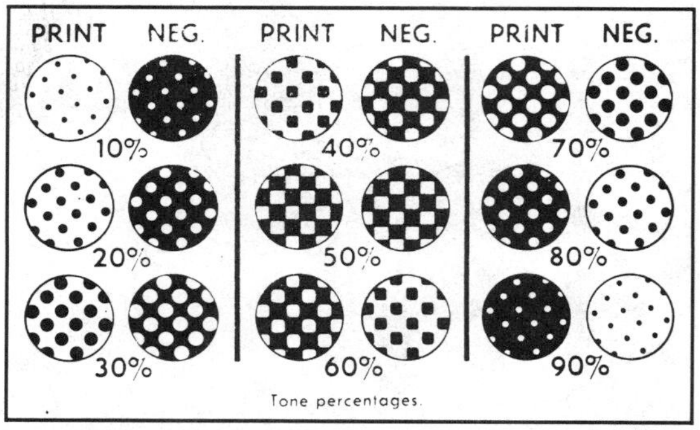

Figure 8.17. A chart showing the comparison of negative and positive dot percentages.

calibrated reflection gray scale and to make visual readings (figure 8.18). A second method is to obtain a commercially produced prepunched gray scale density guide (figure 8.19). Yet another technique is to read densities through a reflection densitometer (see figure 4.2). Each of these methods will help the operator to determine exposures for making the halftone negative.

The operator needs to take the readings of the highlight density (lightest tone) and the shadow density (darkest tone). As discussed earlier, the difference between these two—shadow density minus highlight density—gives the density range of the copy.

• Determining the Basic Density Range of the Screen

The first step in preparing to produce halftone negatives is to determine the **basic density range** (BDR) of the screen. Each screen has a different BDR so this procedure must be performed for each new contact screen.

Several factors controlled by the camera operator can affect screen range, including camera light, darkroom chemistry, variables of time and temperature, and the worker variable of processing film. Many commercial shops have tried to eliminate the darkroom and worker variables with machine processing. For the following example of determining the screen range, tray development will be used:

- Place a calibrated gray scale on the copyboard.
- Set the camera for the same-size (100 percent) reproduction, and make sure the lights are correctly positioned.
- Set the aperture for 100 percent on the f/16 scale.
- Set the exposure time for twenty-five seconds (this is a good starting point with pulse Xenon lights).
- With the safelights on and white lights off, place a sheet of litho (ortho emulsion) film on the vacuum back, emulsion up.
- Place the contact screen emulsion of the screen against the emulsion of film. The screen should be larger than the film to insure good vacuum contact.
- Roll the contact screen and film to insure good contact.
- Close the camera back and make the exposure.
- Develop the film using standard developing procedures as when processing a line negative:

  Develop: 2 3/4 minutes,
  Stop: 5–10 seconds,
  Fix: Twice the time it takes to clear,
  Wash: 10–15 minutes.

- Allow the film to hang to dry, or use a film dryer if one is available.
- Inspect the film after it is dry to determine the BDR of the screen.

For example, in figure 8.20 the smallest printable highlight dot appears in step four—0.15. The largest shadow dot before solid appears in step sixteen—1.20. Now go back to the original copy (gray scale) that was used on the copyboard. Measure the density of steps four and

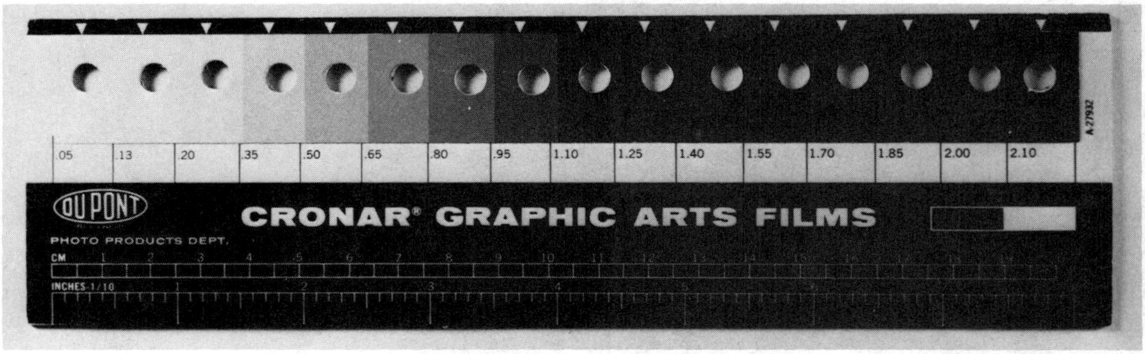

Figure 8.18. Holes drilled in a calibrated reflection gray scale.

sixteen. By subtracting the highlight density reading (0.15) from the shadow density reading (1.20), we have obtained the BDR of the screen 1.20 − 0.15 = 1.05. This screen will reproduce a tonal range of 1.05 with a main exposure. If a job has a density range greater than the screen range, then a flash exposure must be used. The difference between the copy density range and the screen BDR is called **excess density**. For example, if a photo has a copy density range of 1.55 and the screen a BDR of 1.05, then the excess density is 0.50.

The size of target dots depends upon the printing processes to be used. For lithography, for example, 5 percent and 95 percent are the norm. With screen printing, a 12 percent highlight and 85 percent shadow are common. Gravure, however, might hold 2 percent and 98 percent dots.

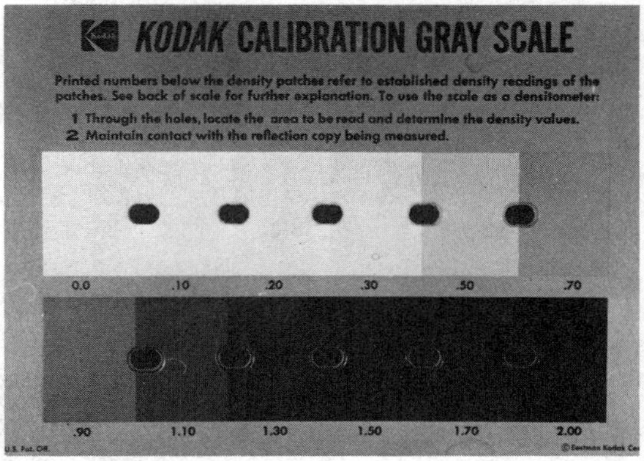

Figure 8.19. A commercially available prepunched calibrated reflection gray scale.

• Determining the Basic Flash Exposure

The next step in preparing to produce halftone negatives is to determine the **basic flash exposure.** Use the following procedures for this purpose:

- Cut small strips of the same type of film used in the previous test.
- Place film, emulsion up, on the camera vacuum back.
- Place the halftone screen over the strip of film as for the previous exposure, and roll it to insure good vacuum contact.
- For this exposure the vacuum back of the camera is open and the exposure will be made with the flashing lamp—try a yellow 00 filter with a 7 1/2-watt bulb.
- Have a piece of black card stock available

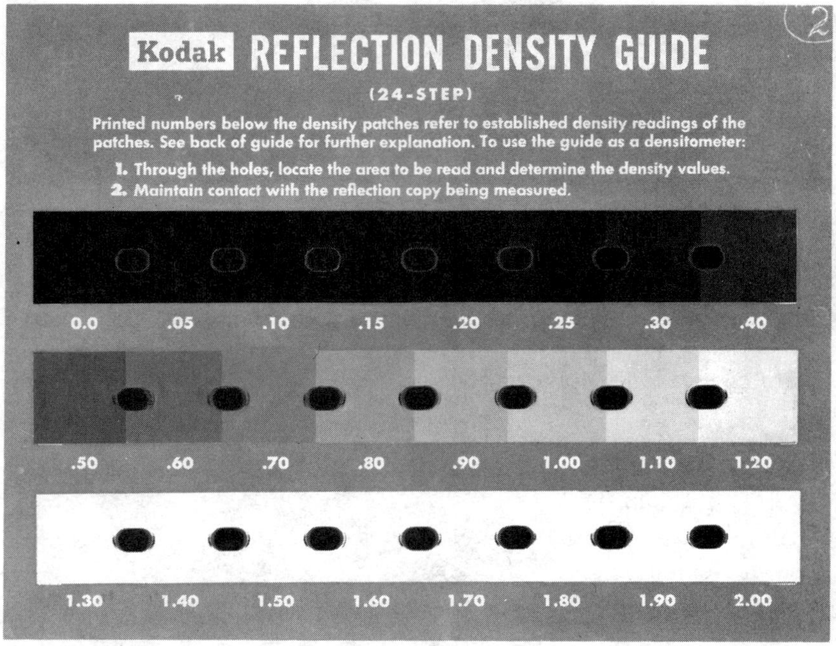

Figure 8.20. A calibrated gray scale used to determine the main exposure and BDR of the screen.

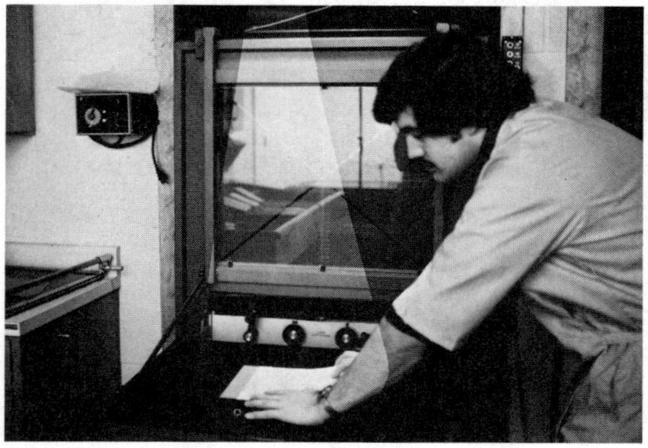

Figure 8.21. Making the flash test.

so you can make a series of exposures (figure 8.21).

- Give a sixteen-second overall exposure to the film. Then step off a series of two-second exposures using a thick piece of black card stock. Hold the stock over all but a small strip of film, make a two-second exposure; move the stock one-half inch, make a two-second exposure; move the stock another one-half inch, repeating the exposure and movement until the entire piece of film has been exposed (figure 8.22).
- Process, wash, and dry the film.
- Inspect the film to determine the basic flash time. Look for the same dot size that was accepted as the shadow dot in the main exposure test. In this example, the shadow dot was located in the fourth step and was obtained with a twenty-two-second exposure. Twenty-two seconds is now the basic flash exposure time for this screen. The test data

for this particular screen are the following:

- Highlight dot area: 0.15,
- Shadow dot area: 1.20,
- Screen BDR: 1.05,
- Basic main exposure: 25 seconds,
- Basic flash exposure: 22 seconds,
- f/16: 100 percent.

There are several ways to use this test information to determine exposure time for a production job. The following sections examine the uses of several different systems to determine exposure times when making halftone negatives.

• The DuPont System

The DuPont system uses two charts to determine the main and flash exposure times (table 8.1 and 8.2). Test data information is the basis for predicting new exposures from the charts. As an example, assume that you want to make a halftone negative for an upcoming job that requires a 50 percent reduction. The following steps outline the procedures.

Table 8.1. Exposure change quick check

Density difference[a]	Exposure factor[b]	New exposure[c]
Basic exposure time ➧		
.02	1.04	———
.04	1.09	———
.06	1.14	———
.08	1.20	———
.10	1.25	———
.12	1.31	———
.14	1.38	———
.16	1.44	———
.18	1.51	———
.20	1.58	———
.22	1.66	———
.24	1.73	———
.26	1.82	———
.28	1.90	———
.30	2.00	———

a. Density difference = difference between test and copy densities

b. Exposure factor = antilog of density difference

c. New exposure = your test exposure time × exposure factor

Source: (Courtesy E.I. DuPont Co.)

Figure 8.22. Step-off negative used to determine basic flash exposure time.

1. Read the highlight and shadow densities of the original photograph. Say you found for this job a highlight of 0.17 and a shadow of 1.52.

Table 8.2. Quick check flash table

For screen ———	
Excess density	Flash time
0.05	———
0.10	———
0.15	———
0.20	———
0.25	———
0.30	———
0.35	———
0.40	———
0.45	———
0.50	———
0.55	———
0.60	———
0.65	———
0.70	———
0.75	———

For use as a quick reference for common excess densities. Use only for the screen tested. To use the quick check flash table: (1) Determine the flash time through tests, (2) Fill in DuPont Flash Computer, and (3) Find flash times using computer for the excess densities listed on the Quick Check Flash Table and Record. (Courtesy of E.I. DuPont Co.)

2. Go to the main exposure chart. The difference between the highlight of the photo and the highlight test data is 0.02 (0.17 − 0.15 = 0.02). Locate 0.02 in the density difference column of Table 8.1, and then read across to find the exposure factor. In this case, the factor is 1.04. Since the test data found a basic main exposure of 25 seconds, the main exposure for this job should be 26 seconds (25 × 1.04 = 26.00).

3. Now go to the Shadow Flash Computer (figure 8.23).

The BDR of this new photograph is 1.35 (1.52 − 0.17 = 1.35). The test data gave a screen BDR of 1.05. Subtract the screen BDR from the print density range (1.35 − 1.05 − 0.30) to find an excess density of 0.30.

This means that the screen can only reproduce 1.05 units of density of the photography and that 0.30 units must be added by a flash exposure. Now find 0.30 on the excess density range scale in figure 8.23. Use a ruler or other straightedge to read up from 0.30 until the line crosses the curve. Where the vertical line intersects the curve, read over to the percentage of basic flash column. In this case, the scale says the flash exposure should be around 52 percent of the basic flash test. The flash exposure for this photograph should be 11 1/2 seconds (22 seconds × 0.52 = 11 1/2 seconds). Both scales are set up so you can write in changes in exposure for each percentage change. If only one screen is being used, then it will save time to write those changes directly on the charts (table 8.2).

4. The final step is to place the photograph on the copyboard, with a gray scale, set the diaphragm control at 50 percent on f/16, adjust the timers for a main of 26 and flash of 11 1/2 seconds, and make the exposures.

• The Kodak Graphic Arts Exposure Computer

Eastman Kodak makes two card-type aids for calculating halftone exposures. The first is the Kodak Graphic Arts Exposure Computer and Calibration Gray Scale (Q–12) (figure 8.24). The following steps illustrate the use of the computer, using the test data from earlier in the chapter. Assume you did test exposures for a different screen in the preceding examples and found:

- Highlight density area: 0.18,
- Shadow density area: 1.30,

- Screen BDR = 1.12,
- Basic main exposure: 30 seconds,
- Basic flash exposure time: 18 seconds,
- f/22: 100 percent.

The following steps show the use of the exposure computer using these test results.

1. Calibrate the computer first by rotating the clear plastic disk so f/22 lines up with 100 percent. Next, move the red wheel so that the highlight density reading (0.18) lines up with the main exposure time (thirty seconds). Then tape both wheels in place so they do not move.

2. Read the highlight and shadow densities of the original photograph. Say, for this example, you found a highlight of 0.05 and a shadow of 1.47.

3. Locate the highlight density of the photo on the red scale of the computer, and read the exposure time in seconds across from the density scale. In this case, the new exposure time would be twenty-five seconds (figure 8.25).

4. To determine the flash exposure, subtract the print density range from the screen BDR. For this example, the print has a density range of 1.42 (1.47 − 0.05 = 1.42). The excess density is 1.42 − 1.30 = 0.12. Refer to the flash exposure table on the computer, and find the horizontal scale. The scale reads "0 0.1 0.2 0.3" and so on, which represents excess density (table 8.3). In this example, the excess density is 0.12. Find 0.12 on the scale, and then find the vertical column labeled basic flash exposure in seconds. Read down until you find your basic flash test results. In this case, we had eighteen seconds. Now read across horizontally from eighteen seconds, and down vertically from 0.12, until the two cross. Then read the required flash exposure of four seconds.

5. The final step is to place the photograph on the copyboard, with a gray scale, set the diaphragm control at 100 percent on f/22, adjust the timers for a main of twenty-five seconds and a flash of four seconds, and make the exposures.

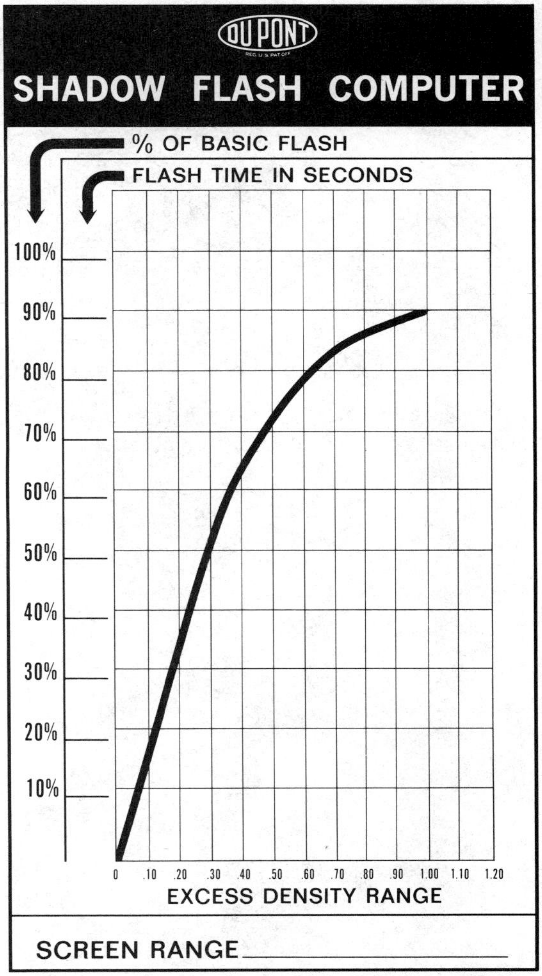

Figure 8.23. Determining flash exposures with the DuPont Shadow Flash computer. (Courtesy of E.I. DuPont Co.)

Figure 8.24. Kodak Graphic Arts Exposure Computer and Calibration Gray Scale.

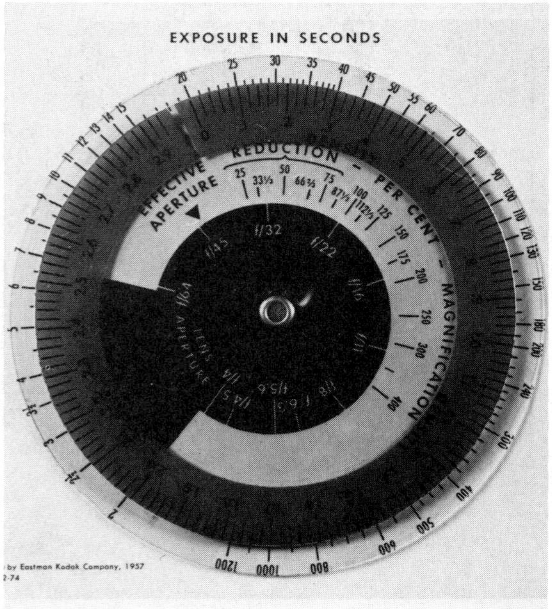

Figure 8.25. Main exposure dial on Kodak Graphic Arts Exposure Computer.

• The Kodak Haltone Negative Computer

The more recent Kodak device is the Q–15, Halftone Negative Computer. This computer has the potential to give more exposure information than the Q–12 since it is set to determine bump exposures, as well as to predict the interaction between the main and flash exposure (for certain situations). The Q–15 is purchased with an excellent instruction manual that describes detailed operation of the computer.

The following example outlines the sequence for using the Q–15 computer. Assume that the following test data were determined:

- Highlight dot area: 0.08,
- Shadow dot area: 1.16,
- Screen BDR: 1.08,
- Basic main exposure: 35 seconds,
- Basic flash exposure: 20 seconds,
- f/16 at 100 percent.

Calibrate the computer by setting the dials from the test data (figure 8.26):

- Position the M pointed at 0.08 on the density scale,
- Move the mask wheel to 1.16 on the density scale,
- Move the calibration tab so that 35 seconds appears in the main exposure window,
- Rotate the clear plastic dial so it reads basic flash 20 seconds and so the 0 number lines up with the mask wheel zero point,
- Now tape the dials and arm in place as shown in figure 8.27.

To determine the main and flash for a new photograph, use the following steps:

1. Read the highlight and shadow densities of the original photograph. Say for this example you found a highlight of 0.04 and a shadow of 1.34.

2. Move the M pointer to the highlight reading of the print—in this case, 0.04 (figure

Table 8.3 Flash exposure table for Kodak Graphic Arts Exposure Computer

Basic flash exposure in seconds*	Flash exposure time in seconds for excess density range								
	0	0.1	0.2	0.3	0.4	0.5	0.6	0.8	1.0
16	0	3½	6	8	9½	11	12	13½	14½
18	0	4	7	9	11	12	13½	15	16
20	0	4	7½	10	12	13½	15	17	18
22	0	4½	8½	11	13	15	16½	18½	20
24	0	5	9	12	14½	16	18	20	22
26	0	5½	10	13	15½	17½	19½	22	23½
28	0	6	10½	14	17	19	21	23½	25
30	0	6½	11	15	18	20½	22½	25	27
35	0	7	13	18	21	24	26	29	32
40	0	8	15	20	24	27	30	34	36
45	0	10	17	23	27	31	34	38	41
50	0	11	19	25	30	34	38	42	45
55	0	12	20	27	33	37	41	46	50
60	0	13	22	30	36	41	45	50	55
70	0	15	26	35	42	48	53	59	63
80	0	17	30	40	48	54	60	67	72

*Flashing-lamp arrangements which give basic flash exposures of less than 16 seconds are not recommended unless accurate timing devices are used, in which case this table can be expanded easily. For example, the times for 14 seconds' basic flash would be 1/2 those in the 28-second row, the times for 10 seconds' basic flash, ½ those in the 20-second row, etc.

8.28). Read the main exposure time in the open window. For this example it is thirty-one seconds.

3. Move the F hairline so it is positioned over the shadow density of the photo—here we found 1.34. Then read the flash exposure time on the transparent scale—seven seconds.

4. Place the photograph on the copyboard with a gray scale. Set the camera controls for a main of thirty-one seconds and a flash of seven seconds, and adjust the diaphragm control for the desired size on the f/16 scale. Make sure the camera enlargement and reduction scales have been set for the required size, and then make the exposures.

There are several other applications for the Q–15, but these steps describe the most basic

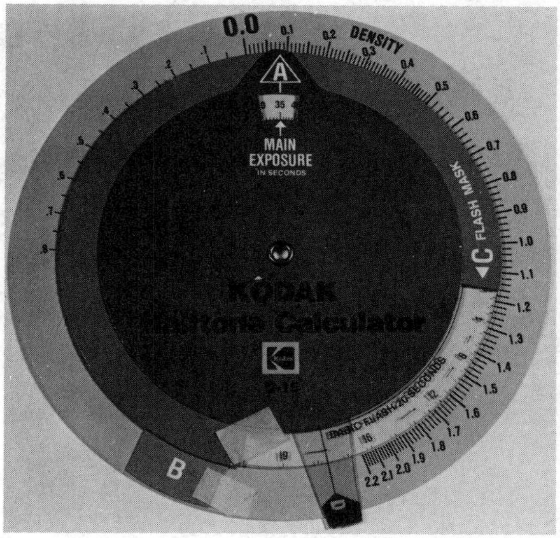

Figure 8.26. Kodak Halftone Negative Computer.

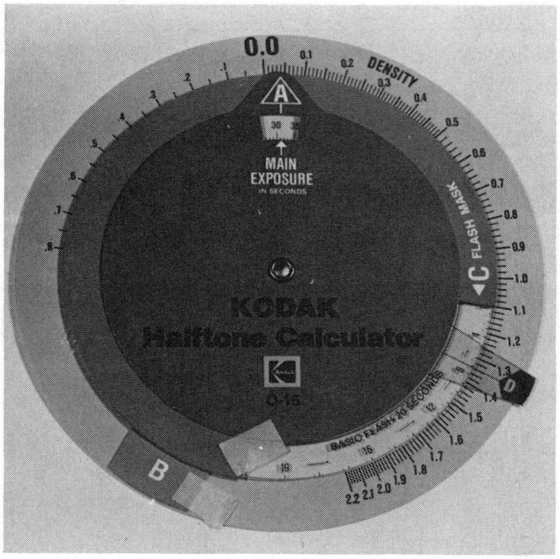

Figure 8.27. Kodak Q–15 Computer.

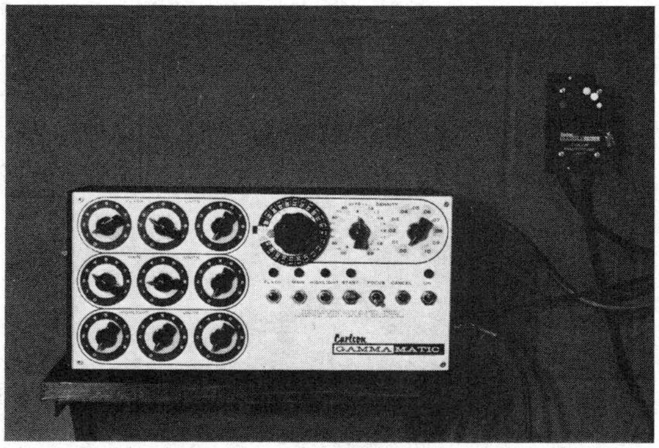

Figure 8.28. Carlson Gammamatic exposure control unit.

operation. Refer to Kodak's manual for more sophisticated operation.

• Other Exposure Devices

In addition to the relatively inexpensive calculators we have discussed, there are a number of excellent camera-timing devices that are useful in producing consistently high-quality halftones. Each of these devices has a series of dials and settings that can be used to dial in main, bump, and flash exposures. Some of them work on density settings and others on time units. They are most helpful in situations with large production volume. These devices also have time units that are activated by the color temperature of the exposing lamps, which is helpful in color separation work. Two examples of these machines are shown in figures 8.28 and 8.29. Each unit comes with complete directions for calibration and production use.

One of the most advanced devices that is now available to assist the camera and darkroom worker is called the Kodak Data Center Q–700 (figure 8.30). This data center uses a programmable electronic calculator and a printout device to provide information on copy scaling, filter selection, chemical mixing, dot-area-density conversion, and camera exposure adjustment.

The unit comes with modules that can be inserted into the calculator. These modules are programmed for the individual shop and store that data for guide access. This quality control device makes repeatable results possible for printers.

• Halftones from Difficult Copy

Up to this point, the discussion has centered upon standard halftone procedures for relatively good copy. Sometimes, however, photos come into the shop for printing that cannot be called good. These pieces can be called difficult or problem copy.

Flat Copy

Flat copy (a gray picture) usually has good highlight detail but has very poor contrast, especially between the middle tones and the shadow (figure 8.31). To handle flat copy, set the camera and controls for a normal halftone. Then set the exposure time for the main exposure for approximately one-third of the normal main time. (Some testing for exact times will be necessary). After the main exposure, if flash is necessary, give the normal flash exposure.

With the vacuum on holding the film and screen, carefully remove the screen and give the negative a 15 percent bump exposure. Process, wash, and dry the film. Evaluate the negative with a magnifying glass. The results should be an improved halftone (figure 8.32).

Dark Copy

This type of photo has very dark highlights, dark middle tones, and shadows with little detail (figure 8.33). The photo looks muddy and lacks contrast. To handle dark copy, set the camera and controls for a normal halftone. Determine the main exposure from the highlight density. Remember, doubling the exposure will move the highlight dots by 0.30 density so that much shift may not be needed. Reduce the flash exposure by at least 50 percent. Process, wash, and dry the negative, and evaluate it (figure 8.34).

Lack of Detail

Figure 8.35 is an example of a photo that comes into the shop with no detail in the sky area. The photo would print better if there was some detail in this washed-out area. To handle this problem, set the camera and controls for a normal halftone. Determine the main exposure by using the sky as the highlight density. This will usually require less main exposure and will place a highlight dot in the sky. Give the normal flash as

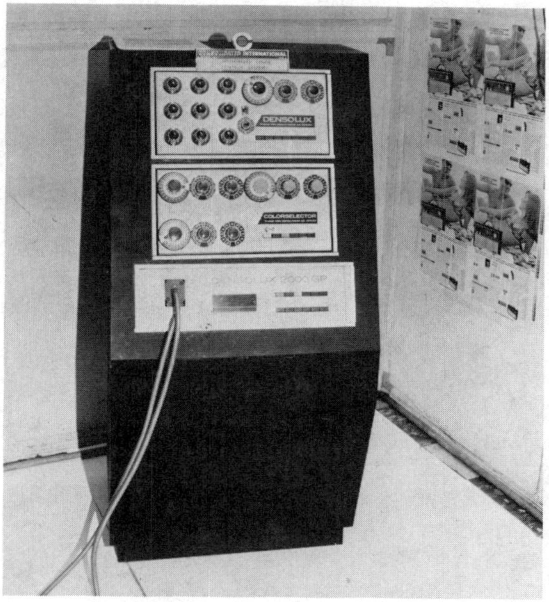

Figure 8.29. Advanced programmable exposure control device. (Courtesy of Consolidated International Corp.)

Figure 8.30. Eastman Kodak Q–700 Data Center for quality camera work. (Courtesy of Eastman Kodak Company, Inc.)

Figure 8.31. Halftone with poor contrast in middle tones to shadows.

Figure 8.32. Improved halftone after proper exposures.

Figure 8.33. Dark halftone in highlights to middle tones.

required by the photo. Process, wash, and dry the negative, and evaluate it (figure 8.36).

In each of these situations, if the shop has an exposure calculator, it can be programmed to handle these as well as the exposure for normal halftones. Full instructions come with these devices.

• Processing Variables

In any craft, the worker will encounter variables in equipment and materials. Controlling these variables is part of knowing the equipment and

Figure 8.34. Improved halftone of the same photo with proper exposures.

Figure 8.35. Halftone with washed-out sky area.

Figure 8.36. Improved halftone after exposure manipulation.

supplies. Changes in some can be made to solve problems (like exposure). Some processing variables, however, must be controlled accurately to give acceptable results.

Developer Temperature

Graphic arts films usually come with an instruction sheet that specifies a working temperature of 68°F. What would happen if the temperature was changed to 60°F or 75°F?

Figure 8.37 shows four halftones that received the same exposure and that were processed for the same time. The only difference is

Figure 8.37. Examples of halftones with different developing temperatures. From upper left proceeding clockwise, temperature increases from 62° to 85°F. The exposures and developing times are identical. (Courtesy of E.I. DuPont Co.)

in the processing temperature. Obviously, temperature control is important.

Agitation

The darkroom worker must control the consistent rate of agitation during the development step. Once you have established an agitation procedure, follow it. Automatic film processors have helped to control this variable, but many shops still use shallow tray processing. See chapter 5 for methods of controlling agitation rates. Figure 8.38 shows three halftones, all with the same exposure. The developer temperature was 68°F. The only difference was in the agitation rates during the developing step, thus illustrating the importance of controlling agitation.

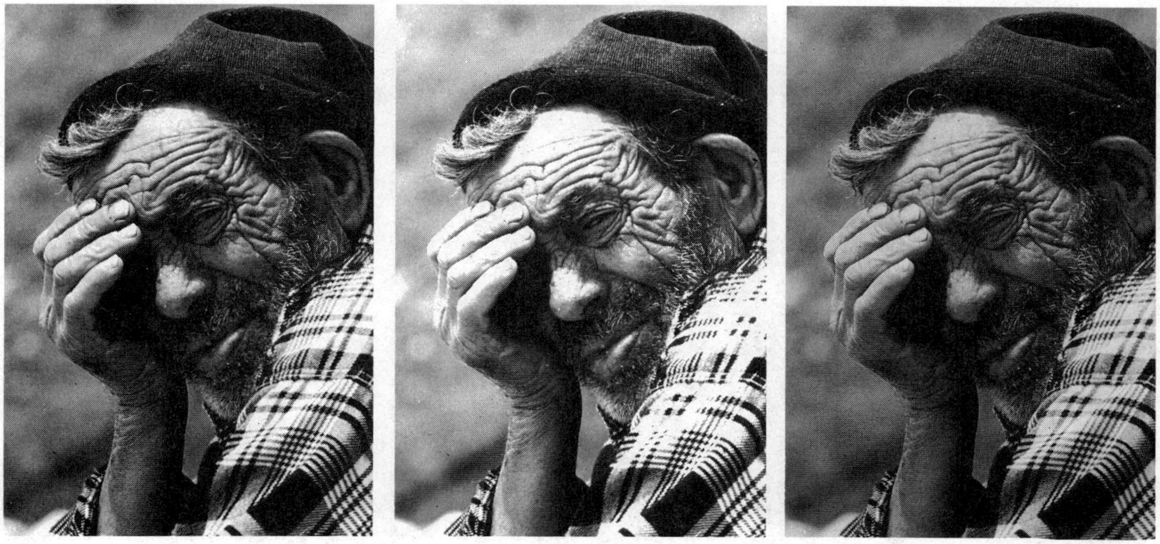

(a) (b) (c)

Figure 8.38. Examples of halftones with different agitation techniques. (a) Normal agitation, (b) brisk agitation, and (c) still development. All the halftones had identical exposures and developing times. (Courtesy of E.I. DuPont Co.)

Developer Exhaustion

Another variable in the processing of film is that of developer exhaustion. It is important to mix only the amount of developer needed for the work at hand. Mixed developer in a shallow tray will deteriorate. Store mixed developer in a tightly sealed container. Each piece of film processed through the developer reduces the chemical activity level. Automatic developer units have a device that replenishes the developer after each piece of film is run through the system (see chapter 5).

What happens if the developer is overused? Figure 8.39 shows three identically exposed halftones. The developer temperature was maintained at 68° and developing times were identical. Using fresh developer will help maintain good quality.

Each of these variables can cause serious quality problems. The problems can be compounded if all three go out of control at the same time.

• Key Points

- A halftone is a copy of a continuous-tone photograph that has been broken up into a series of dots. These dots and clear areas make the copy appear to have shades of gray.
- Halftone copy can be a photograph, a charcoal drawing, a pencil sketch, an oil painting, or any art that has multiple tones.
- A halftone screen is used to break the tones into dots.
- A basic exposure test is used to establish the basic density range (BDR) of each screen.
- Three common exposures are used to make halftones: main, flash, and bump.

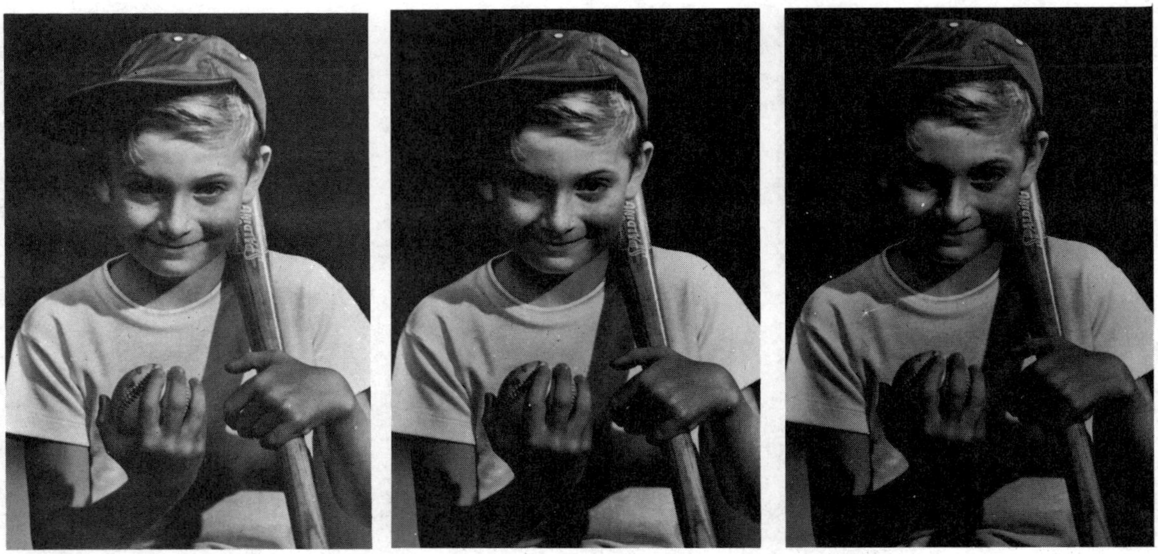

Figure 8.39. Examples of developer exhaustion. All halftones had identical exposures and development times, but were the first, fifth, and fifteenth sheets of film through the same limited quantity of developer. (Courtesy of E.I. DuPont Co.)

• Review Questions

1. Describe what is meant by halftone copy, and explain how it is used in printed products.
2. Describe one procedure that is used to determine basic main and flash exposures. Why is this information important to the camera operator?
3. When the camera operator is evaluating a halftone negative or a contact proof of the negative, what information is being sought? Describe this in dot percentages.
4. When the term *bump exposure* is used, how would you describe it to a person not acquainted with the graphic arts?
5. Three types of difficult copy were explained in the chapter. Give a brief description of each and how you as a camera operator would handle each case.
6. Explain how the dot images are formed on the film by the halftone screen. Why are the dots of varying size?

• Activities

1. With a contact screen selected by your instructor or supervisor, determine the basic exposures for the main and the flash. Determine the screen range. Be sure to record all of this information for further use.

   If your shop has a Kodak Graphic Arts Computer or a Kodak Halftone Negative Computer, use one of these. For copy, use a calibrated reflection gray scale.
2. Select a 4″ × 5″ photograph that will require a normal halftone procedure. From the information determined in activity 1, make a same-size halftone negative. Make a contact print on stabilization paper (or other proofing system) to evaluate the results.

3. Using the same copy as in activity 2, make two more halftones, one at 50 percent and one at 200 percent. Make proofs and compare results with the proof from activity 2. Are the halftones the same in dot quality with the only difference being size?
4. Have your instructor or supervisor give you a piece of difficult copy. Determine how to handle the copy, and proceed to make a halftone negative. Proof and evaluate your results.
5. Select one of the three processing variables discussed in this chapter. Follow the procedure outlined and make your own test. Proof the negatives and evaluate to see if your test shows up the tested variable.

Chapter 9

Contacting

• Objectives

In this chapter you will cover:

- The major types of contacts and uses,
- Contacting equipment,
- Contacting procedures.

After reading the chapter you should be able to:

- Define the process of contacting;
- Describe the two types of contacts;
- Recall, from memory, five uses for contacts;
- Explain the uses of the vacuum frame and the point light source;
- Explain the three types of film orientation;
- Explain the process of determining the basic exposure;
- Make a production contact;
- Make a contact duplicate;
- Make a spread and choke.

Traditionally, graphic arts camera and darkroom workers have not been trained adequately in the skill and technique of making contacts. It often has been viewed as just another task the darkroom worker was expected to perform. However, it is a useful and important technique for the graphic arts industry. The development of specialized contact films has brought a new interest in the techniques of contacting and the role it plays in preplate operations.

• What Is Contacting

Contacting is the process of creating a new film image by exposure through an existing film negative or film positive. The original film sheet is held in direct contact with the unexposed sheet while light is passed through the open images (figure 9.1). To accomplish this operation, the worker must have a vacuum frame to hold the original and film tightly in contact (figure 9.2). Also needed is a light source suitable to expose the material. Some films require a point source light (figure 9.3), and others require a more powerful light source like a quartz bulb (figure 9.4). Some contact materials require a powerful light source like the one used in a platemaker (figure 9.5).

Contacting serves many important functions in the graphic arts. This process also reduces the dependence on the camera for certain operations, thus freeing it for other operations.

There are two major types of contacts. The first is called a **conventional**, or **reversal**, contact print. In this type of contacting, a negative original is used to produce a positive reproduction, or an original positive is used to produce a negative reproduction. The original is usually transparent-based (film), and the reproduction can be on film or a paper base.

The second type of contact is called a **duplicate.** The material that is exposed must be a special film for duplicating. If the original material is a film positive, the exposed duplicating material will process as a positive; if the original is a negative, the reproduction will be a negative. Most duplicating materials are on a film base, but they also can be on a paper base.

Contacting is used in the following graphic arts operations:

- Making negatives from positives or positives from negatives,
- Duplicating high-contrast negatives or positives,
- Changing image orientation from right reading to wrong reading or vice versa,
- Hardening soft-halftone dots,
- Changing the contrast and tone values of the original negative or positive,
- Producing one piece of film from stripped flats,
- Making paper proofs,
- Making step-and-repeat images,
- Making spreads and chokes,
- Making tints,
- Making screened paper prints,
- Making masks for color separation work,
- Making screened positives from continuous-tone separations,
- Making direct screened separations,
- Making stripping keys.

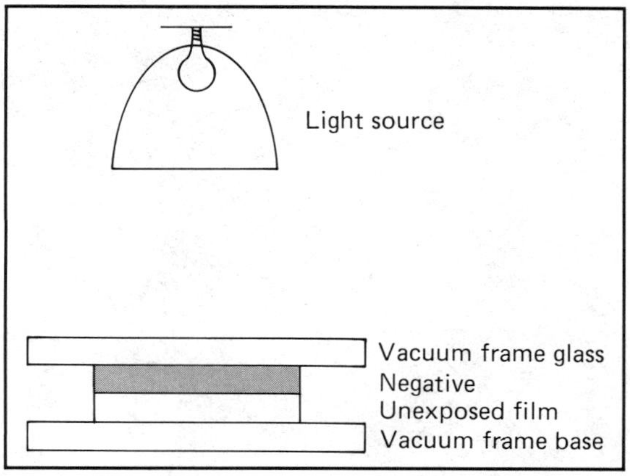

Figure 9.1. Diagram of original and new film orientation for contacting process.

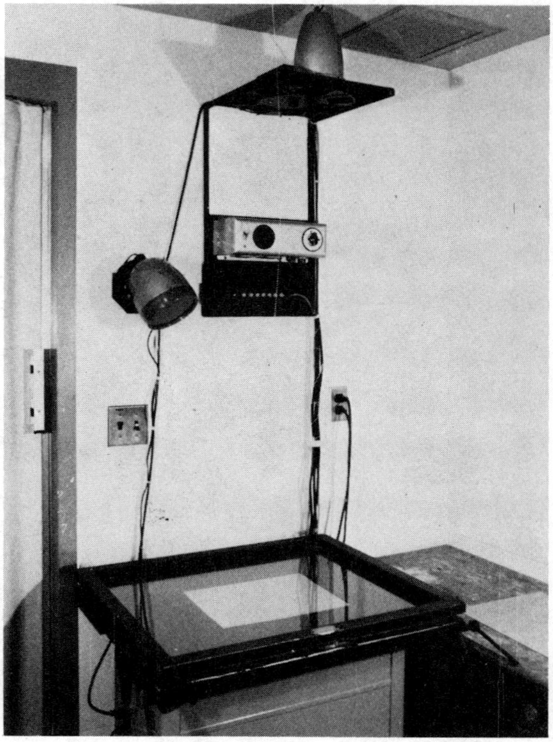

Figure 9.2. Contact area in a shop. Shown are vacuum frame, point source light, timer, filter turret, and safelight.

Figure 9.3. Close-up of point source light used in contacting work.

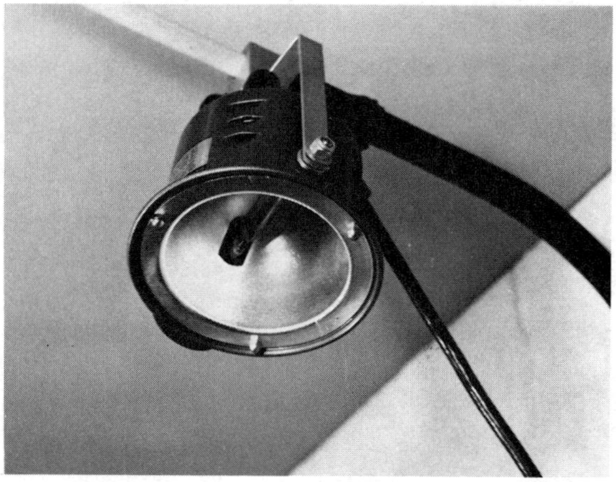

Figure 9.4. Quartz light used in contacting procedures.

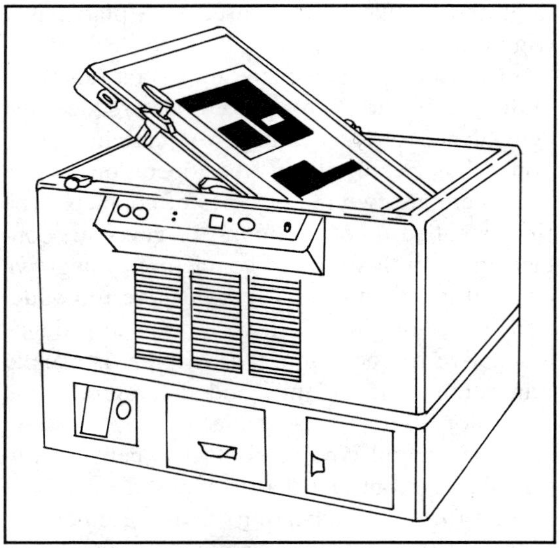

Figure 9.5. Flip-top platemaker used for contacting procedures. (Kimberly Conover-Loar)

• The Contacting Facility and Equipment

This section provides a brief review of some information you have covered in chapter 1. It is important that necessary equipment be located and the work area set up properly.

Some shops have a separate area designated as the contact room. Other shops use a small portion of the darkroom as the contacting area. Since the introduction of so-called room light contacting and duplicating materials, many shops keep their darkroom contacting area and also have another contacting area in the platemaking room where the work can be performed under yellow fluorescent lamps.

The room light, or daylight, working materials are processed just like regular emulsion films. Most of these materials can be processed in regular photographic chemistry as well as in the rapid access chemistry. Read the processing instructions that are packaged with the film.

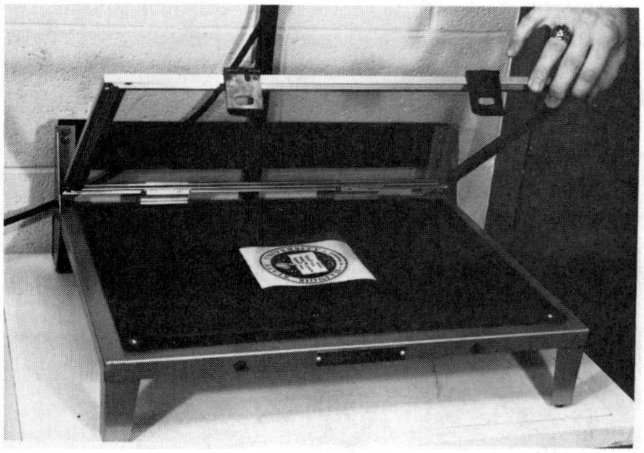

Figure 9.6. Glass-top vacuum frame.

Figure 9.7. Open-face vacuum frame.

For orthochromatic film and high-speed duplicating materials, which require a red 1A safelight, you will need either a glass-top vacuum contact frame (figure 9.6) or an open-face vacuum contact frame (figure 9.7), a point source light and its controls, and a timer. The walls around the vacuum frame should be dark so they will not reflect light and cause exposure problems. For the room light contacting and duplicating materials, a platemaker vacuum frame with an intense light source will be necessary.

For all contacting work, it is important that accurate voltage runs to the contacting lamp. The commercially available contacting lamps have voltage control. The standard three-terminal units have an 8-, 16-, and 20-volt tap (figure 9.8). Tap refers to number settings that rotate light openings. There is also a 6-tap unit light that is voltage controlled (figure 9.8). Its taps are for 4, 8, 16, 20, and 24 volts. The contact lamps are usually set 40 inches from the vacuum frame. Normally, as voltage is increased, so too is light intensity.

One of the worst enemies in contacting is dust because film attracts dust. To help eliminate dust, some companies use a static removal unit (figure 9.9). Passing film through this unit

(a)

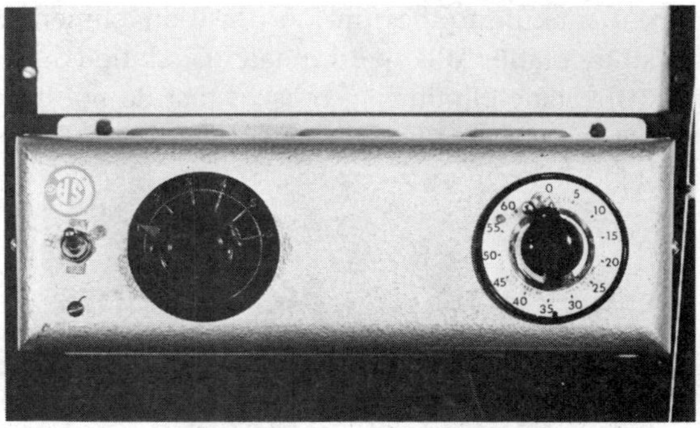

(b)

Figure 9.8. Voltage control units. (a) A three-volt tap for point source light shown with a timer. (b) A six-volt tap for point source light and timer.

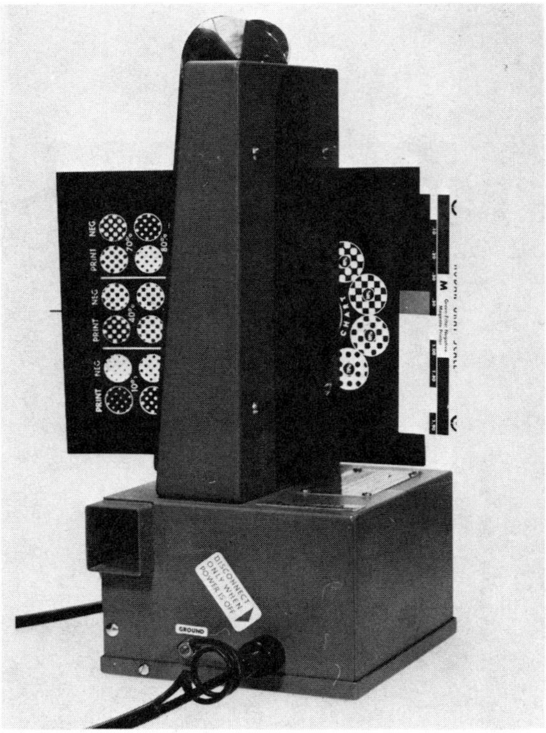

Figure 9.9. Power-driven static removal unit for film.

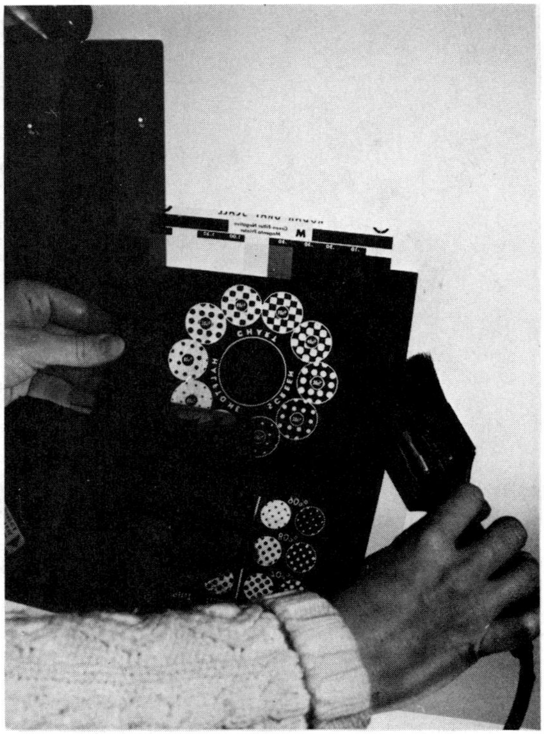

Figure 9.10. Static removal brush attached to power unit.

will eliminate static electricity, preventing dust from sticking to the film. A brush attachment is also available to help eliminate the static (figure 9.10). Static-eliminating brushes that do not have electrical connections are also available (figure 9.11).

• Contacting Procedures

Original and Film Orientations

The first procedure with which the contacting operator must be familiar is how to place the original and the unexposed film in the contact frame. In contacting, the operator has three choices of film/original orientation:

- **E to E**—This means emulsion to emulsion. The emulsion of the original is against the emulsion of the unexposed film or paper (figure 9.12).
- **B to E**—This means base of the original to the emulsion of the unexposed film (figure 9.13).
- **E to B**—This means the emulsion of the original to the base of the unexposed film (figure 9.14).

If the original is a camera-exposed negative, when the emulsion side of the film is held up, the viewer sees it as a wrong-reading negative.

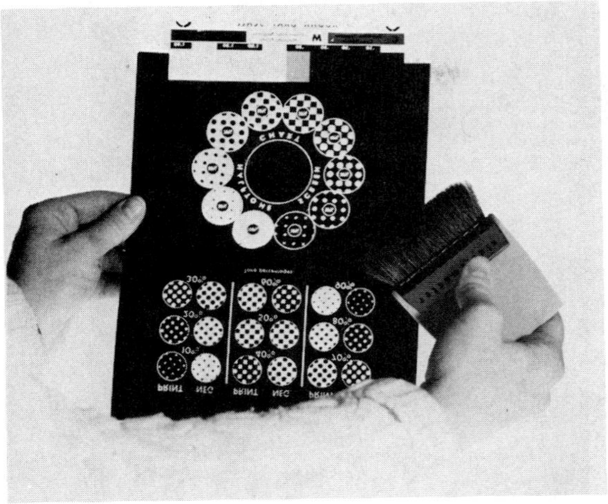

Figure 9.11. Nonelectrical static removal brush.

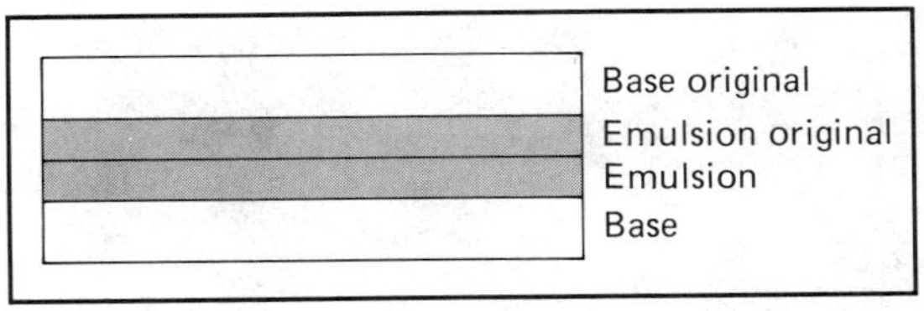

Figure 9.12. Emulsion-to-emulsion (E to E) orientation for contacts.

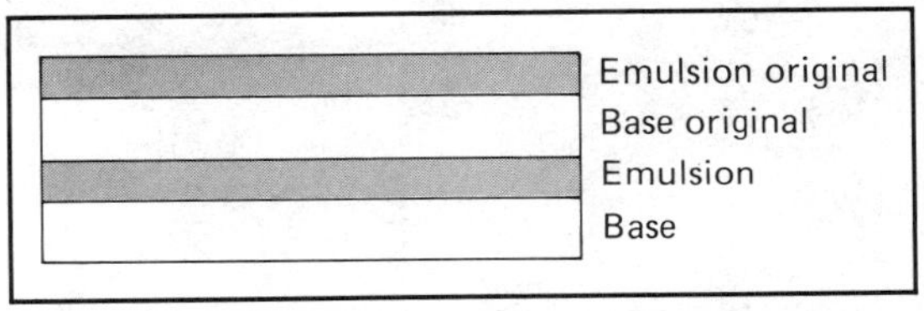

Figure 9.13. Base of original to emulsion (B to E) of unexposed material.

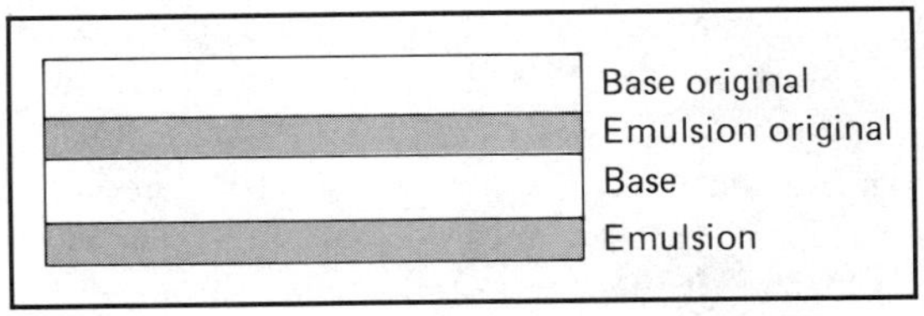

Figure 9.14. Emulsion of original to base (E to B) of unexposed material.

If the film is turned over and viewed through the base side, it reads correctly. A contact negative made by an E-to-E exposure would give a right-reading positive when viewed through the emulsion side. This is an important understanding.

The right-reading and the wrong-reading orientation of a negative or positive is important to the graphic arts worker. If the last product of the contacting procedure is to be used in platemaking for offset, the negative or positive must read correctly when viewed through the base. This is necessary to make a good printing plate.

Determining Basic Exposure

For this first example of contacting, the original will be a contact control negative target (figure 9.15). The result will be a film positive. The developing procedure for contacting work on ortho-type film is identical to the developing procedure used with a line or halftone exposure. As with any film exposure operation, it is necessary to start by determining a basic exposure time for the film being used.

Most film manufacturers have contact targets that can be used to establish contact and duplicating exposure times. You must remember that each film type, whether contacting or duplicating, must have a basic exposure test, which can be performed as follows:

- Clean glass and frame.
- Place a matte black backing sheet in the contact frame.
- Select the desired film (in this example use a sheet of litho film), and place it on the matte sheet in the frame, emulsion up.

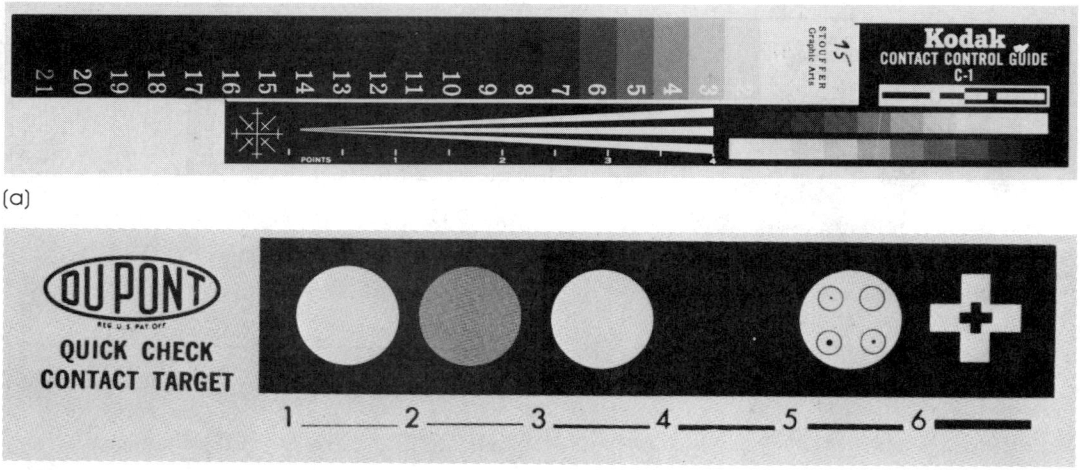

(a)

(b)

Figure 9.15. Examples of control strips. (a) A Stouffer gray scale and a Kodak contact control guide. (b) A DuPont contact control target.

- Place the target over film, emulsion down, and close frame. Use an E-to-E orientation.
- Start the vacuum pump and wait for draw-down.
- Set the timer and expose for five seconds, tap 1.
- Turn off the pump and move the target for second exposure. Repeat steps 5 and 6 until four exposures are on film: Exposure 1, five seconds; exposure 2, ten seconds; exposure 3, fifteen seconds; exposure 4, twenty seconds.
- Process the film.
- After drying, evaluate your results to determine best exposure time.

When evaluating for the best exposure, identify the target with the following characteristics:

- Dot-for-dot reproduction;
- Line thickness on positive the same as opening on the negative;
- Dense black emulsion.

Next, look at the gray scale of the target on the best reproduction. The last solid step becomes the target for all subsequent exposures. For all production work include a transparent gray scale, just as you did for the line negatives, as a quality control device. With the best exposure time established, you should be ready to make production contacts.

Each type of film material you use will need a separate exposure test. It will also be necessary to make an exposure test for each contact orientation—E to E, B to E, and E to B. These orientations require different exposures.

If the tests gave an exposure time that was less than ten seconds on tap 1, it will be necessary to use a #96 ND filter with the point source light. Times less than ten seconds for a contact exposure can cause accuracy errors and give unpredictable results. The table on page 131 will help you select an ND filter to extend your exposure time.

If a 0.60, #96 ND filter were placed over the light source, when the exposure was found to be ten seconds, multiply $10 \times 4 = 40$ seconds to find the new exposure time.

Filter #96 ND	Time extended
0.10 units	1.25 × exposure time
0.20	1.60 × exposure time
0.30	2 × exposure time
0.60	4 × exposure time
1	10 × exposure time

Making a Production Contact

Make a contact positive from a camera-produced negative using the following steps:

- Check the glass and vacuum frame (clean if necessary).
- With the safelight on, select the proper film and place it on the matte black backing sheet in the vacuum frame, emulsion up.
- Place the negative on unexposed film, B to E, with the gray scale in a border area.
- Close the frame, turn on the vacuum pump, and wait for drawdown.
- Set the timer and light tap for the necessary exposure and make the exposure.
- Process the film, watching for the desired gray scale step.
- Evaluate after film is dry.

• Making a Duplicate

The darkroom worker is often called upon to make duplicate negatives and positives (called **dupes**) for jobs that will run multiple copies on a large press sheet (figure 9.16). One way of handling this job would be to make a contact positive and then, from that, to make extra negatives. Another way is through the use of duplicating film that gives negatives from negatives. The photographer will have to go through the testing procedure for setting a basic exposure time since this is a new material.

Emulsion orientation is also a factor to be considered in the duping operation. The major difference is the material being used and the type of product desired. Duplicating film has the density (darkness) built into the emulsion. Exposure removes density in duplicating. It is important to remember in duping that less exposure makes a darker end product; more exposure gives a lighter (less dense) end product. This is just the opposite reaction of regular line film.

Figure 9.16. Multiple identical images on a single press sheet. The images are the back side of a deck of playing cards.

Processing of duplicating film is exactly the same as the processing of regular film and requires the same careful handling that line film requires.

If a point source light is used for exposing the duplicating film, then a high-speed duplicating film will be necessary. Regular-speed duplicating film requires a stronger light source like a 650- to 1,000-watt quartz lamp. Be sure to test for proper exposure with each different film used.

• Contact Proofs on Paper-Base Material

Another important function in contacting is making proofs. One type of proof is a contact print made on photographic paper. Both the printer and the customer can see exactly what the job will look like before making a printing plate and running the job.

While regular photographic print paper can be used for the proofs, a long drying time is needed. One of the quickest methods for making these contact proofs is with the use of **photo-stabilization paper**. The paper is exposed just the same as when making film contacts. Again, for best results when using any material for the first time, test for the basic exposure, using the following procedures:

- Be sure the vacuum frame and glass are clean.
- Place the paper, emulsion up, on the matte black backing paper in the contact frame.
- Place the negative over the paper in E-to-E orientation. Close the frame, turn on the vacuum, and wait for drawdown.
- Set the timer and tap and make the exposure.
- Remove the negative and process the exposed stabilization paper (see chapter 5).

Photostabilization paper is a silver-sensitized material that has the developer chemistry built into the emulsion of the paper. A specialized processor is used to develop (activate the developer) and then to stabilize or stop the developing action (figure 9.17). The processor contains two chemical solutions: an activator to cause development to occur and a stabilizer to stop the development and partially fix the print. Once processed, it can be viewed in room light. The paper will be good for several weeks without further fixing. If permanence is required, the print should be placed in a regular fixing bath, washed, and dried.

These two materials were offered as typical examples of the wide variety of other proof materials.

• Making Spreads and Chokes

While the proper name for this procedure is **spreads and chokes**, some workers call the operation making "fatties and skinnies." The pro-

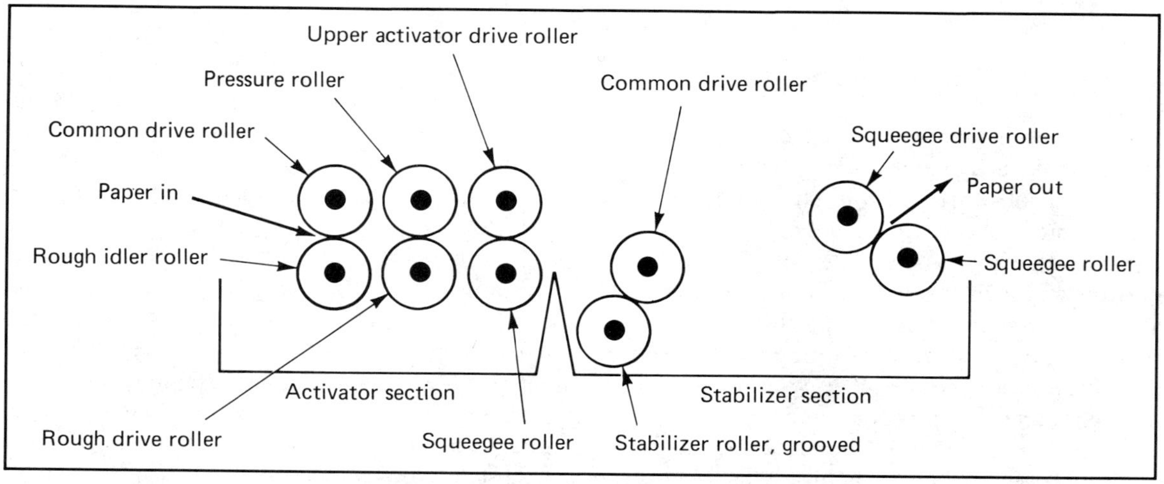

Figure 9.17. Schematic diagram of the stabilization processor.

Figure 9.18. Outline letters. The letters can be produced by the spread and choke technique.

cess is used to produce photographically a thicker or thinner line image than the original. Spreads, or thicker lines, are made from negative originals. Chokes, or thinner lines, are made from positive originals. The technique is used in color printing to make the letters fit more perfectly over the background color. Another use is for the creation of outline letters (figure 9.18).

The most effective method of making a spread or choke is with the use of spacers (figure 9.19). The evaluation of the amount of spread or choke can be determined by the use of the spread and choke target (figure 9.20).

Figures 9.21 through 9.26 illustrate the process of making outline letters. Figure 9.21 is the original negative. Beginning with the original negative, make a same-size positive (figure 9.22). You now have a negative and a positive with equal images. To make a spread, use a duplicating film (figure 9.23). Start with a negative and spacers, and the duplicating film gives a new image that is more open or spread.

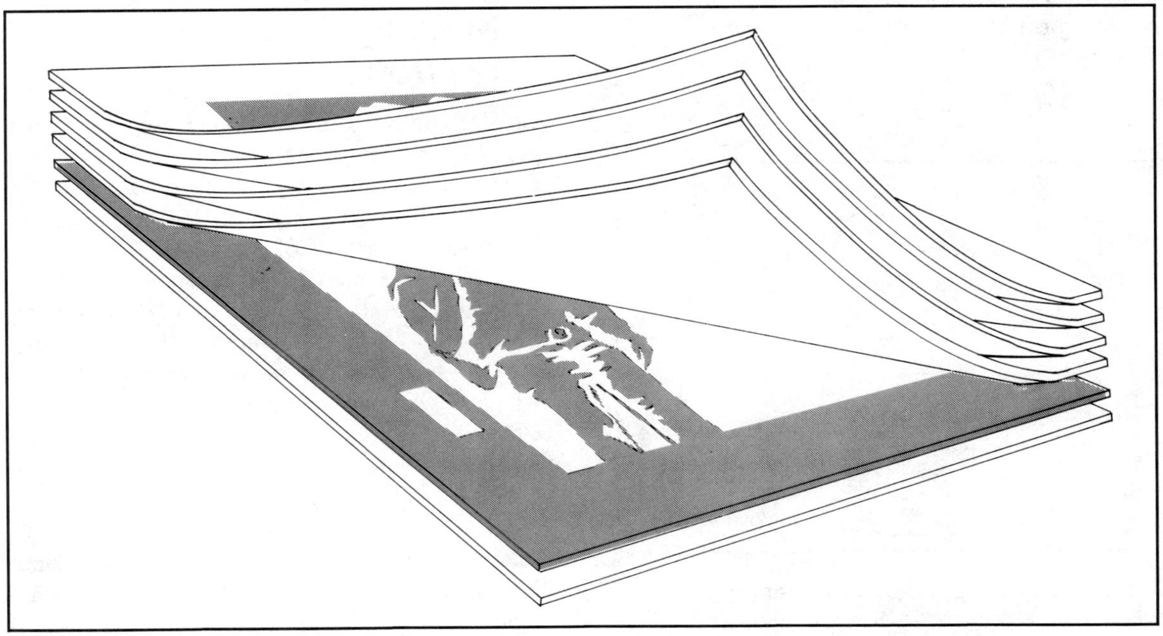

Figure 9.19. Spacers placed between the negative and the positive.

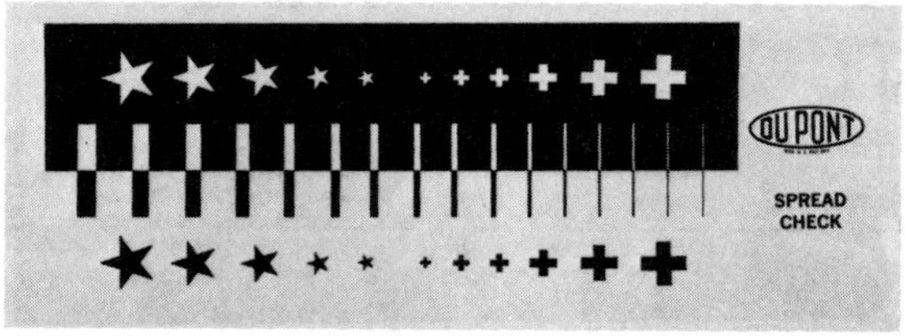

Figure 9.20. DuPont spread check target.

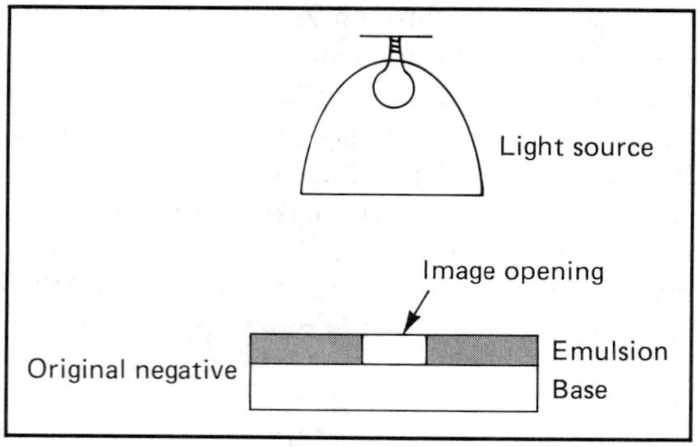

Figure 9.21. Diagram of a film negative showing emulsion and base layers.

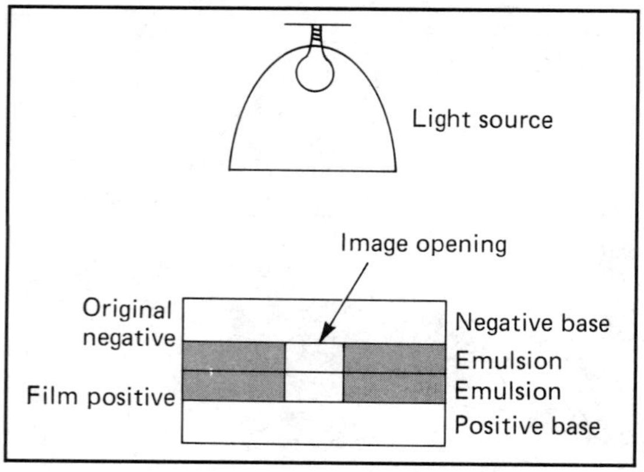

Figure 9.22. Diagram of film orientation when making a same-size positive using contact film.

To make a choke, use the positive that was made as a same-size positive of your original negative. Here again you will use duplicating film. You have the original positive, spacers, and duplicating film (figure 9.24). The product will be a new positive with a smaller, or choke, image.

For a final product of outline letters that will appear as positive images, you will use the following setup. Use the choke positive and a piece of contact or regular ortho film, no spacers (figure 9.25). The end product will be outline letters that are black on clear film—that is, positive images.

If you prefer to have the end product be a negative of the outline letters, use the following setup. Use the spread negative and the choke positive, no spacers, and the new film to be exposed should be a piece of duplicating film (figure 9.26). The end product will be a negative image of the outline letters.

• Contacts and Dupes for Making Hard-Dot Halftones

Soft-dot and **hard-dot** halftones are expressions often heard when working in a graphic arts camera area. On the camera, halftone dots are formed by light passing through the halftone contact screen to the surface of the film. The dot produced by the screen has a ghost or fringe area around it. This dot is called a first generation dot or soft dot. When the camera halftone negative is either contacted or duped, the reproduction will have a hard dot without the ghost area (figure 9.27).

If the photographer is required to produce several duplicate halftone negatives from an original, it is best to make a dupe and then to reproduce the required copies from the first dupe. The hard-dot dupe will make each additional negative an exact duplicate, providing careful exposure and processing procedures are used.

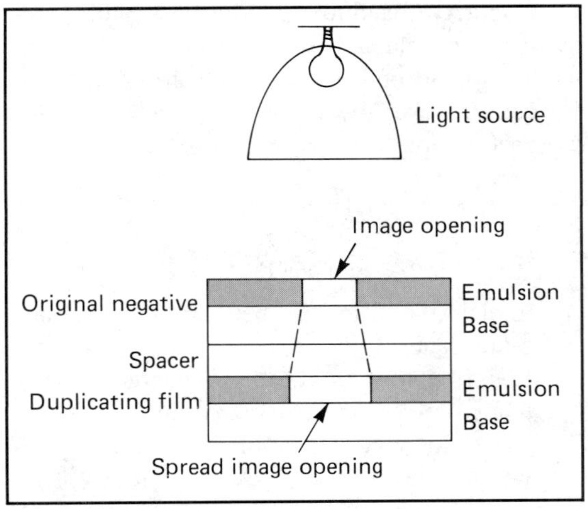

Figure 9.23. Diagram of film orientation and use of spacers when making a spread with duplicating film.

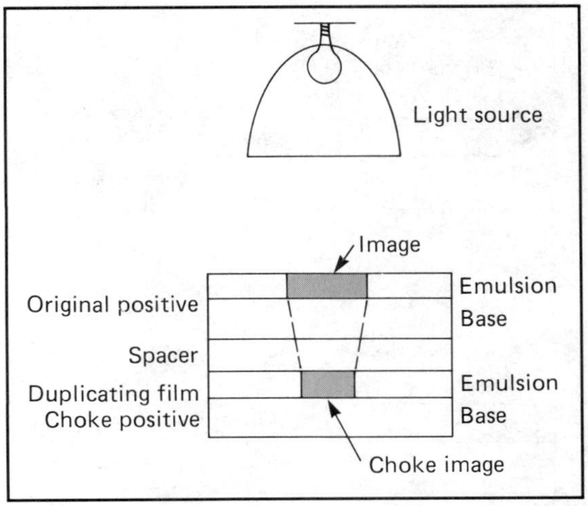

Figure 9.24. Diagram of film orientation and use of spacers when making a choke positive with duplicating film.

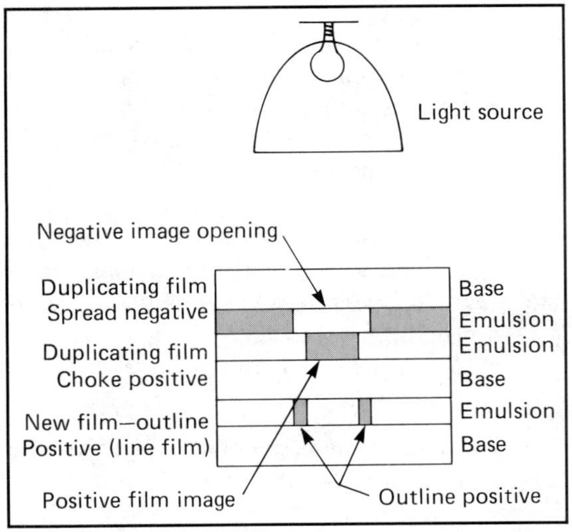

Figure 9.25. Diagram of film orientation when making positive outline letters.

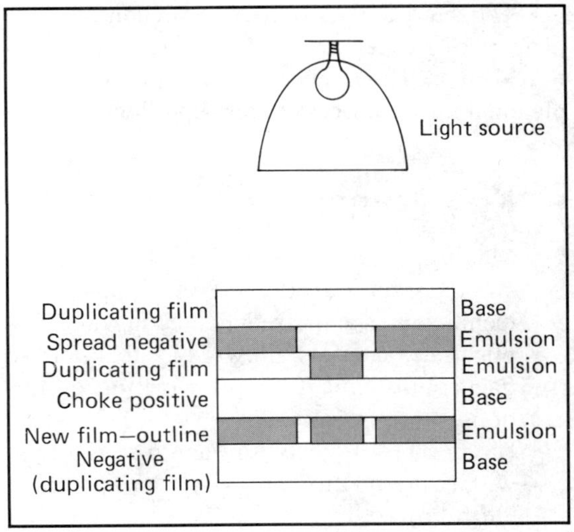

Figure 9.26. Diagram of film orientation when making negative outline letters.

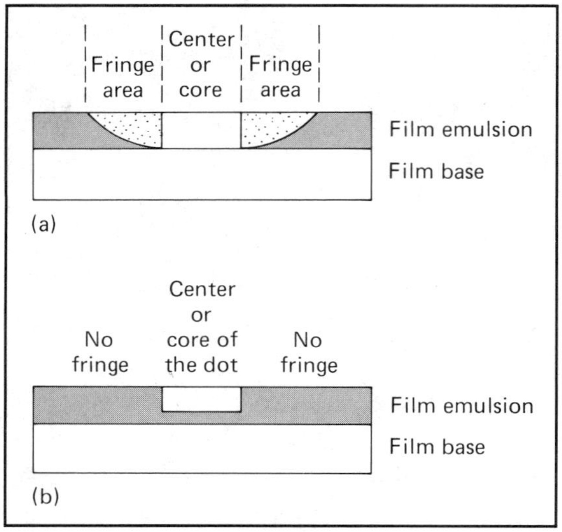

Figure 9.27. Halftone dots. (a) The soft dot created in the camera. (b) The hard dot as it appears in a film contact.

The hard-dot halftone is excellent for the platemaking operation. Most shops use only hard-dot halftone negatives or positives for platemaking in process color reproduction.

• Key Points

- Making contacts and dupes (duplicates) is an important function of the graphic arts technician; specialized contacting and duplicating materials allow exposures both in darkrooms and daylight working conditions.
- Basic exposure tests for each material used will assure quality jobs if standard practices are followed.
- Contact procedures can be used with film-base and paper-base materials.
- To spread and to choke are important procedures used by the contact technician for special applications.

• Review Questions

1. Explain the difference between a contact and a duplicate.
2. List five jobs in the graphic arts industry that involve contacts and/or duplicates.
3. How do you determine right-reading or wrong-reading negatives or positives?
4. Explain what each of the following expressions means: E to E, B to E, and E to B.
5. Describe the process for making a spread and a choke.

• Activities

1. Using the contact control target available in your shop, establish the basic exposure time for making a contact reproduction.
2. Using the same target, establish the basic exposure time for making a duplicate.
3. Using a word set in boldface letters as copy, make the word appear as outline letters using the spread and choke procedure.
4. Make a camera halftone negative to use as an original.
   a. Make a contact film positive.
   b. Make a duplicate negative.

Examine both of these reproductions to see the hard dots compared to the original camera negative.

Chapter 10

Diffusion Transfer

• Objectives

In this chapter you will cover:

- Basic diffusion transfer procedures.

After reading the chapter you should be able to:

- Define diffusion transfer and explain four uses of the process,
- Explain the exposing and processing of diffusion transfer materials,
- Prepare diffusion transfer copy from reflection originals,
- Prepare diffusion transfer prescreened prints,
- Prepare diffusion transfer transparencies,
- Prepare diffusion transfer reflex prints,
- Prepare diffusion transfer special effect prints.

• Introduction

Diffusion transfer, photomechanical transfer, and PMT are names commonly heard in the trade. Whatever it is called, the process permits a camera operator to start with a positive image, make a single exposure, and finish with a positive image. Through the use of the camera, the new image can be the same size, larger, or smaller than the original image (figure 10.1).

The diffusion transfer requires some of the same camera and contacting skills that were covered in previous chapters. The process is a technique used to photograph copy and transfer the image to another carrier. The carrier can be an opaque sheet of paper (made like a piece of photographic paper) or a clear sheet of transparent film. This process also has printing plates that will receive the image so you can go directly to the offset press and print copies. A discussion

Figure 10.1. Size change using PMT process. (a) Original copy, (b) reduction, and (c) enlargement.

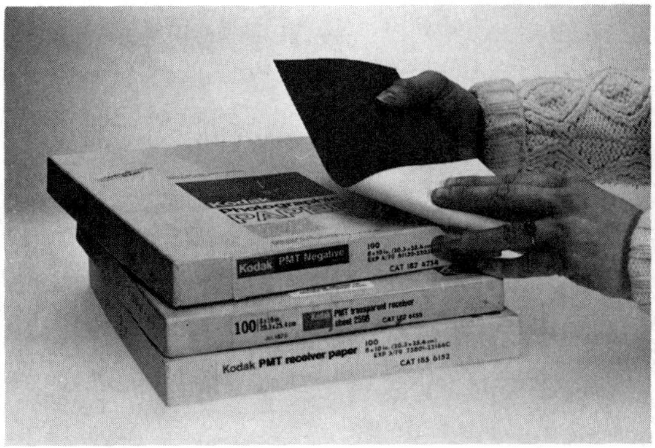

Figure 10.2. PMT negative material. The emulsion side of this material is dark; the base side is light.

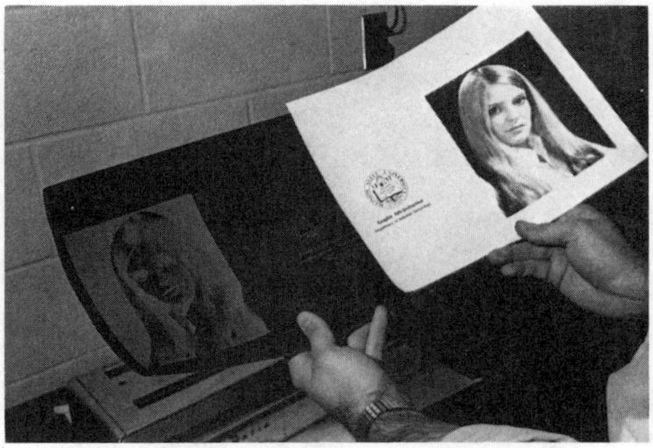

Figure 10.3. Example of image areas on negative and receiver sheet.

of printing plates, however, is beyond the purpose of this book.

Before discussing the operations involved with this process, we need some information on the materials that will be necessary. The first material is the negative paper (figure 10.2). This is a paper material coated with a light-sensitive emulsion. The emulsion side is the dark side. When light strikes the negative material from the white or nonimage area of the copy, the emulsion hardens. The black, or image areas, of the copy do not reflect light, and these areas of the emulsion on the negative paper remain soft. In figure 10.3 the soft areas, or image areas, will transfer to the receiver (using a special chemical bath and processor).

The receiver sheets can be a paper-based material or a piece of transparent film. Both the paper and the film have a chemically coated side that receives the image transfer from the negative paper. The paper receiver has diagonal stripes on the noncoated side. The transparent material is notched in the upper right-hand corner, indicating that the receiving side is toward you (figure 10.4). The other items necessary are a processor and the transfer chemistry (figure 10.5).

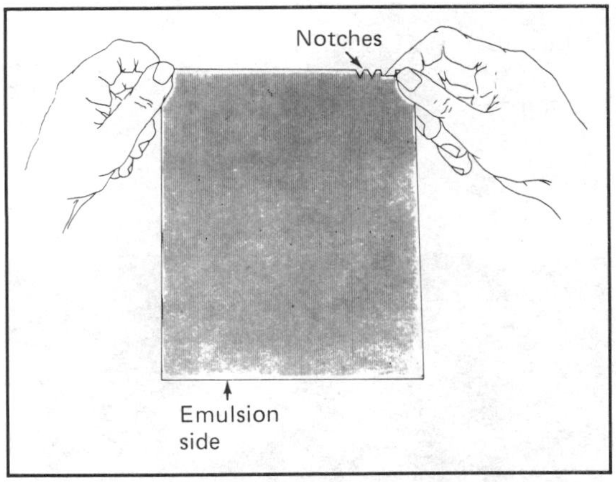

Figure 10.4. Emulsion side of transparent receiver sheet. The emulsion of the material is facing you when the notch is in the upper right corner. However, many new materials are image receptive on both sides. (Kimberly Conover-Loar)

To review briefly the processing steps, the copy is exposed to the negative material in a camera or contact frame. The receiver and the exposed negative material are fed emulsion to emulsion into the processor that is filled with the chemistry. The transfer is made and the op-

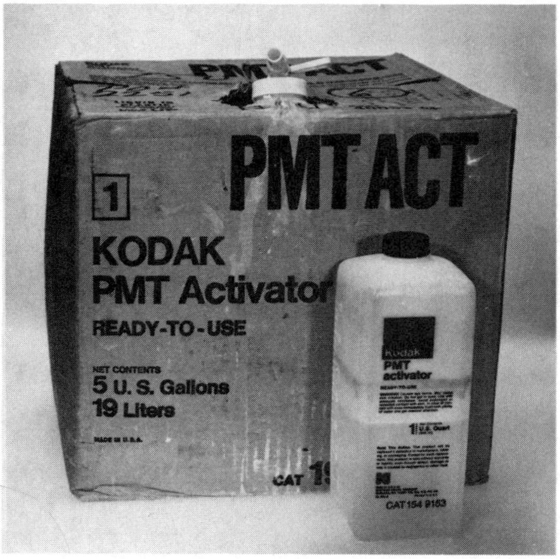

Figure 10.5. PMT activator chemistry. The chemistry is available in quart and five-gallon containers.

Figure 10.6. Camera operator separates negative and receiver sheet.

erator has a new print of the original after separating the negative from the receiver (figure 10.6).

Remember that reflected light from the nonimage areas of the copy (white) passes through the lens and reaches the negative paper. The sheet, then, is exposed in nonimage areas and unexposed in the image areas. When the sheets are passed through the activator solution, a chemical shield, or mask, is formed over the exposed area. This masking leaves the unexposed emulsion of the negative (image area of the original) free to transfer to the receiver sheet.

There are a number of advantages to the diffusion transfer process. The other methods of making a positive image from a positive original require more operator time and the use of more expensive materials. Shop owners like the ease of performing the operations and the saving of operator time.

Graphic arts photographers use diffusion transfer for many different operations such as the following:

- Preparing camera-ready copy (same size, enlarged, or reduced);
- Prescreening halftones for publication work;
- Proofing camera-ready copy;
- Preparing special effects copy;
- Preparing transparent positives for diazo proofing, instructional overheads, screen printing stencil positives, and positive working offset plates.

Diffusion transfer performs another important function in copy preparation. Many times the printer will receive a variety of elements (copy) that must be combined to produce the printed job. Some copy might be good black-and-white images while others are old, stained, or in a variety of colors. The camera operator can expose these pieces to diffusion transfer materials that have the ability to make good new copy. The various elements are then combined to make satisfactory camera-ready copy. The new elements all have the same density and range and help the printer to produce a job of acceptable quality.

The materials, supplies, and the diffusion transfer processors are available from graphic arts supply dealers. The shop should have as a part of its regular equipment a process camera, a vacuum printing frame, darkroom, sinks, and safelight equipment.

It is important to look at the procedures in detail to perform the operations for this process.

• Preparing Reflection Art from Originals

Line copy for the diffusion transfer process should have the same qualities as the copy used when making a line negative. To make a diffusion transfer print using the process camera, the operator should have diffusion transfer negative material, receiver paper, activator chemistry, and the processor unit and should use the following procedures:

1. Place the copy in the center of the copyboard.

2. Set camera controls for size and exposure time (see chapter 7 for a review of camera operation).

3. Set f/stop to the desired reading for the percentage of desired reproduction size. Because light sources on cameras differ and the light distances from copyboard also differ, exact times are difficult to specify. For a first try, use f/22 with an exposure between eight and twelve seconds.

Remember, in this process we start with positive copy and will end up also with a positive image. This means that the operation will have to be different than preparing a negative in terms of exposure times. More exposure in this process will cause the final print to be lighter. Less exposure will cause the print to be darker. This thinking is especially important if the copy is dirty and if some density is picked up in the nonimage areas (this will require more exposure). If, however, the density is poor in the image area, then less exposure is needed to darken the image.

Figure 10.7. Feeding negative and receiver sheet into processor. Notice that the negative (dark side up) is about 1/4 inch forward of the receiver sheet. The two sheets will line up after they go through the processor.

4. Center the negative material on the vacuum back, emulsion side (dark side) toward the lens, close the camera back, and make the exposure.

5. Hold the exposed negative material emulsion up, then place the receiver sheet, chemically treated side down, against the negative (look for the manufacturer's mark indicating the nontreated side).

Before feeding the material into the processor, make sure the negative material is approximately one-quarter inch ahead of the receiver material. This allows for the difference in travel distance of the two sheets through the processor (figure 10.7). The sheets will come out of the processor almost even.

Notice the diagram of the processor (figure 10.8). A separator blade separates the sheets as they are fed into and travel through the processor. The negative material is below and the receiver material is above the separator. The time in the chemistry is controlled by the machine.

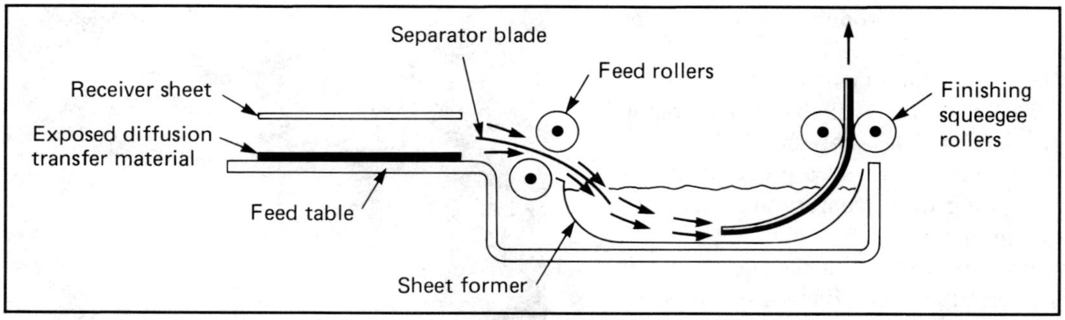

Figure 10.8. Diagram of PMT processor.

6. The two sheets are squeezed together by the feed-out rollers. The sheets should remain together for thirty seconds before they are peeled apart.

At this stage of the process, the unexposed, soft image areas are transferred to the receiver sheet. The hardened nonimage areas do not transfer. After the negative and receiver have been separated, the negative material can be discarded.

Some processor units have register devices so the sheets (negative and receiver) always go through the processor at precisely the same place. If you have one of these processors, you can add material to any receiver sheet (that already carries an image). This is done by using a second negative and then passing the new negative and the old receiver sheet back through the processor. This can be repeated several times, always using a new negative but reusing the receiver. Remember to wait for thirty seconds before separating the two sheets.

• Screening Copy for Prescreened Prints

As was suggested in the earlier discussion of the diffusion transfer process, one of the products is the prescreening of halftones. A **prescreened halftone** is a positive halftone print on a special sheet of paper rather than on a transparent piece of film. The prescreened halftone print can be pasted up with line copy to make up the total page of a publication. This will allow the operator to make a single line negative of the total page and to save time in the negative assembly (stripping) process.

To make a diffusion transfer halftone, the copy should be a photograph with a good contrast range. It is possible, of course, to make a prescreened diffusion transfer halftone from a less than perfect photograph, but as with regular halftone procedures, it requires more skill on the part of the camera operator.

For the halftone process, a diffusion transfer halftone screen is needed in addition to the materials that were used in making the reflection line print. The diffusion transfer screen has been manufactured to produce a flatter-looking halftone than when using film. This is a normal procedure because the diffusion transfer halftone print will gain contrast when it is rephotographed as line copy. Diffusion transfer prescreen halftone prints should be made so no further enlargement or reduction will be necessary. Use the following procedures:

- Center the photograph in the copyboard, close the board, and face it toward the lens.
- Set camera controls for the desired size and exposure time.

- Adjust f/stop for the proper setting.

In adjusting the f/stop, remember that the diffusion transfer halftone exposure will require approximately seven to eight times the exposure of the normal line diffusion transfer exposure. A halftone screen is like a filter. It adds density through which the light must pass to reach the sensitized emulsion of the diffusion transfer negative material. If f/22 for eight-second exposure produced a good line reflecting print, then f/22 for sixty seconds should make a good halftone print. You can shorten the exposure time by opening your aperture to f/16 and exposing for thirty seconds (see chapter 2 for a discussion on this topic). This takes care of the main exposure. A flash exposure of approximately ten seconds should give a good dot in the shadow area of the photograph.

It will be necessary to experiment to determine the best times for both the main and the flash exposures. The flash is made with the same lamp used in making a film halftone flash exposure.

Low-contrast photos will require less flash exposure than the more contrasting photos.

- Place the diffusion transfer negative paper, emulsion side up, on the camera back.
- Cover the negative paper with a diffusion transfer halftone contact screen.
- Turn on the vacuum and roll out any air bubbles.
- Make the main and flash exposures.
- Turn off the vacuum. Carefully remove the screen and place it back in the protective folder.
- Place the negative paper in contact with the receiver paper. Feed the sandwich through the processor. After thirty seconds, peel the sheets apart.
- Evaluate the prescreened halftone for both highlight and shadow dot sizes. The desired size depends upon the printing process to be used. For lithography, a highlight dot of around 12 percent and a shadow dot of 85 percent would be acceptable.

• Producing Transparencies

Quite often a job requires a positive transparency instead of a positive image on a piece of paper. The procedures of producing the transparency print are identical to the diffusion transfer line and halftone procedures just discussed. The major difference is in the type of receiver sheet used. The transparent receiver material is available from the manufacturer or local film distributor. While the transparent sheet looks like a clear sheet of plastic, it is coated on one side with an emulsion to receive the image from the negative during the processing step. Kodak's clear transparent receiver is notched so that when the notch is in the upper right-hand corner, the coated receiver side is facing you (figure 10.4). Agfa-Gavaert's transparent receiver is not notched, and you can use either side.

The transparencies make excellent positives for overheads (visual aids) and making photographic screen printing stencils. They can also be used for lateral reverses. A lateral reversal is a mirror image used in several processes like some photo-engraving processes.

When processing the transparent receiver, a very dense black image can be obtained if the separating of the receiver from the negative material is delayed for sixty seconds. Try ninety seconds instead of the thirty seconds used with the paper receiver.

The activator bath usually leaves a scum (residue) on the transparent receiver. This unwanted material can be removed by washing the transparent receiver in a water rinse. It should then be hung to dry.

• Transfer Prints by Reflex

The making of transfer prints by reflex is a method for making positive copies from positive originals not with a process camera but with a contact-exposing device. The major limitation of this process is that prints can be produced that are only the same size as the original print.

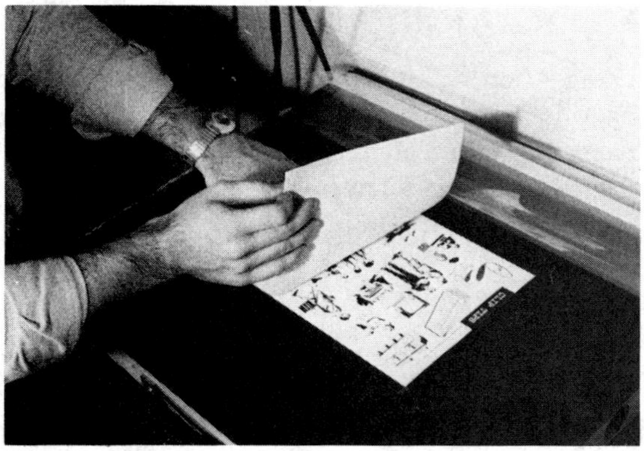

Figure 10.9. Making reflex print. PMT reflex negative material is placed over copy on vacuum frame.

The original is placed face up on a vacuum contact frame. A piece of reflex negative diffusion transfer paper is placed, emulsion down, over the original (emulsion of the transfer sheet against the image on the original). The light source should be 1,000-watt quartz light at approximately 3 1/2 feet from the vacuum frame. Light passes through the negative sheet and is reflected back to the negative material that is on top of the copy. The black image of the original absorbs the light and none is reflected. The negative material is hardened where the light is reflected back from the nonimage area. The negative material remains soft where the light was absorbed on the original, allowing the emulsion to transfer to the receiver sheet.

The following step-by-step method in making a reflex print is easy to use:

- The copy is placed in the vacuum contact frame, image toward the light.
- Place a piece of diffusion transfer reflex paper on the copy, emulsion down (figure 10.9).
- Turn on the vacuum pump and wait for a good contact.
- Expose for approximately thirty seconds. Use a 1,000-watt quartz-iodine bulb at 3 1/2 feet from the frame.
- The exposed reflex negative material and the receiver sheet are held together with the negative material on the bottom and the receiver material on the top. The negative material should be ahead of receiver by approximately 3/8 inch (just as we did with the camera material in the previous section).
- Feed the sheets into the processor with the negative material on one side of the separator and the receiver on the other side.
- After the sheets come out of the processor, keep them together for thirty seconds before separating.

If a transparent receiver is used, be sure the coated receiver side is toward the negative material emulsion and that the two sheets are not separated for ninety seconds.

• Special Techniques with Transfer Materials

Several special effects techniques are possible with the use of diffusion transfer materials. For example, a **ghost halftone** is a very light halftone that appears as a ghost, or phantom, image under a type message (figure 10.10). It is created with a regular main exposure, but the flash exposure is about three times the normal flash exposure. This makes the shadow (black) areas of the photo appear gray. The dark type on this example was placed on the receiver sheet by using a second negative exposure of the type and then feeding the receiver, which already had the halftone image, back through the processor.

There are two possibilities for **line and tint combinations**. In one we can have a dark image with a tint background (figure 10.11). In the second example we can have a clear background with a tinted image (figure 10.12). Both can make effective illustrations for the printing processes. Procedures for making a tint background with a solid image are as follows:

Figure 10.10. Example of ghost halftone. Type appears over a light image of the picture.

Figure 10.11. Tint and line image combination. The background is a tint, the image solid.

Figure 10.12. Tint image on clear background.

- Center the line copy in the copyboard.
- Adjust the camera copyboard, lensboard, and aperture control for size. Set the timer for exposure for a normal line exposure.
- Center the diffusion transfer negative material on the vacuum back. Select a screen tint (in this example, a 40 percent tint that will create a 60 percent dot on the receiver), and place it over the negative material just as you would a halftone screen. Turn on the vacuum and roll out any air bubbles that might be trapped between the screen and the negative.
- Make a normal line exposure.
- Process the negative material and receiver sheet through the processor.
- After the thirty-second waiting period, separate the negative from the receiver.

Procedures for making a clear background, tinted image are as follows:

- Center the line copy in the copyboard.
- Adjust the camera for size, f/stop, and normal line exposure.
- Center the diffusion transfer negative material on the vacuum back.
- Make a normal line exposure, but leave the vacuum on so the negative material stays in place after the exposure. Do not move the negative sheet.
- Go to copyboard and place a large white sheet of paper over the copy.
- Open the vacuum back (with the vacuum still on), place a tint screen (in this example, a 40 percent tint) over the negative material, and remove any air bubbles.
- Close the camera back and make a second exposure (again a normal exposure time).
- Process and then separate in the normal manner.

• Posterization

Posterization is the process of creating a special effects picture from a regular continuous-tone photograph. It is possible to make an image with many tones or shades of gray appear to have only two, three, or even only four tones. A simple line conversion (like a line negative) is an example of a two-tone posterization—all you see is either the image (ink as one tone) or clear

(a)

Figure 10.13. (a) Three-tone posterization, (b) original copy.

(b)

open space (the color of the paper as the second tone). Three- and four-tone posterizations require several steps beyond line procedures.

The topic of photoposterization is discussed in detail in chapter 11. We suggest that you cover that information before attempting the following procedures for posterization with diffusion transfer materials.

Three-Tone Posterization

Three-tone posterization reduces the various gray tones in a photo to three tones—black (the ink), gray (a tint), and white (the paper) (figure 10.13). A posterization is made by the following steps:

- Center the continuous-tone original on the camera copyboard.
- Adjust the camera controls for the required size.
- Center the diffusion transfer negative material on the vacuum back.
- Make a normal line exposure to record the highlight areas in the photo. Leave vacuum on and do not move the negative.
- Cover the negative material with a screen tint (the example shows a 40 percent tint), and be sure it is in perfect contact with the negative diffusion transfer paper.
- Close the camera back and make a second exposure with the tint in place for three times as long as the first exposure.
- Remove the negative material, place it in contact with the receiver paper as with the normal diffusion transfer procedures, and process.
- Separate the negative and receiver after the normal thirty-second wait.

• Key Points

- Diffusion transfer, photomechanical transfer, and PMT are some of the names given to the process of making a positive image from positive copy.
- A basic exposure test determines usable camera settings and exposure times.
- More exposure lightens the diffusion transfer print, and less exposure darkens it.
- Halftones can be screened and placed on a paste-up with other line copy.
- Diffusion transfer can also produce ghost halftones, line and tint combinations, and posterizations.

• Review Questions

1. List three uses of the diffusion transfer process.
2. Describe how the image transfers from the negative material to the receiver sheet.
3. Describe the reflex method of making a diffusion transfer.
4. Why does the operator wait ninety seconds before separating the negative material when using a transparent receiver?
5. Describe the procedure for making a special effects print with a solid image and a tinted background.

• Activities

1. Select a piece of good line copy (or have your instructor assign you a piece of copy). Make a diffusion transfer print on a paper receiver. Follow normal line procedure. Record your exposures, after evaluating the print, and consult with your instructor.
2. Check with your instructor for a piece of copy that will be made into an overhead for instructional use. Follow normal line copy procedures, but use a transparent receiver. Do not forget not to separate the negative and receiver for ninety seconds instead of the standard thirty-second wait.
3. Design an advertisement that is to appear in either your local or school paper. The ad should contain an illustration that must be made using diffusion transfer materials and one of the special effects possible with this material. Consult with your instructor as to size.
4. Select copy for making a reflex print onto a paper receiver. Remember you must use reflex negative material. Record your exposure information, and consult with your instructor.

Chapter 11

Special Effects Photography

• Objectives

In this chapter you will cover:

- Types of special effects photography;
- Special effects screens;
- Line conversion, bas relief, posterization, and duotone special effects photography;
- Proofing procedures.

After reading the chapter you should be able to:

- Recognize and give the correct name for different types of special effects photography;
- Explain the purpose and use of screen tints and special pattern screens;
- Make line conversion photographs;
- Make bas relief photographs;
- Make two-, and three-tone one-color posterizations;
- Make two- and three-tone two-color posterizations;
- Make duotone photographs;
- Proof special effects photographs.

The purpose of printing design is to attract attention. Book covers, standing in a row of racks in a bookstore, compete with each other to make the customer pick up a book and then buy it. Posters must be unique to cause someone who is walking by to take a second look. Ads in magazines must stand out on the page, drawing the reader's attention to a particular product or idea. In order to attract that attention, many graphic designers call for special treatment of illustrations. A great many of those special treatments are in the form of modifications made by photographic means.

The entire area of photographic modifications is called **special effects photography**. Sometimes the special treatment is produced by the commercial photographer, long before the copy arrives at the printing plant (figures 11.1, 11.2, 11.3, 11.4 and 11.5). Other times, the printing photographer is asked to make the modification in the shop darkroom from existing continuous-tone prints. The purpose of this chapter is to examine the most common graphic arts special effects techniques—special effects

Figure 11.1. Photograph made with a fish-eye lens.

Figure 11.2. Example of a close-up photograph.

screens, line conversion, duotone, and posterization—that can be made in the printing plant.

A word of caution should be made: Do not overdo copy modification. While special effects do attract attention, too many special effects can defeat the purpose. If every illustration in a printed piece is a special effect, then the reader will rapidly become tired of the techniques and the illustrations will lose their impact.

• Tint Screens and Patterns

Tint screens and **special pattern screens** are available to the camera and darkroom worker in a great variety of screen rulings and dot percentages for the tints (figure 11.6). A great variety of special pattern designs also are available (figure 11.7).

Tint screens are available on film base (like a film negative) and can be purchased as dry transfer material to be used on art work in the copy preparation area, and they are also available on a paper base (similar to a photographic paper). The paper-based material is also used in the copy preparation area. Special pattern designs are usually available only as dry transfer and on paper-based material. The paper-based and dry transfer materials are used to give special tones to advertising and line illustrations but are not used as part of darkroom work. One trade name for this type of material is Zipatone.

Tint screens (negative type) are used a great deal in platemaking operations to reduce solid areas to tonal values and to give gray tones to otherwise white-appearing areas on illustrations. The addition of a tint screen over a halftone negative will make the halftone appear as a phantom, or grayed-out, picture (see figure 10.10). These platemaking- and contacting-type applications are done in the platemaking area of the shop. Tint negative materials are used by the camera and darkroom worker in some of the special techniques that are explained later in this chapter.

Figure 11.3. Solarized photograph.

Figure 11.4. Example of a double-exposure photograph. (Courtesy of Langhoff Photo)

Figure 11.5. Use of a concentric circle special effects screen.

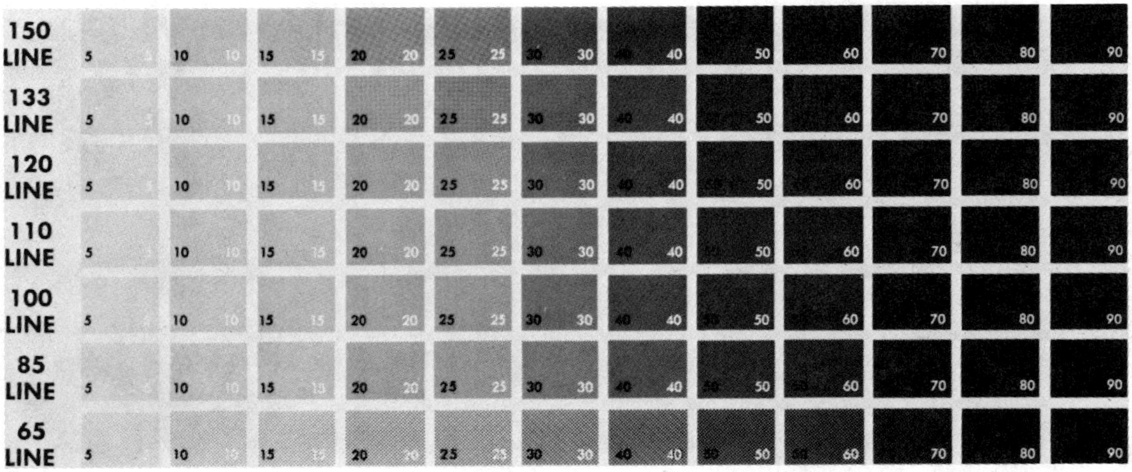

Figure 11.6. Commercially available tint patterns. (Courtesy of ByChrome Co.)

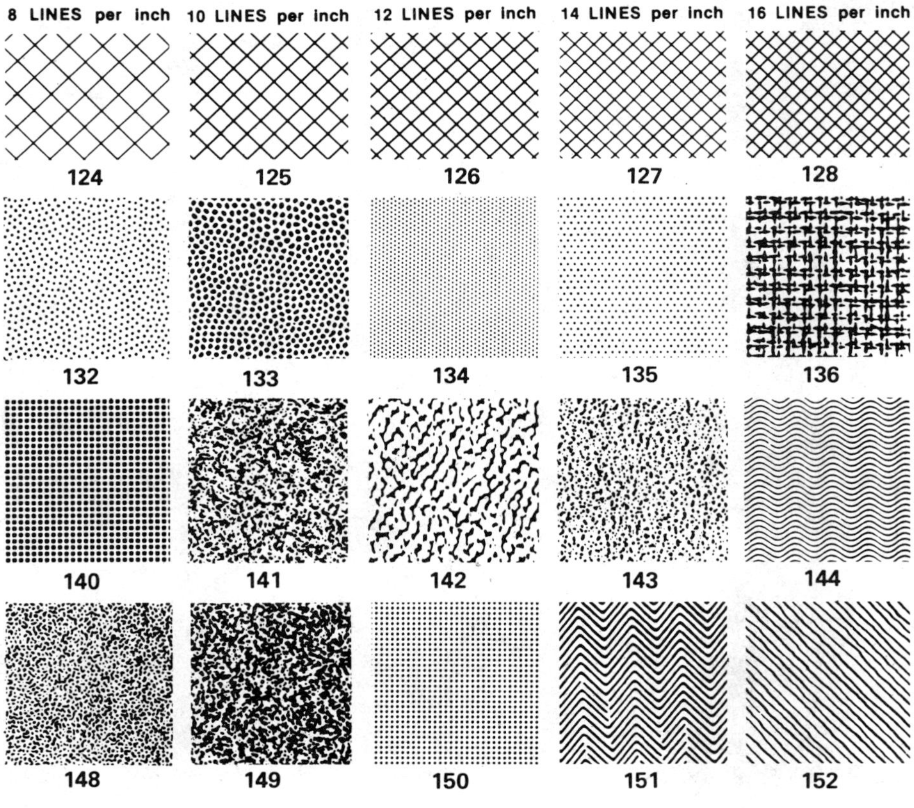

Figure 11.7. Examples of commercially available special design patterns. (Courtesy of Press-sure Graphics)

• Special Effects Screens

One of the most popular methods of obtaining special effects for the graphic arts is the use of commercially prepared **special effect screens**. The procedure for using these screens is the same as using a conventional halftone screen. By varying exposures it is possible to obtain different effects with the same screen.

Camera operators can create their own special effects screens by contacting cloth, silk, wipes, screen wire, and plastic images to film (figure 11.8). The film can then be used just like the commercial screens in creating special effects copy (figure 11.9).

Let us set up the procedures to follow in using either a commercial or shop-created special effects screen:

1. Select suitable copy—usually a good contrasty black-and-white photograph.

2. Set camera for size and timer and aperture control for proper f/stop. Exposure time is usually close to the time for a regular halftone screen, but a test should be made and the results

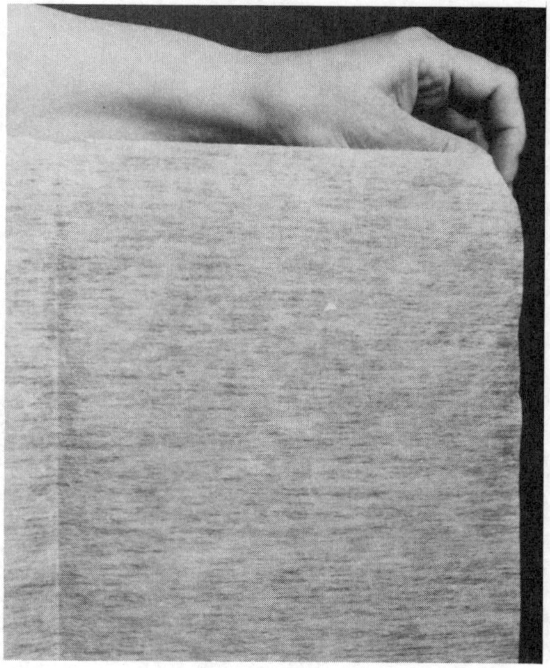

Figure 11.8. Fusible interfacing used for special effects screen. This material is available at fabric stores.

Figure 11.9. Special effect obtained using fusible interfacing as the screen.

(a)

(b)

Figure 11.10. (a) Use of a mezzotint special effects screen. (b) Use of a steel etching special effects screen.

recorded for future use. The f/stop is usually the same setting used for halftones.

3. Select a special effects screen.

4. Using litho-type film (ortho), place the film emulsion up (toward the lens) on the vacuum back. Place the special effects screen over the film (emulsion down). Turn the vacuum on, and using the same techniques as when making a conventional halftone, close the vacuum back and make the exposure.

5. Develop the film using standard halftone-developing procedures.

6. After the negative is dry, make a contact print of the negative on photographic paper or other proofing materials so results can be evaluated.

If the results are too dark, re-expose the negative, giving more exposure. If the results are too light, remake the negative, giving less exposure.

NOTE: There are several methods of proofing graphic arts negatives so you can evaluate your results. Using RC (resin-coated) photographic paper is a satisfactory method. The high-contrast negative is placed on the photo paper. Negative is emulsion down, photographic paper is emulsion up. Exposure requires about ten to twelve seconds of the contact light source (depending upon light and distance). The negative and paper should be in a vacuum frame for good contact. After exposure, the paper is developed in a paper developer, and the operator watches the development. The red litho safelights are safe for the RC paper. Figure 11.10 shows the results of two of the special effects screens with the same copy.

• Line Conversions

Line conversion is the process of changing a continuous-tone photograph into an illustration that appears to be an artist's line drawing. While several techniques can be used to achieve this effect, the procedure shown here does the job with the use of minimum materials:

- Select suitable copy for example, a black-and-white photograph with good contrast (figure 11.11).

Figure 11.11. Photograph selected for line conversion.

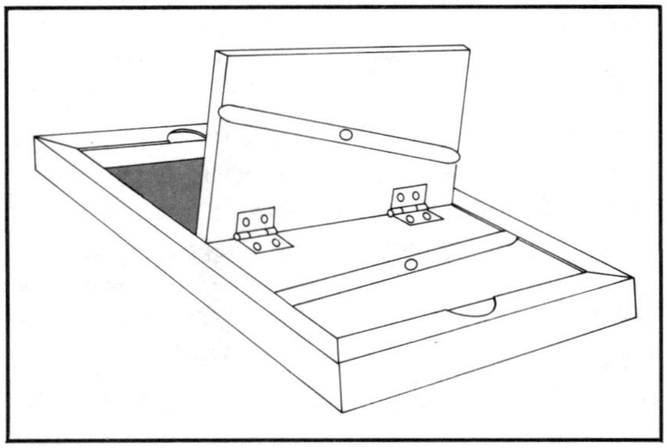

Figure 11.12. Portable contact frame.

Figure 11.13. Contact frame, negative, and lazy-Susan whirling device.

- Place the copy in copyboard, and be sure to include a gray scale.
- Set the camera controls for size, f/stop, and exposure time for the basic line exposure.
- Place a piece of litho-type (ortho) film on the vacuum back, emulsion toward the lens, and make the exposure.
- Process the film, using standard line-exposure-developing procedures, until the gray scale is at a solid step four.
- After the film is dry, make a contact positive on a sheet of litho film (see chapter 8 on contacting).
- Process the positive using standard developing procedures.

You should now have both a negative and a positive image of the original on film. If the two are held together on a light table, they should cancel each other, and you would have what appears to be a black piece of film.

Place three or four sheets of transparent pieces of film or cleared film between the negative and positive (see figure 9.19). The fewer the spacer sheets, the smaller the lines will become in the final result; the more spacers, the broader the lines.

To complete the line conversion process, you will need a contact frame (figure 11.12), a rotating wheel, or lazy Susan (figure 11.13), and a white light source. This can be a safelight unit without a filter, with a fifteen-watt bulb. Use the following steps to complete the line conversion:

- Place a piece of unexposed litho-type film in the contact printer unit, emulsion up.
- Over this film place the negative and positive with the spacers.
- Close the frame and place it on the lazy Susan. This must be done in safelight conditions.
- Hold the white light at a 40° angle from the lazy Susan, at a distance of approximately eighteen inches.
- Rotate the wheel and turn the white light on (figure 11.14). Exposure should be approximately ten seconds.
- After exposure, process the film by standard line-processing procedures.
- The end result should be a line conversion positive image on film (figure 11.15).

If you prefer to have a negative, contact the line conversion positive to another piece of litho film using standard contacting procedures. Process and you will have a negative line conversion (figure 11.16).

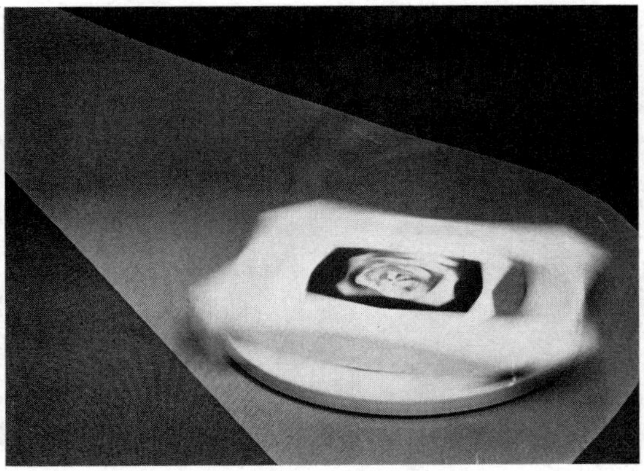

Figure 11.14. Exposing the line conversion. Notice that the lazy-Susan spins during the esposure.

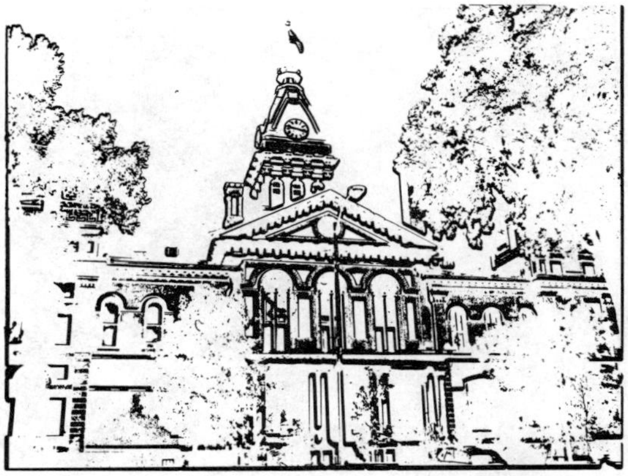

Figure 11.15. Positive line conversion.

• Bas-Relief

A modification of the line conversion techniques is a **bas-relief** image. The procedure for this effect is quite similar to the line conversion.

- Select suitable copy, a black-and-white photograph, with good contrast. Place copy in copyboard.
- Set camera controls for size and exposure.

Exposure time and f/stop setting for this procedure will be different than those for lithotype film. For this process, a film is needed that has a continuous-tone emulsion and that is also red light safe (ortho). The film will be processed in a continuous-tone developer such as a DK50 or HC-110.

Because light sources, developers, and films are different, exact exposure and development should be determined by experimentation. The goal is to produce a normal-contrast continuous-tone negative.

- Place a piece of continuous-tone negative material, emulsion toward the lens, and make the exposure.

Figure 11.16. Negative line conversion.

- Process the film in the continuous-tone developer, stop, fix, and wash baths.
- When the negative is dried, contact it to another piece of the continuous-tone film to produce a continuous-tone positive on film.
- Process and dry the positive.

Figure 11.17. Making a bas-relief. Positive and negative line negatives are held slightly out of register in making a bas-relief.

Figure 11.18. Bas-relief print.

The positive and negative pieces of film are now placed one on top of the other so they are slightly out of register (figure 11.17).

A piece of photographic paper is placed under the two films, they are placed in the contact frame, and a contact print is made. The paper is processed and a positive bas-relief image is formed (figure 11.18). To get this image ready for printing, a halftone negative must be made from the print.

Posterization

Posterization is a process that photographically reduces the many tones of a continuous-tone photograph to a few selected tones. While this process tends to create an abstract-appearing image, the shape and character of the original photograph is maintained. Its purpose is to create a new or different appearing image and not to improve a photograph (figure 11.19).

Posterization techniques can be used in single-color printing such as black ink on white paper, showing two, three, or more tones. The technique is also used in color printing, in which each of the various tones is printed in a different color.

The best copy for the posterization process is a continuous-tone photograph with good contrast. Back-lighted and side-lighted photos usually make good copy for this process. Silhouetted photos will work if the shape of the person or object is recognized without the middle tones.

Two-Tone Posterization

A **two-tone posterization** is a high-contrast line exposure of a continuous-tone photograph. When this process is used to prepare an illustration for printing, the designer will have to decide how many of the white (highlight) areas and the gray (middle-tone) areas can be lost in the picture and still have an effective illustration. The best way to determine this would be to make a series of test exposures to see what various effects you obtain. Avoid extremely complex or abstract images.

By including a gray scale with the photo during the test, it is possible to determine which step in the gray scale matches with the last step to turn black in the negative. (The black in the negative produces the white in the finished print.) In the example shown, each reproduction has more black steps—from two steps black to six steps black (figure 11.20). Which effect are you trying to obtain?

The procedures for making a two-tone posterization follow:

1. Select suitable copy.
2. Decide on the number of tones desired to make the most effective final results. Place the copy on the copyboard, and include a gray scale as a guide.
3. Set the camera controls for proper size. Set the exposure time and f/stop to obtain the desired results determined from the shop trials.
4. Place a sheet of litho film (ortho) on the vacuum back, emulsion toward the lens, close the back, and make the exposure.
5. Process the film using standard line film chemicals and techniques. Watch carefully to remove the film from the developer when the predetermined step on the gray scale turns solid. Finish processing, washing, and drying the film.
6. To check to see if the negative will produce the desired effect, proof the negative.

Figure 11.19. Two-tone posterization print.

Notice that with this process, the only two tones recorded are the white of the paper and the black areas. Some graphic arts technicians call this a single-tone posterization because they think of it as being toned only where the black image is located. It is really two tones: white and black.

Three-Tone Posterization

Three-tone posterization can be used with a single ink color or with several ink colors. If the job is to be run in a single ink color, the photographic operations can be performed on a single piece of sensitized material (film). If the job is being planned for several colors of ink, a negative for each printed tone must be exposed sep-

Figure 11.20. Making negatives for posterization.
(a) Original copy, (b) 15-second exposure, (c) 20-second exposure, and (d) 25-second exposure.

(a)

(b)

.05
.13
.20
.35
.50
.65
.80
.95
1.10
1.25
1.40
1.55
1.70
1.85
2.00
2.10

(c)

.05
.13
.20
.35
.50
.65
.80
.95
1.10
1.25
1.40
1.55
1.70
1.85
2.00
2.10

(d)

(a) (b)

Figure 11.21. (a) Three-tone posterization printed in a single-color ink. (b) The original.

arately. A three-tone posterization using a single ink color has two ink tones plus the paper on which it is printed (figure 11.21).

The procedures for making a three-tone posterization using a single ink color follow:

1. Select suitable copy.

2. For the third tone, select a tint screen (hard dot) with a 30 to 40 percent dot size. This range is selected so that the three tones will be distinctive. The final three-tone result will be the white of the paper, the solid black, and the gray screen tint. Screen tints over 50 percent value tend to appear almost solid; those lighter than 30 percent appear whiter.

3. Set camera controls for size, and place the copy on the copyboard.

4. In this process, two exposures will be made on a single piece of ortho film. In order to minimize the chance for the film to move, tape the film in position after turning on the vacuum.

5. With the vacuum still on, place the tint screen over the film as you would with a halftone screen.

6. The first exposure should be the same time as for a normal halftone main exposure. The purpose here is to record dots in all areas of the photo that are reflecting light back to the

film. After the first exposure, open the vacuum back without turning off the vacuum pump. Remove the tint screen and close the back.

7. You are now ready for the second exposure. This exposure will record images from only the very white parts of the photograph. When the exposure is complete, process the film as with a normal halftone negative.

8. After drying, make a photographic contact proof of the combined exposures to make sure the effect is what you wanted. Keep records of exposures so the process can be repeated.

In three-tone posterization in several ink colors, each of the colors to be reproduced will be exposed as a distinct image on a separate piece of film. The negative images will then be combined on the printing press. Because more than a single negative will be used to make the posterization, register marks must be placed on the copy (figure 11.22). These marks are used by the negative assembly department (stripping) to make sure the two colors will print together in the proper positions. The procedures for making a three-tone posterization in several ink colors follow:

1. Select suitable copy and place at least two register marks in opposite corners.

2. Decide on the tones to appear in the second color and the solid color (refer to the shop test sheet). Assume, for this example, that we will expose the first negative to a solid step two. This will be the light-color-ink printer (light printer). The second negative will be exposed to a solid step six. This will be for the dark-color-ink printer (dark printer). No tints will be used during the exposure of these negatives. If tints are desired, they will be added at the proofing or platemaking stages.

3. Set camera controls for size, exposure time, and f/stop.

4. Place film on the camera back, emulsion toward the lens, and make the first exposure.

Figure 11.22. Posterization copy showing register marks.

To alter the exposure to just darken the second step, remember that for each 0.30 density of the gray scale you want to expose or not expose, it is necessary to either double or halve the exposure time. For example, if the step you wish to darken is 0.30 units of density less than the step four you usually develop to, then cut the time in half. If step six is 0.30 density more than the step four, then double the exposure time.

5. Remove the first negative, place a second piece of film in the camera, and make the second exposure.

6. Process both pieces of film, watching for the proper gray scale steps to appear. Move the film through the stop, fix, and wash steps.

7. After the film has dried, it is best to take the two negatives to a light table and to align them, using the register marks. Secure them in position, using whatever methods are used in the shop.

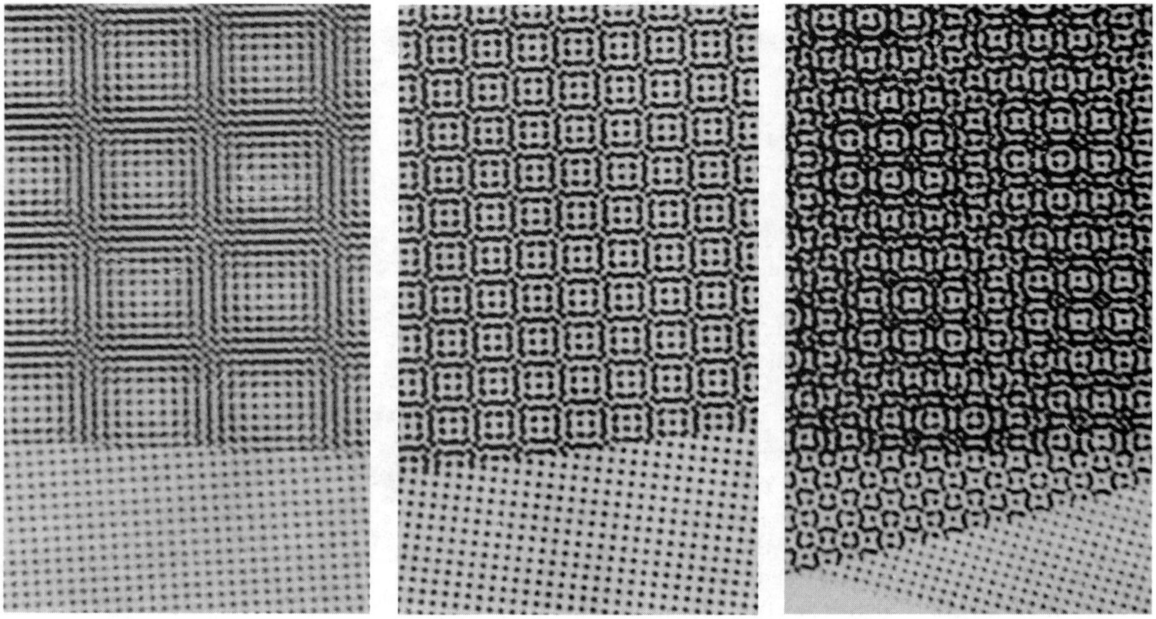

Figure 11.23. Examples of moiré patterns. The patterns appear when screen angles are not the proper degrees apart.

Posterization with More Than Three Tones

Sometimes the designer requests a posterization effect with more than three tones or colors for the illustration being used. Four colors are usually considered the limit because most color presses are set up to print only four colors of ink in a single pass. The technique for four tones is the same as explained for the three-tone posterization where the separate negatives are used. In the case of a four-tone posterization, the operator would make three separate line exposures—that is, negative A to a step two, negative B to a step four, and negative C to a step six. The first negative would be for the lightest color, the second negative for the intermediate color, and the third negative for the darkest color (plate 1).

Sometimes the job calls for a four-tone posterization but in a single color. Here the operator would usually make the three negatives as in the previous example. Instead of proofing this in color, the proof and the printed job would be a single color.

Screen tints selected for this type of job would probably be a 20 percent tint and a 40 percent tint. The last negative would print solid. First, the negative and proof paper are placed in contact. Then the 20 percent tint is placed between these two, making sure the angle of the tint was 45°, with the emulsion against the emulsion of the paper. The last negative is exposed without a screen tint.

When exposing the second negative, use the 40 percent tint and make sure the angle of the tint is at 75° (30° from the first tint). It is important that the angles are 30° apart to prevent the appearance of a **moiré pattern**. Figure 11.23 shows the various moiré patterns that appear when the tint screen angles are incorrect.

Posterization images are effective for attracting attention, but each additional color requires an extra press run.

• Posterization Proofing

Proofs for a posterization can be made in black, gray, and white, or in color. The procedures for making a three tone proof in black, gray, and white follow:

- In the darkroom contact area, tape a piece of photographic paper to the vacuum board. This sheet of paper will be used for two exposures.
- When making the first exposure for the light printer, insert a tint screen between the negative and the proof paper.
- Make the next exposure by aligning the second negative in register; do not use a screen tint with this exposure.
- Expose and develop.
- Examine the results.

There are a number of methods to make color proofs. While many multicolor proofing systems exist, one method called Color Key is used widely by industry and schools. Color Key is a 3M product. Several other manufacturers also make a similar product. Some of the other major color-proofing materials that are widely used in industry include 3M's Transfer Key and DuPont's Chromalin. These two products make a color proof on a single receiver sheet.

The Transfer Key material comes in sheet form with the color dye already in the proofing material. The pigmented sheet is adhered to a receiver, and the mylar carrier sheet is removed. The negative or positive, according to shop procedures, is exposed for that color, and the material is developed. The next color sheet is applied, and the procedure is repeated until the four colors are completed. This makes an excellent proof on a single sheet.

The DuPont Chromalin material uses a different procedure. Chromalin can also be purchased for work with negatives or positives. With

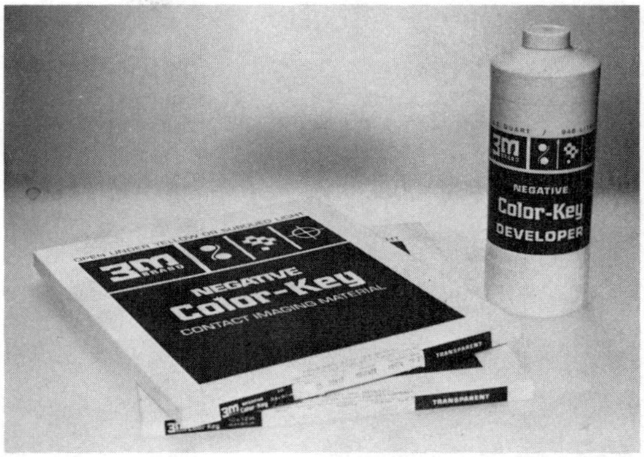

Figure 11.24. Color Key developer and a box of negative Color Key material.

Chromalin, the shop needs a special laydown machine that uses heat and pressure to place the clear Chromalin material on the receiver sheet. For each color, another sheet of the material has to be laid on the receiver sheet. After the first sheet is adhered, the first exposure is made, and no visible image can be seen. The sheet is then dusted with color pigment powder that gives the image its color. This process is repeated for each color using the different color pigments.

Each of the systems has advantages and disadvantages. Transparent-based proofs can be laid over the paper for printing and can give a clear idea of the final color effect. They are, however, limited in the color hues that can be duplicated. Materials like Chromalin can produce a wide range of color hues, but they cannot show the result of combination with a color base paper. Both processes deliver excellent proofs that look more like press proofs.

Color Key is a transparent-based material coated with a light-sensitive color emulsion. It is purchased in sheets, according to color. The developer comes in bottles and is used for all colors (figure 11.24). This material can be worked with under yellow safelights like those

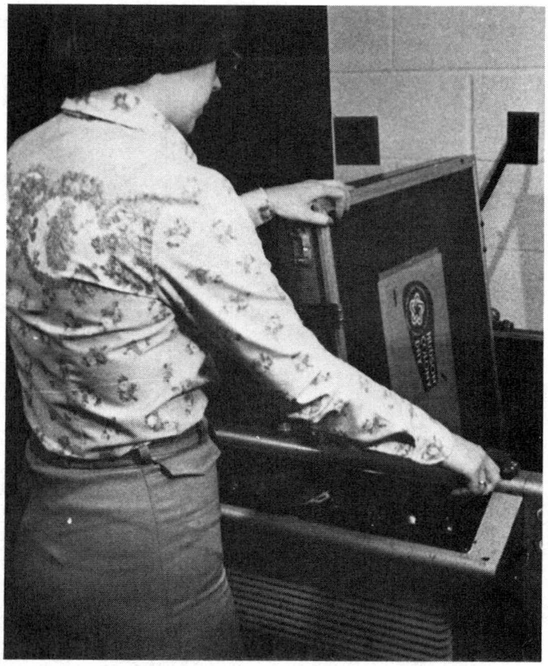

Figure 11.25. Operator using flip-top platemaker to make a Color Key proof.

found in offset plate-developing areas. The exposure of the Color Key must be done in a vacuum frame—the type used for platemaking—with an intense light source. Exact exposures for this material must be determined by tests with shop equipment.

The procedures for making a Color Key Proof follow:

1. Determine the two colors to be used for the printed job, and select Color Key materials to match the inks.

2. Place the least exposed (step two on gray scale) negative over the lightest color ink (Color Key) selected. *Caution:* For proper exposure of Color Key material, the emulsion of the film negative must be placed against the base (nonemulsion side) of the Color Key. The two sheets are then placed on the platemaking vacuum base (emulsion of the Color Key down), the glass is closed, and the vacuum pump is turned on. After the correct vacuum is reached (25 pounds of vacuum), the top is flipped (figure 11.25) and the exposure is made.

3. After exposure, the first Color Key sheet is placed in a box and the second negative (the step six on the gray scale) is placed on the darkest ink (matching Color Key). Emulsion of the negative is again next to the base of the Color Key. The vacuum is turned on, the top is flipped, and the exposure is made.

4. The Color Key sheets are then developed one at a time in the plate sink (figure 11.26). The exposed material is placed emulsion up on a flat surface such as a piece of glass or stainless steel sheet. Wet the surface with water before laying the material down, which will help to hold it in position.

Pour Color Key developer over the sheet and gently wipe with a cotton swab, rubbing the developer over the Color Key. The developer will remove all of the unexposed emulsion and will leave the image that was hardened by the light. Rinse the Color Key with water, place it on absorbent paper, and blot dry. Repeat this operation for the second Color Key sheet. Be sure to cap the developer bottle and clean the sink area.

5. Place the lightest color material down on a sheet of paper similar to the paper on which the job is to be printed. Place the second color in register (use the register marks placed on copy) over the first color. The final result should then be viewed by reflected light and should give a good indication of how the job will appear when printed.

• Duotones

Duotone printing is another effective way of adding appealing color to a printed job, and it requires only two press runs. The technique employs two separate halftones, each printed in a

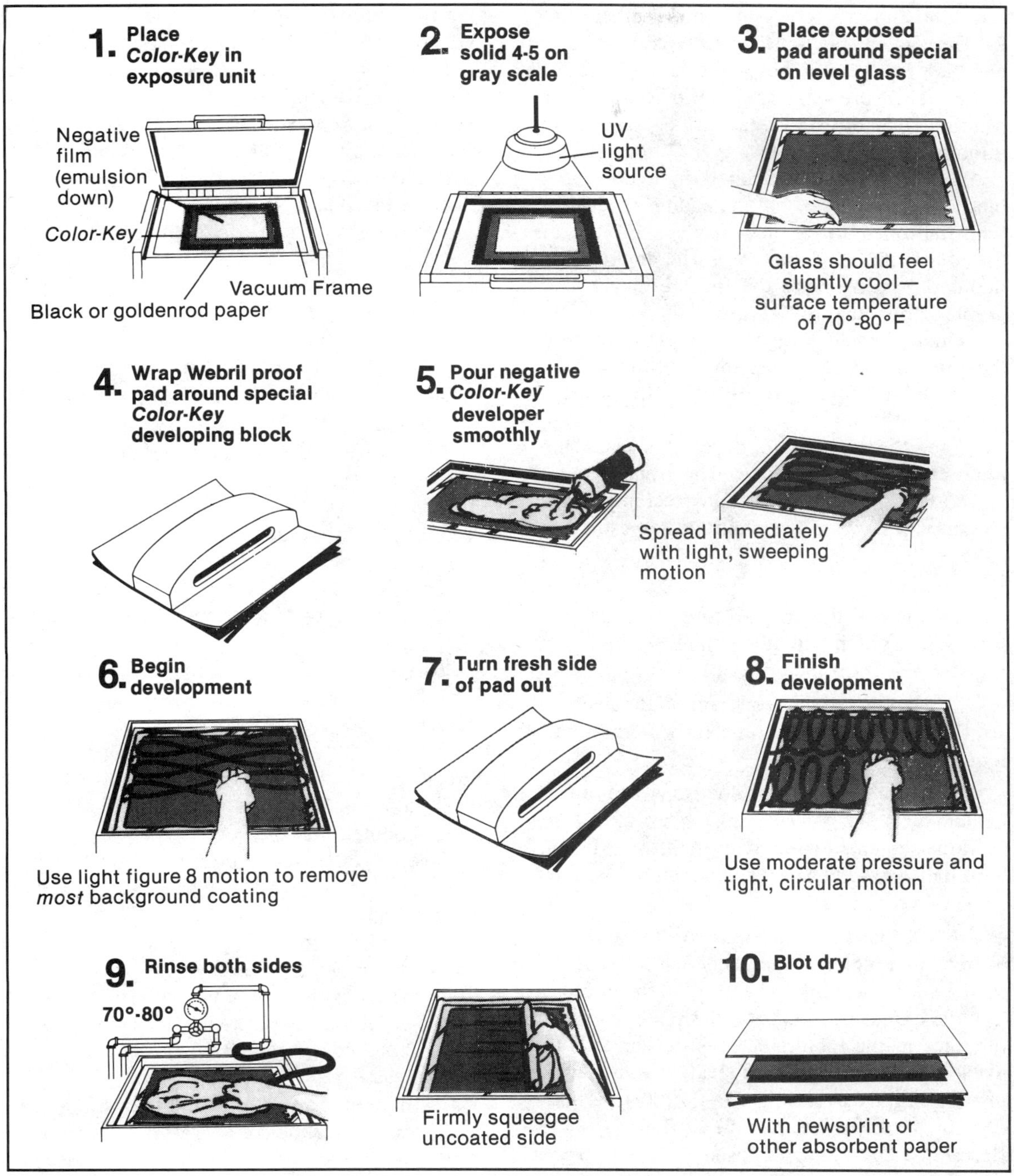

Figure 11.26. The 3M procedure chart for making Color Key proofs.
(Courtesy of Graphic Preparation Systems Division, 3M Company)

different color run, one on top of the other (plate 2). Here again, the halftone screens must be rotated 30° from each other when the halftones are made. This prevents the halftone dots from printing right on top of each other, and it also diminishes moiré patterns.

Duotones can be printed in a color plus black, in two separate colors, and in some cases, both halftones are printed in black ink (this is called a **double-dot duotone**). The double black duotone printing gives the final result a photographic print quality.

Duotones add a high-quality appearance to the printed job at a cost much reduced when compared to full-color (four-color process) printed work.

Each camera operator develops special techniques for making duotones. The procedure suggested here is just one of many techniques that an operator can use to obtain the same final results:

1. Select appropriate copy (a black-and-white photograph with good contrast), and place register marks on the edges of the print.

2. Adjust all camera controls for size, and set f/stop and exposure time for a normal halftone exposure.

3. Place litho (ortho) halftone film on the camera vacuum back, emulsion up. Place the halftone screen squarely over the film. All standard halftone screens are manufactured with the screen pattern at 45°.

4. Expose the first halftone for a slightly overexposed highlight dot. This first halftone will be for the darkest ink to be used on the duotone. The dark areas of the negative should have only pinholes in the highlight areas, rather than the usual 5 percent target. The shadow areas should also be slightly overexposed, giving large black dots in the clear areas. This is done by overflashing. Remove the exposed film and place it in a light-tight container.

5. Place a second piece of film on the vacuum back for the second halftone. This halftone will be for the lightest ink. When the screen is placed over this second sheet, it must be positioned at a 30° angle from the way it was placed for the first exposure. This position will help to diminish the moiré pattern and to insure that the screen dots do not print on top of the first set of dots on the final reproduction.

For this exposure, the highlight areas (dark areas of the negative) should have larger openings when compared to the first negative. Slightly underexpose the main exposure. The shadow areas (open areas of the negative) should have only pinpoint shadow dots. This effect is achieved by underflashing or by giving *no flash* exposure.

6. Process both halftone exposures by standard halftone-processing procedures. When the film is dry, the next step is to proof so you can inspect the results.

Choosing the proper color of inks for the final job is a very important part of the task if the duotone is to be effective. Water scenes, snow scenes, and sky and mountain scenes appear best when blue and black inks are selected. Desert scenes look good with warm colors such as red or yellow. Farm scenes work well with green and black. If you are in doubt about the best color combinations, try proofs with different combinations of color.

Follow the same procedures for making Color Key proofs given in the section on posterization proofing.

A variation of the duotone that is practiced by some shops is to use only one halftone. A solid ink block the size of the halftone is printed, and the halftone is printed right over the block in a second color (plate 3). This is called a **fake duotone**.

Still another type of fake duotone is to print a tint pattern for the solid color then to print the halftone over this. If this technique is used, remember that the tint must be positioned 30° from the halftone screen pattern.

Yellow printer

Magenta printer

Black printer

Four-tone posterization

Light printer

Duotone

Dark printer

Halftone

Fake duotone

Color patch

 Plate 4. Example of four-color reproduction.

Yellow printer

Magenta printer

Yellow plus magenta

(Color separations for Plates 4 and 5 courtesy of Shanebrook Graphics.)

Cyan printer

Black printer

Yellow, magenta plus cyan

Yellow, magenta, cyan plus black

Plate 5. Example of color-corrected four-color reproduction.

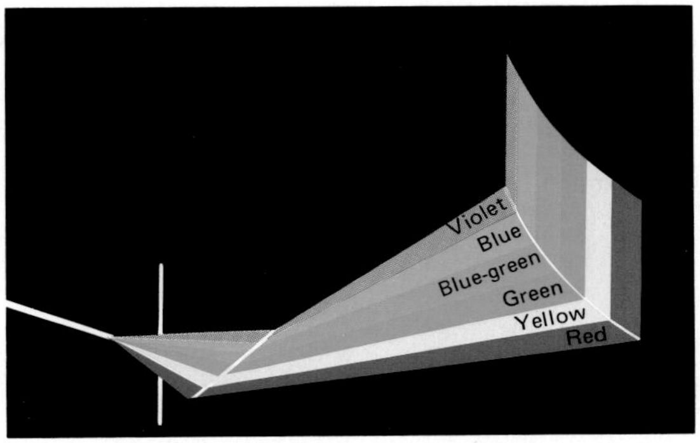

(a) Schematic of white light broken into primary additive colors by a prism.

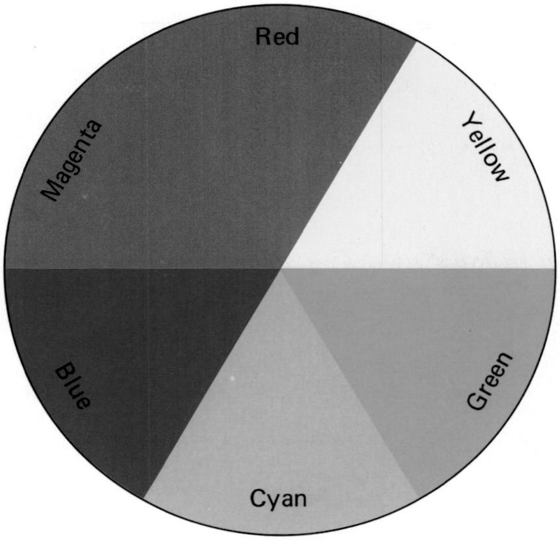

(b) Color wheel. Opposite the three primary additive colors are the complementary colors of cyan, magenta, and yellow.

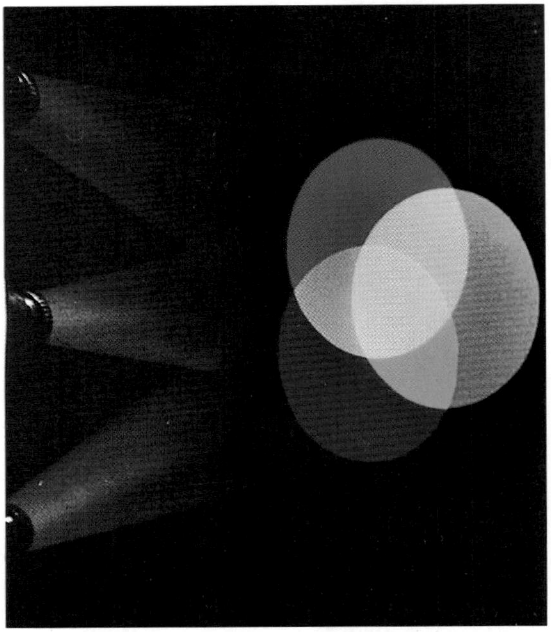

(c) Projected light of primary additive colors. Overlapping two beams produce cyan, magenta, or yellow. Overlapping three beams produces white.

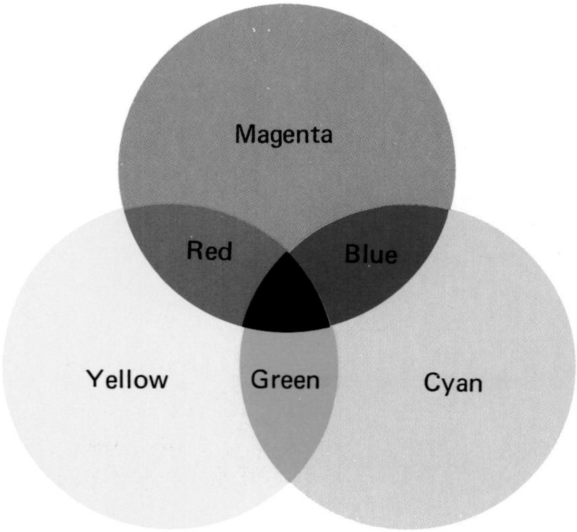

(d) Primary subtractive colors. Overlapping of two primary subtractive colors produces the additive colors of red, green, or blue.

(a) Example of 35-millimeter transparency for use in a four-color job.

(b) Example of color negative used for separations.

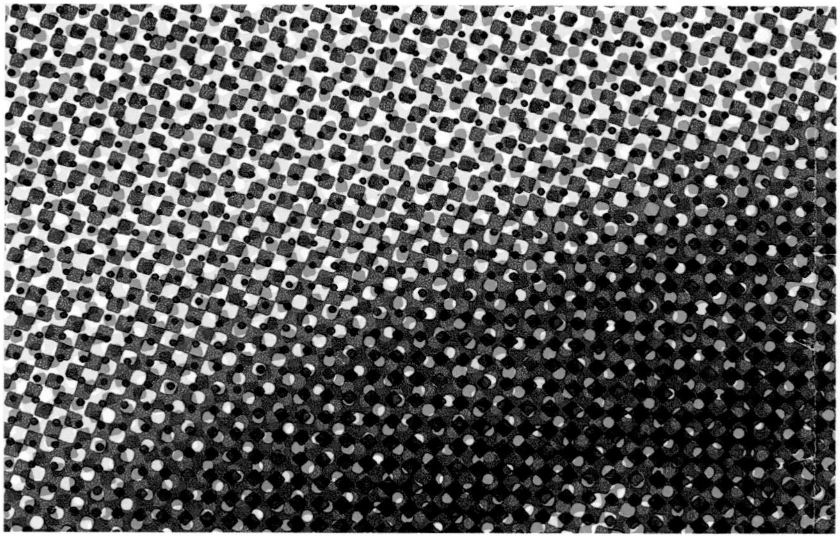

(c) Enlarged view of 4-color print showing color dot clusters.

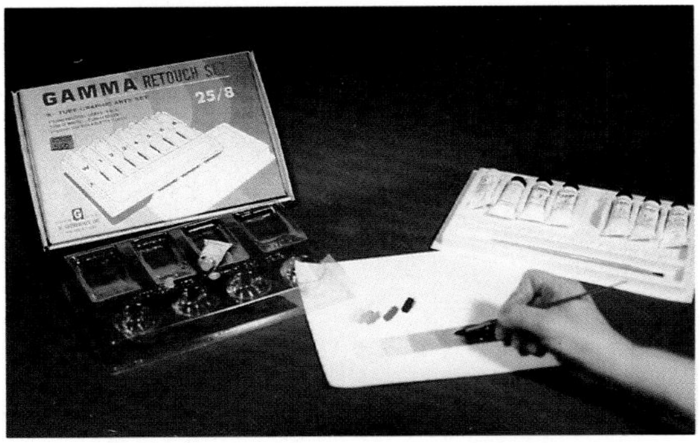

(a) Making a gray scale using standard gray retouch colors.

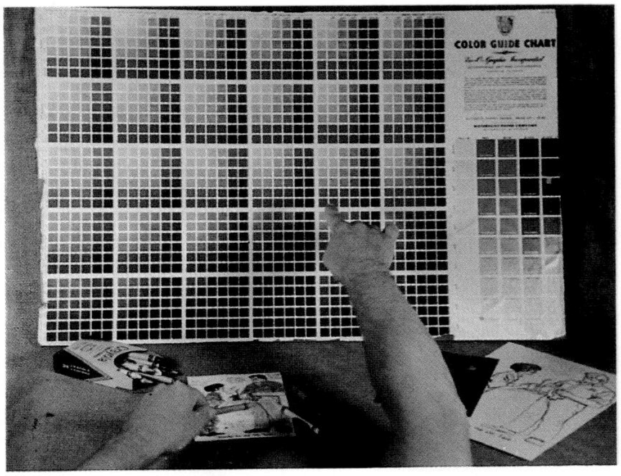

(b) Determining dot percentages using a color guide chart.

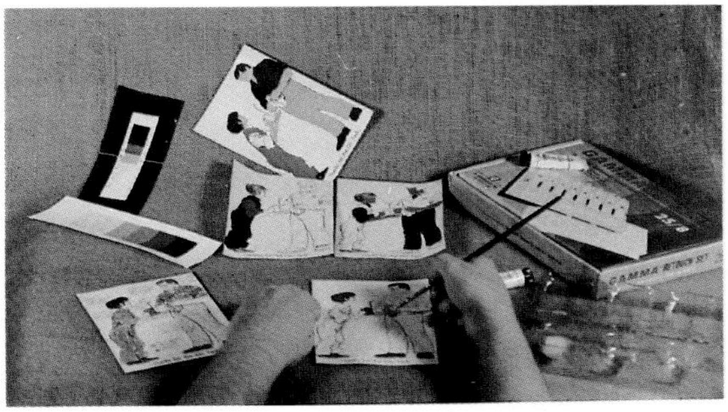

(c) Adding gray values for each color separation.

(d) Color Key proofs. Individual proofs are combined to form final proof.

(e) Comparing final proof to original colored copy.

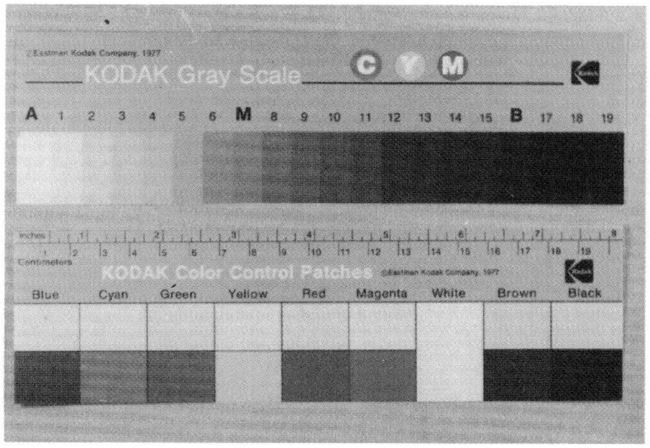

(a) Kodak reflection gray scale and color control patches. (Courtesy of Eastman Kodak, Co.)

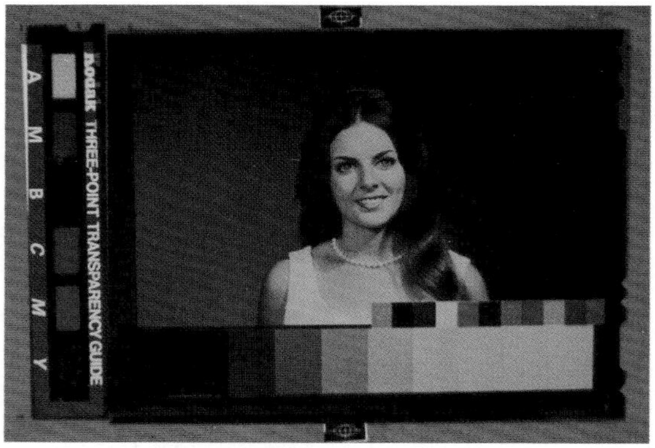

(c) Carrier with a 4″ × 4″ transparency. An AMB and color control guide are stripped in the carrier.

(b) Color reflection copy in copyboard. Notice the color control patches and the gray scale.

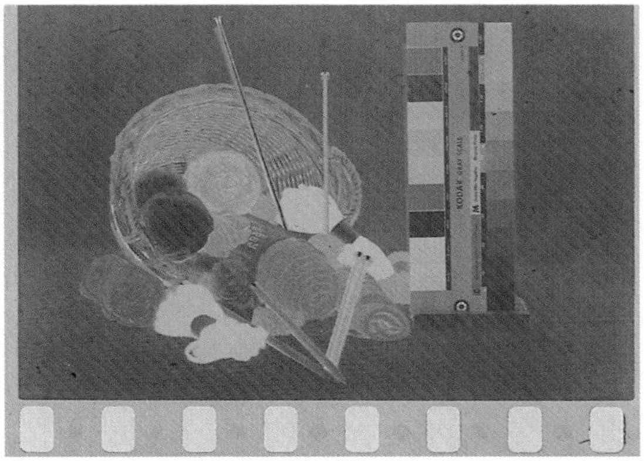

(a) Color negative photographed as standard in making ROP separations.

(d) Yellow

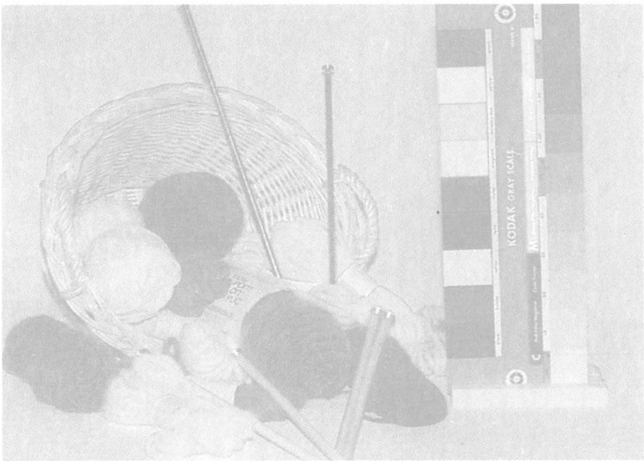

(b) Cyan

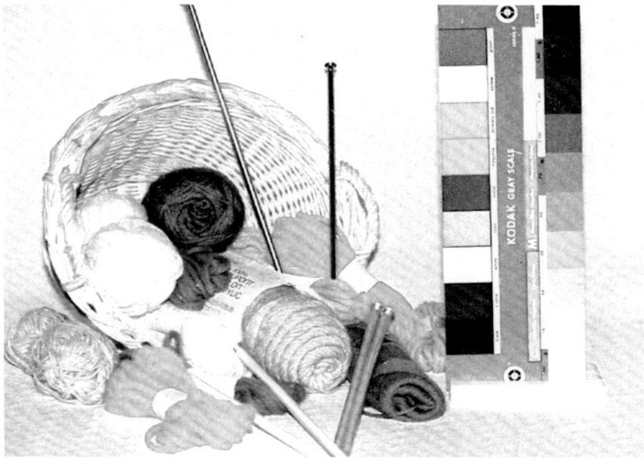

(e) Black

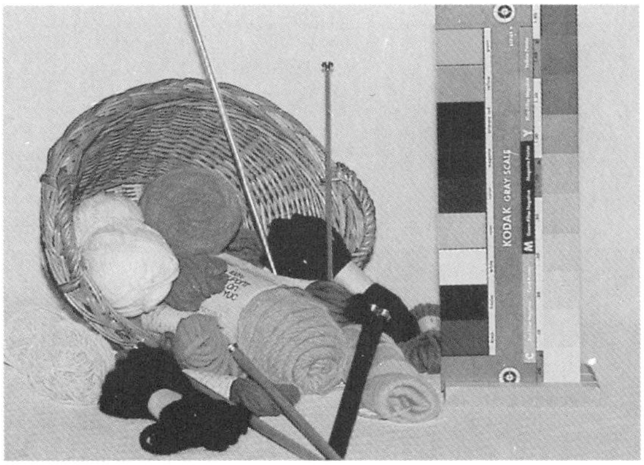

(c) Magenta

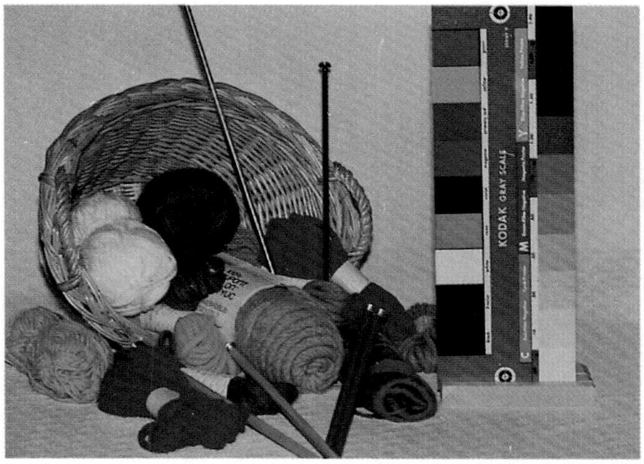

(f) Final print

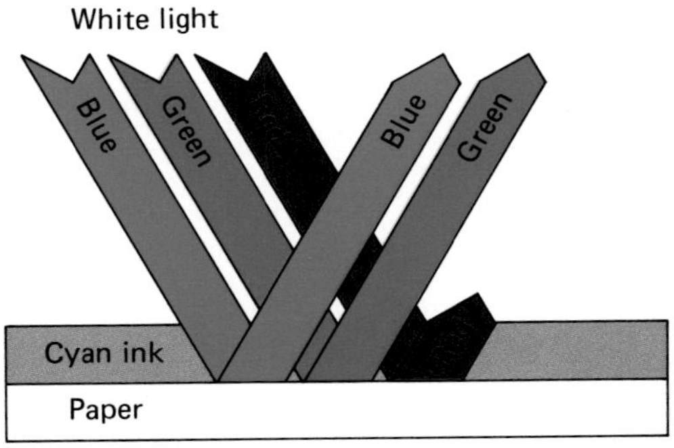

(a) Theoretical reflection and absorption qualities of perfect cyan ink.

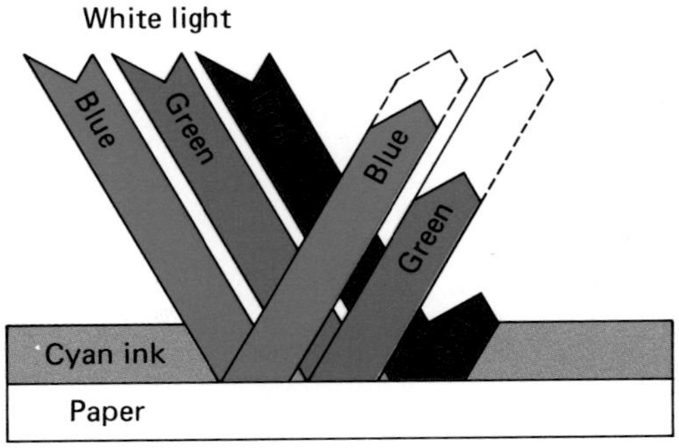

(b) Actual absorption and reflection qualities of cyan ink.

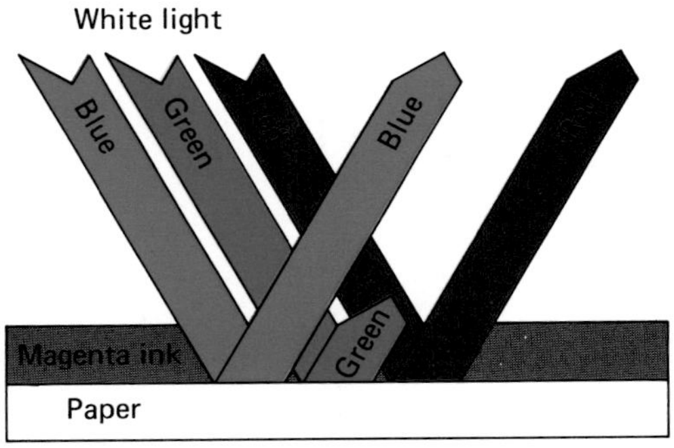

(c) Theoretical reflection and absorption qualities of perfect magenta ink.

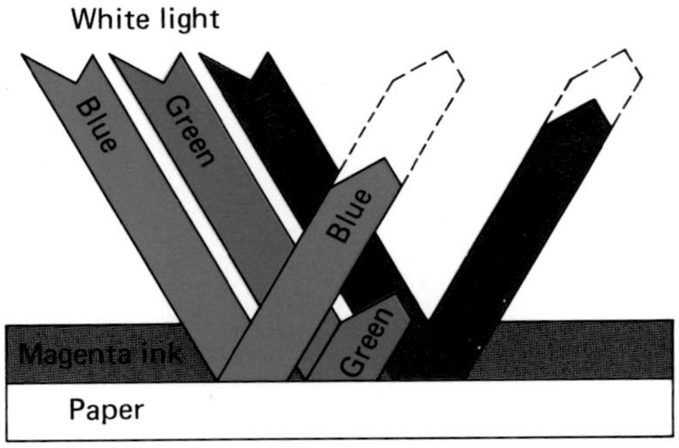

(d) Actual absorption and reflection qualities of magenta ink.

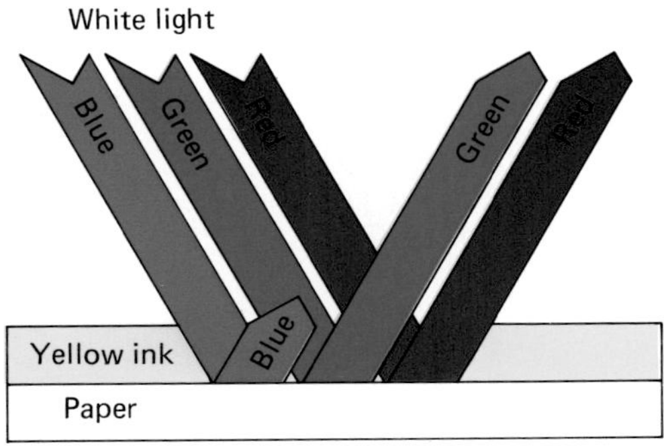

(e) Theoretical reflection and absorption qualities of perfect yellow ink.

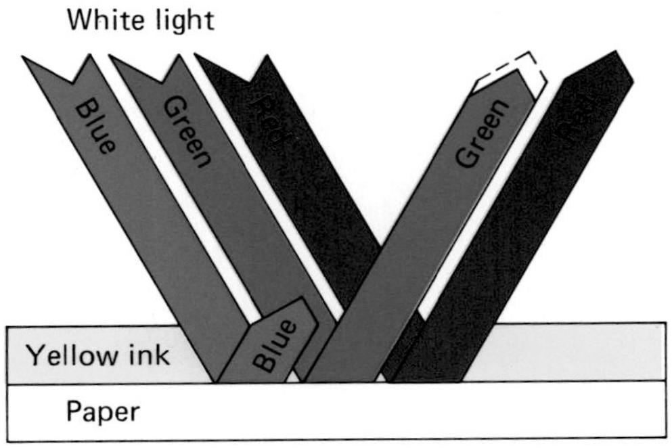

(f) Actual absorption and reflection qualities of yellow ink.

Key Points

- Special effects, or modified, copy can be produced by the commercial photographer and the graphic arts photographer; these techniques attract the reader of printed products.
- Special effects screens, tints, and patterns are available to assist the camera worker in producing the special effects copy.
- Techniques for special effects used by the graphic arts technician include special screens, duotones, line conversions, and posterization.
- Copy modifications can be produced in multiple colors if careful register procedures are used by the graphic arts worker.

Review Questions

1. In your own words, describe what is meant by special effects photography. List three techniques and give examples of where they might be used.
2. Describe the line conversion of a continuous-tone photograph.
3. How would you make a two-tone posterization?
4. Describe the procedure when handling and using a special effects screen. If a commercially produced screen was not available, what could you do?
5. Describe the duotone process, using two different halftone negatives.

Activities

Each of the following activities should use a different special effect technique. Obtain continuous-tone photographs from your instructor that can be used for the major illustration to be modified. Prepare a layout for the entire project, and indicate which special effect technique will be used. When the camera work is complete, be sure to make the appropriate proof of your work.

- Use a cover page for the annual report of a large corporation. The company you select can be real or fictitious.
- Use a record cover for a current album. This can be a real record or a record you have created. Browse through a record store for ideas.
- Use a food advertisement for a national magazine. The food can be packaged or prepared for the table.

Chapter 12

Color Separation

• Objectives

In this chapter you will cover:

- Uses of color material,
- Color principles,
- Types of color copy,
- The theory of color separation,
- Basic color separation procedures for several different operations.

After reading the chapter you should be able to:

- Explain the relationship of color to white light;
- Recall the primary subtractive colors and the primary additive colors;
- List the types of color copy printers use;
- Outline the basic color separation procedures;
- Define *tone balance*, *gray balance*, and *color correction*;
- Explain and perform mechanical separation using gamma gray tones;
- Explain and perform color separation from reflection copy;
- Explain and perform color separation from transparent copy;
- Recognize the term *color scanning*.

The purpose of this chapter is to introduce the theory and practice of color separation. **Color separation** is the technology of photographically separating a color original into three black-and-white film records of the three primary subtractive colors of cyan, magenta, and yellow plus black. The printing process will then bring the elements back together as the press places ink layers on the paper, one on top of the other, duplicating the appearance of the original (plate 4). We concentrate here on the photomechanical aspects of the process and not on the printing of color on a press. The process is called by different names: **Process color**, **four-color printing**, and **color reproduction of originals**.

We live in a world of color. While color makes objects and people seem real, it also affects the way we feel. Red is the color of passion and rage. White is associated with innocence, black with mourning. Purple is the color of royalty. Hues (colors)—the reds, yellows, and oranges—are called **warm colors**; the blues and greens are called **cool colors**.

Advertisers, who purchase printing, know that colors affect the way people feel, as well as the way their products look. The aim is to get the readers to remember and purchase the products they saw. While process color printing costs more to produce than single- or two-color work, it will be more effective in moving the reader to buy. Think for a moment of how you react to color in advertising when reading books and magazines or watching color TV. Does color affect you when shopping for the products you saw?

Color is an important process in producing graphic arts products. Technicians in the graphic arts need a knowledge of color and an understanding of the equipment and the skills required to reproduce it on the printed sheet.

• Color Principles

In order to work in color reproduction, a knowledge of color principles is important. The problem is knowing where to start a discussion of color because so many ideas are related closely with each other. One common starting point is a review of visible light.

Electromagnetic Spectrum

Electromagnetic waves carry energy in all directions throughout our universe. Recall from chapter 2 that a small portion of these waves—from 400–700 millimicrons—stimulates our sense of sight (figure 2.9). This part of the **electromagnetic spectrum** is called the **visible spectrum**. We see white light as a combination of relatively equal parts of all wavelengths in the visible spectrum. If a beam of white light is passed through a prism, the individual wavelengths are refracted into a rainbow of light-red, orange, yellow, green, blue, and violet (plate 6a).

All of the different colors are made up of just three colors of light: red, green, and blue. These are called the **primary additive colors**. Television projects the three beams of primary additive light onto the viewing tube to give full-color images. Incandescent and fluorescent bulbs emit the three additive colors also but not in the same proportion of red, green, and blue as the sun. The photographer selects film according to the light source under which the picture will be taken. The film's sensitivity must match the light source emission.

Seeing Color

The Greeks once thought that all objects emitted particles of light, that colored objects gave off colored particles. When they walked into the path of these particles, they thought, it was possible to see. Scientists now know a great deal about how we see. The objects we see are registered on the retina of the eye by reflected light form the object. The retina is made up of cells called rods and cones. Sensitivity is equally divided among these cells to the red, green, and blue wavelengths of light. If only red cells are energized, we see red; if all the cells are equally energized, we see white. As the wavelengths of light energize different numbers and combinations of these cells, we see a variety of hues.

The Color Wheel

A good way to learn basic color identification and relationships is to construct a color wheel (plate 6b). Artists, photographers, and printers use the color wheel as a tool in their work.

The three complementary colors, or colors directly opposite the primary additive colors of red, green, and blue, are known as the **primary subtractive colors**: cyan, magenta, and yellow. They are subtractive because they represent two of the three wavelengths of light minus one: Cyan is blue and green minus red, magenta is red and blue minus green, and yellow is green and red minus blue.

Cyan, magenta, and yellow are the colors used in color printing and color photography; in printing they are known as **process colors**. It is important to understand that process colors are special transparent inks that act as a filter on the printed page: White light (red-green-blue) is projected onto the paper where the subtractive color images are printed.

- Cyan absorbs red and reflects blue and green.
- Magenta absorbs green and reflects red and blue.
- Yellow absorbs blue and reflects green and red.

The white light is reflected from the paper through the filters (ink). The result is that our eyes see proportions of various wavelengths to make the printed job appear as the original color object. Where the three inks overlap equally, all color is absorbed and will appear to be black.

When we project three beams of light—red, blue, and green—onto a white screen, we produce our full array of colors from the primary colors (plate 6c). We can also produce a full array of color from reflected light with the primary subtractive colors (plate 6d).

• Type of Color Copy

For color reproduction, the printer has to work with a variety of types of original copy. Each type poses special problems. Basically, there are only two categories—transparent (positive transparencies and negatives) and reflection (photographs and artist's drawings)—but within each are several types. All color originals should be viewed in controlled light for exact results (figure 12.1). This is also true of color proofs. A color-viewing booth has light at 5,000°K for accurate color evaluation.

Figure 12.1. Viewing booth. Color material should be viewed in a standard viewing booth. The booth makes it possible to standardize view and color interpretation.

Positive Transparent Copy

One type of original copy with which the graphic arts photographer works is a **positive color transparency**. These transparencies, or **slides**, can come in a variety of sizes from 35 millimeters to 8″ × 10″. Slides are excellent to work with because it is possible to see how the finished job should appear (plate 7a). Slides, however, do create some special problems. For example, slides have a longer density range, usually greater than the printing processes can reproduce. The small-sized transparencies must be enlarged for printing and, therefore, must be extremely sharp in their focus when delivered to the printer. Many times, if a small transparency is to be used in the printed job, the slide can be duped. This process makes a duplicate transparency that is enlarged to the size needed for the printed job. Another method is to make an **internegative** from the slide. The negative is then placed in an enlarger and a new, full-size positive produced.

Reflection Copy

Recall from chapter 4 that **reflection copy** is an image we view from reflected light. It can be either a color photograph or an artist's original. Reflection copy usually has a density range close to the limits the printing operations can reproduce. The printer can also see how the final job should appear. Such copy does, however, have some drawbacks in some of the color correction processes (discussed in chapter 13).

Color Negative Copy

A **color negative transparency** is another form of original copy for the color separation process. Some newspapers work directly from the color negative to make color separations. This process has the advantage of using the conventional continuous-tone darkroom enlarging equipment for making the separations. The continuous-tone separations are made on a special Resisto Rapid Pan paper. **Resisto Rapid Pan paper** is a water-resistant paper made especially for color separation for this process. It is panchromatic and will react to all light waves. It must be processed in near total darkness. A #10 or #13 safelight can be used. The difficulty in using this process is not knowing how the final result should appear because the color negative is the color opposite the final reproduction (plate 7b).

• Color Reproduction

Before viewing the processing steps in color separation, some basic information is necessary. What is the function of the ink? What is the function of paper in the process? How important is the halftone process?

Ink

The process color inks cyan, magenta, and yellow are transparent based. That means the vehicle and the color pigment will transmit light. When these inks are laid down on the paper in the printing process, they will act as filters to absorb or transmit the white light reflecting from the paper. Because these inks transmit and absorb certain parts of the projected light, the viewer will receive an image that resembles the original color copy. Black ink is added to the three colors to give the proper density in the shadow areas and to increase the reproduction range.

Paper

In viewing a color-printed job, the paper performs an important part of the job. The surface of the paper both carries the ink and reflects the light when we view the printed piece. Most color jobs are printed on white paper so that all wavelengths of light are reflected. However, consider what happens to the color accuracy if blue paper is used: Blue light is reflected back through the ink (acting like a filter), disturbing the color balance.

The Halftone Process

The illusion of seeing a printed halftone as a continuous-tone black-and-white print was discussed in chapter 8. In color reproduction, this same illusion is at work. Each color is separated from the original copy photographically and is made into a monochromatic (black-and-white)

Figure 12.2. Camera with transparent copyboard used for separating transparencies.

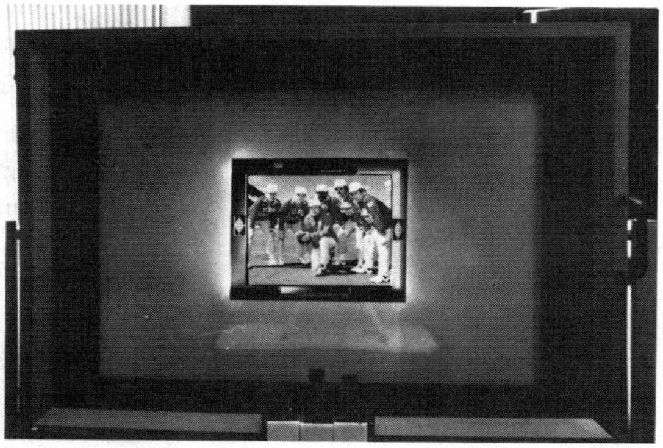

Figure 12.3. Transparency in the copyboard. Notice masks are used to allow light only through the transparency. Copy has a gray scale and control steps.

negative. A halftone of each separation is made. The screen angle of the dots is changed to avoid a moiré. This angle change also allows the dots to appear in a cluster instead of printing one on top of the other (plate 7c). If the dots were printed in register with the others, the dots would appear as black.

The combination of the screen angles, transparent inks, and white paper reflecting the light gives the viewer the full-color reproduction. If these variables are not controlled, then accurate color duplication of the original is not possible.

• A Review of the Separation Process

Basic Procedures

When one begins to learn a new subject, an overview of the full operation must first be established before exceptions or problems are considered. Let us work through an ideal set of procedures for color separations—there are enough variations and problems to deal with later. Assume that we have perfect inks so that special techniques for color correction are unnecessary. For this example, a 4″ × 5″ color positive transparency will be separated for same-size reproduction. The easiest way to begin is to explain the direct screen separation technique. Equipment in the example will be the process camera with a transparent copyboard (figure 12.2). To make a direct screen separation use the following procedures:

1. Place the transparency in the copyboard with a mask around it so only the transparency is showing (figure 12.3). Swing the camera lights so they will shine through the transparency toward the lens.

2. Adjust the camera setting for same size—100 percent. Set the lens aperture for proper f/stop (try f/16).

3. Set up the darkroom and sink for processing panchromatic film. Knowing where every tool is located is important since the film will be handled in total darkness.

4. Obtain a set of pre-angled contact gray negative screens of the desired ruling. Each of the four records (negatives) will require a different screen angle: Cyan, 105°; magenta, 75°; yellow, 90°; black, 45°. Each screen in this set has the dots at these prescribed angles. The screen angles suggested are not absolutes; some shops use different colors at other than the suggested angles. It is best to use the darker colors of magenta, cyan, and black at the angles that are 30° apart to eliminate the moirés. The yellow, which is the lightest color ink used, is always at the angle that is only 15° from the others. Because of the limited number of degrees in the circle to work with, these angles have become the accepted angles for the manufacturers to make the pre-angled screens.

5. Set exposure for the main, flash, and bump. It is assumed at this point that exposures have been determined previously by tests. The pan film will allow us to record exposure for all the colors since it has color sensitivity across the visible spectrum (see chapter 4).

6. Place a sheet of panchromatic film on the vacuum back; and mount a halftone screen into place. Remember that this operation is performed in total darkness. The contact screen angle should be 105°. Place the red filter in front of the lens and make the main exposure. Next, open the camera back and make the flash exposure.

The red filter will pass red light to the film, exposing the areas where red light hits the film. The red filter does not allow blue and green light (cyan color) to reach the film; these will be the transparent areas of the negative. These open areas represent the amount of green and blue that appears in the original copy. When the printing plate is made from this negative, it is printed with cyan ink.

7. Make a second negative with a green filter in front of the lens. Use pan film with a screen angle of 75°. Make the main and flash exposure. This filter will pass green light and will hold back, or absorb, red and blue light. The processed negative will be dark in the green areas and clear in the red-blue (magenta) areas. When this negative is used to make a printing plate, the ink to be printed is magenta.

8. Place a blue filter in front of the lens. Use pan film with a screen angle of 90°. Make the main and flash exposure. The blue light coming from the copy will expose the film. The red and green light (yellow) will be absorbed by the filter and will leave those areas of the negative transparent. When this negative is used to make a printing plate, yellow ink will be used on the press.

9. For the black printer, you have several choices of filters that can be used, including a yellow filter, a #85B, or you can make a short exposure through each of the filters used for the other negatives—red, green, blue. This is called the split filter method. Be sure to use pan film and a screen with a 45° angle. The black printer negative should be somewhat overexposed. The highlight dots should appear in the middle tones—0.70 density. The highlight areas should be completely closed.

The four negatives should appear as shown in figure 12.4. The basic process has been discussed without emphasizing the detail and precision required to get the job done. The topics of tone balance, gray balance, and color correction must be covered first.

Tone Balance

Tone balance refers to the goal that the tones (densities) of the reproduction should be approximately the same tones that are in the original. Tone balance is controlled by the halftoning process.

(a)

(b)

Figure 12.4. Examples of separations negatives. This set of negatives is a black-and-white record of the standard colors. (a) Cyan, (b) magenta, (c) yellow, and (d) black.

Gray Balance

Gray balance is the task of making the gray tones in the reproduction appear gray to the eye. The tones are controlled in the exposures by making the cyan printer print more ink in the set than the yellow and magenta printers. This means the cyan halftone negative must appear more open and less dense than the others. This difference makes a darker printer, but we need a darker printer because of the lack of perfect inks. If the three printers were made equal in the dots values, the printed job would appear reddish.

To make the cyan halftone different from the magenta and yellow halftones, the camera operator must alter the cyan exposures. This is done by a reduced main exposure that opens up the middle tones in the negative. The bump (no-screen) exposure is then made to close the highlight dots to the desired densities. The flash exposure must also be adjusted to give the desired shadow dots.

(c) (d)

Figure 12.4. (continued)

Color Correction

Several film manufacturers have developed systems and quality control guides to assist the camera operator (figure 12.5). The most important variable in color reproduction is the relationship between the highlight, middle-tone, and shadow densities. The DuPont Company uses a step wedge with three densities labeled H (highlight), M (middle tone), and B (shadow). If the camera operator controls the densities in these three steps, a reasonably good set of separations can be produced.

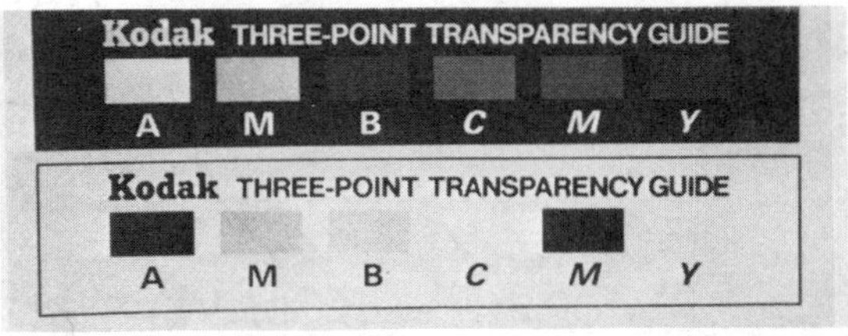

Figure 12.5. Kodak three-point control target and three-point color guide. The lower picture shows how the target appears in the negative. The M (magenta) is dark. This was made with a green filter. (Courtesy of Eastman Kodak Co.)

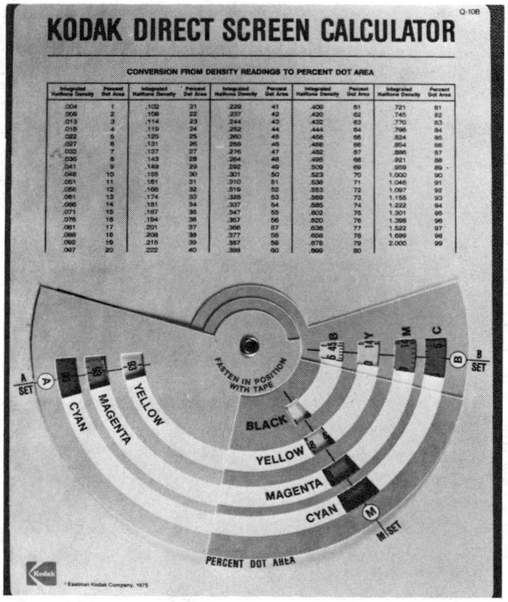

Figure 12.6. Eastman Kodak direct screen calculator. (Courtesy of Eastman Kodak Co.)

In addition to the aim (target) point scale used in the photographic separation steps, computers (dial type) have been developed to assist the operator in giving targets for densities in these steps. A computer is shown in figure 12.6.

Color correction is a specialized operation that uses these aim points to control color quality. Unfortunately, not everything in the system is operationally ideal. Process color inks are not perfect light filters; halftone screens cannot record the full tonal range of most color originals; press ink densities cannot match the densities of color originals. **Color correction** is thus a specialized operation that attempts to account for these limitations.

• Separation Processes

Two approaches can be used in making a set of separation negatives or positives. The first process is called **direct screen separation** (figure 12.7). In this procedure, the separation of color

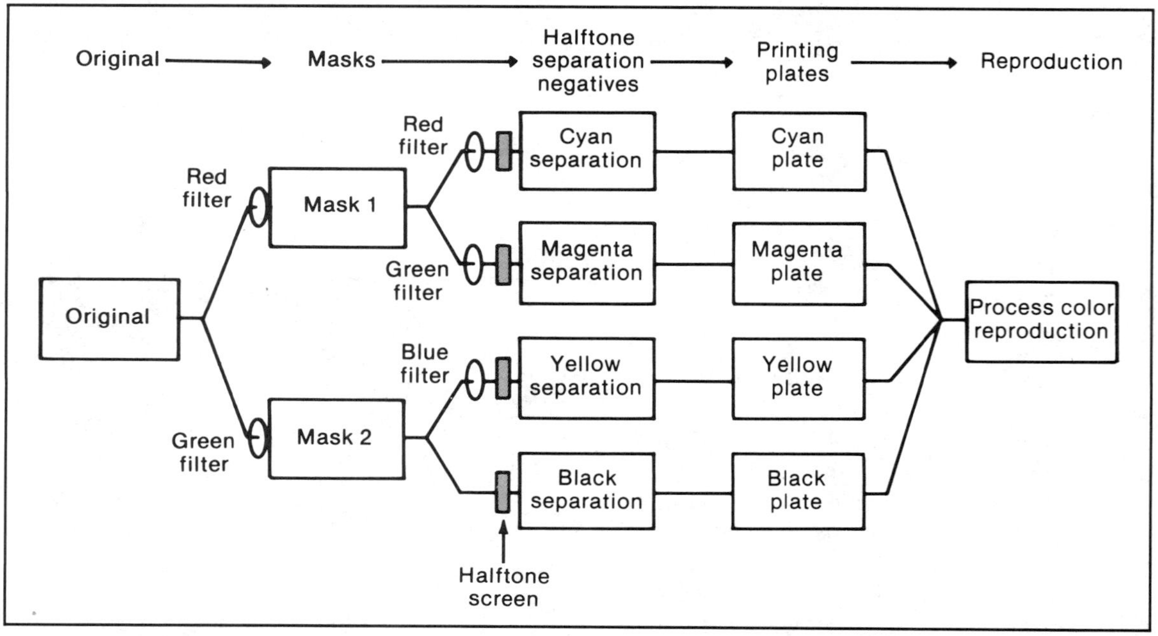

Figure 12.7. Diagram of steps for direct screen separations.

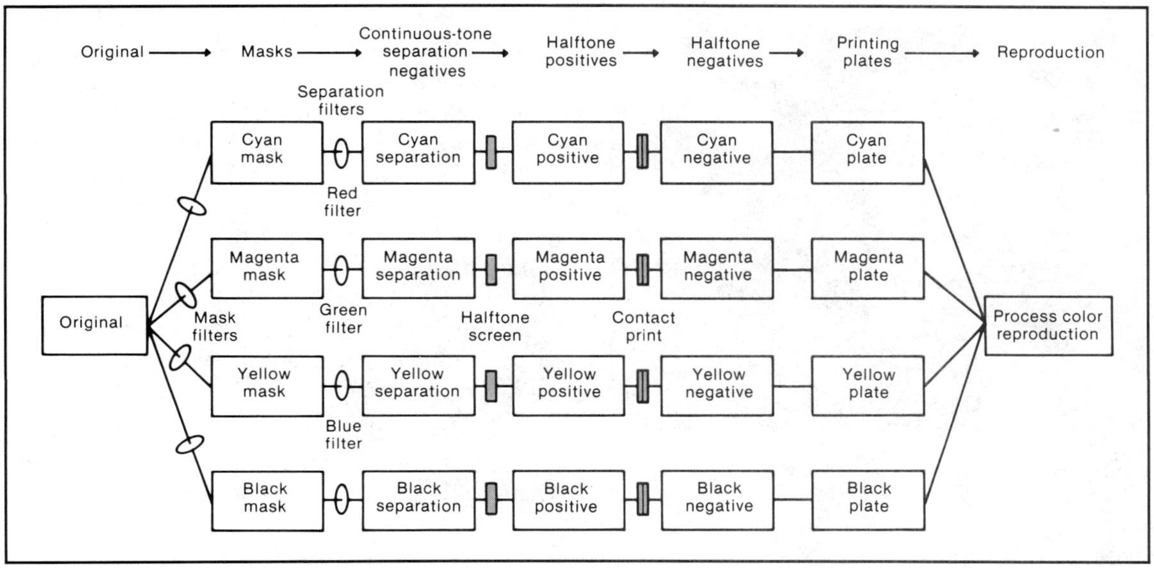

Figure 12.8. Diagram of steps for indirect separations.

and making of halftones are done together. This method is the fastest and most direct. If the ad or illlustration is to be used in several different-sized publications, the entire process must be performed for each size. Direct screen separation is currently the most widely used process.

The second process is called **indirect color separation** (figure 12.8). Here, continuous-tone separations are made for each color. Screened positives are then made. Next halftone negatives are contacted or projected in the camera from the positives. The advantage of this method is that the separation step is separate from the halftone step. If different sizes of the illustration are needed, only the halftoning needs to be done for those sizes. The disadvantage is the cost, both in time and material.

Mechanical Separation Using Gamma Gray Tones

While the gamma gray tone process is not used in large production situations, it provides a great deal of fundamental information and practice in the color separation process. To complete a set of separations using this technique, a set of gamma gray paints is needed in addition to the graphic arts darkroom, camera, and films. Use the following procedures:

1. Using the gamma gray colors, make a step gray scale (plate 8a). Be sure to allow the paints to dry thoroughly.

2. Using the gray scale as copy, follow regular halftone procedures and make a halftone negative of the step gray scale.

3. Follow contacting procedures and make a contact print on photographic print paper.

4. Using a reflection densitometer, read the halftone density of each step, then convert the density readings to dot percentages of each step (table 4.1), or measure dot size with a dot area meter.

5. Obtain a line drawing (like a drawing in a coloring book) and make a line negative. When the film is dry, make four contact prints.

6. Using color pencils, color the original drawing.

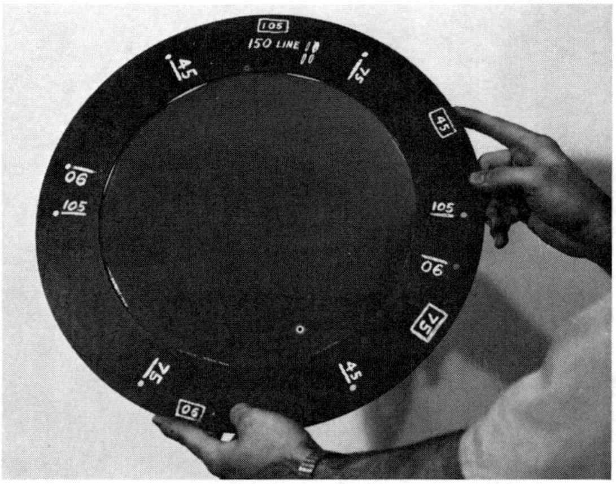

Figure 12.9. Rotating screen device. A single screen is mounted in a cardboard or vinyl circle and punched to obtain the various screen angles.

7. Using an ink percentage chart, identify the colors on the chart that are close to a particular color on your original. Mark the percentages of cyan, magenta, yellow, and black necessary to match your color closely (plate 8b). Do this for all elements of your original.

8. Using the four line prints, label one for each of the colors cyan, magenta, yellow, and black. Using the gamma grays, place the grays on the four proofs in their proper gray percentages (plate 8c).

9. Make regular halftone negatives of each of the four gray prints. (These prints are actually black-and-white records of each of the four colors.)

You will have to use a set of pre-angled halftone screens or a single screen that can be rotated to give each color its own screen angle (figure 12.9): cyan, 105°; magenta, 75°; yellow, 90°; black, 45°. When the negatives are dry, they can be used for making a set of color proofs.

Again, one of the most satisfactory proofing methods for the small or low-volume shop is the 3M negative Color Key or similar materials.

10. After exposure, each sheet is developed, using a soft wiping device or cotton pad and Color Key developer. The exposed areas are hardened and remain on the base. The unexposed areas are soft and will be washed away. Use a water wash after development, and blot dry with a paper towel. The material should be viewed by reflected light. Lay the yellow down first on a piece of stock to be run or on a piece of white stock (plate 8d). Then place the colors magenta, cyan, and black over the first in register. Compare the proof to the original and see how closely the colors match (plate 8e).

Understanding this basic procedure, even though it was performed mechanically, is fundamental to attempting more complex methods.

Making Separations in Your 35-Millimeter Camera

While this technique is not being used in industry, schools or small shops with limited equipment can make a pleasing four-color job of still-life-type setups. The person doing this will learn and practice the principles of color separation.

For an example of this technique, assemble a display that will not be subjected to movement. We have arranged a bowl of fruit and some napkins. A backdrop was used as a background (figure 12.10). The following procedures describe this separation technique:

1. Load your camera with a medium-speed film like ASA/ISO 125. Set your camera on a tripod, and focus on your display. We included a gray scale and color bar on our test.

2. Expose the first frame, after setting your flood lamps, to make a good black-and-white print. Most cameras have a built-in light meter. Set your aperture at f/8 and your shutter at the appropriate setting for a good exposure.

3. For your second shot, move the film to the next frame. Keep your aperture at f/8. Change your exposure time the equivalent of two f/stops

over exposure. This will give you a very overexposed negative. The print of this negative will become the black printer.

4. For the third shot, advance the film to the next frame. (Do this carefully so you do not move the camera.) Hold a #25 red filter in front of the lens. Do not change the f/stop, but adjust the shutter speed for the correct exposure. The same amount of the scene remains in focus for all your shots if the f/stop is not changed. This negative will make the cyan printer.

5. For the fourth shot, advance the film to the next frame. For this exposure, hold a #58 green filter in front of the lens. Do not change the f/stop, but change the shutter speed to set the light meter for the correct exposure. The internal light meter reads the filtered light, which is why it is different with each filter. The negative that is exposed with the green filter will be for the magenta printer.

6. For the final exposure, move the film to the next frame. This time you will use a #47B blue filter. Adjust the exposure time and not the f/stop. The blue filter negative will become the yellow printer negative.

7. Rewind the film back into the cassette for removal from the camera. Process the film according to instructions that came with your roll of film. After the processing cycle, and when the film is dry, you will be ready to make enlargements of each of the exposures.

8. The first negative was for a straight black-and-white print. Make the best print possible, keeping a good record of your exposure and developing time. When you are satisfied that you have a good print, use the same exposure and developing time for each of the negatives.

9. Make a print of each of the negatives at the exposure and developing time used earlier in this example. These will be your continuous-tone separation prints. Use RC paper when making the prints. The overexposed second negative should be a very light print, which is what you want. The three other prints will be correct densities, but each will appear different because of the use of the filters. When these prints are dry, you will be ready to make halftone negatives (figure 12.11). (If you have not had any experience with continuous-tone photography, ask your instructor or supervisor for help with these techniques.)

Figure 12.10. Still-life setup for separation by 35-millimeter camera. Notice camera is on a tripod to prevent movement.

10. Because these separation prints are black-and-white records of where the various colors are in the original scene, the halftones can be made with ortho (litho) film under a red safelight.

Using the same halftoning techniques you

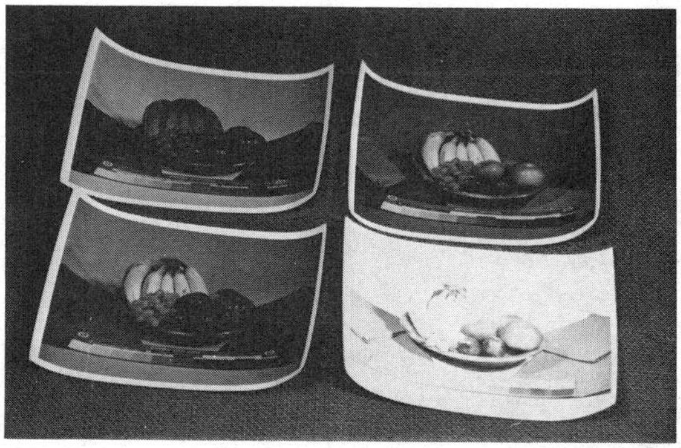

Figure 12.11. Continuous-tone, black-and-white prints of separated colors.

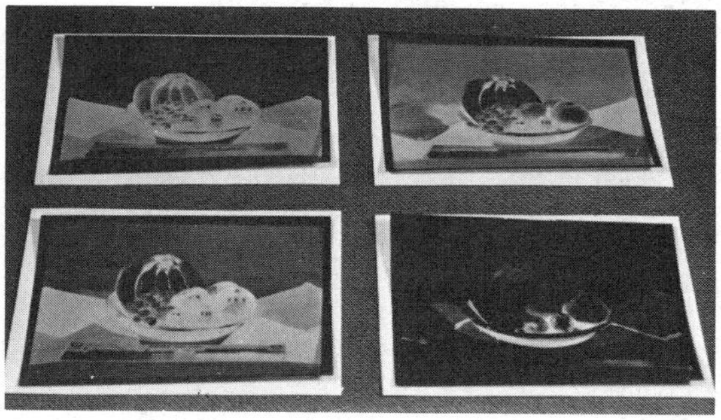

Figure 12.12. Halftone negatives of separation prints.

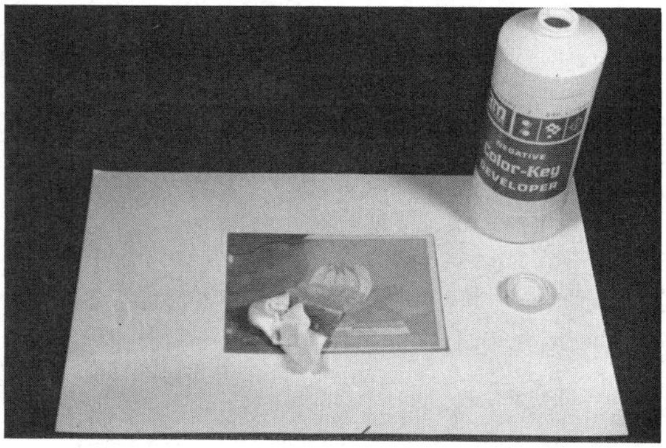

Figure 12.13. Color Key colored proofs being developed.

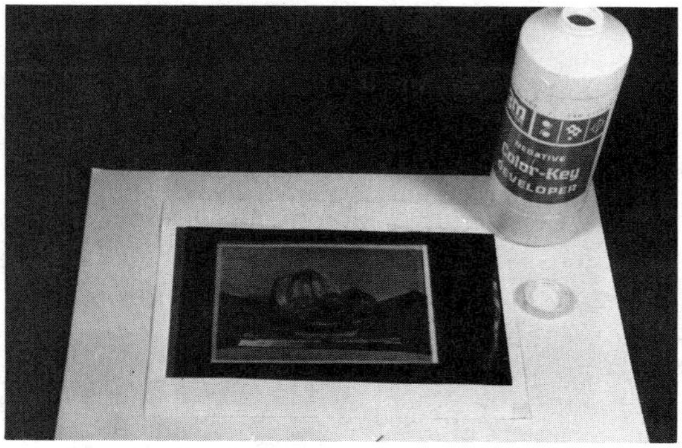

Figure 12.14. Four Color Key proofs in register. The four proofs are combined to show the appearance of the final job.

used in the gamma gray separation procedures, make a halftone negative of each of the four prints. When evaluating the prints for highlight and shadow areas, assume the four prints to be one. Find the one highlight and the one shadow area, and screen all the prints at the same exposure. The four processed negatives should appear as those in figure 12.12.

After the negatives are dried, make a set of color proofs. Do not forget to expose the Color Key material through the base. Develop each proof with the proper chemical and a soft wipe (figure 12.13). The assembled Color Keys should make the completed proofs appear as the original copy (figure 12.14).

• Direct Screen Separations

Color Separation from Reflection Copy without Color Correction

Color separation from reflection copy is a frequent shop assignment. The process is used in making a set of separations from a color photographic print or an artist's original painting.

The most common procedure is to work with this copy in the graphic arts camera.

Before starting this process, a discussion of filter factors and filter ratios is necessary since filters will be used to separate the colors of the original picture into black-and-white film records. Because filters used in graphic arts photography subtract some of the light passing through the filter and lens back to the film, you will need either to increase the exposure time or to open the lens to compensate for the loss of light.

The number by which you need to make these changes is called a **filter factor**. Filter factor numbers are used also in continuous-tone photography.

These numbers depend upon the film and light sources you are using. Table 12.1 shows the filter factors and the light sources for lithographic panchromatic film

In using the filter factor numbers, the camera operator must first establish the exposure for the film without the use of a filter. You have done this for litho orthochromatic film. You must now do this for litho panchromatic film. Ortho litho film has a film speed of ASA/ISO 6. Pan litho film has an ASA/ISO 40. The doubling of an ASA/ISO number is the equivalent of one f/stop smaller or the halving of the exposure time. The difference between ortho film and pan film is approximately 2 1/3 stops. Try a pan halftone without using a filter to establish your exposure time. Do a flash test on the pan film also because of the faster film.

Now back to the filter factors. The factor

Table 12.1. Filters and filter factors for lithographic pan film.

	Filters		
Light source	#25 red	#58 green	#47 blue
Plused xenone	2	12	12
Tungsten-quartz-iodine	2	12	40

number for the #25 red filter with pulsed xenon lights is 2 (table 12.1). That means the exposure with that filter is one f/stop more open or twice the exposure time for that film.

Another term with which the color worker will become familiar when working with filters and graphic arts film is **filter ratio**. The filter ratio differs from the filter factor. The ratio numbers appear on the data sheet that comes with a package of film (see table 12.2).

Table 12.2. Filter ratios based on the red #25 exposure as 1.0.

	Filters		
Light source	#25 red	#58 green	#47 blue
Pulsed xenone	1.0	2.0	4.0
Tungsten-quartz-iodine	1.0	4.0	12.0

Multiply the #25 exposure by the ratio number for the other filters.

After you have established the correct red #25 filter exposure, this is considered a ratio of 1. The exposures for the other filters—#58 green and #47B blue—are based on the time for the red #25. An example would be a #25 exposure of fifteen seconds. The exposure time for the green #58 filter shot would be doubled, or thirty seconds.

The filter factor numbers are used for finding the exposure when using that particular filter under certain lights. The ratio numbers are used for finding exposures after establishing an exposure for the #25 red filter in graphic arts photography.

Include with the color copy a step gray scale and color bar (plate 9a). (The three-step color bar will indicate which separation negative you have.) The three marked steps—A, 0; M, 0.70; and B, 1.60—are the target steps that will help to produce satisfactory results, using the following procedures:

1. Using a color densitometer, determine highlight and shadow densities. Determine your

Table 12.3. Target aim points for steps A, M, and B.

	A		M		B	
Printer	Dot%	Density	Dot%	Density	Dot%	Density
Cyan	90	1.0	32	0.16	5	0.02
Magenta	93	1.15	45	0.26	17	0.08
Yellow	93	1.15	45	0.26	17	0.08
Black			90	1.0	45	0.26

main and flash exposures for the three color halftones. The black exposure is made to place the highlight dot in the middle tone of the picture. Record these readings for future reference.

2. Place the copy and gray scale in the copyboard (plate 9b). Be sure the copy has register marks in the margins.

3. Set the camera, lights, and controls for the desired size. Set the timer for exposure (determined by test). Then make the following:

- The first exposure for the red filter negative (cyan printer),
- The second exposure for the green filter negative (magenta printer),
- The third exposure for the blue filter negative (yellow printer),
- The fourth exposure for the yellow filter negative (black printer).

Each exposure will require a separate piece of film and the appropriate exposures to obtain the described results. The target aim points are shown as negative readings in table 12.3.

These targets in table 12.3 are to be used for the pieces of film. The density readings are above-base density, or the density of the emulsion and not the film base. This means the densitometer must be zeroed on a clear section of the film. Refer to chapter 4 for a discussion on zeroing.

Another precaution is that each exposed negative must have the screen set at a precise angle:

- Red filter negative, 105°;
- Green filter negative, 75°;
- Blue filter negative, 90°;
- Yellow filter negative, 45°.

Screen angles were discussed briefly in the mechanical separation procedures. The pre-angled screens should be punched so that register pins will make the angles precise when mounted on the camera vacuum back. If using a circular screen, it must be punched on each edge (see figure 12.22).

4. Register punch four pieces of pan litho film in total darkness. With the film punched, place three pieces in a light-tight box, and mount the fourth, emulsion up, on the vacuum back pins. Place the halftone screen over the film on the pins, and turn on the vacuum. Carefully roll out the sandwich, and check that the filter being used matches the screen angle.

5. Make each of the four exposures, always returning the exposed film to storage and checking to insure that the correct filter and screen angles are being used. Then process the film using regular halftone development procedures.

For all film developing in total darkness with panchromatic materials, it would be ideal to have a film processor. Most small shops can not afford the processor and the great quantity of chemistry that is required to keep the processor in balance.

A suggestion, which is not a standard practice in the industry, would be to do totally dark processing in a color-print-developing drum (figure 12.15). These developing drums are available from many manufacturers. The film is loaded into the drum after exposure. The drum is closed, and the processing can be done in the light. Developing times and the chemistry used would be the same as that used in tray processing. It is much more convenient if you have a motorized agitator base that will rotate the drum during the processing cycle (figure 12.16). If this is not available, the drum can be rolled on a level surface.

The chemistry required for an 8″ × 10″ drum is two ounces for each of the three required chemistries: developer, stop, and fix. The chemistry is poured into the drum, and the timer is set for each step.

This unit has worked well in many shops for small pan-film-size work. This process also works well for the Resisto Pan Prints used in the ROP negative color separation process (see the section on color separation from a color negative original).

6. After the film is dry, visually examine the set for obvious defects and make Color Key proofs for color evaluations. All exposures must be made while the camera remains set up for that copy. If one separation must be reshot, then it must be made before the camera settings are changed. It is not possible to reset the camera to the exact position so that halftone dots align correctly on a remake.

Color Separation by Contact from a Transparency without Color Correction

This process is a popular method in the industry, but the separations are limited to the same size as the original picture. Because of the satisfactory results from this process, the photographic industry is called upon to make duplicate transparencies for the graphic arts. These transparency duplicates can be made to any specific size

Figure 12.15. Example of color print developing drum.

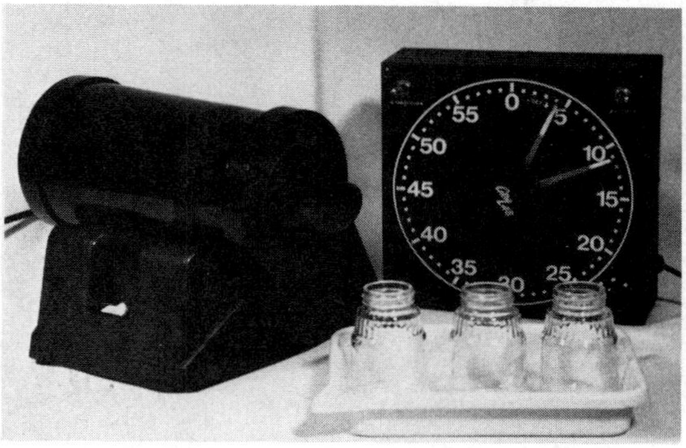

Figure 12.16. Motorized processor with developing drum.

from any size original. A 35-millimeter slide can be duplicated to an 8″ × 10″ size or larger.

Direct screen separation by contact is extremely important in publication printing where even a single page may carry twelve full-color illustrations (figure 12.17). The transparency duplicates are each made to reproduction size and then are stripped into position. The separations are made by contacting the entire page.

These separations are best accomplished using an open-face vacuum frame with a point source light. Most shops that do this work have a filter turret where push buttons bring the proper filters into position for exposures (figure 12.18). Register pins for both film and screens should be used to keep the work in register (figure

Figure 12.17. Example of advertisement to be printed from multiple color illustrations.

Figure 12.18. Multiple filter turret used in contact separation work.

Figure 12.19. Kodak register pin punch, pins, and punched sheet.

12.19). A cutout overlay sheet assures good contact and vacuum holddown.

All materials must be in place and the sink set up because the operations are performed in total darkness. Before operations begin, make a carrier for the transparency, the aim point scale, and the color bar. To make the carrier, a piece of ortho (litho) film is exposed by the point source light in the vacuum frame. Make a step off to determine how much exposure is necessary to give an overall 0.70–1 density to the film (see figure 8.22). Develop the film in a continuous-tone developer like Dektol. After determining the text exposure and development times, expose a complete piece of film of the proper size for a carrier so that it has a density between 0.70 and 1. A 5″ × 7″ piece of film is a satisfactory size for a 4″ × 5″ transparency, with the three-point transparency guide (plate 9c).

1. Carefully strip the transparency into the center of the carrier, placing the tape on the base side of both pieces. Try to use as little cellophane tape as possible.

2. Expose a piece of pan masking film, using the white light from the point light source, to the transparency after the carrier and masking film have been register punched. Pan masking

film is a specialized film material that will develop into a slightly out-of-focus mask to be placed over the transparency. The softness, or lack of sharpness, in the masking film will allow the sandwich of the mask and transparency to make a good halftone without any lines showing where the images of the mask and original blend together.

The transparency and the masking film should be emulsion up. Give a trial exposure of twenty seconds on tap 2. Your time may vary because of your point source light setup. The density range of the mask should be 0.90 ± 0.05 (45° mask of the usable density of the transparency 2). The white light mask is used only to reduce the density of the transparency. The printing process can only print approximately a 1.6 density. A transparency usually has a range of 2.40 or more. The masking film should be developed in a continuous-tone developer HC = 110 dilution D. If the density range of the mask is less than or more than a 0.90 ± 0.05, remake the mask. The range is measured on the A–B patches.

Use this mask in register with all subsequent separation operations. More detail on masking is presented in chapter 13.

3. Place the red filter #25, the 0.60 ND filter, and the 1.00 ND filter in a filter holder. Register punch a piece of high-contrast pan film and place it emulsion up in the vacuum frame on the pins. Place the transparency and mask on the pins (no screen) for the bump exposure and the two ND filters. A bump exposure is performed with the red filter. Try fifteen seconds on tap 3.

Remove only the 1.00 ND filter, and place a halftone screen in position (105°) on the pins. Make a main exposure for fifteen seconds. The #25 and 0.60 ND are in the filter holder.

Next, remove the mask and transparency, leaving the screen for the flash exposure of twenty seconds. The filter for the flash exposure should be a 3.5 ND without a color filter in position.

All of these operations should be performed in total darkness. The advantage of having a filter turret allows all filter changes to be made by pushing buttons.

The final negative can be processed as a regular halftone. It must be processed in total darkness. Use the recommended developer for the brand of film being used.

4. For the magenta printer negative, follow the same procedure as in step 2, except do not use the bump exposure. The green filter #58 is used instead of #25. Try a main exposure of twenty-five seconds and a flash of twenty seconds. Use a screen angle of 75° (flash must be made with a 3.5 ND filter).

5. For the yellow printer negative, use the same procedures (no bump exposure). Use a #47B blue filter with an eighty-second main exposure and a twenty-second flash. Screen angle is 90°.

6. For the black printer negative, use a #85B filter with a twenty-second main exposure. No flash is necessary for the black printer halftone. The screen angle should be 45°. Aim points can be taken from the Direct Screen Calculator. Table 12.4 shows such aim points.

If the trial set of negatives is close to these readings, make a set of Color Key proofs. Check the proofs against the copy. A set of color separation negatives without color correction is said to have **eye-pleasing color**.

Color Separation from a Color Negative Original

One method to separate color negatives is called **ROP color**, which means "run of the paper". ROP is a quick and relatively simple method of making color separations. The separations are made as continuous-tone black-and-white prints. A black printer can be made but is not necessary. The separation operations must be done in almost total darkness with a #10 or #13 safe-

Table 12.4. Direct screen aim points

	A		M		B	
Printer	Dot%	Density	Dot%	Density	Dot%	Density
Cyan	90	1.00	32	0.170	7	0.032
Magenta	93	1.15	45	0.264	17	0.083
Yellow	93	1.15	45	0.264	17	0.083
Black			90	1.00	49	0.292

light filter. The separation prints are then converted to halftones with ortho film under red safelight conditions. Pre-angled screens are necessary. ROP color has been used by newspapers and small commercial shops that need to print eye-pleasing color.

Making separations from color negatives requires a special photographic paper made only by the Kodak Company: Resisto Rapid Pan paper. The paper is a panchromatic material that has an emulsion speed fast enough that a regular photographic enlarger (tungsten light source) can be used.

For establishing standards in this process, it is best to have a test color negative with a gray scale in the negative (plate 10a). A correctly exposed color negative will have the following readings of these steps when the densitometer is zeroed on the unexposed border: white step, 1.10 to 1.30; black step, 0.30 to 0.50. While masking for color correction can be used in this process, the following procedures will be for an unmasked set:

1. Make a carrier for the negative as was done during the contacting operations. Use a glass negative carrier to keep the negative from buckling under the heat of the enlarger lamp. A register punch system should be used to place and hold the paper on the enlarging easel. Focus the negative on the easel for the desired size.

2. Make exposures for the three prints on separate sheets of Resisto Rapid Pan paper for the times indicated. Set the f/stop at f/8. Because we are working with negative color originals in this process, two of the filters are different than those used in conventional separation from positive originals (table 12.5).

Develop the cyan printer negative in Dektol developer (stock) for 2 minutes. Develop the magenta negative in Dektol developer 1:1 dilution for 2 minutes. The yellow printer is developed in Dektol 1:2 dilution for 1 1/2 minutes. After the prints have dried, check the density on a reflection densitometer for the aim points shown in table 12.6.
The prints will appear as in plate 10b.

If the prints are close to these readings, proceed to make the halftone negatives. Remember to use pre-angled screens.

In all subsequent separation work, be sure to make density readings and compare them to the standard set. Lighter copy will need less exposure, and denser copy will require more exposure.

After the halftones are produced, make a set of Color Key proofs to view the results (plate 10c).

Separations for Scanning

A **color scanner** is rapidly becoming the most used machine for making separations in the industry. The scanner performs the color separation procedures electronically. Many of the

Table 12.5. ROP filter selection

Separations	Filter	Suggested exposure (seconds)
Cyan printer	#92 red	13
Magenta printer	#99 green	15
Yellow printer	#47B blue	30

Table 12.6. Aim points

Printer	White Step	Shadow Step
Cyan	0.12	1.40
Magenta	0.08	1.30
Yellow	0.08	1.25

photographic steps that have been necessary to complete the set of separations are handled by the scanner's computer circuits (figure 12.20).

A number of companies manufacture scanners. Shown in figures 12.21–12.23 are three machines that are available.

Scanners are expensive machines and very few schools have them, but the fundamentals learned by camera and contact methods will give you the basis for operating these units should you find a job in color separation. Figure 12.24 shows a small, inexpensive scanner that has been adapted for instruction.

Scanners operate and produce separations by three methods. Some scanners produce continuous-tone separations. Others use the contact screen to produce halftones. The third type has a laser light and electronically generates the dots for the halftone. Many of the scanners can produce either negatives or positives. Because of the high speed of the laser-type scanners, and because of their ability to use inexpensive rapid access developing film, these units are doing a major share of the work.

The scanners can accept transparencies and reflection copy (figure 12.25) as originals. The operator sets the controls for the proper highlight, middle-tone, and shadow areas (figure 12.26). These readings are stored in the com-

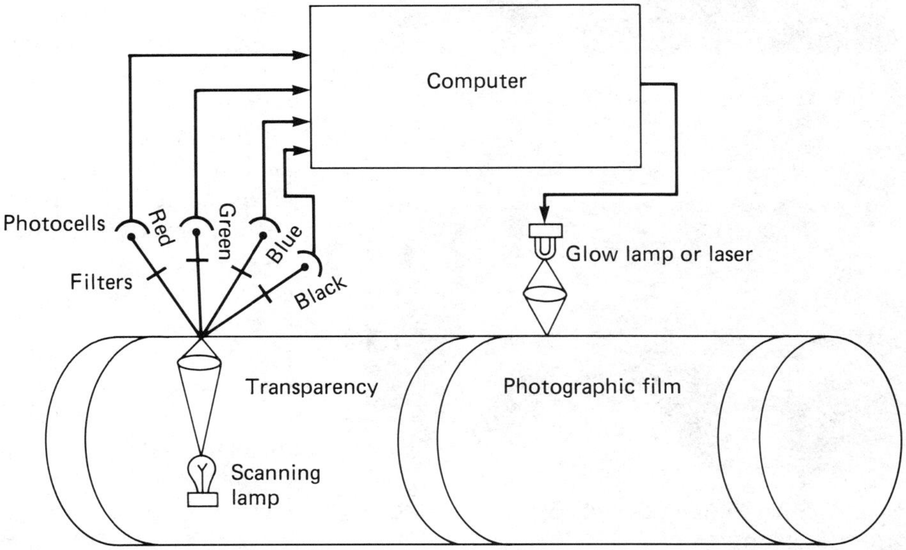

Figure 12.20. Schematic drawing of basic elements of color separation scanner.

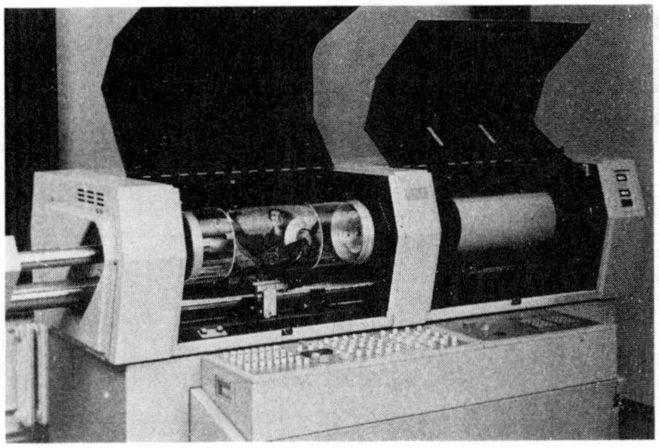

Figure 12.21. HCM 299 scanner copy, and film areas.

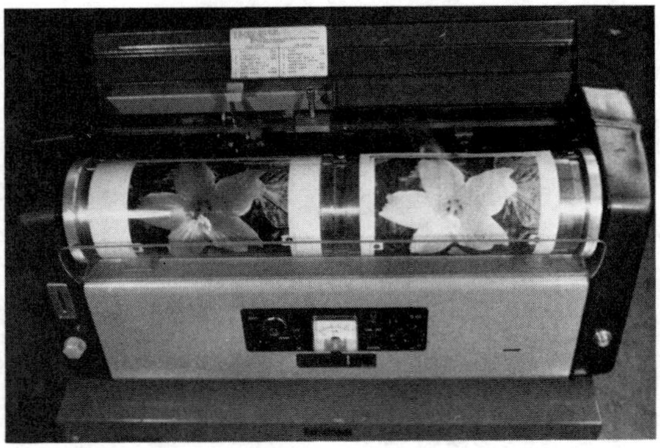

Figure 12.24. Roneotronic scanner. This scanner, made for mimeograph stencils, can be adapted for basic scanner instruction.

Figure 12.22. Linotype-Paul color scanner.

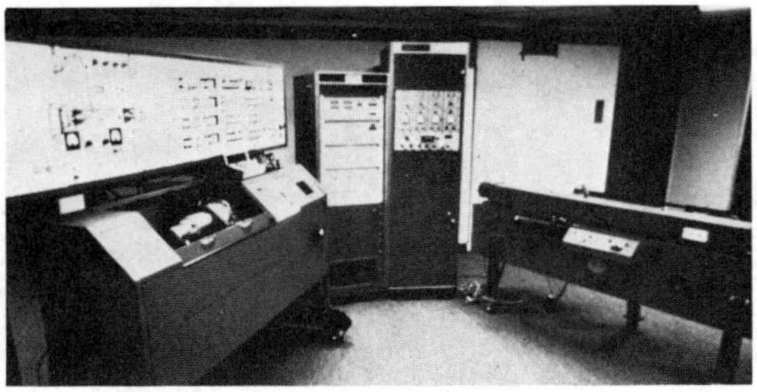

Figure 12.23. Printing Development, Inc. (PDI) scanner complex.

puter area of the machine and control the output to produce the desired negative or positive dot values.

Scanners handle the color correction problems (see chapter 13) through electronics. The operator is able to dial into the machine the amount of correction that is necessary to produce a quality job. The scanner eliminates the many photographic steps that are necessary in color correction. The PDI scanner is able to scan the copy and produce the four separations on one pass through the machine.

Most scanners on the market operate similarly to a lathe—that is, the copy and the film revolve on a central shaft (figure 12.27). A glow lamp reads the densities of the original for the particular color that is being separated. An output light exposes the film and creates the halftone negative or positive. The scanner can both enlarge and reduce to fit the printer's need for size changes within the limits of the machine. For the gravure industry, the scanner can engrave the cylinder and skip the film step.

Scanners are being developed that will not rotate as a lathe but that will work on a moving, or scanning, light. The scanned information can then be stored, and the output of the machine will not have to be working with the input units.

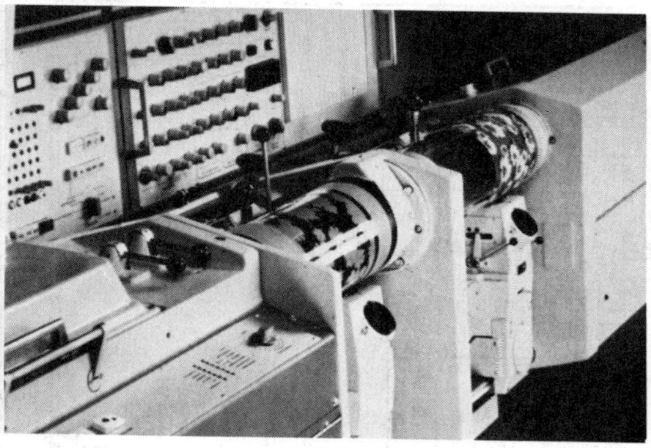

Figure 12.25. Scanner for both transparencies and reflection copy.

Figure 12.26. Setting up HCM D–300 scanner for separation job.

This device will allow the scanned data to be sent over wires or microwave so that the output part of the scanner can be miles away from where the copy was scanned.

Using the Densitometer in Color Work

Chapter 4 discussed sensitometry and the use of the densitometer in measuring continuous-tone density as well as halftone density. Densitometers that are used for color work have built into the mechanism a provision for measuring the density of the primary colors. Transparencies are read on the transmission unit. Reflection copy color prints are read on the reflection densitometer.

The color knobs on the transmission device are marked R, red; G, green; B, blue; and Y, yellow. The first three are the primary additive colors that we view by transmitted light. The Y setting is where the probe should be set for making black-and-white readings.

On the reflection densitometer head, the colors of the knobs are C, cyan; M, magenta; Y, yellow; and B, black. The readings of reflection copy are giving you values of the primary subtractive colors: cyan, magenta, and yellow. The black knob is for reading the black-and-white copy. The filters for taking these readings are built into the densitometer heads.

The camera department must read the densities of the original color copy in each of the color areas. A black reading on color material is not necessary if good records are kept of the density readings of the various jobs. These records can become the basis of repeatable results, as well as how to expose new color copy as it comes into the shop. Denser color originals will require more exposure, and lighter new copy will require less exposure.

The densitometer's built-in filters read copy. For example, if the transmission densitometer is set on the red filter, only the red in the copy is transmitted to the instrument; the blue and green is absorbed by the filter. The instrument reads the density of what is absorbed, giving the operator the cyan densities. This same principle works with all of the other colors.

It is important to remember that when you are evaluating a separation negative, whether continuous tone or halftone, this negative should be dealt with as a black-and-white negative or print because it is a black-and-white record of the particular color.

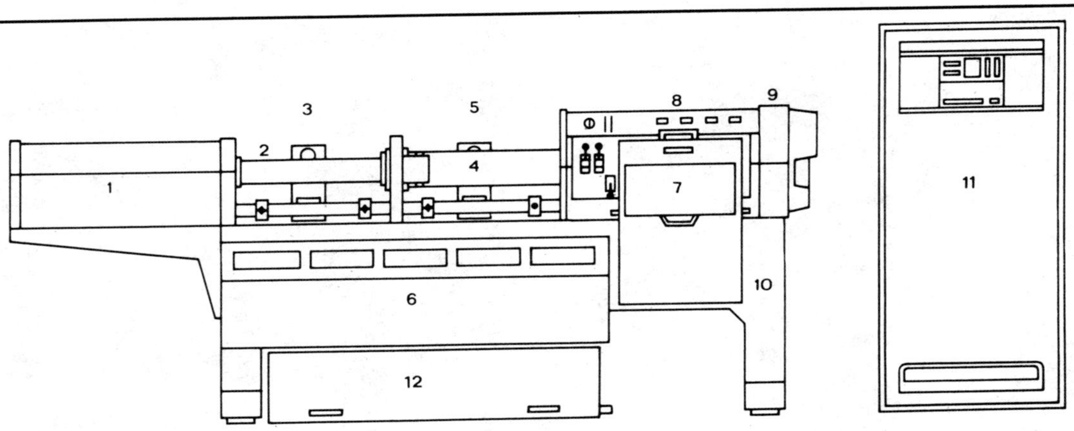

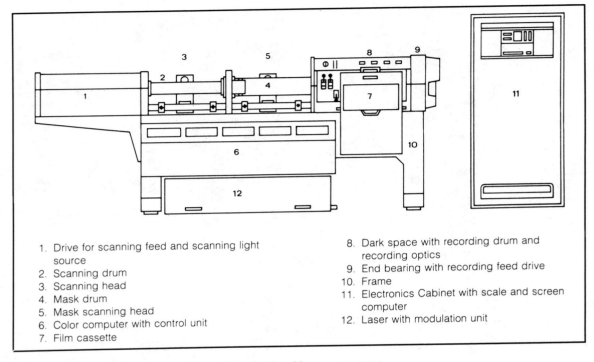

1. Drive for scanning feed and scanning light source
2. Scanning drum
3. Scanning head
4. Mask drum
5. Mask scanning head
6. Color computer with control unit
7. Film cassette
8. Dark space with recording drum and recording optics
9. End bearing with recording feed drive
10. Frame
11. Electronics Cabinet with scale and screen computer
12. Laser with modulation unit

Figure 12.27. Diagram of major compontents of laser scanner.

• Key Points

- Because we live in a world of color, color printing makes the printed page seem real; what appears to be white light is really three beams of light: red, green, and blue (primary additive colors); when we see equal parts of each, the light is white. Only a small part of the electromagnetic spectrum, 400–700 millimicrons, produces visible light. All colors we see are made from the mixture of the red, green, and blue light.
- Ink and paper are important ingredients in color printing along with the halftone process. Color printing depends upon the breaking of the original color copy into four black-and-white records of the color in the copy. The printing process recombines the colors by using inks and halftones.
- The inks used in process printing are called the primary subtractive colors—cyan, magenta, and yellow plus black.
- A number of methods are used in the industry to produce color printing from transparencies, color negatives, and reflection copy originals.
- Use of electronic scanning equipment is a popular and efficient way to produce four-color separation work.
- The use of sensitometric instruments can help to organize the color separation process into a measurable, repeatable system.

• Review Questions

1. List the primary additive colors. List the complementary colors of these primaries.

Explain what colors make the color complement.

2. How do we perceive (view) color? What is the electromagnetic spectrum?
3. Briefly describe what happens when red, green, and blue filters are used in the photographic separation of color copy.
4. Describe the different types of original copy used for color separation.
5. Select one separation method, and describe the steps necessary to complete a set of separations.

• Activity

Because the projects in this area take considerable time for completion, just one activity is suggested here. Take into consideration the equipment and materials available in the shop. Then select a piece of copy—either reflection or transparent, negative or positive.

1. Make a set of uncorrected screened separations.
2. When the separations are complete and have satisfactory aim points, make a set of Color Key proofs to evaluate your results.

Chapter 13

Color Correction

• Objectives

In this chapter you will cover:

- The reason for color correction,
- The purpose of color masking,
- Color-masking procedures for different systems.

After reading the chapter you should be able to:

- Explain the major problem in color reproduction,
- Define color correction,
- Explain the basic photo-masking concept,
- Outline the indirect separation system using positive masks,
- Make color-corrected indirect separations from transparencies,
- Make color-corrected direct separations from transparencies,
- Make color-corrected direct separations from reflection copy,
- Recognize other color correction techniques.

Chapter 12 dealt with the practices and procedures of separating the color originals (transparency or reflection art) into the three primary subtractive colors of cyan, magenta, and yellow. A black printer was added to give the picture depth and good shadows. It was assumed that good separations could be made and that the inks used in the printing were the correct colors that would faithfully reproduce the original art. If in practice this were true, we would not need a chapter on color correction. However, the system does not faithfully reproduce the originals. The major problem in color reproduction is that the inks are not perfect in their reflection and absorption properties.

• Ink Deficiency in Color Reproduction

The first step is to examine the three primary subtractive ink colors in order to analyze the problems.

Cyan Ink

If cyan ink were a perfect ink, it would absorb only red light when printed on a sheet. Reflecting from the paper would be blue and green light (plate 11a). Cyan ink does absorb the red light as it should, but it also absorbs some green light and a bit of blue light. Cyan ink acts as if it contains some magenta pigment (the green light absorber) and some yellow pigment (the blue light absorber) (plate 11b).

Magenta Ink

If magenta ink were a perfect ink, it would absorb only the green light when printed on a sheet. Reflecting from this paper would be blue and red light (plate 11c). Magenta ink does absorb the green light as it should, but it also absorbs some blue light and just a bit of red light. The magenta ink acts as if it contained some yellow pigment (the blue light absorber) and some cyan pigment (the red light absorber) (plate 11d).

Yellow Ink

If yellow ink were a perfect ink, it would absorb only the blue light (plate 11e). Yellow ink absorbs blue light as it should, but it also absorbs a trace of green. The yellow ink acts as though it contained some magenta pigment (the green light absorber) (plate 11f). Of all the inks used in the color reproduction process, yellow comes closest to being pure in its color-absorbing qualities.

Because inks are imperfect, graphic arts technicians must do color correction work when making color separations to compensate for ink deficiencies (Plate 4). Color correction makes the job appear more like the original and the colors more vivid (Plate 5). **Photographic masking** is the popular method of color correction.

• Color Masking

Recall the discussion on bas relief in chapter 10 that placed a film positive over a film negative. When a contact positive is placed in register over the original negative, the result, if the two were held over a light table, would be a black sheet of film. This would be called a 100 percent mask (figure 13.1). A mask is anything that blocks the passage of light. Photographic masks in color work are never 100 percent but are usually in the range of a 40–50 percent mask (figure 13.2). This percentage allows a controlled amount of light to pass through the two pieces of film when they are held together. They do not cancel each other as in the 100 percent mask. If color filters are used when making the masks, it is possible to control where the density of the cancelling effect is placed in the tonal range of the original.

Masks are made by contact when the original copy is a transparency and when the halftone negative to be produced will be made either on a camera, on an enlarger, or in a contact frame. Masks that are used with reflection copy must be made in the process camera.

Photographic Masking for Color Correction

While several techniques can be used for color correction, the most common is called **silver masking**. Silver masking is popular because the masking film can be processed with the same processor equipment already in the shop. Additionally, silver masking helps to solve the problem of contrast reduction, which is just as important as color correction. Most printing pro-

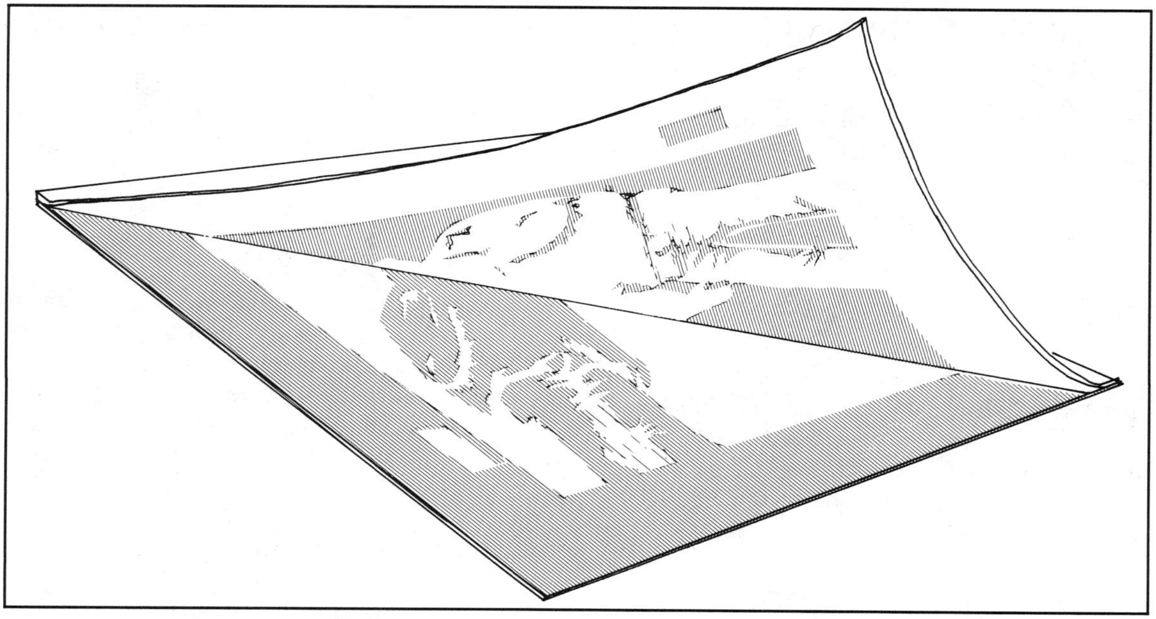

Figure 13.1. Negative and positive of the same image held together in register. If the densities of the two are the same, there would be a 100 percent mask. (Kimberly Conover-Loar)

Figure 13.2. 45 percent silver mask. The soft-appearing focus is characteristic of masking film.

cesses can reproduce a color image on paper that exceeds a density of 1.6 to 2. Most color transparencies used as color copy have a density range in excess of that figure; some copy has density range as high as 3. Consider an example that shows how masking will improve the ability to work with the copy.

Assume the screen BDR is 1.10 (see chapter 4) and the color transparency has a 0.40 highlight density and a shadow density of 3. Also assume that the printing process can reproduce a density range of 2. We will have to accept the area of the copy for reproduction with the highlight of 0.40 and the shadow area of 2.40 (0.40 + 2). Anything denser than 2.40 (2.40 to 3) will show as black, and the eye will not detect any detail. Remember that the screen range is 1.10 but that it is possible to extend this range by the use of a flash exposure for the shadow area. Thus, the task in this example is to make the best reproduction.

In making the mask, we must expose and process the film to obtain a density range that is 45 percent (the recommended percentage) of the usable range of the transparency. The press can only reproduce a range of 2; 45 percent of 2 is 0.90.

The following is a summary of example data:

	Highlight density	Shadow density
Transparency copy	0.40	2.40
Mask (negative)	1.20	0.30
Totals	1.60	2.70

(Shadow density) − (highlight density) must be within the BDR of the halftone screen:

$$2.70 - 1.60 = 1.10,$$

which matches the BDR of this example.

This manipulation of mask highlight and shadow densities reduces the density range of the original to a manageable size. Without this change an acceptable halftone could not be made.

When making the halftone negative, the mask is placed over the transparency in close register. The halftone can be made in a backlighted camera or in an enlarger device that projects the image onto an easel (figure 13.3). The halftone can also be made in the vacuum contact frame. In contacting, the halftone will be made the same size as the mask and transparency.

If the printing inks were perfect, and if no color correction was necessary, a **contrast-reducing mask** alone would improve the color printing job. A contrast-reducing mask can be made by exposing the masking film by white

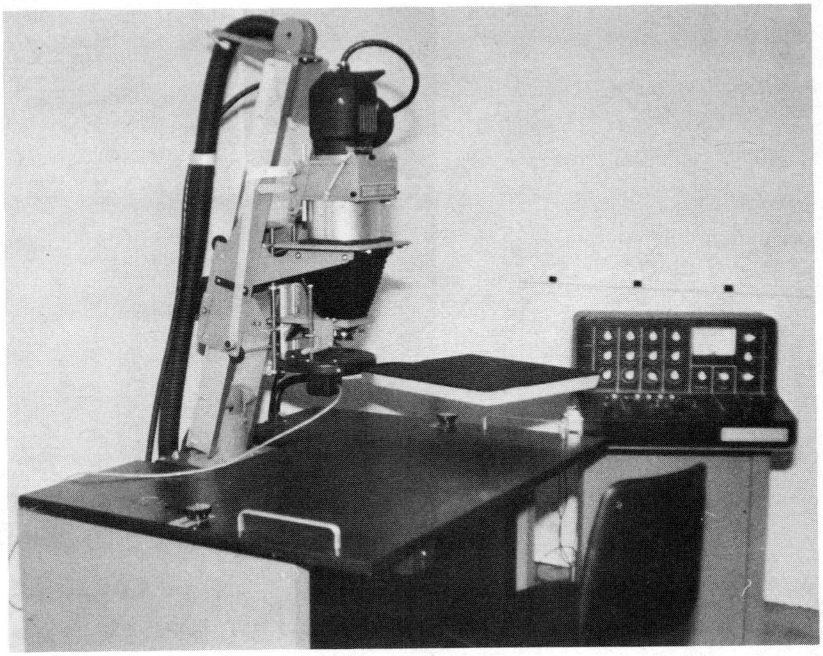

Figure 13.3. Enlarging device with exposure control panel for color separation production.

light (contacting light) or by using a warming filter #85B in the contact light. Remember, pan masking film is panchromatic and must be handled in total darkness. Be sure to read the film manufacturer's specification sheet for trial exposure time and developing instructions.

• Color-Corrected Indirect Screen Separation from Transparencies

Technicians use many masking systems. The more masks used, naturally, the more exacting the color correction. However, each mask adds to the cost of the color job because of additional materials and technician time. For the purpose of understanding the principles of color correction by masking, it is best to begin by discussing a positive masking system. The essential feature of masking for color correction is that a negative or positive image made with a filter is combined with the original to control densities in selected areas or combined with a negative that was made with a filter from the original.

Look at the diagram of the separation and masking process in figure 13.4. The first step is to make a set of continuous-tone separation negatives from the original transparency. This can be done by contacting with a large original trans-

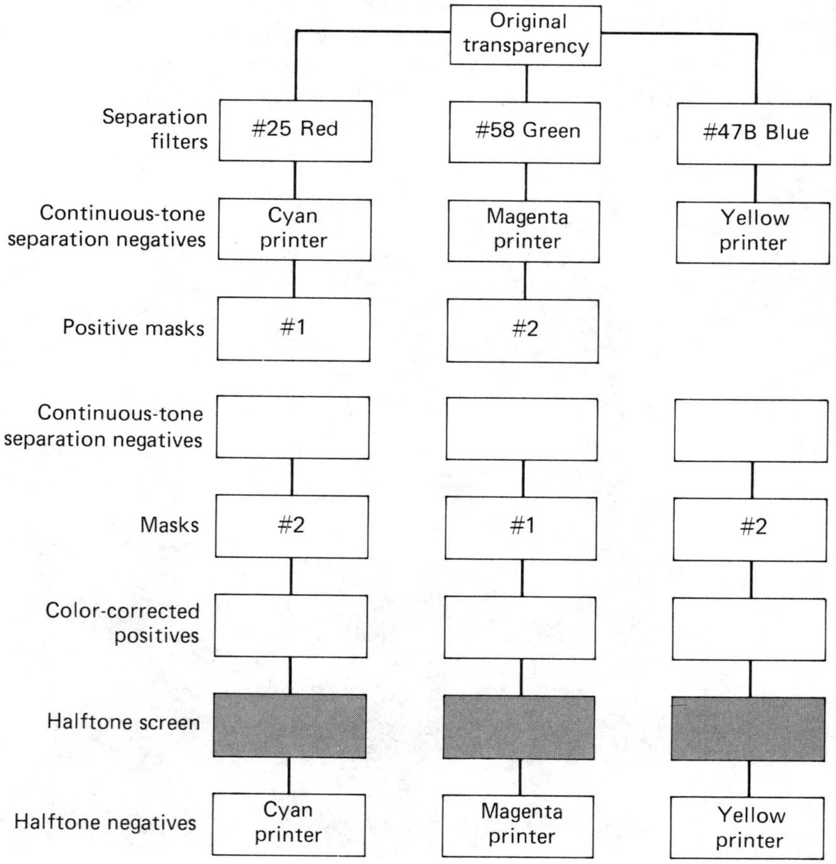

Figure 13.4. Steps in indirect separation with positive masks.

parency, or if the transparency is small, this step can be accomplished in the enlarger or the camera.

The next step is to make a contact positive from each of these separation negatives on masking film. When positive masks are made from continuous-tone separation negatives, a blue-sensitive masking film can be used. This film allows the operator to expose and develop these masks in red safelight. You can work in a red safelight because the masks are made from black-and-white separation negatives and not from the original color transparency. The blue-sensitive masking film is also a continuous-tone film that develops an unsharp image, which is correct for masking purposes. First look at the magenta printer (green filter negative). If you remember, the magenta printer is the green light absorber, but magenta ink also absorbs blue light, which should in theory only be absorbed by the yellow ink. The remedy for this problem is to print less yellow ink wherever the magenta ink is to print. By using the positive mask made from the green filter negative we have a record of where the magenta ink is to print. If we combine this mask with the blue filter (yellow printer) negative when we make a corrected blue filter positive, we have added density where magenta will print. In this way, the corrected positive will be lighter (print less yellow in the magenta ink areas).

The red-absorbing areas of the original transparency (cyan-reproducing areas) always absorb some green light, so these areas will also be recorded in the making of green filter masks (these are not as strong as the magenta areas). The mask, therefore, is also a record of where cyan will be printed and will compensate for the slight contamination of the cyan ink with yellow ink. This corrects the blue filter positive.

The red filter positive mask, combined with the green filter negative, will compensate for the other major color error, which is the contamination of the cyan ink with the green light absorber. When the corrected positive is made, density is added in the cyan areas so less magenta will be printed in these areas to compensate for the green-light-absorbing qualities of the cyan ink.

The cyan printer is the final corrected positive to be made. The mask made from the green filter negative is used to compensate for the unwanted red-light-absorption (cyan printer) of the magenta ink. No correcting positive mask was necessary from the blue filter negative since the other two masks do the color correcting.

After the corrected positives are made from the negatives and masks, halftone negatives (screened) are produced. These negatives will be used in the platemaking steps.

While correction is best explained by this process, the number of steps (amount of time) and sheets of film make this technique impractical and costly. However some advertising agencies will specify the separations to be made by the indirect method, because the work turned out using it is of very high quality. In production today, the direct screen method and electronic scanning are used by most shops. The direct screen method requires fewer steps and much less film.

• Color-Corrected Direct Screen Separations from Transparencies

With the method shown in figure 13.5, two masks are made by contact with the original transparency. Both of these masks are negative masks, and when placed in contact with the original transparency, they will add density in certain areas of the original when the halftone negative is made. This additional density changes the dot structure of the halftone and thus controls the amount of color that will be printed. This technique provides color correction.

One of the two filters used in making negative masks is the #33 magenta filter. This filter passes red and blue light and absorbs green light. The second filter used is the #58 green filter.

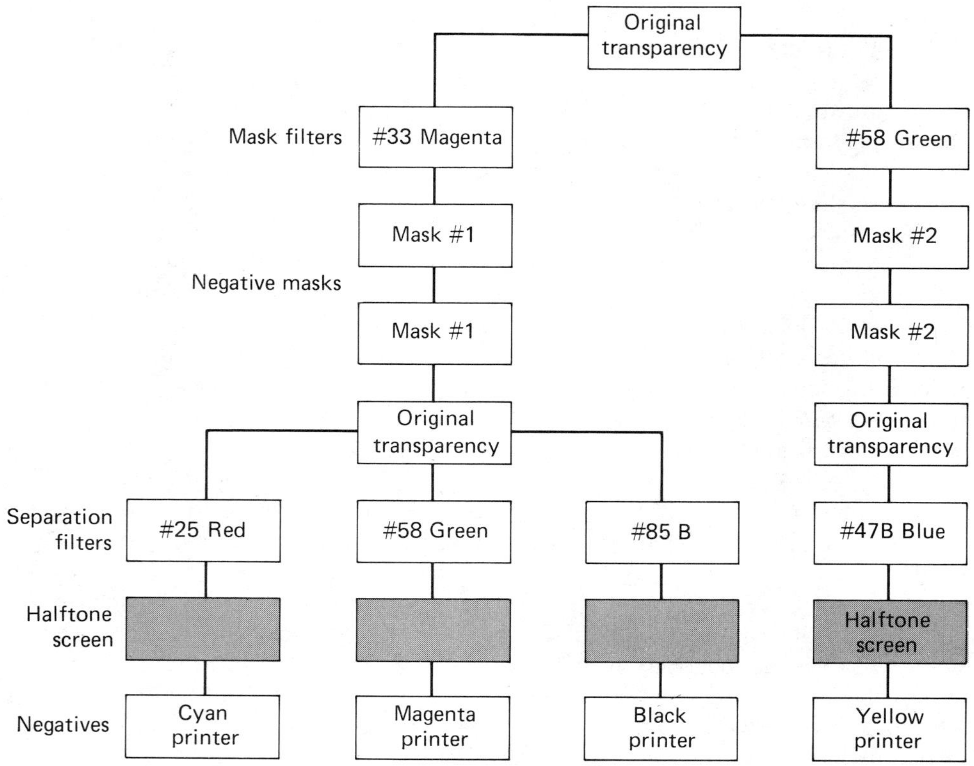

Figure 13.5. Steps in color-corrected direct screen separation.

This filter passes green light and absorbs blue and red light.

The magenta filter mask #1 is used with the red filter (cyan printer) separation negative. This same mask is used with the green filter (magenta printer) separation negative. Mask #2, made with the green filter #58, is used with the blue filter (yellow printer) separation negative. The #1 mask is used when making the black printer separation negative. It is used mainly as a contrast-reducing mask since no color correction is necessary in this printer.

These masks accomplish the same job as the positive masks in changing densities to compensate for ink deficiencies. These masks also serve in the capacity of contrast reducers. This method uses less film and operator time than the indirect method. The use of the mask with the black printer halftone negative is for contrast reduction. The mask also keeps the exposure times for the four halftones evenly balanced.

The procedure for making a color-corrected direct screen separation from a transparency is as follows:

- After the transparency has been selected for separation, the transparency, register marks, and a three-step control and color bar are placed in a special transparent carrier (figure 13.6).
- Strip the elements in the carrier.
- Expose and process the masks by contact, using a pan masking film. It is important to remember that the film, special carrier, and

Figure 13.6. Transparent carrier with register marks and three-aim point control.

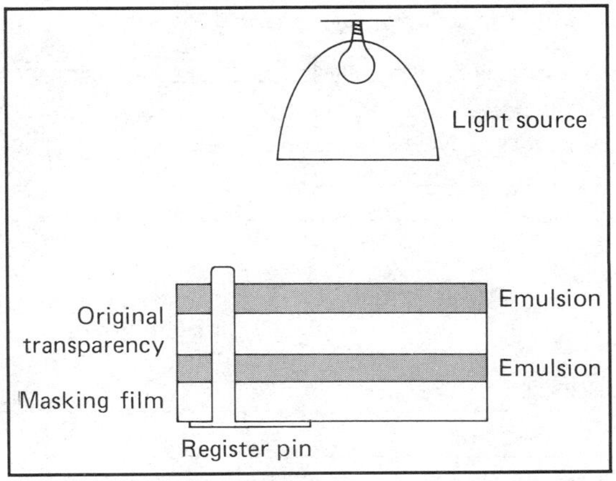

Figure 13.7. Diagram of film and emulsion orientation when making contact masks.

screens must be pin registered when making exposures.

This step requires total darkness so be sure to know where filters are stored, set the timer, and prepare the sink area.

Evaluating the Masks

The best procedure for preparing the masks is to expose both masks (use a light-tight box to store the exposed sheets) then to develop each one separately. Figure 13.7 shows the contacting orientation of the transparency and the masking film.

Exact exposure and processing times for any shop must be determined by testing procedures. However, it is necessary to have some starting point (see table 13.1).

The three-point control and color guide, which was stripped into the carrier, is used as a tool to evaluate the mask. It is important

Table 13.1. Recommended starting points for exposure and development

		Trial exposure times	
Mask	Filter	Time in seconds	Lamp
1	33	25	Try tap 3 (in a 3-tap unit, set 40 inches above the vacuum table)
2	58	25	

	Recommended processing times (68°F, or 20°C)		
Developer*	Stop	Fix	Wash
3¼ minutes	10 seconds	5 to 10 minutes	5 minutes

Note: Developer is Kodak HC-110 Developer, Dilution D (1 part developer to 9 parts water)

Figure 13.8. Color Separation Record Sheet*

Color original: Negative__________ Transparency__________ Reflection print__________
Subject____ Date__________________
Film or print type__________ Remarks (original exposure, lighting, filters used)__________
____
____

Densitometer readings of original

Area	Red-Cyan	Green-Magenta	Blue-Yellow
Highlight			
Middle tone			
Shadow			

Graphic arts equipment settings

Camera__________ Enlarger__________ Contact__________
Lighting______________________________ Lamp distance__________________
Size settings__________ Screen__________ Screen range__________

Masks

Contact__________ Camera back__________ Film__________

	Mask number 1	Mask number 2
Filters		
Exposure time		
F/stop scale		
Developing time		
Developer/Dilution		
Density A		
Density B		
Density C		

throughout this process to keep accurate records; figure 13.8 shows a data sheet that can be used to maintain an ongoing data system.

Begin by taking density readings of the A, M, and B patches on the mask. These three numbers are used to determine the acceptability of the mask. The mask should have an A–B density range of 0.90 ± 0.05. This means that a density range from 0.85 to 0.95 would be acceptable. To find the A–B range, simply subtract the density of the B patch from the density of the A patch.

Figure 13.8. (continued)

Separations (Halftone)

Film____________________ Developer____________________

	Cyan	Magenta	Yellow	Black
Filters				
F/stop scale				
Main Exposure time				
Flash Exposure time				
Bump Exposure time				
Developing time				
Screen angle				
Density Highlight (A)				
Middle tone (M)				
Shadow (B)				

Separations (Continuous Tone)

Film____________________ Developer____________________

	Cyan	Magenta	Yellow	Black
Filters				
F/stop scale				
Exposure time				
Developing time				
Density Highlight (A)				
Middle tone (M)				
Shadow (B)				

*This form may be reproduced.

The next concern is the relationship between the highlights and middle tones and between the middle tones and shadows. This relationship is called the mask number. Table 13.2 shows the steps in determining a mask number, and typical density readings are shown. While these are exact target points, some judgment is necessary by the darkroom worker to accept or reject a mask that does not meet these guidelines. If the masks numbers are a bit off, then it is best to have them both off in the same direction (e.g., 0.26 and 0.27 rather than 0.14 and 0.26).

Table 13.2. Determining the mask number

A-B range		M-B range		Mask number	
A density	1.15	M density	0.80	M–B range	0.55
M density	−0.80	B density	−0.25	A–M range	−0.35
A–M range	0.35	M–B range	0.55	Mask number	0.20*

*An acceptable mask number is ±0.05, or 0.15 to 0.25

The mask number is mainly controlled by exposure. The A–B range is mainly controlled by development time. A change of 3 percent in development will change the A–B range by approximately 0.02 density. A change of 5 percent in exposure will change the mask number by approximately 0.01. Large changes in either exposure or development will affect both A–B range and mask number. Table 13.3 gives the direction of changes in exposure or development time, or both, to correct an unsatisfactory mask.

• Screening the Separations

When the masks are complete, the halftone negative separations can be made. It is best to make the red filter halftone first. From this halftone, establish the dot values for the other negatives by going to the table on the direct screen calculator (figure 12.6). This device suggests highlight, middle-tone, and shadow values for the three colors and black.

The #23A red filter is substituted for the #25 red filter used in this process. The two red filters are very similar in their transmission and absorption qualities of the colors. Because of the differences, most shops use the #23A when working with color-corrected masked transparencies.

The red filter negative is the only step that requires a no-screen (bump) exposure. This procedure will allow for a reduced main exposure and will give the cyan printer more ink in the middle tone.

- After the four exposures are complete, follow standard halftone-developing procedures.
- After drying, evaluate your results for desired aim points.
- Remake any halftones that are not close to the density readings. This is easily possible with direct screen contacting because the operator is always working same size with no focusing adjustments.
- Make color proofs for a final evaluation of the work.

Table 13.4 gives suggested exposure times.

• Color-Corrected Direct Screen Separation from Reflection Copy

For this method of separation, discussion centers upon preparation of the masks. Masks have to be made in the camera and are referred to as **camera back masks**. The steps involved with making the separation negatives were discussed in chapter 12.

Table 13.3. Changing exposure or development to correct an unsatisfactory mask

If mask number is	and A–B range is	Procedure
	Low	Increase development time to increase the A–B range. If the mask number is only slightly low, no exposure change is needed. The increased development will raise the mask number slightly. If the mask number is very low, increase exposure time slightly.
Low	Correct	Increase exposure time to raise the mask number. If you use a very large exposure increase, decrease development time slightly to hold the A–B range constant.
	High	Increase exposure time to raise the mask number. Decrease development time to decrease the A–B range.
	Low	Increase development time to increase the A–B range. This development increase will also tend to raise the mask number. You may need to decrease exposure time slightly to hold the mask number constant.
Correct	Correct	No change is necessary.
	High	Decrease development time to decrease the A–B range. Since decreased development will tend to lower the mask number, you may need to increase exposure time to hold the mask number constant.
	Low	Decrease exposure time to lower the mask number. Increase development time to increase the A–B range.
High	Correct	Decrease the exposure time to lower the mask number. If you use a very large exposure decrease, you may need to increase development time slightly to hold the A–B range constant.
	High	Decrease development time to decrease the A–B range. If the mask number is only slightly high, this development decrease will also tend to correct the mask number. If the mask number is very high, decrease exposure time slightly.

Table 13.4. Suggested halftone negative exposures

Printer	Mask	Filters	Bump	Main exposure	Flash exposure	Contact lamp
Cyan	1	#23A and 0.60 ND	10 percent of main use 15 seconds	15 seconds	20 seconds	Lamp 40 inches above vacuum board, use tap 3 at 20 volts
Magenta	1	#58	None	25 seconds	20 seconds	
Black	1	#85B	None	20 seconds	None	
Yellow	2	#47B	None	80 seconds	20 seconds	

Figure 13.9. Camera overlay sheet prepared to hold sandwich in place. The notched areas allow register pins to be used.

In order to color correct it is necessary to make two masks from the reflection copy. These will be silver masks, just as we made when contacting, with a #33 filter and a #58 filter. However, now the masks will be made in the camera.

- First, the copy is placed in the copyboard just as was done with the uncorrected separations from reflection copy.
- Prepare an overlay (figure 13.9). This is a transparent sheet that will assure good vacuum holddown on the camera back. Be sure to make cutouts for the register pins.
- Place spacers on the vacuum back (figure 13.10). These will put the masking film in the correct position for proper focus. Notice that the first spacer is for the halftone film and that the second is for the screen.

Later, when the halftone negative is made, the mask will be in the correct position.

The following exposure times are based on pulse xenon lights. Exposure times will be different depending upon the light source.

Mask	Filter	Exposure
1	PM 33	180 seconds
2	PM 58	180 seconds

Note: Be sure to use photomechanical (PM) filters because they are optically clear.

- Process the masks, using the same procedures for those made by contact.
- Aim points for masks for reflection copy should be different than those made by direct contact. The A–B range should be 0.50 ± 0.05 (0.45–0.55). The mask number should be 0.10 ± 0.05. (0.05–0.15).

The separation negatives are then made as discussed earlier. Exposure times for corrected negatives are not necessarily the same than those for uncorrected negatives because of the addition of the density of the mask.

• OTHER COLOR CORRECTION TECHNIQUES

Tri-Mask Film

Tri-mask film is a specialized masking film produced only for color correcting for the color separation process. It is a multiple-layer film made much like a color negative or color transparency film. The colors of the image formed by this film after exposure and processing do not look like those produced by the conventional color materials.

The main advantage with tri-mask film is that it reduces registration errors in masking. One of these masks does the work of several silver masks. Tri-mask material requires tray development and chemistry suitable only for the tri-mask materials. Recall that silver masks can be processed in automatic units; this difference prevents the wide acceptance of the tri-mask materials.

Masks for transparencies to be used in enlarger-type units are made by contact the same as when making masks for contact procedures.

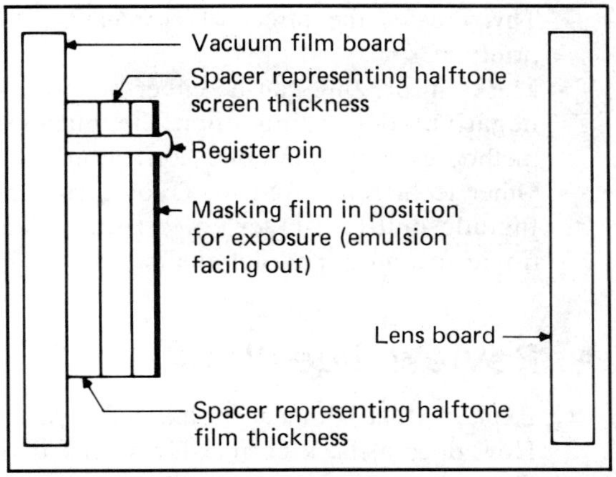

Figure 13.10. Diagram of film layer orientation in camera back masking.

Dot Etching

A highly skilled technique used by some color houses is a hand correction procedure called **dot etching**. In this procedure, the color correction is done by changing the size of the halftone dots. The graphic arts technician uses a chemical like Farmer's Reducer (potassium ferricyanide) and a small swab or brush to change the dot shape (see chapter 5). Since it is relatively simple to reduce the dots on a positive, this is the usual procedure. It is also possible, however, to enlarge the dots, which must be done on negatives. The altered dots will in turn print more or less ink in selected areas and, thus, will change the final appearance of the job.

Color correction by this procedure was once very popular, but because of high labor costs, it has been replaced by the masking method.

Scanners

The discussion in chapter 12 covered separation and color correction by scanning devices. The actual correction procedures are done electronically and not photographically. The theory behind the correction procedure is the same as for the photographic steps.

• Key Points

- Color inks are not perfect absorbers and reflectors of light; because of the ink deficiencies, color correction procedures must be used to produce quality color printing.
- The most popular method for color correction is the use of photographic masks. Masks help to control the amount of density in areas of the halftones and in turn allow more or less ink to print in selected areas of the job.

This creates the effect of corrected color printing.

- Masks in printing can be either positive or negative, depending upon the masking method employed in color correction.
- Other techniques used for color correction include multiple-layer color films, electronic scanning, and dot etching.

• Review Questions

1. Explain what is meant by ink deficiencies.
2. How does a mask correct for an ink deficiency?
3. Describe the correction necessary for the following inks:
   a. Cyan,
   b. Magenta,
   c. Yellow.
4. Diagram the color-corrected direct screen separation system from transparent copy.
5. You have just completed making a mask that has a correct mask number but too low an A–B range. What should you do to correct this?

• Activities

Using the copy you have available in your shop (reflection or transparencies), select one piece and do the following:

1. Make a set of masks and a set of separation direct screen negatives, giving the job color correction.
2. Make a set of Color Key proofs for comparison with the original.

Chapter 14

Stripping Transparent Images

• Objectives

In this chapter you will cover:

- Uses of film images after leaving the camera room,
- The general sequence of stripping steps,
- Stripping equipment and supplies,
- Fundamental stripping techniques.

After reading the chapter you should be able to:

- Explain the importance of camera room quality control,
- Describe the general sequence of steps when stripping any type of printing job,
- Identify common stripping equipment and supplies,
- Describe common stripping techniques for a basic printing job.

• Review of the Printing Cycle

The purpose of this book was to take a detailed look at the range of tasks performed in process photography. By this time in your study, you have been introduced to those tasks and should understand the terms and procedures used in most printers' darkrooms. It is important that with this knowledge you also understand the next step for any job.

Recall from chapter 1 that most jobs follow the same production sequence. The steps in the sequence are:

- Image design,
- Image assembly,
- Image conversion,
- Image carrier preparation,

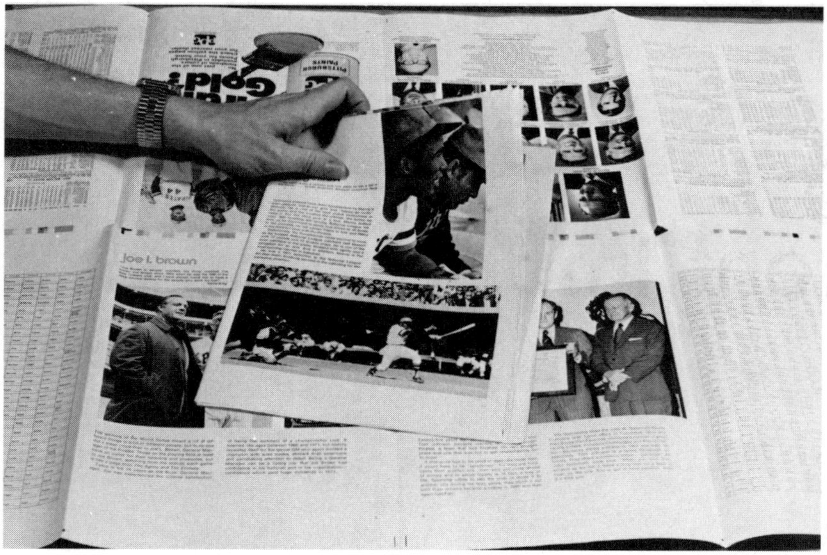

Figure 14.1. Printed signature sheet before and after folding. Printed signatures that will be folded and used as part of a book require careful page imposition.

- Image transfer,
- Finishing.

The conversion of the image to a transparent form is only one of the basic steps in the production sequence. Skilled process photographer's can save time and money in the next step if they understand the stripping operation. The purpose of this chapter is to examine those operations.

• Goals of the Stripper

The next person who works with the film negatives or positives is called a **stripper**. Remember, the point of the job is to reproduce the images carried by the film onto paper or some other material. The job of the stripper is to assemble all pieces of film into the correct positions so the film images will appear in the correct positions on the printed stock.

In order to accomplish this goal, the stripper uses a **masking sheet** to hold the pieces of film in place while a printing plate is made from the images. The masking sheet, with pieces of film attached, is called a **flat**. Most jobs use more than one piece of film (figure 4.3). The stripper must make sure not only that each piece of film is in the right location next to each other but also that all images will print in the correct position on the final material.

The process of placing pieces of film in the right positions in reference to each other is called **image imposition**. Lines must be parallel to each other, images must not overlap, and every detail must appear as specified by the designer.

Page imposition is a term sometimes used to describe the placement of all job images in the right position. If the job is a signature for a book (figure 14.1), then all pages must be placed correctly so they will appear in the right order after folding. Each page must also be parallel to every other page and must be positioned in such a way that, when you open the book, the top line is always the same distance from top of the page.

The following sections examine the job of

the stripper. Knowing where each piece of film is to be used, and why, will help you to be more effective in the darkroom.

• Sequence of Stripping Steps

All effective strippers follow five main steps when working on a job:

- Examine the work order,
- Determine that all elements of the job are complete and of acceptable quality;
- Plan the stripping sequence;
- Strip the job;
- Make a proof.

The most difficult part of any stripping assignment is planning the order of each operation, not the actual placement of pieces of film. Most jobs arrive in the stripping department in a large envelope. The first step is to examine the work order from the envelope. The stripper will look for specifications that tell the plate size to be used, number of colors, and use of screens, tints, halftones, surprints, reverses, or any other special techniques that require attention. The work order is the key to all stripping operations.

The second step followed by most skillful strippers is to check that all elements of the job are in the envelope and are of acceptable quality. It is time consuming and expensive to discover, halfway through a job, that one part of the job was not shot. All pieces of film or copy are laid out on a table and are checked against the work order or job specifications. The stripper also begins to organize the pieces into logical groups. The images to be printed the same color are placed with each other. All screen tint images may be grouped together. The halftones might be placed in a single pile. The system will differ, depending upon the specific job, but the checking of each piece of film for job readiness is always done.

The third step is to plan the actual stripping sequence. If it is a multicolor job, then a master color is identified to be used as a guide for stripping all other colors. When surprints are used, the main image must be stripped first and then the overprint. Halftones are almost always stripped into windows on a main negative. The order of stripping does make a difference. A few minutes spent planning can save hours of work redoing a job that did not work because of a forgotten step.

The fourth step is to strip the job. Guidelines are drawn on masking sheets, and the pieces of film are attached. The specific procedures of this step are covered in the rest of the chapter.

The final step in any stripping operation is proofing. The finished flats are exposed to inexpensive photosensitive paper prior to being used to make printing plates. The proof is checked for image imposition and to insure that all image areas are printing clearly and cleanly. If there are errors, the stripper will correct them and proof again. This process of testing the job before it reaches the press is extremely important.

• Equipment and Supplies

The stripper uses a variety of tools. The most common are a quality **T-square** and **triangle**. Tools made of plastic are not used because they must serve as cutting edges for razor blades or Exacto knives when trimming pieces of film or masking sheets. Most printers use one high-quality steel T-square and one steel 30°–60°–90° triangle. Mesurements are commonly made using stainless steel straightedges with fractional gradations to one-hundredth of an inch. For greater accuracy, an ordinary needle or a special purpose **etching needle** is used to mark the masking sheet when laying out a flat. An etching needle can also be used to remove unwanted emulsion from a film negative or positive. Detail

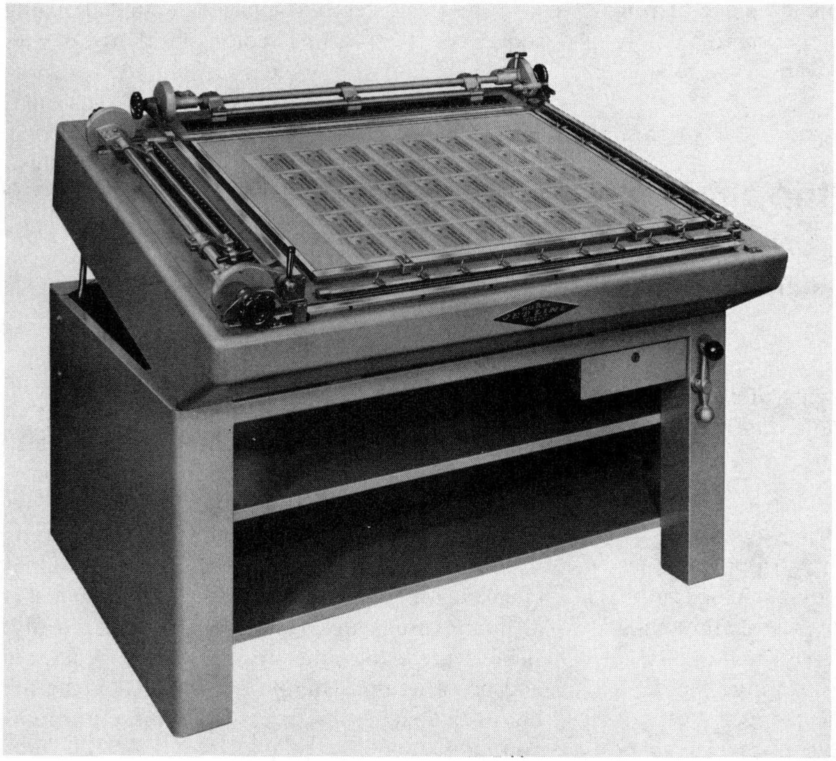

Figure 14.2. Mechanical line-up table. (Courtesy of nuArc Company, Inc.)

is added to a piece of film with a brush. Most strippers have an assortment of **red sable water-color brushes** on hand. Start your collection of brushes with #0, 2, 4, and 6 brushes. In addition, the stripping area should include items such as a scissors, a supply of single-edged razor blades, a low-power magnifying glass (10X), pencils (#2H and 4H), erasers, and several felt-tip marking pens for labeling flats.

Almost all stripping is done on a **glass-topped light table**. One side of the glass is frosted, and a light source, under the glass, evenly illuminates the surface. When a piece of film is placed on the lighted glass, it is easy to view the image and to detect any film defect. More sophisticated models called mechanical line-up tables (figure 14.2) come equipped with rolling carriages, micrometer adjustments, and attachments for ruling or scribing parallel or perpendicular lines.

A variety of supplies are needed for stripping operations. For negative stripping, masking sheets that do not pass light to the printing plate must be used. The most common material is **goldenrod paper**, which blocks actinic light (any light that exposes light-sensitive emulsions) because of its color. For jobs that require greater dimensional stability, **orange-colored vinyl masking sheets** are used. When you are stripping positives, the masking sheet and film must pass light in all but the image areas. Most positive stripping is done on **clear acetate** or **mylar support sheets**. In most positive stripping, tracing paper is used for the initial image layout. Clear tape is used to secure the film to the flat. With negatives, special red translucent tape is sometimes used to secure the pieces to the flat. This red tape blocks actinic light. **Opaque** is a liquid material used to cover pinholes and other unwanted detail on film negatives. Red opaque is easier to apply, but black colloidal-graphite opaque is thinner and more efficient for extremely small areas like when retouching halftones. Both water- and alcohol-based opaques are available.

All tools and supplies should be located centrally near the light table so the stripper can reach any item easily.

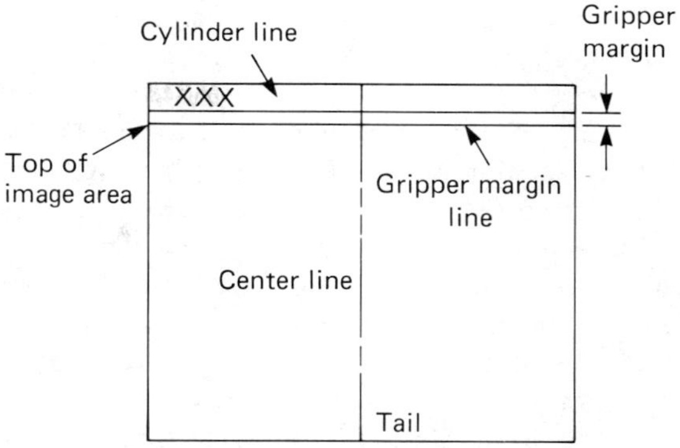

Figure 14.3. Marking blank masking sheets. Many strippers lay out blank masking sheets using the specifications for a particular press. The cylinder line, gripper margin, center line, and top of the image area are carefully located. Preprinted masking sheets are also used with these guidelines provided.

• Fundamental Stripping Techniques

It is important to keep in mind that there is no single correct way to strip a flat. In fact, it often seems that there are as many different stripping techniques as there are strippers. The techniques presented in this section are intended to introduce you to some fundamental procedures to use when stripping negatives, but you should understand that they represent only one approach.

Masking Sheets

In order to place pieces of film in the correct printing positions on the final flat, you must identify four areas on the masking sheet (figure 14.3):

- Cylinder line (or plate clamp area),
- Gripper margin (or gripper bite area),
- Plate center line,
- Point where the image begins on the printed piece.

The **cylinder line** identifies the area of the masking sheet that covers the part of the lithographic plate clamped onto the press to hold the plate on the plate cylinder. Most offset lithographic plates are flexible and wrap around a press cylinder called the **plate cylinder**. The top and bottom portions of the plate are covered by the clamps, so no image can be printed from these areas. The **gripper margin** is the area of the paper held by the mechanical fingers that pull the sheet through the printing unit. Since these fingers cover part of the paper, it is not possible to print an image in the gripper margin area.

The top of the uppermost image on the printed piece dictates how far down from the bottom of the gripper edge the film image is stripped onto the masking sheet. Information on this dimension should be included on the rough. The center line of the masking sheet is used to line up the center of the film image area so that it is exposed squarely in the center of the plate and, consequently, so that it prints in the center of the press sheet. Once these four areas are marked on the masking sheet, film can be stripped onto the sheet with confidence that the images will appear in the correct location on the printing plate and the final press sheet.

Masking sheets can be purchased with or

without preprinted guidelines. Preprinted masking sheets are typically made in specific sizes for specific presses. For example, preprinted masking sheets can be purchased for an 11″ × 17″ offset duplicator. These numbers indicate that the press can print a page up to 11 inches wide and 17 inches long. The plate for such a press would be about 11 inches wide and more than 17 inches long. The plate is longer than 17 inches to allow for space to clamp it to the plate cylinder.

The stripper's job is to create a flat by positioning the film on the masking sheet so the plate will transfer images in the required locations on the final press sheet. Press adjustments to change image location are possible, but they are time consuming and costly. Press adjustments for image location are also limited. Often an incorrectly stripped flat must be completely restripped and a new plate made. This wastes both time and money. The problem becomes even more critical when several flats are used to expose images on the same plate.

Preprinted masking sheets of the type mentioned earlier are usually made only for small duplicator presses (images up to 11″ × 17″ in size) although some larger sizes are available. Stripping for larger presses requires the use of unlined masking sheets. Whether or not the masking sheets have preprinted guidelines, the stripper's tasks remain the same: The cylinder line, center line, gripper margin, and top image line must be identified, and the images must be stripped into their correct positions. Stripping for both lined and unlined masking sheets is discussed later, but first we cover stripping procedures for lined masking sheets.

Laying Out a Preprinted Masking Sheet

For this explanation, assume we are stripping a single film negative to be printed on 8 1/2″ × 11″ paper, using a common duplicator press. The first task is to select the correct masking sheet. If there is only one size of press in the shop, this is no problem. However, if the shop has several different-sized presses, careful selection becomes important. The masking sheet should be the same size as, or slightly larger than, the plate that will be used on the particular press. If the masking sheets are not marked for each press in your shop, then simply compare each sheet with a plate from the press to be used.

Place the masking sheet on a light table, and line up one edge of the sheet with a T-square. Tape the sheet securely in two places on the edge opposite the T-square (figure 14.4). Masking tape can be used for this purpose.

Most prelined masking sheets use a one-quarter-inch grid. This grid can be used as an indicator of measurements on the sheet, but exacting measurements should always be made with a rule. Not only is the one-quarter-inch grid not perfectly accurate, but also you should tape the masking sheet in place based on the location of the edge of the sheet against the T-square, not the printed grid. There is no reason to assume that the grid printed on the masking sheet is parallel to the edge of the masking sheet. It may be close but probably not perfectly parallel.

After the masking sheet is taped in place, look it over carefully. As in figure 14.4, the cylinder lines, gripper margin, and center line should be clearly identified. It is often a good idea to draw a line over the bottom of the gripper margin line and down the center line on the masking sheet. This will help you to refer back to these locations as you lay out the sheet.

Now check the rough layout to determine the top margin—that is, the distance from the top of the paper to the top of the image on the printed piece (figure 14.5). A line representing the top of the image should be drawn across the masking sheet, below the bottom of the gripper margin; lines representing side and bottom margins should also be drawn (figure 14.6).

For this example, there will be only one film negative. Lay it emulsion down near the mask-

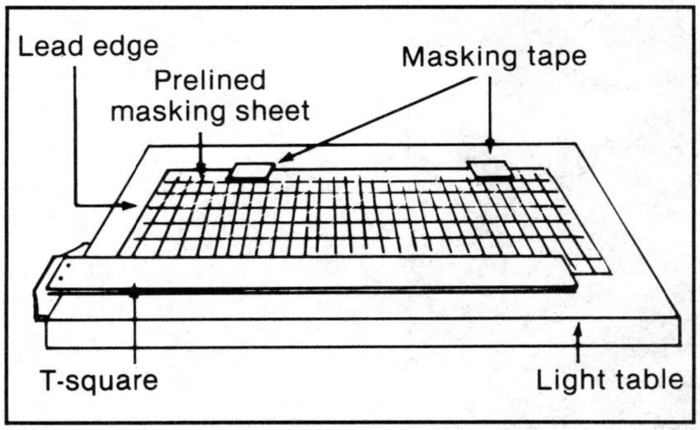

Figure 14.4. Placing masking sheet on light table. Line the masking sheet up against the edge of a T-square and tape it on one side.

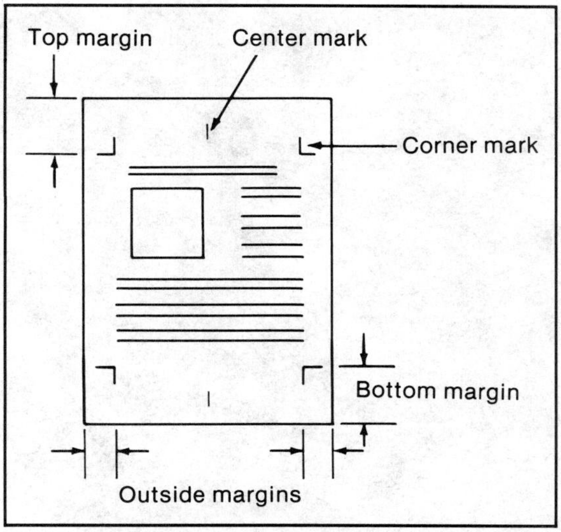

Figure 14.5. Rough layout with margins identified.

ing sheet on the light table. Examine the negative carefully. Corner marks that indicate image extremes or center lines (or both) should be recorded on the negative (figure 14.7). These marks will help you position the film negative in the proper location under the masking sheet. These marks should have been placed on the copy in the paste-up, or **keylining**, stage of the work.

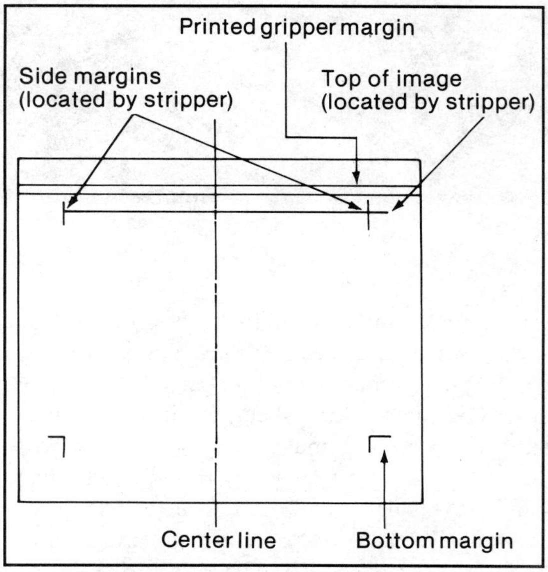

Figure 14.6. Diagram of masking sheet. Lines representing the top, sides, and bottom margins are first drawn on the masking sheet. The top image margin should always be below the gripper margin.

Attaching Film Negatives

With rare exception, all offset lithographic plates are exposed with the emulsion side of the plate against the emulsion side of the film. Negatives are right reading through the base. In other words, if the piece of film is placed on the light table so that the images can be read from left to right, the base side is up and the emulsion side is against the glass. If there is any question about which is the emulsion side of a film negative, the emulsion side can be identified in one of two ways. The first is by comparing the finish; the duller of the two sides is usually the emulsion. Second, the emulsion side can be identified by scratching a portion of the film, well away from any image. The emulsion side of the film can be scratched away, but the base cannot. In fact,

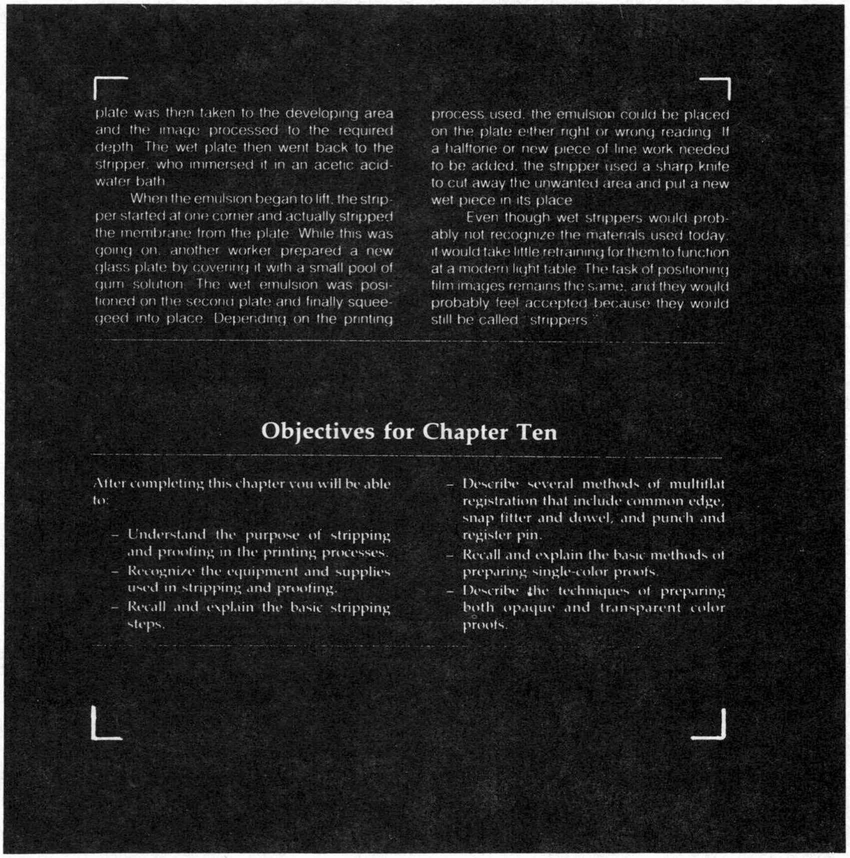
plate was then taken to the developing area and the image processed to the required depth. The wet plate then went back to the stripper, who immersed it in an acetic acid-water bath.

When the emulsion began to lift, the stripper started at one corner and actually stripped the membrane from the plate. While this was going on, another worker prepared a new glass plate by covering it with a small pool of gum solution. The wet emulsion was positioned on the second plate and finally squeegeed into place. Depending on the printing process used, the emulsion could be placed on the plate either right or wrong reading. If a halftone or new piece of line work needed to be added, the stripper used a sharp knife to cut away the unwanted area and put a new wet piece in its place.

Even though wet strippers would probably not recognize the materials used today, it would take little retraining for them to function at a modern light table. The task of positioning film images remains the same, and they would probably feel accepted because they would still be called "strippers."

Objectives for Chapter Ten

After completing this chapter you will be able to:

- Understand the purpose of stripping and proofing in the printing processes.
- Recognize the equipment and supplies used in stripping and proofing.
- Recall and explain the basic stripping steps.
- Describe several methods of multiflat registration that include common edge, snap fitter and dowel, and punch and register pin.
- Recall and explain the basic methods of preparing single-color proofs.
- Describe the techniques of preparing both opaque and transparent color proofs.

Figure 14.7. Example of negative with corner marks. Corner marks placed on the paste-up board will appear as images on the film negative. These negative corner marks can then be lined up with the top, sides, and bottom margins on the masking sheet.

scribing the emulsion is a common method for adding image areas to a film negative.

Begin by placing all negatives, emulsion down, on the masking sheet. Position each negative in its approximate printing position with the images falling in place with the image margins. Never allow pieces of film to overlap on the flat. If the overlap is near an image area, there may be some distortion as the plate exposure is made. With all negatives in place, mark where any pieces overlap. If possible, cut any overlapping sheets to within one-half inch of any film image.

Because the masking sheet is translucent, it is possible to see through the material to the glass surface below. With right-reading stripping, untape the masking sheet and set it aside. Place the negative, emulsion down, on the light table. Accurately align the image margins, or tick marks, with the T-square and triangle, and tape just the edges of the film to the table (figure 14.8). Next, move the masking sheet over the film until the image lines are positioned with the image margins on the negative. It should be easy to see both marks line up as you look down through the flat. Use a T-square to ensure that the margins and type lines run parallel to the edge of the masking sheet. After the negatives are in place, smooth the masking sheet down and cut two small triangular openings over the negative in the nonimage areas (figure 14.9). It is important that you cut only through the masking sheet and not into the film. Practice several times on a scrap sheet. Still holding the film in position under the masking sheet, place a small piece of red tape over each triangular opening and apply pressure. This will temporarily attach the negative to the flat.

Before untaping the flat from the light table, again check all film images for position and squareness. Improper image placement at this stage will be reflected throughout the rest of the job.

After all negatives have been attached temporarily and checked for accuracy, release the flat from the light table and carefully turn it over. Each negative should now be secured to the masking sheet at each corner with a small piece of cellophane tape (figure 14.10). Be sure to smooth each negative as the tape is applied to ensure that there are no buckles in the film. Once the film is securely taped in place, turn the masking sheet over again (lined side up) and recheck the image placement.

If two pieces of film overlap, it is necessary to cut the negatives so they will butt against each other. To do this without cutting into the masking sheet, insert a piece of scrap film or acetate beneath the overlapping portions, and with a steel straightedge and a single-edged razor blade or frisket knife, cut both pieces of film (figure 14.11). Do not remove the straightedge until you are certain that you have cut completely through

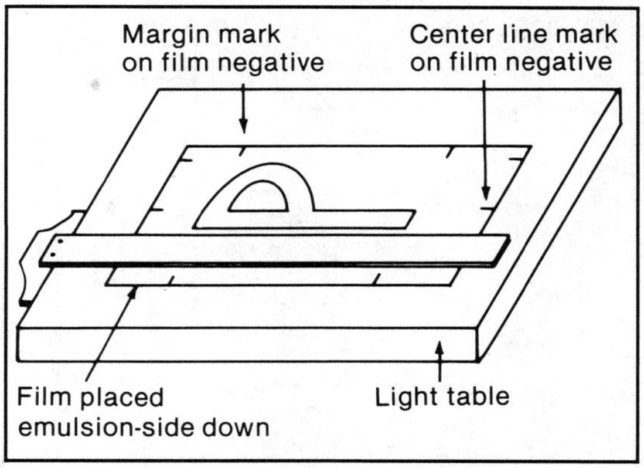

Figure 14.8. Positioning the negative on the light table.

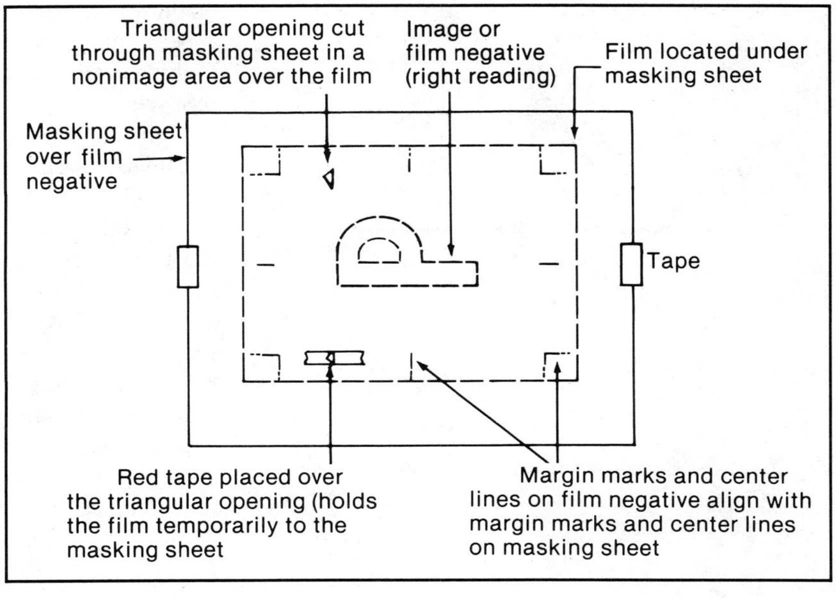

Figure 14.9. Cutting triangular openings.

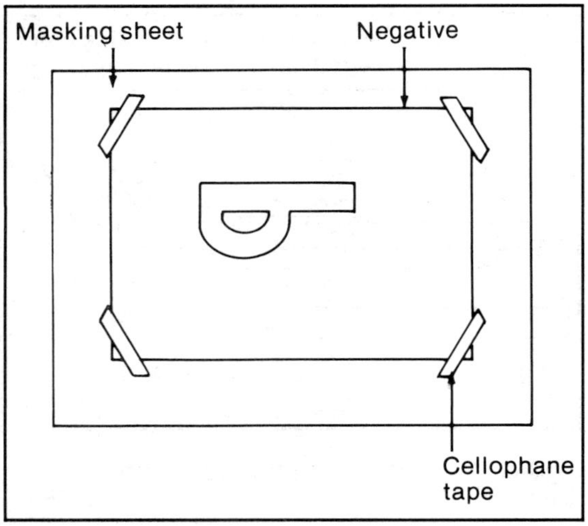

Figure 14.10. Taping negative to the masking sheet. Turn the masking sheet over and tape each corner of the film negative with cellophane tape.

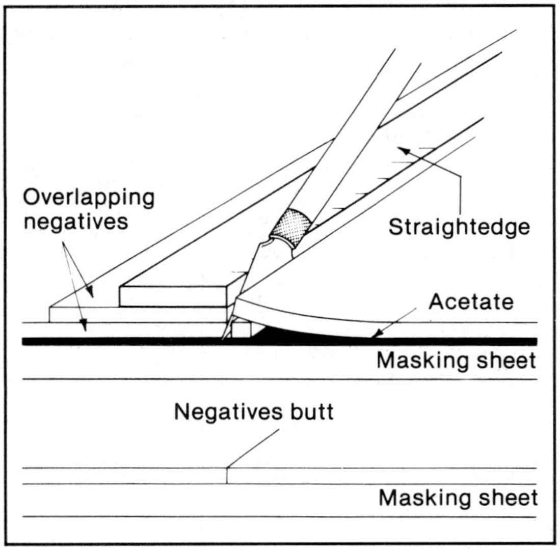

Figure 14.11. Cutting overlapping negatives

both sheets of film. Remove the loose pieces and scrap of film, and tape the negatives to the masking sheet. Tape the negatives on the nonimage edges only.

After all negatives have been located and taped in place, turn the flat over again so the film emulsion is against the light table, and cut away the masking sheet in the image areas. Some strippers slide a piece of scrap plastic between the masking sheet and the film during this operation to ensure that only the masking sheet is cut. With practice and a sharp cutting tool, however, there should be no need for a plastic insert. The fewer open nonprinting areas exposed, the better (figure 14.12).

Opaquing and Etching

Although the flat will appear complete, in practice there are usually small defects that must be corrected. The most common defect is **pinholes**. These are small openings in the emulsion that pass light. They may be caused by dust on the copyboard when the camera exposure was made or by dirty original copy. Special care by the camera operator can save a great deal of problems in stripping. Whatever the cause, any openings that pass light to the printing plate will appear ultimately as ink on the final press sheets. Pinholes are undesired images and must be blocked out with opaque.

Most opaques are water based. The opaque should be applied in as thin a coat as possible yet still block light through the negative. If properly mixed, water-based opaque should dry on the film in fifteen to thirty seconds. Although some strippers opaque on the emulsion side of the film, we recommend that you opaque only on the base side when first learning. The emulsion of any film is frail and cannot withstand a great deal of manipulation. If opaque is mistakenly placed over a desired image on the base side of the film, the opaque can be washed off or scratched away with a razor blade without damage to the film.

New strippers sometimes have trouble deciding whether or not to opaque an area. As a rule of thumb, when someone standing over the light table looking straight down at an eye-to-flat distance of about two feet can see light through a pinhole, then opaque it. If you can see it at this distance, it will probably pass enough light to expose a plate emulsion.

The fact that a film's emulsion is fragile can be used to advantage. There are frequent situations when detail needs to be added to a negative. Images can be created in the film emulsion by scraping away the emulsion with an etching tool. An overdeveloped area on a character can be opened with the tool, and new letters or symbols can even be added, although they must be etched in reverse. Lines can be added by etching against a straightedge.

The final step, after all opaquing and etching are completed, is to label the flat. The platemaker typically handles many flats in a single day, so each must be identified. Place all information in the trailing edge of the masking sheet, out of the paper limits. The notations made depend on the individual shop, but information such as a name of the account, job title or production number, sequence of the flat, ink color, or any special instructions like the inclusion of a screen tint are all commonly included (figure 14.13).

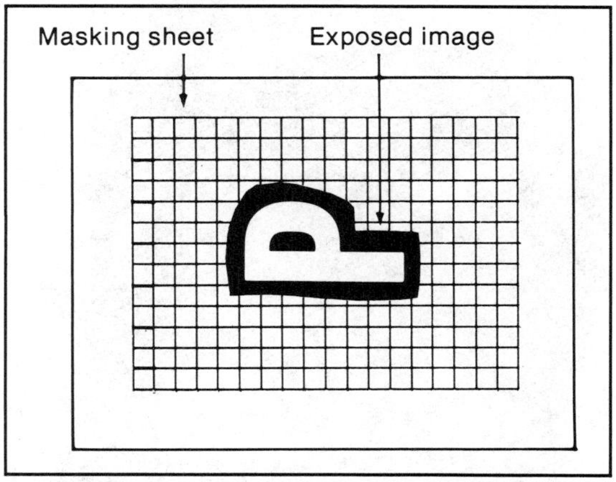

Figure 14.12. Exposing image area. The masking sheet is cut away to expose the image area of the film negative

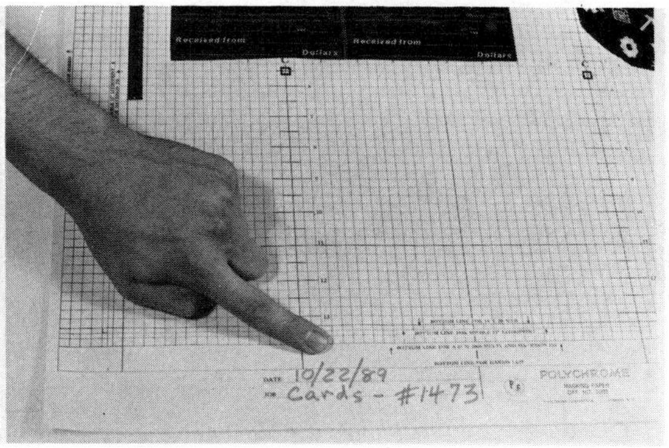

Figure 14.13. Properly labeled flat.

Stripping Halftones

Printers use several different techniques to combine halftones with line negatives. The most common is to attach the halftone to a window previously created on the line negative (figure 14.14). They are created by placing red or black pressure-sensitive material on the paste-up. Red or black on the paste-up would reproduce on the film as a perfectly clear area.

To add a halftone negative to a window in a line negative, first prepare the masking sheet, add the line negative(s), and complete all cutting, opaquing, and etching. Then turn the flat

Figure 14.14. Window on a film negative.

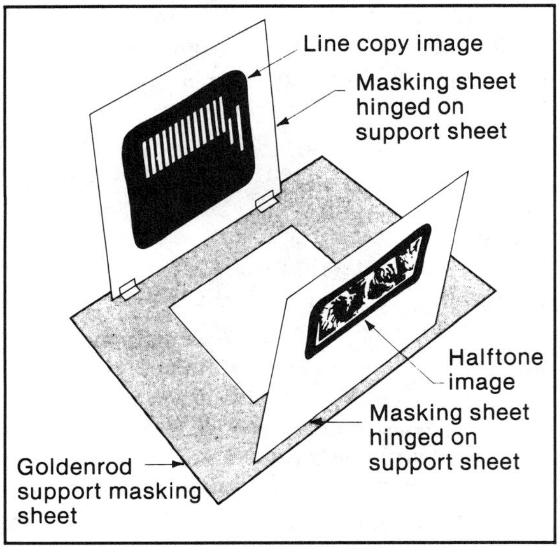

Figure 14.16. Complementary flats. In this example of complementary flats, the two masking sheets are hinged on a larger support sheet.

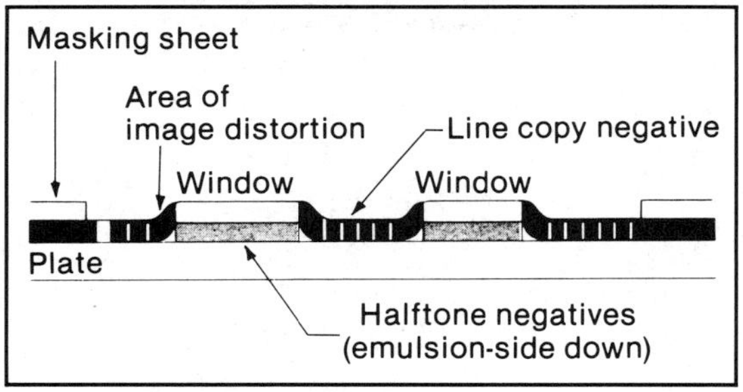

Figure 14.15. Positioning the negatives. The emulsions of both the line copy and the halftone negatives must contact the emulsion of the printing plate.

over on the light table so that the film is emulsion side up. Trim the halftone that is to be stripped into the window so that it is larger than the window opening and yet does not overlap any image detail near the window. Position the trimmed negative over the window, emulsion up, in line with the rest of the image detail on the flat, and tape it in place with clear cellophane tape. The halftone must be mounted in this position because the emulsions of both the line negative and the halftone negative must be in contact with the printing plate when the plate exposure is made (figure 14.15).

Check to be sure that the halftone image completely fills the window. Any open area around the edges of the window will print as a solid line on the final reproduction.

It is often not possible to add a halftone negative to an existing flat without overlapping image detail and creating an area of image dis-

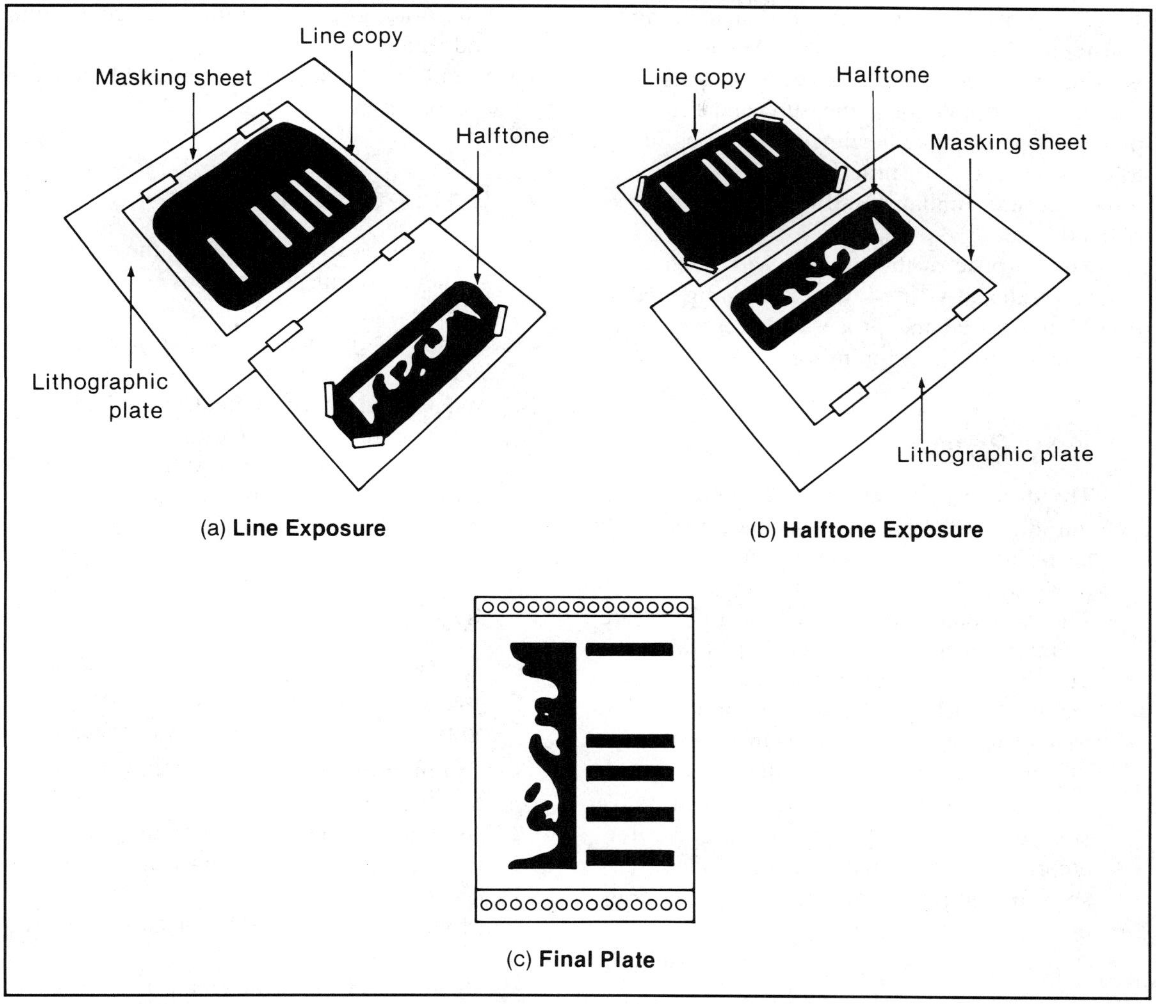

Figure 14.17. Using complementary flats for double exposures. The complementary flat uses one exposure to record the line copy (a) and one exposure to record the halftone (b). The final plate carries both images (c).

tortion. This happens when two halftones are to be butted together on the final printed sheet or the halftone window is positioned too closely to other image detail. In such cases, the stripper cannot work with the halftones on a single flat. The solution is to use two complementary flats. One flat carries the line-printing detail; the second holds the halftone image (figure 14.16). If properly stripped, each flat can be exposed in succession in the platemaker in order to combine the two images in their proper positions on a single printing plate (figure 14.17).

The procedures outlined in this section are considered basic in the industry. Most stripping is done on large, unprinted masking sheets on which the stripper must measure and draw the plate, gripper, and center lines before beginning to position pieces of film. The basic techniques, however, are fundamentally the same as explained here.

The purpose of this section was not to provide an exhaustive review of stripping operations but to give the process photographer an introduction to the stripping operation.

• Key Points

- The stripper must assemble all pieces of film into the correct positions so the images will be printed in the required locations on the press stock.
- The two major concerns of the stripper are image imposition and page imposition.
- The five main stripping steps are (1) examine the work order, (2) check all job components, (3) plan the stripping sequence, (4) strip the job, (5) proof the job.
- The most common stripping tools are a T-square and triangle, straightedge, ruler, etching needles, brushes, razor blades, scissors, a low-power magnifying glass, erasers, and marking pens.
- Negative stripping is done on masking sheets.
- The stripper must always check for the cylinder line, gripper margin, plate center line, and image lines.
- Detail can be added or removed by etching and opaquing.

• Review Questions

1. Where does stripping fit into the production sequence of all printed jobs?
2. What is the job of the stripper?
3. Define *image imposition* and *page imposition*.
4. What are the five main stripping steps?
5. What is the gripper margin?
6. Describe the steps in positioning a single film negative on a masking sheet.
7. What is the purpose of opaquing?

• Activities

Strip a simple single-flat job for reproduction by lithography, screen printing, relief, or gravure by completing each of the following steps.

1. Examine the quality of the film images for reproduction.
2. Assemble all necessary stripping tools.
3. Lay out the flat, following work order specifications.
4. Mount the film, and cut any necessary openings.
5. Opaque and mark the flat with appropriate job information.

Glossary

Actinic light. Any light that exposes light-sensitive emulsions.

Actinic output. Energy that activates or hardens light-sensitive coatings; consists of shorter wave lengths of visible spectrum.

Additive colors. Colors that make up white light; red, blue, and green are the additive primary colors.

Aerial oxidation. The process of increasing the chemical action of a solution because of surface exposure to air; a developer bath can become exhausted because of aerial oxidation.

Agitation. Flow of solution back and forth over film during chemical processing.

Angstrom units (A or A.U.). A measure of wavelengths; One millimicron equals ten Angstrom units.

Antihalation dye. Dye that is generally coated on back of most transparent based film to absorb light that passes through emulsion and base during exposure.

Aperture. Opening in the lens of the camera through which light passes.

Back-lighted copyboard. Equipment on some process cameras for photographing transparent copy; light is projected through the back of the copyboard and the lens to the new film.

Basic density range (BDR). Range of detail produced from halftone screen by main exposure.

Basic exposure. Camera aperture and shutter speed combination that will produce a quality film image of normal line copy with standardized chemical processing.

Baume. Density scale used by Antoine Baume, a French chemist, in graduating his hydrometers.

Blueline flat. Special flat prepared as part of one multiflat registration system; carries all important detail, including register marks.

Blueprint. Inexpensive photomechanical proofing material; is exposed through the flat on a platemaker, developed in water, fixed in photographic hypo, and then washed to remove fixer stains.

Blue-sensitive material. Photographic material that reacts to the blue part of a white-light exposure.

Brownline. Inexpensive photomechanical proofing material; is exposed through the flat on a platemaker, developed in water, fixed in photographic hypo, and then washed in water to remove fixer stains; the longer the exposure, the more intense the brownline image.

Bump exposure. No-screen image exposure made through the lens; used to change contrast by compressing the screen range.

Camera. A machine used to control the passage of light to some form of film material.

Camera-ready copy. Finished paste-up used to create the images of the final job.

Carbon arc. A common graphic arts light source created by passing an electrical current through two carbon rods.

Carbon arcs. Rods whose electromagnetic emission is heavy in blue and violet light; are commonly used as a light source for the graphic arts industry.

Carousel carrier. Multicolor screen printing equipment that holds individual screen frames, one for each color; rotates around a central axis and sequentially moves each screen into position over object to be printed.

Center lines. Lines drawn on a paste-up in light-blue pencil to represent the center of each dimension of the illustration board.

Characteristic curve. Visual interpretation of exposure/density relationship of a light-sensitive material.

Cold type composition. Preparation of any printing form intended to be reproduced photographically.

Collodion. Viscous solution of cellulose nitrates and ether and alcohol used as a coating for photographic plates.

Colloid. Any substance in a certain state of fine division.

Color Corrections. An operation used to overcome by altering the characteristics of the individual color separations the limitations of inks and plates in the reproduction process.

Color-Key. A commercial color proofing system that produces transparent-based images.

Color sensitivity. Chemical change response in a particular silver halide emulsion to an area of the visible electromagnetic spectrum.

Color separation. Photographically separating a color original into three black-and-white film records of the three primary subtractive colors of cyan, magenta, and yellow, plus black.

Color temperature. Measure of the sum color effect of the visible light emitted by any source.

Composition. Process of assembling symbols (whether letters or drawings) in the position defined on the rough layout during image design.

Comprehensive. Artist's rendering that attempts to duplicate appearance of final product.

Contact frame. A special piece of equipment used to hold pieces of film in perfect contact during a contact exposure.

Contact printing. The process of placing one transparent-based film image directly against an unexposed sheet of film, and then passing light through the film. Also referred to as contacting.

Continuous-tone photograph. Image created from many different tones or shades and reproduced through photography.

Continuous-tone photography. Process of recording images of differing density on pieces of film; continuous-tone negatives show varying shades of gray or different hues of color.

Contrast. Refers to the relative range of tones in a photographic image.

Control strip. Piece of film used in automatic film processing to gauge the activity level of solutions in the machine; several times a day the photographer sends a preexposed control strip through the machine and then examines the processed piece to determine whether machine adjustments need to be made.

Copy. Words to be included on a rough layout; final paste-up; or, in some situations, final press sheet.

Copyboard. Part of a process camera that opens to hold material to be photographed (the copy) during exposure.

Copy density range (CDR). Difference between the lightest highlight and the darkest shadow of a photograph or continuous-tone copy.

Cromalin. A commercial color proofing system that produces opaque-based images through the use of special powders that are rubbed into the sheet after each exposure.

CRT (cathode ray tube) character generation. Third-generation typesetting system that generates images by utilizing a computer coupled with a cathode ray tube.

Cyan. One of the three subtractive primary colors, sometimes called process blue.

Dark printer. One of the halftones used to make a duotone; usually printed with the use of black or another dark color; often contains the lower-middle tones to shadow detail of the continuous-tone original.

Darkroom camera. Type of process camera designed to be used under the safelights of a darkroom; can be either vertical or horizontal.

Deep tank process. A method of holding developing chemicals in large, rectangular tanks with only a small amount of solution surface exposed to the air.

Densitometry. Measurement of transmitted or reflected light with precision instruments and the expression of these measurements in numbers.

Density. Ability of a photographic image to absorb or transmit light.

Developer. Chemical bath used to make the image on a light-sensitive emulsion visible and useful to the printer; some developers are used in the darkroom to process line film; others are used in proofing, plate making, stencil preparation in screen printing, and some areas of masking in gravure.

Developer adjacency effect. Underdevelopment caused by chemical exhaustion of small, lightly exposed areas when surrounded by large, heavily exposed areas.

Diaphragm. Device that adjusts the aperture, or opening size, in the camera lens.

Diaphragm control. A scale attached to the lens that allows the operator to adjust the aperture size for changes in copy size.

Diazo. Light-sensitive material developed by exposing to ammonia fumes; also, a material used in one of the proofing processes.

Diffusion transfer. Photographic process that produces quality opaque positives from positive originals.

Direct image photographic plate. Short-to-medium-run surface plate exposed and processed in a special camera and processor unit; used mainly in quick print area of printing industry.

Direct/indirect process. Method of photographic screen printing stencil preparation in which stencil emulsion is applied to clean screen from precoated base sheet; when dry, base is removed and stencil is exposed and developed directly on fabric; *see also* Photographic stencils.

Direct process. Method of photographic screen printing stencil preparation in which stencil emulsion is applied wet to screen fabric, dried, and then exposed and developed; *see also* Photographic stencils.

Direct screen color separation. Color separation method that produces a color-separated halftone negative in a single step.

Dot area meter. Transmission or reflection densitometer designed to display actual dot sizes.

Dot etching. Chemical process used to change dot sizes on halftone negatives and positives.

Dot-for-dot registration. Process of passing a sheet through the press twice and fitting halftone dots over each other on the second pass.

Double-dot black duotone. Reproduction of a continuous-tone original made by printing two halftones, both with black ink; its purpose, when compared with a halftone, is to improve quality in tone reproduction.

Drying time. Time it takes for something to dry or for liquid to harden.

Duotone. Reproduction of a continuous-tone image that consists of two halftones printed in register and that adds color and quality to the image.

Dup film (or dupe). *See* Reversal film.

Electromagnetic spectrum. The range of known energy, measured in wavelengths.

Emulsified. Condition in which something has become paste-like from contact with a highly acidic substance.

Emulsion. Coating over a base material that carries the light-sensitive chemicals in photography; emulsion in mechanical masking film and hand-cut stencil material is not light sensitive.

Evaporation. Conversion that occurs when a liquid combines with oxygen in the air and passes from the solution as a vapor.

Excess density. Density difference after the basic density range of the screen is subtracted from the copy density range (CDR).

Exposure index. *See* Speed.

Fake color. One-color reproduction printed on a colored sheet.

Fake duotone. Halftone printed over a block of colored tint or a solid block of color.

Filmboard. Part of process camera that opens to hold the film during exposure; a vacuum base usually holds the film firmly in place.

Film speed. Number assigned to light-sensitive materials that indicates sensitivity to light; large numbers (like 400) indicate high sensitivity; low numbers (like 6 or 12) indicate low sensitivity.

Filter. A material used to control the passage of light, either by selectively blocking or passing certain wavelengths (colors) or diminishing the quantity of light.

Fixing bath. Acid solution that removes all unexposed emulsion in film processing; is the third step in the process and follows the developer and stop-bath; also called fixer.

Flare. Exposure problem caused by uncontrolled reflection of stray light passing through the camera's lens.

Flash exposure. Nonimage exposure made on the film through a halftone screen; regulates detail in the shadow area.

Flat. Assembled masking sheet with attached pieces of film; is the product of the stripping operation.

Flexography. Primarily a relief, package printing method based on a combination of rubber plates, solvent-evaporating inks, and web printing.

Focal length. Distance from center of lens to filmboard when lens is focused at infinity.

Focusing. Process of adjusting the lens so reflected light from the object or copy will be sharp and clear on the film.

Fogging. A light background exposure over the entire emulsion surface.

Form. Grouping of symbols, letters, numbers, and spaces that make up a job or a complete segment of a job (such as one page set to be printed in a book).

Four-color process printing. Technique using cyan, magenta, yellow, and black process inks to reproduce images as they would appear in a color photograph.

f/stop system. Mathematically based way of measuring aperture size in the lens of a camera; f/stop numbers predict the amount of light that will pass through any lens; moving from one f/stop number to another always either doubles the amount of light or halves it.

Galley camera. Type of process camera used in a normally lighted room; film is carried to the camera in a light-tight case, the exposure is made, and the case is carried to the darkroom for processing.

Ghost halftone. A very light halftone that appears as a tint image but has the appearance of tonal variation; commonly used with a solid type overprint.

Gray scale. Continuous-tone picture of shades of gray used by graphic arts photographers to gauge exposure and development during chemical processing; also known as step table or step wedge. *See also* Sensitivity guide.

Gripper margin. Area of paper held by mechanical fingers that pull sheet through printing unit of press.

Grippers. Mechanical fingers that pull a sheet through the printing unit of a press.

Ground glass screen. A frosted (or sandblasted) glass plate that can be moved into the position of the filmboard to view the size and focus of the image passing through the lens.

Halftone photography. Process of breaking continuous-tone images into high-contrast dots of varying shapes and sizes so they can be reproduced on a printing press.

Highlight area. Lighter parts of a continuous-tone image or its halftone reproduction.

Holding lines. Small red or black lines made on a paste-up to serve as guides for mounting halftone negatives in the stripping operation; are carried as an image on the film and are covered prior to plate making.

Horizontal process camera. Type of darkroom camera that has a long, stationary bed; film end is usually in the darkroom, and lights and lens protrude through a wall into a normally lighted room.

Hypo. Fixing bath of sodium thiosulfate.

Image assembly. Second step in the printing process; involves bringing all pieces of a job into final form as it will appear on the product delivered to the customer.

Image carrier preparation. Fourth step in the printing process; involves photographically recording the image to be reproduced on an image carrier (or plate).

Image conversion. Third step in the printing process; involves creating a transparent film image of a job from the image assembly step.

Image design. First step in the printing process; involves conceptual creation of a job and approval by the customer.

Image guidelines. Lines used in paste-up to position artwork and composition on illlustration board; are drawn in light-blue pencil and are not reproduced as a film image.

Image transfer. Fifth step in the printing process; involves transfer of the image onto the final job material (often paper).

Imposition. Placement of images in position so they will be in desired locations on the final printed sheet.

Indirect process. Method of photographic screen printing stencil preparation in which stencil is exposed and developed on a support base and then mounted on the screen; *see also* Photographic stencils.

Indirect screen color separation. Color separation method that produces a continuous-tone separation negative; requires additional steps to produce color-separated halftone negatives.

Instant image proof. Proofing material that creates an image when exposed to light and does not require special equipment or chemicals.

Latent image. Invisible change made in film emulsion by exposure to light; development makes latent image visible to the human eye.

Lateral reverse. Changing of a right-reading sheet of film to wrong-reading.

Lens. Element of a camera through which light passes and is focused onto the film.

Letterpress. Process that prints from a raised or relief surface.

Light integrator. An instrument that measures with a photoelectric cell the quantity of light that passes through the lens; used to control exposure.

Light printer. One of the halftones used to make a duotone; is usually printed with a light-colored ink and often contains the highlight to upper-middle tones of the continuous-tone original.

Light table. Special table with frosted glass surface and a light that projects up through the glass for viewing and working with film negatives and positives.

Line conversion. The process of changing a continuous-tone photograph to a high-contrast image; also a special effects technique that converts a photograph to a highly-detailed line drawing.

Linen tester. Magnifying glass used for visual inspection.

Line photography. Process of recording high-contrast images on pieces of film; line negatives are either clear in the image areas or solid black in the nonimage areas.

Line work. Any image made only from lines, such as type and clear inked drawings.

Lithography. Transfer of an image from a flat surface by chemistry.

Litho-type film. High contrast orthochromatic materials used in graphic arts photography.

Magenta. One of the three subtractive primary colors, sometimes called process red.

Main exposure. Image exposure made through

the lens and a halftone screen; records detail from the highlights or white parts of a photograph to the upper-middle tones; also called a highlight or detail exposure.

Mask. Any material that blocks the passage of light; is used in paste-up, stripping, and plate making; is generally cut by hand and positioned over an image; photomechanical masks used in color separation are produced in the darkroom.

Masking. Continuous-tone photographic image that is used mainly to correct color and compress tonal range of a color original in process color photography.

Masking sheets. Special pieces of paper or plastic that block the passage of actinic light; are most commonly used in the stripping operation.

Masterflat. In multiflat registration, the flat with the most detail.

Mechanical. Board holding all elements of composition and artwork that meet job specifications and are of sufficient quality to be photographically reproduced; also called a paste-up, final layout, or camera-ready copy.

Mechanical line-up table. Special piece of equipment used in the stripping operation; comes equipped with roller carriages, micrometer adjustments, and attachments for ruling or scribing parallel or perpendicular lines.

Mercury vapor. Popular light source for the graphic arts industry that operates when current passes through a mercury gas in a quartz envelope; a mercury vapor lamp emits massive peaks in the blue-violet and ultraviolet regions of the visible spectrum.

Metal halide. Recent development in light sources for the graphic arts; a metal halide lamp is a mercury lamp with a metal halide additive and is rich in blue-violet emissions.

Middle-tone area. Intermediate tones between highlights and shadows.

Moiré pattern. Undesirable image produced when two different or randomly positioned screen patterns (or dots) are overprinted.

Negative-acting plate. Plate formulated to produce a positive image from a flat containing negatives.

Neuton's rings. An optical effect that creates circular distortions when a small amount of moisture is trapped within a vacuum frame.

Neutral density filter. A material that diminishes the intensity of light passing through the filter.

No-screen exposure. *See* Bump.

Offset. Press design in which an image is transferred from a plate to a rubber blanket that moves the image to the press sheet; offset principle allows plates to be right reading and generally gives a better-quality image than does direct transfer.

Opaque. Used as adjective meaning not transparent or translucent under normal viewing; also liquid used to ''paint out'' pinholes on film negatives.

Opaque color proofs. Proofs used to check multicolor jobs by adhering, exposing, and developing each successive color emulsion on a special solid-base sheet.

Orthochromatic. Condition in which photographic materials are sensitive to all wave lengths of the visible spectrum other than red.

Overcoating. Protective coating placed on most transparent-based film to protect film emulsion from grease and dirt.

Overlay sheet. Sheet often used in paste-up to carry images for a second color; clear or frosted plastic overlay sheet is hinged over the first color and carries artwork and composition for the second.

Oxidation. Process of combining with oxygen; in aerial oxidation, a solution or ink combines with oxygen in the air to evaporate.

Panchromatic. Condition in which photographic materials are sensitive to all visible wavelengths of light plus some invisible wavelengths.

Pan masking film. *See* Pan separation film.

Pan separation film. A continuous-tone film used in the color separation process.

Pantone Matching System (PMS). Widely accepted method for specifying and mixing colors from a numbering system listed in a swatch book.

Percentage tapes. The mechanical system on a process camera that is used to read size changes.

Photoelectric densitometer. Instrument that produces density readings by means of a cell or vacuum tube whose electrical properties are modified by the action of light.

Photoengraving. Relief form made by photochemical process, after being exposed through laterally reversed negative, nonimage portion of plate is acid etched, allowing image area to stand out in relief.

Photographic stencils. Screen printing stencils produced by use of a thick, light-sensitive, gelatine-based emulsion that is exposed and developed either on a supporting film or directly on the screen itself; the three types include direct, indirect, and direct/indirect stencils.

Photomechanical proofs. Proofs that use light-sensitive emulsions to check image position and quality of stripped flats; are usually exposed through the flat on a standard platemaking device.

Photomechanical transfer. *See* Diffusion transfer.

Photopolymer plates. Plates formed by bonding a light-reactive polymer plastic to a film or metal base; polymer emulsion is hardened upon ultraviolet exposure; and unexposed areas are washed away, leaving image area in relief.

Photostat. Photographic copy of a portion of a paste-up; images are sometimes enlarged or reduced and then positioned on the board as a photostat, also called ''stat.''

Phototypesetting. Cold type composition process that creates images by projecting light through a negative and a lens and from mirrors onto light-sensitive material.

Pica. Unit of measurement used by printers to measure linear dimensions; 6 picas equal (approximately) 1 inch; 1 pica is divided into 12 points.

Pinholes. Small openings in film emulsion that pass light; are caused by dust in the air during camera exposure, a dirty copyboard, or sometimes, acidic action in the fixing bath; must be painted out with opaque in the stripping operation.

Platemaker. Any machine with an intensive light source and some system to hold the flat against the printing plate; light source is used to expose the film image on the plate; most platemakers use a vacuum board with a glass cover to hold the flat and plate.

PMT. A trade name for diffusion transfer materials.

Point. Unit of measurement used by printer to measure type size and leading (space between lines); 12 points equals 1 pica; 72 points equals 1 inch.

Point light source. A device that projects a small, controlled beam of light.

Positive-acting plate. Plate formulated to produce a positive image from a flat containing positives.

Posterization. A photographic process that reduces the many tones of a continuous-tone photograph to a few selected tones; a special effects technique; usually consists of two, three, or four tones and is reproduced in one, two, or three colors.

Prepunched tab strips. Strips of film punched with holes and used to hold flat in place over pins attached to light table.

Printing. Permanent, graphic, visual communication medium; includes all the ideas, methods, and devices used to manipulate or reproduce graphic visual messages.

Printing processes. Relief, intaglio, screen, and lithographic printing.

Process camera. A device used by graphic arts photographers to record film images; can enlarge or reduce images from the copy's original size and can be used to expose all types of film.

Process color. Use of ink with a translucent base that allows for creation of many colors by overprinting only four (cyan, magenta, yellow, and black).

Process color photography. Photographic reproduction of color originals by manipulation of light, filters, and chemistry.

Proof. Sample print of a job yet to be printed.

Proofing. Process of testing final stripped images from flat on inexpensive photosensitive material to check image position and quality.

Proportion scale. Device used to determine percentage of enlargement or reduction for piece of copy.

Proportion wheel. *See* Proportion scale.

Pulsed xenon. Recently developed light source for the graphic arts; xenon lamps are made by filling quartz tubing with low-pressure xenon gas; output is similar to sunlight.

Punch-and-register pin. Method of multiflat registration in which holes are punched in the tail of the flat or in strips of scrap film taped to the flat; the punched holes fit over metal pins taped to light table surface and cause the flat to fall in correct position.

Rapid access. A type of film that reaches maximum density, based upon exposure, in the development step, and cannot be overdeveloped.

RC (resin coated) photographic paper. A special finish that is applied to print papers that produces a perfect, glossy finish without the use of a hot print—drying system.

Receiver sheet. The second part of a diffusion transfer product; it might be an opaque paper sheet, an aluminum plate, or a piece of clear plastic.

Reduction. The process of removing density from the film emulsion after the developing process has been completed.

Reflectance. Measure of ability of a surface or material to reflect light.

Reflection densitometer. Meter that measures light reflected from a surface.

Register marks. Targets applied to the pasteup board and used in stripping, plate making, and on the press to ensure that multicolor images fit together in perfect register.

Registration. The process of assemblying and securing all film pieces so that each image is in the required position on the printing plate.

Relief printing. Transferring an image from a raised surface.

Repeating timer. A device that can be set to a unit of time and then activated for that time period to control a light exposure; without changing the time setting, the device can be started again to repeat the exposure.

Resist. Material that will block or retard the action of some chemical.

Retouching pencil. Special pencil used by retouch artists to add detail or repair continuous-tone images.

Reversal film. A special photographic material that duplicates the original; sometimes called dupe film.

Reverse. Technique of creating an image by use of an open area in the midst of another ink image.

Right reading. Visual organization of copy (or film) from left to right so that it can be read normally; see wrong reading.

ROP color. A system of preparing color separations from color negatives; means Run Of the Paper.

Safelight. Fixture used in the darkroom to allow the photographer to see, but not expose, film; color and intensity of safelight vary with type of film used.

Scanner. An electronic device that is used to separate a continuous-tone print or transparency into its three subtractive primary colors (cyan, magenta, and yellow) and black.

Screen angle. The angle of ruling (horizontal or vertical) of the dots in a halftone or solid-line screen.

Screen printing. Transferring an image by allowing ink to pass through an opening or stencil.

Screen ruling. Number of dots per inch produced by a halftone screen or a screen tint.

Screen tint. Solid line screen capable of producing evenly spaced dots and of representing tone values of 3 percent to 97 percent in various line rulings.

Sensitivity guide. Transparent gray scale often stripped into a flat to be used as a means of gauging plate exposure; also used in one method of direct color separation.

Sensitometer. An instrument that exposes a step tablet or gray scale onto light-sensitive materials.

Sensitometry. An area of photography concerned with the measurement of film reaction to light.

Shadow area. Darker parts of a continuous-tone image or its halftone reproduction.

Shallow tray process. A method of holding developing chemicals in small pans, with a large amount of solution surface exposed to the air.

Shelf life. The length of time a stock or working solution can be stored without losing its usability.

Short-stop. *See* Stop-bath.

Shutter. Mechanism that controls the passage of light through the lens by opening and closing the aperture.

Shutter speed. Length of time the lens allows light to pass to the film; is adjusted by use of a shutter.

Snap fitters and dowels. Method of multiflat registration in which adhesive dowels are attached to the light table surface; plastic snap fitters that fit over the dowels are stripped into the tail of the flat; exact image position can be controlled, since the flats will always fall in the same position on the dowels.

Special effects photography. Modification of a continuous-tone photograph to attract attention, or create a unique image; examples are duotone, posterization, use of screen tints and patterns, and bas-relief.

Special effects screen patterns. Solid line

screens that pass light to create unique background images, such as concentric circles, burlap, mezzotint, and many others.

Spectral highlight. White portion of a photograph with no detail, such as the bright, shiny reflection from a metal object.

Speed. Film speed refers to the relative amount of light necessary to cause an image to be recorded; a measure of film speed is the exposure index—ASA.

Stabilization. A special processing technique that uses a two-bath system—the first is an activator, the second is a stabilizer. A special machine is designed to carry the stabilization sheet through the two baths.

Stable-base jig. Exposed piece of stable-base film containing register marks, with a density between 0.7 and 1.0; used as a carrier for color transparencies during color separation process.

Stable-base sheet. Sheet that will not change size with changes in temperature.

Stain. Black liquid used by retouch artists to add detail on continuous-tone images.

Stat. *See* Photostat.

Step-and-repeat plate making. Method of making identical multiple plate images on a single printing plate with one master negative; special machines move the negative to the required position, expose it, and then move it to the next location.

Step-tablet. *See* Sensitivity guide.

Step-wedge. *See* Sensitivity guide.

Stock solutions. Concentrated chemicals supplied by a manufacturer in either powder or liquid form.

Stop bath. Slight acidic solution used to halt development in film processing; is sometimes called the short-stop.

Stripping. Process of assembling all pieces of film containing images that will be carried on the same printing plate and securing them on a masking sheet that will hold them in their appropriate printing positions during the plate-making process.

Surprint. Technique of printing one image over another.

Substrate. Any base material used in printing processes to receive an image transferred from a printing plate; common substrates are paper, foil, fabric, and plastic sheet.

Subtractive primary colors. Colors formed when any two additive primary colors of light are mixed; subtractive colors are yellow, magenta, and cyan; yellow is the additive mixture of red and green light; magenta is the additive mixture of red and blue light; cyan is the additive mixture of blue and green light.

Sweep timer. A clock-like device used to control a light exposure. The time must be reset each time it is used.

Tape system. *See* Percentage tapes.

Tone balance. The goal that the tones (densities) of the final reproduction will nearly match the tones of the original copy.

Transfer lithographic plate. Plate formed from a light-sensitive coating on an intermediate carrier; after exposure, an image is transferred from the intermediate carrier to the printing plate.

Transmission densitometer. Meter that measures light passing through a material.

Transmittance. Measure of the ability of a material to pass light.

Transparent-based image. Any image carried on a base that passes light; transparent-based sheets can be seen through.

Transparent color proofs. Proofs used to check

multicolor jobs; each color is carried on a transparent plastic sheet, and all sheets are positioned over each other to give the illusion of the final multicolor job.

Vacuum back. A special unit on some cameras that holds film in place by use of a vacuum during exposure.

Velox. Prescreened halftone print used to mount on a paste-up board; looks like a regular photographic print but has been broken into small dots for reproduction.

Vertical process camera. Type of darkroom camera that is contained entirely in the darkroom; is a self-contained unit that takes up little space because the filmboard, lens, and copyboard are parallel to each other in a vertical line.

Vignetted screen pattern. Pattern made up of gradually tapering density and found in halftone screens; produces the variety of dots found in typical halftone reproduction.

Visible spectrum. That portion of the electromagnetic spectrum that can be seen by the human eye.

Wedge spectrogram. Visual representation of a film's reaction to light across the visible spectrum.

Working solution. Diluted stock solution ready for use by the photographer.

Wrong reading. Backwards visual organization of copy (or film) from right to left; *see* Right reading.

Yellow. One of the three subtractive primary colors.

Zeroing. Setting or calibrating a densitometer to a known value.

Index